PERSONALITY
AND POLITICS

GORDON J. DiRENZO is Professor of Sociology at the University of Delaware. A certified social psychologist, he specializes in the fields of personality and social systems and social psychiatry.

Professor DiRenzo is a *cum laude* graduate of the University of Notre Dame from which he also received his M.A. and Ph.D. He has done graduate work at Harvard and postdoctoral studies at Columbia and the University of Colorado. He joined the faculty of the University of Delaware in 1970 after appointments at several colleges and universities, including Indiana University, Fairfield University, the University of Portland (Oregon), Brooklyn College (CUNY), and the University of Notre Dame.

Dr. DiRenzo has studied and traveled extensively in Europe and served at the University of Rome in 1960–61 as Visiting Research Sociologist and again in 1968–69 as Senior Fulbright-Hays Professor of Sociology. He is the author of *Personality, Power and Politics,* and *Concepts, Theory and Explanation in the Behavioral Sciences.*

PERSONALITY AND POLITICS

Gordon J. DiRenzo

ANCHOR BOOKS
ANCHOR PRESS/DOUBLEDAY
GARDEN CITY, NEW YORK
1974

Library of Congress Cataloging in Publication Data

DiRenzo, Gordon J.
  Personality and politics.

  Bibliography: p.
  1. Political psychology—Addresses, essays, lectures. 2. Person-
ality—Addresses, essays, lectures. I. Title.
JA74.5.D55   320'.01'9
ISBN 0-385-06516-7
Library of Congress Catalog Card Number 73–15479

To my beloved
Mary Kathleen Ryan
whose personality
is congruent with my politics

Acknowledgments

Patience and persistence have been the watchwords of this project. The presentation of this volume, perhaps reflecting the nature of its contents and the issues surrounding them, has been a long time in coming. But here now is the fruit of our hopes and toils. For the realization of these efforts I am indebted to a number of people for their assistance; but, unfortunately, here I can record my particular appreciation to only a few:

To my distinguished colleague, Professor Seymour Martin Lipset of Harvard University, for his belief in the need and utility of a work of this kind—and, more especially, for his belief in me.

To Elizabeth Knappman, the jovial and sagacious editor of Anchor Press/Doubleday, for her enthusiasm about this project, her keen interest, her wise counsel, and particularly her patience with this sometimes tardy author.

To my former colleague at the University of Delaware, Professor Shigeo Nohara, now of the State University of New York at Oswego, for his critical reading of earlier drafts of my manuscript, and the helpful suggestions which he offered.

To my research assistant, Judi DiIorio Steigerwalt, for her efficiency and resourcefulness in a host of ways, and her good cheer at all times.

To Diane Iffland for her excellent skills in preparing the typescript for publication.

Faculty grants from the General University Research Fund of the University of Delaware and Indiana University have enabled me to complete work on some of my own research projects which in part are reported herein. I am grateful for this generous assistance.

Not the least of my obligations is a profound gratitude to the individual authors—my "co-authors"—of the several selections, and their publishers, for permission to reprint their material and for thereby contributing so indispensably to this volume.

My greatest debt is to my wife, and our daughters, Maria Giulia and Chiara Veronica, who in their own ways not only made this project possible, but together really make it all worthwhile.

G.J.D.

Devon Place
Newark, Delaware
February 1974

Contents

PART THREE:
POLITICAL MAN AND PERSONALITY TYPES

PART FOUR:
PERSONALITY AND POLITICAL IDEOLOGY

PART FIVE:
PERSONALITY AND POLITICAL DYNAMICS

Foreword

Interest in the social psychology of politics has been growing steadily in recent years. A rapidly expanding body of literature, consisting of both research findings and theoretical statements, has been accumulated in this new field. Simultaneously, an increasing number of colleges and universities have instituted courses of various kinds to cover the broad domain of the psychology of politics; although these developments have taken place principally in departments of political science and psychology, the same type of interest is being shown in the areas of political sociology and social psychology.

Given this scientific development and academic curiosity, the time has come for an inventory of this expanding field of scholarship. We offer in these pages a modest effort toward this goal. We will delineate major issues and problems, describe empirical findings, assess formulated principles, and provide theoretical and methodological statements in this new area of inquiry.

To give focus to our volume, we have limited our concerns to one phase of the social psychology of politics and to the one in which there has been the most interest—personality and politics. Unlike other students who have plowed some of this ground, we do not equate "personality" with "psychology." Personality, in our view, represents only one part of what has been labeled the "psychology of politics." There are a number of areas of this more extensive field, however, which are beyond our specific concerns in this volume. We are not interested here, for example, with such areas as political socialization, psychological biography, and political psychiatry—although we deny neither the value, nor the indispensability, of these areas for the explanation of certain kinds of political phenomena. Nonetheless, even within the more delimited field of personality and politics, we have had to be selective.

This volume concentrates on a few of the principal dimensions of the relationship of personality to politics: (1) psychological motivation in recruitment to political roles and careers, (2) personality types among politically active people, (3) the relationship of personality to particular political ideologies, (4) the interaction of personality and various political dynamics, (5) the functional interrelationships of personality and different kinds of political systems, and (6) methodological and theoretical issues that currently characterize this field of behavioral inquiry.

The categorization of these concerns, while facile enough on the analytical level, are not mutually exclusive in the empirical realm. The themes in any selection we provide may overlap one or more of the divisions of the volume. For example, the question of motivations for political activity cannot be completely divorced from that of personality types, which in turn cannot be practically separated from the question of which sorts of personality are suited more ideally for the efficient function of particular kinds of political systems. In this regard, our classification of readings in some instances may appear somewhat arbitrary; but, in all cases, they have been made on the basis of their over-all appropriateness as well as their particular suitability for our specific, analytical considerations. Hence, some of our selections will have application for more than one of our focal areas; but, hopefully, this extended concern will serve to illustrate the complex interconnection and interaction of personality and political dynamics, which itself is one of the principal aspects of these phenomena which we wish to emphasize.

Our selection of articles has been made in terms of their value for demonstrating the relationship of personality to politics as regards the particular issues which constitute the foci of our concerns. Generally, we have tried to use more recently published material; in many cases, however, we felt that "older" selections were a better choice, not only because they constitute the superior writings that are available, but also because, retaining much of their empirical validity and theoretical utility, they provide a necessary historical perspective to our general and specific topics.

The approach of this volume is more demonstrative and constructive than argumentative and controversial. Accordingly, we have adopted a basically text-type format; and, despite a conscious attempt to remain objective in the presentation of the relevant issues and data, we are fully aware that we have tried to state the more positive argument for the determinative role of personality in political behavior.

Consistent with our admitted bias, we have utilized selections that for the most part make a positive contribution to the theoretical development of the interaction of personality and political behavior; nevertheless, we give what we hope is a fair presentation and honest exposure to the more speculative and controversial aspects of the several issues which we discuss. This material is provided in the editor's introductory essay to each of the subdivisions of the volume. In these statements, the editor attempts to synthesize, and to put into focus, the hypothetical and theoretical issues relevant to each topical question, and to interrelate the particular selections which are presented. These editorial essays reflect and extend the assumptions and arguments which are put forth by the editor in Part One.

Part One, presented in a historical perspective, delimits the field of "personality and politics" and assesses several of the major conceptual and methodological issues concerning the conjoint study of personality and politics.

The fundamental thesis of this volume is that the comprehensive explanation of political behavior and political systems requires an analysis of the personality and psychology of the actors behaving in particular political systems and situations, along with political, and other sociocultural, factors. Our intent in the pages that follow, however, is to stimulate rather than to inculcate, to excite more than to convince, and to question more than to resolve.

PART ONE
INTRODUCTION

Perspectives on Personality and Political Behavior
Gordon J. DiRenzo

No analysis of political behavior can be complete without an examination of the political actor who is the agent of that behavior. For what a person does, or can do, is linked to what that person is—not only in respect to human nature, but in terms of the unique psychological structure and dynamics of the individual.

The relationship of human psychological nature to political behavior has been recognized as a fundamental question of both theoretical and practical importance since at least the days of classical Greek thought. Plato, as far as can be determined, was the first of several political thinkers to delineate the importance of understanding the role of human nature in the study of politics, when, in his *Republic,* he discussed the problem of developing in young people those human qualities that were thought to be indispensable for effective political leadership. And Aristotle in his *Politics* remarked on the necessity of fitting the constitution of a city-state to the character of its people. But, while the teachings of these men, in these respects, have not been completely overlooked, their lessons—apart from some limited concerns shown by a few much more recent figures, such as Hobbes (1651), Tocqueville (1840), and Mill (1861)—have gone unheeded throughout the history of political scholarship in the civilizations of the Western world.

HISTORICAL PERSPECTIVES

The study of political behavior in the light of modern psychological concepts and methods has been undertaken seriously only during the past thirty years and nearly exclusively in the United States. Moreover, despite the growing evidence that psychological dynamics play an important role in politics, political scholars have paid little attention to the psychological aspects of political behavior. Political psychology, therefore, has been relatively slow to develop in any systematic fashion as a subdivision of the fields of political studies.

Political analysis, nonetheless, as it becomes more complex and probes deeper into the explanation of social behavior, inevitably reaches a stage where psychological considerations must be taken into account and placed in proper theoretical perspective in relationship to other variables. Personality is of prime concern in such considerations.

Yet, unfortunately, despite the encouraging research on the questions of personality and politics, only a few modern scholars seem willing to entertain the hypothesis that political behavior is a function, at least in part, of the personality of its agents. Political scientists have described many of the roles involved in political activity, but they have not given major attention to the personality of the individuals performing these roles, or concerned themselves with the personality of political actors as regards the structure and function of political processes and systems, which have comprised their focal interests.

The same type of explanatory pattern characterizes the field of sociology. Political sociology is one of the oldest areas of systematic concern with human behavior, but even here—as in nearly all other areas of sociology—classical models of explanation have remained paramount. Human personality, as with other allegedly "psychological" variables, was excluded from the early sociological theories and methodologies which have become the fundamentals of sociological analysis today.

This explanatory model is exemplified, indeed founded, in the classical works of Emile Durkheim, the distinguished French sociologist of the late nineteenth century, and those of Max Weber, an equally renowned German sociologist, whose contributions, while gaining widespread attention only during the past few decades, have served as a major source of current thinking regarding the behavioral dynamics of social organization. The theoretical contributions of these men have had a dominant influence in shaping the theoretical and methodological orientations of contemporary analysis in the field of political sociology. Durkheim (1895) stressed the analysis of social behavior and social systems in terms of "social facts," that is, elements external to the individual and ones which were realities *sui generis*—originating apart from, and not dependent upon, the individual. In this view, personality, despite its widely acknowledged social nature and origins, is considered to be a subjective, or "psychological," phenomenon. Weber (1947) advanced a similar view for the exclusion of personality in his theory of bureaucracy. Bureaucratic organizations operate according to the principle of conformity and in a spirit of impersonal rationality, while elements such as motivations and emotions are hindrances and dysfunctions that need to be eradicated at all costs.

In these classical perspectives of organizational analysis,[1] little concern is shown for the social agents as status-role occupants operating within the social systems. Accordingly, only minor attention is given to the individuality and the diversity of the members of political and social organizations; or to the consequences, for organizational function, of such individual personality matters as motivations for role-taking, attitudes and conceptions vis à vis the particular role and organization, and the nature of personal values which may be

[1] There are some inconsistencies in these formulations, even though the thrust of the anti-psychologistic arguments of Durkheim and Weber are clear. Durkheim (1951), in contending that certain kinds of social structure (degrees of social cohesion and integration) are causally related to certain forms of behavior (e.g., suicide), implicitly asserts that the human being, in his fundamentally psychological nature, functionally requires a particular kind of social structure. And for Weber (1947), in his conception of bureaucratic man, the motivations of conformity (automatic acceptance of structural norms) and status seeking (desire to advance oneself by the acquisition and exercise of technical competence) are postulated as universal drives in human nature.

serving as the instruments and the goals of one's organizational behavior. As Gouldner (1954:16) has stated, "Indeed, the social scene described [in the analysis of bureaucratic organizations] has sometimes been so completely stripped of people that the impression is [perhaps] unintentionally rendered that there are disembodied forces afoot, able to realize their ambitions apart from human nature." But political systems, like all other social systems, are not realities *sui generis;* they do not exist apart from individuals, nor do they function without human dynamism. Consequently, the comprehensive explanation of sociopolitical systems cannot be properly and completely achieved without the consideration of their human sources of energy.

Contemporary objections of a more concrete nature to the study of personality and politics have been elaborated and well answered by Greenstein (1967a, 1967b). Some of these objections are based on conceptual and theoretical concerns (e.g., "What is personality?"), while others have dealt with methodological procedures (e.g., the efficacy of personality inventories). Beyond these more valid kinds of considerations, many of the objections are simply *a priori* assumptions which can be resolved only by empirical investigations. For examples, as Greenstein details, it is frequently contended that (1) political actors are severely limited in the impact that they have, or can have, on political events, and (2) individuals with different personalities act similarly in the same political situation. The principal shortcoming of objections of this kind is that they are stated in absolute terms—that is to say, as applying to all political situations and at any time. Yet, a more justified criticism, derivable from the inconsistencies in the empirical evidence which thus far has been accumulated, would temper such objections with the qualification that "it depends on the particular political situation."

One needs to specify the particular social situations and conditions in which personality does or does not play an instrumental role; and, furthermore, to specify the degree to which the particular kind of interaction may or may not be true. Many studies which have sought to test the relationship of personality to political behavior assume, for example, that there is a personal involvement, on the part of the respective subjects, in the political issues or events in question. No significant interaction between personality and politics, however, should be expected if this assumption is not true. Hence, whatever truth or falsity these categorical objections have, they constitute, from a scientific perspective, theoretical hypotheses that can be resolved—indeed, need to be resolved—only by empirical analysis.

THE ROLE OF SOCIAL CHARACTERISTICS

Nobody seriously denies that, in a given sequence of behavior, the personality of the actor may make a difference in the performance of his role; but it has been difficult to find allegiance to the more critical hypothesis that personality factors enter systematically as significant influences into the performance of whole sets of roles, such as those of particular sociopolitical systems.

The principal objection is that personality and other "psychological" phenomena are less productive than social phenomena in the analysis and explanation of social behavior.[2] Most social scientists are dubious that personality elements possess anything like the influence exerted by more "objective" forces, such as the social backgrounds of social actors. Yet, as several studies (see Inkeles, 1964) have shown, role recruitment and subsequent role performance cannot be safely predicted solely on the basis of the extrinsic features of a social position and its typical occupants.

Modern political scientists, as with the political sociologists after whom they have modeled themselves in turning to more empirical analyses of politics, have concentrated heavily on the social backgrounds and other social characteristics of the political actor in their search for the causal connection between the individual and his political behavior. Yet, knowledge about social backgrounds and other social characteristics

[2] These two "kinds" of phenomena are by no means mutually exclusive. For example, while political scientists, like their sociological colleagues, do not object to "value and attitudinal" data which psychologists would include within even a most elementary conception of personality, they prefer, as we shall see, not to conceive of personality in such terms.

is not in itself sufficiently enlightening for the more complex questions—those that ask "why?" rather than "who?" or "what?"—regarding political phenomena and man's involvement in and relationship to them. The preliminary "who" and "what" explanations provide merely *descriptions* which, involving the definition and classification of phenomena, make statements of the empirical relationships associated with the given phenomena; however, the subsequent "why" explanations provide *interpretations* that determine the nature of the relationships observed among phenomena, such as whether these are causative, purposive, structural, and so forth.[3] As Lane (1959:98) has pointed out: "Explanations of political decisions which rely wholly upon analysis of the social environment, while they have high predictive value, neglect a vital link: they never explain why an individual responds to the environment the way he does. Such purely external analysis tends to presume that two individuals behaving in the same way in a given situation are responding identically. But as seen from the inside out, from the point of view of the individuals, the forces to which they respond might be quite dissimilar." These kinds of "sociological" studies, moreover, have been limited in scope, considering only a few of the variables of social background, such as age, sex, occupation, income, social class, religion, and ethnicity.

All social behavior in these more "sociological" perspectives is determined by forces "outside" of the individual. The political actor, ruled by his own group and categorical affiliations, is regarded as having no "internal" dynamics of his own—other than perhaps a primitive and hedonistic motivation to avoid (or to minimize) pain and to seek (or to maximize) pleasure. The view represented here reflects what Wrong (1961) has criticized as the "oversocialized conception of man." Yet, as difficult as it may be to accept, man has not been made, nor has he evolved, in the image of any one academic department or field of scholarship. Rather he is the product of a complex field of forces, including biological, anthropological, sociological, and psychological ones—among others.

[3] For a more elaborate statement on these theoretical distinctions, see DiRenzo (1966:245–59).

Social backgrounds in themselves cannot directly effect or affect social behavior. As Allport (1931:173) has stated: ". . . background factors never directly cause behavior; they cause attitudes (and other mental sets) and the latter in turn determine behavior." The question that must be answered is *why* some people are affected by a given set of social background factors in a particular way, and others are not. Since not all individuals with the same social backgrounds act in the same way, or react to an objective situation in the same manner, the influence of social backgrounds is selective. This "selection" involves mediation by personality. It is personality which constitutes the more immediate and dynamic force in social behavior, and the source of human energy for social systems.

Personality, as the intermediary mechanism for whatever indirect influence social backgrounds may have on political and social behavior, is the more direct agent of such behavior. The social environment is reflected in individual action only to the extent that it is mediated via the personal system. Accordingly, while social categories frequently do vary on the basis of characteristic patterns of personality, knowing the social foundations of political behavior, such as social class, gives no reliable indication of the "psychological basis" of this behavior, or more specifically, of its personality foundations. Similarly, knowing the personality or other psychological characteristics of political behavior is no clue to its social bases.

Personality, notwithstanding its biological and physiological foundations, is essentially a social product: a consequence of human interaction with particular social backgrounds and social experiences.[4] Yet personality systems have dynamics—psychological dynamics—of their own. Hence for the explanation of political and social behavior, it is not a question of

---

[4] The origin and sources of personality, although central and crucial questions in themselves, are not part of our concerns here. The reader may consult any of the several contemporary theories of personality for various perspectives on these considerations. See, e.g., Hall and Lindzey (1970). For a treatment on how the social environment is tied to political behavior via the intermediary mechanism of personality, see Froman (1961). Niemi (1973) provides an even more recent statement on political socialization.

whether or not "social characteristics" or "psychological traits" provide the more fruitful answer. Rather, we need to recognize both sets of factors as indispensable to the determination of political and social behavior. And, accordingly, we need to specify precisely how social backgrounds and personality work together to determine political and social behavior.

It is also important to understand the development of personality via the social environment and social processes and to view the one as antecedent to the other. The problem here is the sociopsychological variety of the chicken-or-the-egg dilemma. But social factors and personality factors need not be treated so much categorically as either independent or dependent variables as much as interdependent and interacting variables—mutually influencing the structure and dynamics of both social and psychological processes.

Sociologism, the view against which we caution, amounts to a partial, and hence distorted, perspective in the analysis of both social and personal behavior. This one-sided approach needs to be replaced with a balanced, non-reductionistic orientation in which both the sociological and the psychological dimensions are viewed in a mutual state of reciprocal cause-and-effect relationships. Accordingly, we must inquire into how the social environment affects personality (in its development, structure, and function) and individual behavior; and, simultaneously, into how personality and even other psychological factors affect social systems and environments (in their development, structure, and function).

Research and theory development in the social sciences, however, has not been devoid of personality considerations. It has been a common tendency to introduce personality and other "psychological" explanations in the analysis of political and social behavior usually only when "deviation" (i.e., abnormal, undesirable, non-conforming activity, or whatever is arbitrarily so labeled) is involved in the social process; or whenever the researcher seeks—or, more likely, is forced —to account for the atypical cases which otherwise remain uncodable within the conceptual categories of the political and social theory being utilized or developed.

This "last resort" technique is due to the fact that often

the researcher-scholar does not have a sufficiently viable "political" or "sociological" explanation for the "deviant" behavior and hence makes the easy assertion that the deviant is undoubtedly psychotic, neurotic, or at the very least has serious "personality problems."[5]

Little use of these personality and psychological approaches has been made to account for regularity or "normality" of social behavior, processes, and organization. Yet, if personality and psychological explanations have any validity for the explanation of human behavior, then it should be just as legitimate to use them to explain "normal" behavior—the everyday political and social phenomena. The dichotomy of "normal" and "abnormal" behavior is a false one, consisting more frequently than not of arbitrary designations which are imposed externally upon the phenomena in question by the researcher rather than stemming necessarily from any intrinsic quality of the phenomena under investigation. Hence our fundamental concerns in the social and behavioral sciences should be to explain human behavior as objectively and as empirically as our scientific epistemology permits.

AN INTEGRATED APPROACH

But there has been an extensive aversion on the part of social and behavioral scientists in every field to co-ordinate personality and other psychological perspectives with social perspectives, and vice versa.[6] The singular fields of inquiry, and consequently to a great extent academic discourse, have been delimited quite provincially, but not very realistically: psychology presumably deals with "individual" behavior; economics with "economic" behavior; anthropology with "cul-

[5] This orientation frequently is involved in biographical analyses, even on the part of political scientists who place much positive value on the personality and politics approach. See, e.g., the study of Woodrow Wilson by George and George (1956b) and the assessment of James Forrestal by Rogow (1963).

[6] Levinson (1963) has suggested that an "identity crisis" is the common ailment in all academic professions—for both faculty and students—and that territorial rights are fought for and preserved no less fiercely than elsewhere in the animal world.

tural" behavior; political science with one "kind" of human social behavior, namely, all those aspects that relate to authority and governance in the social order; and sociology, as the generalizing science, supposedly has the "enviable" distinction of dealing with any and all "social or collective" behavior. Of course, the arbitrary, and hence artificial, categorical distinctions between these various fields of behavior —quite apart from not necessarily mirroring the reality which they purport to explain—are by no means mutually exclusive nor definitive. And, fortunately, there are in actuality few "pure" practitioners in any one of these disciplines; for each of them, reflecting the realistic nature of the phenomena which constitutes its subject matter, is necessarily multidisciplinary—even though this fact has not always been acknowledged in the *de facto* order of operations.

A broader theoretical perspective is needed. We believe that interdisciplinary and multidisciplinary analyses are able to account for much more of the political and social dynamics about which we are so curious. Considerations of personality, we submit, are fundamental to this type of approach. But personality is not the only, nor even necessarily the most crucial, factor in determining and explaining political behavior. There are many areas of politics for which personality considerations are not relevant or, at least, so it appears at the moment. For example, political demography and political philosophy are two subfields of the discipline in which personality considerations seem not to be applicable. Moreover, even in concrete situations, political decisions and actions often derive from legal, economic, and even "political" (expedient) considerations, rather than as products of personality phenomena. (Of course, for a given theoretical analysis, the researcher may wish to focus exclusively on one kind of variable while excluding, or holding under control, the others.)

As the personality approach is not meant to be reductive, neither is it meant to be exhaustive. Other factors—cultural, social, historical, economic, philosophical, and so forth—also must be taken into account in any effort to comprehend human social behavior in general and political behavior in particular. What needs to be done, therefore, is to assess, in an effective and relevant manner, the specific contribution and relative importance of the various kinds of phenomena as they vary with the particular, or particular kind of, situation.

Our fundamental perspective here is that of scientific convergence: We wish to enhance the role of interdisciplinary and multidisciplinary orientations in the scientific analysis and theoretical explanation of political, and other kinds, of social behavior. What is required is not the reduction of one mode of analysis to another, but rather a co-ordination and integration of the basic data and conjoint perspectives of psychology, political science, sociology, and even anthropology into a more complex and more sophisticated explanatory scheme.

A sociopsychological approach of this nature, we believe, tends to preclude premature and arbitrary closure of the fields of investigation. It avoids, on the one hand, the extreme position—advanced primarily by psychologists—which sees human, political, and social behavior as deriving exclusively from unconscious forces, and considers social elements, such as ideologies and values, as mere epiphenomena, or by-products, of these "internal" dynamics, devoid of any relationship to social reality. On the other hand, it avoids the antithetically extreme position—advanced primarily by political scientists and sociologists—that political and social behavior results exclusively from social factors, and that personality variables, such as values and ideologies, are mere reflections of social learning which are directly and mechanically absorbed by the individual, uninfluenced by the psychological forces of the human personal system in which they are found.[7]

Political organizations represent psychosocial systems that need to be analyzed in traditional sociological perspectives, i.e., in terms of structural dimensions, such as statuses and cohesion, and dynamic elements, such as roles, norms, and processes—as well as in psychologically meaningful terms, such as motivations, values, ideologies, and the psychodynamics and personality structures of the actors and agents of these systems.

The interdisciplinary concern with personality in the social

---

[7] Levinson (1958) has labeled these approaches respectively as "mirage" and "sponge" theories.

and behavioral sciences, up to quite recent times, has been confined to studies of a more anthropological nature, such as those concerned with "national character," in which political scientists[8] and political sociologists have not played a major role. The personality approach, in a multifocal orientation, however, need not be so restricted. More comprehensive political and sociological analyses in the same dimension can be applied quite fruitfully to particular types of social systems, such as those of the polity. Within this tradition, and utilizing similar perspectives, we seek to encourage the application of the same theoretical principles to various kinds and dimensions of political systems.

PERSONALITY: WHAT IS IT?

The acceptance of the personality approach, as is advocated here, rests fundamentally on the field of discourse. And, as no doubt would be expected, "personality" is the focal concept involved in the contemporary objections and rejections of the personality approach in political analysis. We need to explain the nature of personality and to distinguish the concept in both its denotative and connotative aspects. What then is meant by "personality"?

The criticism of the jargonistic proclivities of social scientists is, undoubtedly, too well known, although in our own defensive judgment not well founded, to require elaboration here. Nevertheless, the problems of conceptual clarification and specification have been fundamental and pervasive ones for all of the behavioral sciences, and these difficulties are no less evident in the pivotal concept of personality than they are anywhere else.

The term "personality" has been defined and is used in a host of ways. As is rather well known, Allport, in 1937, categorized nearly fifty types of definitions for this term, not to mention the far greater number of individual definitions which

[8] One classic exception for the political scientists is Tocqueville (1840). For an excellent review and evaluation of earlier work on the relationship of personality, in terms of "national character," to politics, see Inkeles (1961).

he uncovered. Since his census, the progeny have increased and multiplied many fold. More often than not, however, the definition of "personality" is bound inextricably to a particular theory or conceptual orientation, and this fact seems to eliminate some of the apparent conceptual chaos.

But what about the particular meanings of "personality" for political scientists, and other students of social behavior who are antipsychological in their theoretical orientations. Political scientists, according to Greenstein (1969:4–5), tend to equate personality in a rather limited fashion to more unconscious dynamics, such as "ego strength" and "ego defense"; and they correspondingly tend to equate the field of "personality and politics" with the effects of psychopathology on political behavior, and to think of this area of scholarship primarily in terms of clinical case studies of psychological and psychoanalytic biography. Perhaps to some extent, even in great part, these conceptions derive from the early and pioneering work of Harold D. Lasswell (1930), the first modern political scientist who, with training in psychoanalysis, explored such questions in attempting to unite political and psychological concepts and may have set the dominant tone and the course of much of the scholarship in this area of political inquiry.

Be that as it may, the more fundamental question in each of the many conceptual formulations of personality concerns the metaphysical nature of the concept of "personality." Is personality a real or a nominal concept? That is to say, is personality a real phenomenon or simply a mental construct? While this question is far from resolved, and one which represents several cardinal issues in the epistemology of science, we take the position that personality is a real, ontological, and metaphysical phenomenon. By this we mean that personality is not a purely synthetic formulation. Rather personality refers to denotata, corresponds to actuality, and its definitions are convertible *sempliciter* with the concept, and the phenomena to which it applies.[9] Moreover, lest we be misunderstood, personality, as a universal property of human

[9] A more elaborate statement on these questions of conceptualization can be found in DiRenzo (1966:3–8 and 264–75).

beings and in the conception presented here, is essentially a qualitative variable and not a quantitative one. Everyone has personality; it is not a question of how much, but rather of what kind.

By and large, in terms of essential elements, the current definitions of personality are fundamentally consistent with each other, and they have substantially much in common—although one may wish to quibble with the specifics of the formulation. Personality may be defined fundamentally as follows: one's acquired, relatively enduring, yet dynamic, unique system of predispositions to psychological and social behavior.

"Predispositions" imply that personality is not behavioral response, but rather that which comes before, or lies behind, the concrete action of the individual—that which produces or determines the action. Personality is willingness or readiness for response or behavior but not actual behavior itself.

"System" refers to the scientific postulation that the phenomena of personality are organized into an integrated whole and function as a unit. This aspect of organization is the salient feature of the basic facts and theories of personality.

"Unique" implies that, despite fundamental universals, and while individuals may share very similar social and cultural experiences that in great part are responsible for the formation of personality, the total set of developmental and formative forces are never identical for any two individuals. It is the totality of the personality system, particularly in its structural or organizational dimensions, wherein the uniqueness resides.

"Relatively enduring, yet dynamic" perhaps at first glance sounds paradoxical; but the reference here for stability is to basic and central dimensions of the personality (e.g., personality structures and foundational elements, such as genetic endowments) rather than to highly changeable elements (e.g., attitudes). Once formed, personality tends to endure, unless intentionally—or even unintentionally due to traumatic experiences—radical modifications, such as through psychotherapy, are attempted; "dynamic" implies that the personality as a total systemic entity is not static, but rather that it can, and does, experience change, although primarily in the non-basic or non-foundational elements, such as attitudes, values, beliefs, and so forth.

"Acquired" implies that personality, despite its genetic foundations, is not in itself innately given, but rather is the product, often a latent one, of social learning and other forms of social interaction, principally during the very early years of one's life.

As with any other kind of system, personality systems may be analyzed in terms of two fundamental dimensions: *content* and *structure*. Personality content refers to the specific elements or units that comprise the personality system and which in many cases constitute personality subsystems: motivations, values, attitudes, ideologies, emotions, cognitions, and so forth; while personality structure refers to the co-ordinated arrangement and dynamic relationships among the components of content, which includes such dimensions as complexity, integration, isolation, cohesion, consonance, unity, and so forth. It is the interaction of personality structure and personality content that yields personality function, which ultimately accounts for or produces the concrete, "psychological"[10] behavior of the individual.

An analogy for this distinction between systemic content and systemic structure can be had in the organization of a timepiece. The gears, jewels, and hands constitute content elements; the co-ordination and organization of these parts constitute structure. The interconnection of the parts and structure, when provided with energy (a tensioned spring), produces the movement or action of the watch or clock; but its more or less efficient function, that is, the degree to which it keeps fast, slow, or accurate time, stems from the quality of the interconnections, that is, from the "goodness of fit" among the individual elements and between the two systemic components.

Among personality theorists today there is general agreement that personality is an exclusive, comprehensive system that consists of parts, elements, units, subsystems, and processes, which are organized, patterned, and structured. What these elements are, however, and how they are structured is

10 This qualification is intended to exclude behavior at the chemical and biological levels, such as reflexes, which are beyond the voluntary control of the actor.

another question, the answers to which may be characterized as much less homogeneous.[11]

The two analytical dimensions of content and structure, however, are not of equal value in attempts to explain the interaction of personality systems and sociopolitical systems. The more viable dimension for this theoretical question, we believe, appears to be that of personality structure. One of the major reasons for this position is that the measurable dimensions of psychological structure and sociological structure, such as cohesion and integration, are substantially the same, and hence easily amenable to theoretical juxtaposition, while the contents of the two systems consist in great part of mutually exclusive variables (e.g., emotions and physiological elements on the one hand, and norms and roles on the other). One example of this type of structural rapprochement, both conceptually and empirically, involves the phenomena of "anomie" and "anomia" as *structural* states of "normlessness" in both the social and personality systems respectively.[12]

Secondly, it is the dimension of structure which, as the fundamental property of organization in the personality system, accounts for, or gives, the personality system its uniqueness. The emphasis on content, or the trait approach, completely ignores the fact that the same content element (e.g., so-called personality traits) will function differently in personalities that are organized or structured differentially; and the implicit misconception of the nature of personality, as consisting merely in the sum of the individual's personality traits or characteristics (content variables), with no attention to the systemic dimensions of structure and organization, produces certain theoretical problems in that it yields data that do not fall into mutually exclusive or non-overlapping categories. The structural approach, while by no means devoid of this shortcoming, nonetheless, makes it possible to talk about different types of personality in more absolute terms, which

[11] Sanford (1970) provides an interesting assessment of current issues in personality theory.
[12] See Srole (1956) on these conceptions. Interesting treatments on the relationship of anomie to political behavior can be found in Yinger (1973) and Schwartz (1973).

in turn facilitates the explanation of the dynamic rapprochement between personality systems and social systems in a much more comprehensive manner.

Research on personality with this kind of orientation has been lacking in the social sciences, especially in the sphere of political behavior; and this neglect of the crucial dimension of structure is one of the principal reasons why, in our estimation, attempts to relate personality to social roles and systems have not been more successful than they have. As Lasswell (1954) has stated: "The study of political roles has not been planned or extended to the consideration of the total personality structure of the politician or its developmental history." We believe that, in the light of scientific developments, both in terms of personality theory and political and social research, the dimension of personality structure has greater viability and holds much more promise than the elements of personality content for theoretical development and explanation in the field of personality and politics.

One of the more common objections to the study of "personality and politics" on the part of political scientists is the belief that personality is distributed randomly in all political statuses and systems. This assumption, frankly, is not borne out by the evidence which is available. In fact, the bulk of the empirical data are to the contrary; and, more specifically, they indicate that certain kinds of personalities are attracted so disproportionately to particular social roles and statuses as to constitute distinct personality types for these statuses and roles.

The concept of "modal personality"[13] is one of the fundamental assumptions underlying much of the work in the field of personality and politics. Modal personality refers to that type of personality which is found so extensively within a particular range of personality types, in a given social situation or population, as to constitute the typical, average, or dominant psychological expression.

[13] This concept of "modal personality" has descended from the earlier anthropological concerns with "national character" and now "national modal character." See Inkeles (1961) for a review and evaluation of early work attempting to explain political behavior in terms of these conceptual orientations.

Personality is the property of the individual, and in this sense it may be viewed justifiably as a psychological variable; but modal personality is a property of the collectivity and, hence, as an element of social organization and sociopolitical systems, is essentially a sociological variable. The crucial theoretical question, of course, concerns the fundamental significance of the presence and dynamics of this sociological variable of a distinct modal personality type, or types, for the political and social systems, or situations, in which they are found.

PERSONALITY THEORY AND FOCAL PERSONALITY VARIABLES

We are not concerned here with evaluating the merits of the various theories of personality. Many formulations (see, e.g., Hall and Lindzey, 1970) have been offered to explain the origin and dynamics of personality, and nearly all current theories except for a few, such as that of the constitutional school, are potentially useful for the analysis and explanation of behavior in the field of personality and politics.

We subscribe, however, to no particular theory of personality, and prefer to utilize an eclectic approach to the problems of investigation. Yet, an "eclectic" orientation for us would be one that is consistent with the "field theory" of personality as developed by the late Kurt Lewin (1951) and his followers. Field theory, one of the most sociopsychological personality theories today, posits that human behavior is a function of both the forces of the environmental situations in which actors find themselves and the psychological predispositions which the actors bring to these situations.

Much of the extant work, however, in the field of personality and politics—as in nearly all other areas in which personality has been the focus of analysis—has direct or indirect roots in the still empirically problematical theories of psychoanalysis. Indeed, much of the controversy—alas, even the intrigue in more receptive quarters—surrounding the literature in the area of personality and politics has been due to the fact that the major portion of it has been based on psychoanalytic concepts and theories. Yet, for the same reason, these theoretical orientations have led to considerable skepticism and even outright rejection of much of the work in the field of personality and politics.

A number of singular variables of personality have been explored in terms of their relevance for political behavior. But the concept and dynamics of authoritarianism, again in the psychoanalytic tradition, have received more attention than any other personality variable.[14] Indeed, a considerable amount of research on personality and politics during the past twenty-five years already has established authoritarianism as a personality constellation which has significant implications for political behavior.[15]

One reason for the extensive concentration on authoritarianism in political analysis concerns the focal elements of power and authority in the authoritarian syndrome and their significance in terms of the study of non-democratic ideologies and political systems. Another reason is the relevance of authoritarianism to the dimension of personality structure and its utility in this respect as a more viable means for the theoretical explanation of the interactional analysis of personality and social systems.

The first systematic attempts to formulate a conception of authoritarianism as a personality syndrome was made in the 1930s by two German psychologists, Erich Fromm (1936) and Wilhelm Reich (1946), who working independently, but with common interests and orientations in the psychoanalytic tradition, used politics, particularly the politics of fascism, as their vehicle in seeking to develop a psychoanalytic social psychology.

In his well-received book *Escape from Freedom,* Fromm (1941) delimited the "authoritarian character," particularly in reference to the Nazi political movement, and his work became the most significant contribution, at least in terms of its impact in stimulating the principal empirical research that

---

[14] For a review of the literature on authoritarianism, at least until 1956, see Christie and Cook (1958).
[15] For a discussion of the methodological and theoretical value of authoritarianism as an explanatory variable for political behavior, see Farris (1956).

has become the conceptual, theoretical, and methodological foundation for the introduction of authoritarianism into the field of political analysis.

The principal study of authoritarianism in this tradition was that undertaken during the 1940s by a team of social psychologists (Adorno, 1950) at the University of California in Berkeley: *The Authoritarian Personality* has generated one of the most widely used typologies of personality structure and was the first study to provide concrete evidence that political ideologies, values, and attitudes are intimately related to personality, both structurally and dynamically. The now classic study, with its famous F scale, despite widespread criticism (see Christie and Jahoda, 1954), has stimulated an enormous amount of social psychological research in many different areas of social behavior, including in particular the field of politics.

Emerging out of the tradition of *The Authoritarian Personality,* but utilizing a different theoretical orientation, is the work of Milton Rokeach (1960) on the concept and dynamics of dogmatism, and its empirical measure, the D scale, which he offers as alternative approaches to authoritarianism, and which have received a substantial amount of attention in studies concerned with relating personality to political behavior. Rokeach's formulations, rooted in a strongly cognitive orientation that derives from the work of Lewin, are concerned with the openness and closedness of belief systems, and deals primarily with modes of cognitive functioning rather than with the unconscious dynamics and processes of psychoanalytic theory. The dynamics of dogmatism focus on ideological structure rather than on ideological content; and in this regard, Rokeach's conceptual contributions are consistent with the systemic dimension of structure as the more viable route for the theoretical explanation of the interaction of personality and politics.

Unfortunately, the terms "authoritarian" and "dogmatic" more often than not are perjorative in connotation. Labels such as these, particularly in a liberal democracy, are negatively evaluated and equated to the "bad" or the "undesirable." These connotations interfere with scientific efforts to use them as neutral instruments for the analysis and description of empirical phenomena. Nonetheless, as we shall see in the subsequent sections of this volume, much of the empirical analysis in the field of personality and politics has concerned itself with structural dimensions of personality that have their bases in the dynamics of authoritarianism and dogmatism, and several of the individual selections in this volume will be concerned with a more detailed explication of these personality variables and their particular utility for the study of personality and politics.

LIMITATIONS OF PERSONALITY EXPLANATIONS

Personality, as only one of several factors determining human social behavior, does not play the same instrumental role in each concrete situation. There are a number of other factors that individually and collectively account for human behavior—and in the individual case, as well as in certain types of cases, one or more of these factors may play the dominant role, while the contributions of personality are minimized.

When is the influence of personality on political activity minimized or maximized? Research in social psychology has provided some answers to this question. First, the instrumentality of personality is related to the degree of personal involvement in the political situation at hand. No relationship between personality and politics should be expected when the individual actor is not actively involved, subjectively or objectively, in the relevant political issues and behavior. For example, Scott (1958) argues that Americans, on the whole, do not have sufficient interest in, nor knowledge about, foreign policy to permit them to relate psychologically to such matters; and that, accordingly, personality does not normally come into play for Americans when they are required to respond to events in the international realm.

Political ignorance and/or apathy, for whatever reasons, counteract the dynamic interplay of personality; consequently, all other things being equal, the greater the degree of political involvement, the greater the expectation of a significant interaction between personality and political behavior. Similarly, when one is not freely or willingly involved in political activity, differential patterns in terms of personality will not be revealed. An example of such political coercion can be had in those countries in which the individual citizen is legally "required," even if only by mild social sanctions or social pressures, such as "civic duty," to vote. Another example from the recent history of our own country was the widespread practice by American colleges and universities, and other quasi-public organizations, of "compulsory" subscription to loyalty oaths, on the part of their faculty and other employees as a condition of employment, to defend the Constitution of the United States. Political behavior such as this often is devoid of any internal dynamics and has little personal meaning for the individuals involved.

Secondly, the role of personality in political behavior is an inverse function of social structure: the more highly structured, defined, or delimited the sociopolitical situation (norms, roles, values), the more explicit is the expected behavior in a given situation, and the more minimal is the instrumental role of personality. And, conversely, the more unstructured and ambiguous the social situation, the greater the role of personality in structuring the behavior which will be manifested in a given situation. For example, some political situations, such as authoritarian institutions, are so highly structured in terms of prescribed and proscribed behavior that there is relatively little room for personality factors to enter into the definition of the many situations that confront the individual actor.

Sherif (1953) has demonstrated that the contribution of internal (psychological and personality) factors increases as the external stimulus situation becomes more unstructured. Hence, ambiguous and unstructured political situations are more likely to elicit personality elements in the definition and structuring of a situation and the appropriate behavior which is manifested within it. One should not expect personality to play an instrumental role in political behavior unless the individual actor is provided that kind of political situation— "psychological space"—that not only facilitates but, first of all, permits the personality room to operate.

One kind of political situation in which personality dynamics are not provided ample room in which to interact is that which is not only relatively unstructured sociologically, but also correspondingly psychologically ambiguous, for the actor. In this kind of sociopsychological situation the actor is not able to apply ready-made definitions of the situation in terms of providing the socially appropriate or expected behavior. Accordingly, as a general rule, the more unstructured and ambiguous a political situation, the more likely it is that the response of the individual actor will involve personality elements.

Some of the specific kinds of sociologically unstructured, and correspondingly psychologically ambiguous, situations are the following:

1) New situations: ones in which the actor has had no previous experience and hence can find no familiar cues to aid in the definition and structure of the situation.[16]

2) Complex situations: ones which, at least for the individual confronting them, are too difficult to structure either adequately or satisfactorily because of a relatively large number of familiar cues.

3) Contradictory situations: ones in which largely unfamiliar or comprehensive elements preclude adequate definition or structure of inherent inconsistencies and incompatibilities.

4) Situations devoid of social sanctions: ones in which the actor is not constrained to choose among socially sanctioned alternatives. When the social expectations and corresponding social sanctions are clearly specified, the actor is likely to act as expected in terms of the social norms—all other things being equal.

Finally, the involvement of personality in political activity is related directly to the richness and complexity of the external stimulus field (see Levinson, 1964). Personality is maximized when, in choosing a course of action, the individual actor is confronted with a wide range of alternatives, all of which are socially acceptable. Hence, the greater the number of socially acceptable options for political participation,

[16] For more on this question, see Budner (1962).

the more likely is the probability that the political actor will make his selection on the basis of personal congeniality.

The fundamental goal of research in the field of personality and politics is to specify in greater detail, and in more concrete terms, the particular kinds of political and social situations in which personality variables are instrumental in structuring and determining specific courses of political action, and to delimit even further the circumstances in which this dynamic role is maximized or minimized.

CONCLUSION

The study of personality and politics, despite its ancient history, is in its youth. Before this area of scientific scholarship reaches a level of maturation at which it can bear prolific progeny and become theoretically and predictively productive, a number of questions need to be answered, and a host of problems—both conceptual and methodological—need to be resolved. Fortunately, the fertilization of the field has been an extensive one—in breadth if not in depth—and the outlook for the future is one that promises a rich harvest of scientific and theoretical rewards.

We hope that the perspectives provided here, admittedly selective, as well as being more reflective of our own orientations to the social psychology of politics, provide a sufficient conception of the issues and problems in the intriguing study of personality and politics so that the reader can find intellectual meaning, and indeed stimulation and enthusiasm, from the remainder of this volume.

PART TWO

POWER MOTIVATION: A BASIS FOR POLITICAL PERSONALITY

Introduction

Why do people engage in political activity? Our concern in this section is with the role of motivations for political behavior. In pursuing this question we hope to learn something about the patterns of political recruitment, as well as about the personality of political actors: how they conceive of their roles, and the nature of the instrumental values attached to them.

The search for psychological motivation does not deny the role of social factors, such as family tradition or environment, in shaping political activity and careers. For example, children who are reared in strongly politically oriented families are more likely to be imbued with motives and attitudes favorable to politics than those with other kinds of social backgrounds. And family name and experience may be a decided advantage in achieving political goals as professional careers. Sufficient instances of this situation in our own country document the point quite well. Nonetheless, in the current context, social factors are seen as the external stimuli which provide the circumstantial answer for the selection of politics, rather than another form of activity, as the vehicle for the fulfillment of internal, psychological wants or needs.

Political activity, as with almost all other types of behavior, can be used to achieve a number of different kinds of personal goals: prestige, popularity, money, fame, and so on. Most politicians, of course, contend that they are in politics to be of altruistic service to the public. Their frequently stated motives are such things as civic duty, defense of nation, and social reform.[1] But politics offers also, as Matthews (1960:49) indicates, a number of psychic lures, such as a sense of power, excitement, camaraderie, "love of the game," a sense of "being in on things," a sense of importance, and so forth. Of course, none of these attractions is unique to the political arena. Just as the same goal (e.g., politics) may be cathected by different motives, so too may the same motive (e.g., fame) cathect different goals.

Notwithstanding this motivational heterogeneity, the pursuit of power is the most apparent goal in the political arena. Power,[2] of course, is a fundamental dimension of all behavior, but within the political sphere it constitutes the "name of the game." As Weber (1958:116) rightly stated, "the power instinct" is a normal quality of the politician, since the striving for power is one of the basic driving forces of all politics. Power, then, as the unavoidable means of politics is the basic goal of the politician. Yet, for our considerations, the more crucial questions concern the significance which such means and goal have for the political man. That is, what are the value-conception and the orientation which the political actor has toward power? For example, Mahatma Gandhi, in many senses a political leader, viewed power as an evil; while Lenin and Stalin considered power to be a supreme good.

The unmistakable contention in much of the relevant literature is that political man has an authoritarian conception of power and a Machiavellian orientation toward it. Political man, more frequently than not, is presented as an essen-

---

[1] See, e.g., Harned (1961), DiRenzo (1967a), and Payne and Woshinsky (1972).

[2] "Power" is the influence or control that one has, or may exercise, on the behavior of another. As such, power resides in the very essence of the social process and is essentially sociological. Orientations to power, however, are a psychological matter; and, in this respect, as well as in the sense of being a value, power may become an element of anyone's personality. Political power is but one "kind" of power which is distinguished by the domain of its exercise. For a statement on "Types of Power," see Goldhamer and Shils (1939).

tially power-lusting individual. This view dates back to Eduard Spranger, the German psychologist, who contended that every personality is characterized by the dominance of a cultural value, of which he distinguished six: wealth, religion, art, science, love, and power. This arrangement yielded a classification of six basic types of men. Power became the dominant or supreme value for the "political type" of man. Says Spranger (1928:28) of this type: "The purely political type makes all value regions of life serve his will to power."

The most extensive writings on the concept of political man in this perspective are those of Harold D. Lasswell (1930), who similarly conceives of political man as one distinguished by virtue of his pursuit of personal power; but his classic formulation of the problem is that political involvement is a compensation against low personal estimates (feelings of personal deprivation and insubordination) and that private motives (intense and ungratified cravings for power and deference) are displaced onto public objects (persons and practices connected with the power process) and rationalized in terms of the public interest. The attainment of power is expected to overcome low estimates of self. A similar psychoanalytic view is offered by Erich Fromm (1941: 162) as a pivotal dynamic of the "authoritarian character" that, in a psychological sense, the lust for power is rooted in weakness and not in strength, and that fundamentally this motive is a desperate attempt to gain secondary strength where genuine strength is lacking.

In the Lasswellian view, political man shares the private motives in common with every man, and the displacement mechanism with some, but the distinctive mark of the political man is the rationalization of the displacement in terms of the public interest.[3] In a similar vein Schumpeter (1950) maintains that the competitive struggle for power is primary in political behavior, and that the social function of legislating is fulfilled incidentally, as somewhat of a latent consequence. This particular conception of the power-centered political personality has been stated more recently by Downs

[3] For a recent study which supports Lasswell's formulations of political man as a displacer and externalizer, see Rutherford (1966).

(1957). For his model of an economic theory of democracy, Downs accepts the self-interest axiom as the basis of human behavior: private ambitions are the ends of human actions, social functions are usually the by-products. He contends, in this conception, that politicians are motivated solely by the desires for power, prestige, and income which come from being in office. "Thus politicians in our model," says Downs, "never seek office as a means of carrying out particular policies; their only goal is to reap the rewards of holding office per se. They treat policies as means to the attainment of their private ends, which they can reach only by being elected" (1957:28–30). The general proposition of personal power orientation as the distinctive mark of the politician has been stated to a lesser extent by several other political scholars.[4]

Lasswell's thesis of the personally power-oriented political man is presented more thoroughly in his *Power and Personality*, from which is taken our first selection for this section. Therein Lasswell contends that "in a political type in [his] sense, the basic characteristic will be the accentuation of power in relation to other values within the personality when compared with other persons" (1948:22). Such an accentuation of power, nevertheless, must be seen in its cultural context. In a particular culture, power may be a dominant or central value which as such would be manifested in a more modal fashion in the national character of that society.

In a later work, Lasswell (1954) offered a restatement of the theory of the development of the power-centered man, and qualifies his position by suggesting that power is a nonprimary motive; and that considering it the sole or major motive for entering politics is too inflexible an explanation. Contending that those individuals seeking personal power would be restrained by their colleagues and relegated to positions of lesser worth, Lasswell thought it more likely that political leaders ". . . of large scale modern politics where comparatively free institutions exist are oriented toward

---

[4] See, e.g., Michels (1962), Gottfried (1955), and Morgenthau (1956).

power as a co-ordinate or secondary value with other values, such as respect (popularity), rectitude (reputation as servants of the public good), and wealth (livelihood)" (1954: 221). He says: "We now speak of power demands in the primary circle as being directed toward secondary circles and justified in terms of common values. (We have substituted less 'clinical' terms for 'displacement' and 'rationalization,' and we use 'defense' of the self against low self-appraisals.) It is clearer that the 'public objects' are the institutional patterns of power in a given social process" (1954:215–216).

Negative arguments on the thesis of power motivation as the distinctive mark of political man are not wanting.[5] Those who take the contrary view, but offer no supporting evidence, contend that there is too little opportunity for direct power gratification in the field of politics—a view apparently restricted to "democratic politics"—and suggest that such worlds as those of finance, industry, and the military might provide more efficacious avenues toward this personal goal.[6] Lasswell, of course, did not limit his formulations of political man to the political arena. In this regard, he distinguished between "conventional" and "functional" politics. Politics in his conventional sense refers to all personnel of governmental departments or agencies, while "functional politics" refers to important decisions made by "politicians" who do not hold office.

We offer in the selection which follows an excerpt from one of Lasswell's early works in order that not only this question of power motivation but also much of the topic of personality and politics may be put into historical perspective.

The hypothesis of the power-oriented political man has been explored by a number of people on the level of political biography.[7] In our second selection, Alexander George

[5] See, e.g., the comments of Lane (1962a) and Milbrath (1965).
[6] Politics is not the only way one may seek and achieve power. Power-oriented people can be found in all walks of life. For a consideration of why political activity might be particularly attractive and selected as the primary route for the attainment of personal power, see DiRenzo (1967a:110–115).
[7] For an essay on contributions of psychobiography, see Glad (1973).

attempts to broaden, while at the same time evaluating, the theoretical framework of Lasswell's general hypotheses. Case studies, of course, do not in themselves constitute modal types, but George, in drawing heavily on his own biographical work of Woodrow Wilson, suggests a method for employing and extending the Lasswellian formulation in research on political leaders in the perspective of political biography.

Empirical evidence that the personally power-motivated individual is attracted to politics is not easy to come by; and the available research results are inconsistent. Much of what has been done on this question has involved an indirect analysis by means of instruments, such as measures of authoritarianism, in which power motivation is incorporated as a central, but not exclusive, element. And, aside from the conceptual and methodological biases of some of these instruments, one of the more important problems is that actual professional politicians—or, as Lasswell calls them, the "active elite" of government or political parties—have not been studied for the most part.

One of the first attempts to test the hypothesis of power motivation was made by McConaughy (1950), who, with a very small sample of only eighteen men, administered the Edwards Unlabelled Fascist Attitudes Test to state legislators in South Carolina and to a non-political control group. He found no statistically significant differences either way, but concluded that the politicians were less fascistic, and hence less power-oriented, than the control group.

Hennessy (1959), on the other hand, in an exploratory study of party workers, officials, and candidates in Arizona, found that politicians as a whole have statistically significantly stronger orientations toward power than non-politicians, and have stronger desires for direct influence over persons and things, but that the two categories did not differ on a number of other personality dimensions. DiRenzo (1967a), in a study of Italian parliamentarians which is reported in the next section, found that authoritarian power motivation was a modal attribute of his political subjects. And Parker (1972), in a study of the motivations of political candidates for seeking initial office in county and state elections, found that the highest factor loading was that for the "desire for leadership position."

Our third selection for this section, incorporating a number of methodological refinements as well as some conceptual and sociological specifications of the political role, provides strong support for the hypothesis of power motivation. Browning and Jacob report on research that involved the administration of projective techniques, designed to tap power motivation along with motives for achievement and affiliation needs, to samples of unsuccessful candidates, of former appointed and elected officials at the local level, and of politically inactive businessmen. These researchers found no differences in power motivation between politicians and non-politicians in terms of general categorization; but, they suggest, power motivation needs to be specified in terms of particular kinds, or levels, of politicians, and in terms of different kinds of political systems.

The strongly power-motivated individuals, argue Browning and Jacob, are likely to be attracted to only certain kinds of political systems, and then only to certain offices or roles within that system. Their data show that the motivation for political power is related to the patterns of political and non-political opportunities in different communities, the distribution of opportunities among political offices, and the opportunities for power gratification in other areas of social activity, such as in the economic fields.[8] Browning and Jacob make the following conclusions: (1) In communities where political and non-political issues are at the center of attention and interest, individuals attracted to politics are likely to be the more strongly power-motivated and achievement-motivated than in those communities where politics commands only peripheral interests. (2) Political systems that offer upward political mobility attract men with relatively strong power motivation. (3) Offices with high potential for power are occupied by men who are strongly power-oriented, as compared to the politically inactive from the same occupational and socioeconomic strata. (4) Relatively

[8] For references to the struggle for power in business organizations, see, e.g., Zaleznik (1970).

plentiful opportunities for power in other arenas (here the economic) will attract power-oriented individuals to those areas.

These qualifications for the hypothesis of power motivation which Browning and Jacob provide are somewhat consistent with our own suggestions (DiRenzo, 1967a:103–110) that differences in the level and function of political offices, and differences in the modes (methods, procedures, and structures) of recruitment, may attract individuals with different motivations and personality. At any rate, the hypothesis of power motivation as the distinctive mark of the political man—given the paucity and inconsistency of relevant empirical data—has not been adequately tested, and hence the general thesis remains a valid and viable one for further research.

The fundamental problem in terms of inconsistency, we believe, has been the conception of the political role in absolute terms. What is needed is a specification of it on the basis of such things as level of office, type of political and ideological system involved, elective or appointive political roles, vocational or avocational occupants, full-time or part-time activity, as well as cultural specifications. For, as George contends in his essay, the dynamics of power motivation do not operate uniformly in all situations, and perhaps are subject to highly specific arousal conditions. Our immediate need is the specification of these arousal and non-arousal conditions in terms of particular roles, systems, and situations.

Meanwhile, the conception of the political man as a power-monger remains much alive in the minds of many people, and its threat is equally real and feared—in democratic as well as in non-democratic political systems. These fears are exemplified in our own country by recent concerns about maintaining a balance of power between the various branches of government, particularly at the national level. And an even more vivid and active concern was manifested in the rather extreme proposal by a recent president of the American Psychological Association, who, in his presidential address (Clark, 1971), making an analogy to the use of drugs as vaccines in preventive medicine against physical ills and disease, advocated biochemical intervention into the inner psychological recesses of the motivational and temperamental systems of human beings.[9] His suggestion amounts to the development of a pill for compulsory and periodic administration to the political leaders of the nation, as well as to those who aspire to positions of leadership, as a preventive medication against their use of power for personal and socially destructive ends. This type of internally imposed disarmament against absurd or barbaric use of power is intended to provide the masses of human beings with the security that their leaders would not, indeed could not, sacrifice them on the altars of their personal ego pathos, vulnerability, and instability. Yet, taking the positive side of this argument, George asserts that political personalities of the power-motivated type, once successful in obtaining office, often emerge as reformers and innovators.

As we explore the relationship of personality to politics in the several dimensions that comprise the contents of this volume, we shall need to keep a balanced perspective on the question of power motivation in terms of its social and political functions. This issue will be a focal consideration for us in Part Six wherein we shall consider the question of the "right kind" of political man for a given political process and system.

[9] Lasswell (1948:187), claiming that human freedom requires the elimination of power, made a similar suggestion nearly twenty-five years ago, when he proposed the establishment of a "National Personnel Assessment Board" to select, and to supervise the work of, competent experts in the description of suitable personality types for democratic governments.

The Political Personality
Harold D. Lasswell

POWER AS COMPENSATION

Our key hypothesis about the power seeker is that he pursues power as a means of compensation against deprivation. *Power is expected to overcome low estimates of the self,* by changing either the traits of the self or the environment in which it functions.

The self typically includes more than the primary ego, which is the symbol used by a person to refer to his irreducible "I," "me."[1] The self takes in whatever is included with the primary ego as belonging with it. The boundaries of the self ordinarily include—besides the primary ego symbols —symbols that refer to parents, wife, children, friends, countrymen, coreligionists and other groups and individuals. These are the symbols of identification.

The personality includes demands made *by* the self *on* the primary ego and on each constituent part of the self. Everyone makes demands on every member of a group with which he is identified, including himself.

Reprinted from *Power and Personality* by Harold Dwight Lasswell by permission of W. W. Norton and Company, Inc. Copyright 1948 by W. W. Norton and Company, Inc. Pp. 39–58.
[1] On the self, see especially Mead (1934). Recent social psychology has moved increasingly in this direction, as in Sherif and Cantril (1941).

Besides identifications and demands, there are expectations about the self in relation to the world. The primary ego or the constituent elements are deprived to the extent that they do not enjoy the value position demanded, whether the value in question is well-being or any other in the list we have been using for descriptive purposes. Furthermore, the self is regarded as deprived when it is moving into a future in which loss of value position is held likely, or failure to overcome obstacles in the way of expanding values is foreseen. (Deprivations are endured or threatened losses, and endured or threatened obstructions to an improved value position.)

Our hypothesis about the power-accentuating type is that power is resorted to when it is expected to contribute more than any alternative value to overcoming or obviating deprivations of the self.[2] The deprivations may be appraised in terms of any value, and any component of the self-structure may be involved.

WHEN COMPENSATION OCCURS

Deprivations may be met not by compensatory strivings but by withdrawal from active participation in human relationships. What are the conditions favoring compensation rather than acquiescence?

One set of conditions is related to the deprivation: *compensation is favored when the deprivation is not overwhelming.* For if the blows of fortune are too hard to bear, the individual and the group may withdraw from the arena of power. The individual may commit suicide, even when not threatened by retaliation; and the group may abandon its own

[2] This applies the basic postulate of response, the $I:D$ ratio, which expresses the ratio of indulgence to deprivation and states the principle that response maximizes net indulgence over deprivation. Under the impact of behaviorism the older "pleasure-pain" postulate is often rephrased as "abolishing stimuli" in modern systems of psychology. Unconscious as well as conscious dimensions are included, and in this way equivalency is achieved with the Benthamite "calculus of felicity."

institutions, either taking over the culture of another or physically disappearing.[3]

Deprivations are not regarded as overwhelming *when lost or denied indulgences are not demanded absolutely.* The man who kills himself when he is rejected at the polls has made an absolutely rigid demand upon himself; this *or else.*

Deprivations are not regarded as overwhelming *when they are not wholly attributed to the self.* If it is possible to absolve the self from responsibility by blaming superior forces at the disposal of an enemy, or immoral conduct on the part of the antagonist, the demand on the self is sufficiently flexible to permit life to go on.

It is also true that deprivations can be better borne when they are *accompanied by some indulgences.* The man who fights a good fight can sometimes save his self-respect when he loses power or wealth. Losses can sometimes be minimized, as when they are less than expected.

A second set of conditions is favorable to compensation; *compensation by the use of power is facilitated when it is expected to yield more net values than can be obtained by the use of other alternatives.*

Favorable expectations about power occur among those who have *successfully used power* in the past under similar circumstances, or who know of such use by others. Professional soldiers are often more calm in military disaster than civilians who imagine "all is lost." Seasoned party politicians are famous for the cold-bloodedness with which they can survive defeat.

INDOCTRINATION WITH A MISSION

The conception of political type that has just been outlined is put forward as a means of unifying the data of history, social science, psychology and medicine. It appears to be confirmed by what we know of many of the outstanding

[3] See Lasswell (1935) and Kluckhohn (1944). Responses to deprivation may be predominantly *object orientations, adjustive thinking, autistic reactions* or *somatic reactions.* (They may involve one or more values and institutions.) See DeGrazia (1948).

figures in the history of political life, especially in the case of men who were indoctrinated from the earliest years with a political mission. In these instances all of our specifications are met. The individual was identified with the destiny of a group larger than his primary ego. The emphasis on mission rose from the discrepancy between the goals of the group and the present or prospective situation in which the group appeared to be. Group losses or obstructions, it was believed, could be removed by power (though not necessarily to the exclusion of other means). Moreover, power was glorified as a probable—if not inevitable—means of fulfilling the collective mission and hence of removing and preventing deprivation. The focus of attention of the developing young-ster has been absorbed with symbols of reference to power and with rationalizations of power. Immediate indulgences have been granted to him as he acquired the skills deemed appropriate to the mission to be fulfilled. Such intense in-doctrination usually occurs when a changing political situa-tion is surcharged with conflict, or when checks and losses are fresh.

Recall the story of Hannibal, indoctrinated from child-hood with burning hatred of Rome and loyalty to Carthage by his able father, the Carthaginian general Hamilcar Barcas. This occurred in the thick of the duel which ultimately led to the extinction of Carthage in the struggle for Mediter-ranean primacy between the two great super powers of the time.[4]

Gustavus Adolphus of Sweden was trained from the first by his austere parents (Charles IX and Christina) to be a champion of Protestantism. He learned Swedish and Ger-man as his mother tongues, and at twelve had mastered Latin, Italian and Dutch. Later he acquired a working knowl-edge of Spanish, Russian and Polish. The boy began to take a responsible place in public ceremonies during his ninth year. At thirteen he received petitions and conversed offi-cially with foreign ministers. Two years later he administered a Duchy, and within a year was practically coregent. He was trained in martial and chivalric skills, and his subsequent

[4] On the political pattern referred to, consult Fox (1944).

record speaks for itself in the struggle against the Catholic powers.

The importance of ambitious and loving parents in shaping the ego ideal (the demands made on the self) is a commonplace of everyday wisdom and scientific observation. Although we know little of the details of the early life of Genghis Khan, everything points to the decisive influence of his mother in preparing him to restore the position of the family. It was a period in which the great clans were giving way to smaller social units, the family. Families with large herds of horses were able to support a large following of armed riders as well as slaves to do the menial work of the camp. Weaker families were compelled to get on as best they could outside the lands of the aristocrats. Temujin (later Genghis Khan) was born into a broken-down family of Mongols with memories of a heroic past but surrounded by present adversity. Temujin's father was poisoned by enemies before the boy went on his first hunt. Temujin and his brothers hunted marmots and mice, and they even caught fish in the streams, which no self-respecting Mongol was supposed to eat. The mother kept them alive and did what she could to inspire them with the pride and self-confidence that came from the heroic legends of past greatness. She tried to keep together the small band that had still clustered around her husband. In the rough and tumble of the steppes, Genghis formed his whole life in the struggle to survive, to overcome, to bend men to his will. As he once declared, "a man's highest job in life is to break his enemies, to drive them before him, to take from them all the things that have been theirs, to hear the weeping of those who cherished them, to take their horses between his knees, and to press in his arms the most desirable of their women."

This is typical of the burning ambition for restoration and revenge of those who have been deprived of the power to which they believed themselves entitled. And in fashioning the instrument of restoring the family fortunes, the role of the mother, as in the case of the great Khan, is often exemplified. A more humble instance is the life of Napoleon III, who was so profoundly shaped by his mother. Louis Bonaparte, his father, was a brother of Napoleon I and had been king of

Holland. At one point in Louis's career, he had compelled his wife, by a "scandalous" legal action, to give up to him the elder of her two children. With Charles she wandered from Geneva to Aix, Carlsruhe to Augsburg, and supervised the son's education, whether he studied in a school or with tutors.

EXTREMES OF INDULGENCE AND DEPRIVATION

Our recent advances in studying personality development have given us greater understanding of the process by which extreme cravings for power, respect and related deference values come into existence and find outlet in positive forms of activity, rather than in total withdrawal. An essential factor is the balancing of deprivation by indulgence; and, more particularly, the tensions arising from extremes of both. Without a compensating flow of affection and admiration, deprivations may appear too overwhelming to justify the exertions necessary to acquire the skills essential to eventual success. And if the flow swings erratically from extreme to extreme, the tensions of uncertainty can be kept within bearable limits, so that energies are concentrated upon the task of mastering the environment.

We know that one of the tension-inducing environments is created when affection, respect and other values are (or are felt to be) contingent upon the acquisition and exercise of skills. To some degree, of course, this process is inseparable from the early contact of the infant and child with the standards imposed upon him by the carriers of the culture into which he is born. Unless some obedience is given, there is punishment in the form of bodily chastisement, withdrawal of affection and other deprivations. With conformity, on the other hand, rewards are forthcoming in the form of food, affection and other indulgences. It is a question, here, not of this process in general but of the special form given to it when the young person is exposed to a relatively elaborate set of requirements, which are rewarded or punished with special intensity. Almost all learning of set tasks gives rise to characteristic deprivations. One must practice grammar, for instance, at a set time whether one is in the mood or not. The inhibiting of impulses to run and play or to study something else often carries with it rage reactions, reactions which may never rise to full expression in what is said and done or even thought. But these answers to a command, whether emanating from outside or from the internalized commander (the conscience), characteristically arouse tendencies to get out of the situation, either by escape or by destruction. Such tendencies, if not deliberately recognized and rejected, may give rise to a recurring level of tension against which defensive measures are spontaneously taken. One of these measures is a blind urge to act with intensity and rigidity; in short, the dynamisms of compulsiveness. The primary ego, caught in the tug of conflicting impulses and requirements, can develop a very extreme set of expectations about the characteristics of the ego: on the one hand, the ego may appear to be loving and admired; on the other, the same ego can appear as unloved, shameful, guilty and weak. Pessimism may rest on the idea that one is loved only "conditionally"; that is, that love can only be received as part of a bargain or a battle.

Certain eminent historical figures were subjected to great extremes of indulgence and deprivation, and they responded to the tension by great, even though reluctant, concentration upon power. Frederick the Great is a conspicuous example. His father, Frederick William I of Prussia, was reacting against the "French" standards that he thought had too much influenced his own father. Hence Frederick William imposed a regime of Spartan rigor on his son, hoping to make him a model soldier and a man of "thrift and frugality" after his own pattern. But the young Frederick sought and found indulgence in other pursuits. Encouraged by his mother and his governess, Madame de Roucouille, and his first tutor, Duhan, a French refugee, Frederick acquired a taste for music and literature, secretly learned Latin, which had been forbidden by his father, scoffed at religion, refused to ride or shoot and affected the French language, dress and manners, while deriding German uncouthness. Revolting against the harsh treatment received from his father, Frederick planned to run away to the English. But the secret was betrayed, with well-known results. One of the conspirators, Frederick's friend

Katte, was beheaded in his presence. Eventually the crown prince began to conform as a means of obtaining power.

The impact of exposure to extreme indulgence and deprivation during formative years is exemplified further in such a career as that of Peter the Great. He saw one of his uncles dragged from the palace and butchered by a mob in 1682. He witnessed his mother's mentor and own best friend torn from his grasp and hacked to pieces in his presence. Exposed to the contempt of the boyars, and knowing of the contempt in which Russia was held abroad, Peter groped toward a career devoted to the internal consolidation of the Crown and the laying of the foundation for Russian power and fame abroad.

An interesting test case is Alexander the Great. Although we cannot completely penetrate the cloud of glorification with which his career is veiled, several strong indications can be found. His father, Philip of Macedon, was a strong and successful king in the very process of enlarging and consolidating his domain, taking advantage of the shifting constellation of power throughout the known world. In the full stride of conflict, he did not underrate the importance of having a successor properly equipped to deal with his new and heavy responsibilities. Alexander was not only given distinguished tutors, like Aristotle, but from early times he was subjected to a busy and by no means "soft" life. Of decisive significance, perhaps, was the soaring ambition of Alexander's mother, who was well acquainted with Eastern mystery cults, if not indeed a priestess before her marriage to Philip. How seriously Alexander took the tales of his divinity and his mission in the world, we cannot say. (When he gave encouragement to the belief in his divine attributes, he may have been deliberately employing a myth to consolidate his empire.)

We know that the devaluation of power among those born to power has been most conspicuous among those whose power is unchallenged, leaving them comparatively free to pursue other values.

When we consider less glamorous careers among those born to or claiming great power, the result is in harmony with our hypothetical picture of the political type. We know that middle-class homes are hothouses of ambition, holding their children to high standards of achievement, thus providing the tension between indulgence and deprivation so congenial to the accentuation of power.[5]

We know, too, that a disproportionately large contribution is made to the public service by professional families, especially by clergymen and teachers. Many factors affect this result. One element is exposure to a stream of talk that typically contains many of the dominant rationalizations of public life. Facility in the use of words and familiarity with the history and traditions of public life are skills that expedite the shaping of an active career in politics. Contrast the articulateness of the clergyman or the teacher with the inarticulateness of the typical manual toiler. The symbols of reference to public targets and to plausible means of rationalizing power foster the displacement of private affects upon public objects. Middle-class professional families are the custodians of the dominant myths of the community; and more. They emphasize the public interest and glorify the professional standard of serving collective rather than purely private advantage. This means that business activity, for instance, is looked down upon, however much the economic advantages of wealth are openly or covertly desired. To be professional is to curb the business standard of "charging what the traffic will bear." The ideal is some form of direct public service, as in law, medicine, education; and law, in particular, leads to active participation in the power process.

Where crisis conditions prevail in modern society, the educated and professional middle class has contributed heavily to the leadership of political movements. Those who sacrifice for the acquisition of any skill undergo self-discipline; and they develop a moral claim on the world for reward. Moreover, they are equipped with the symbols most appropriate to the making of these claims plausible to themselves and their fellows. When deprivations fall upon them, they tend to respond with moral indignation. Not only do they see that they are worse off; they believe it is unjust that they should be subject to deprivation. Hence it is easy for articulate professional

[5] The literature on middle-class ambitiousness is large. A methodologically interesting application of contextual analysis is found in Smith (1946).

families to rationalize their assertiveness in terms of the public good.

Furthermore, young people who have been reared in such an environment, even when they are unable or unwilling to acquire a long education, continue to apply strenuous standards to themselves. Whether they admit it or not, they feel acutely inferior when they fail to follow the accepted path. And their modes of compensation frequently take the form of what they conceive to be short cuts to the seizure of power and the regaining of a sense of total worth.

It is not to be forgotten that the tension between demands on the ego for both independence and dependence is intensified by a disciplinary-indulgent environment. This increases the likelihood of those vigorous compensations against dependency that enable many persons to impress upon others their seeming courage, intensity of conviction and strength of will. The child of our middle classes, for instance, is somewhat baffled by the intricate code that is forced upon him. On the one hand he is supposed to "be a nice boy" and not fight or engage in perversity, but on the other he is supposed to "stand up for himself" in altercations with other boys. And the niceties of the conduct appropriate to these commands are as intricate as the code of what is phrased as "selfishness" or "service." We laud business, yet deplore selfishness in the sense of outspoken pursuit of personal advantage. And our double standards create problems of adjustment that not infrequently are resolved by ruthless determination to escape from quandaries into action, and to use action as a means of silencing doubts by the fact and the fame of power.

"Mobility upward" along the power ladder is fostered by a home in which one member of the family, usually the mother, feels that she has married "beneath" her social (respect) class. These women are sensitive to the blight in their careers and obstinately determined to vindicate themselves by the vicarious triumphs of their children. Whether or not such ambitions are explicitly connected with the power myths and operations of society, they frequently create that taut internal state (that bifurcation of the ego into the secure and the insecure part) that favors the use of power as a way of relief.

A variant of the same compensatory response is the drive of the "provincial" or the "small-town boy" or the "country boy" to succeed against the stigma of rusticity.[6] One advantage of a marginal position in terms both of class structure and territory is that new power opportunities may be perceived and utilized free of older commitments. But the advantage from the side of motivation is the overcoming of a low-respect position through the use of power and other available means. Commentators have not failed to recognize that Napoleon came from the periphery of French power, Corsica, and that his family had long opposed the inclusion of the island in France. More recently the rise of Hitler and Rosenberg has emphasized certain advantages of a peripheral starting point.

That blighted careers make politicians is another observation in accord with our basic idea of the dynamic factors in leadership. A career is blighted when expectations are thwarted and when the responsibility can readily be projected from the self upon society. When power is the frustrator, restitution and retaliation in terms of power are plausible possibilities. The failure of the established order to put Doctor of Philosophy Marx in a Prussian university post was of no small consequence in launching him on his career. And this is not untypical of the response to be expected of men who have sacrificed to acquire a skill for which society provides no suitable scope. Hence the dynamic role so often noted of students and unemployed intellectuals in movements of political protest.[7]

The person who has not passed the preliminary qualifications expected for a recognized place in society is another potential recruit in the power struggle. Sometimes disturbed times or economic adversity has prevented the completion of a regular education. Or the person is rebellious against the exactions of a teacher and falls by the wayside on the way to

[6] See Hutchinson (1938). In general, on social mobility and power consult Sorokin (1927).
[7] For example: Heinbert (1939, 1938); Rosten (1937); Neumann (1942).

a degree. As Bismarck contemptuously remarked, such a one may join the profession of the untrained—journalism; political journalism continues to be an avenue to power in modern societies.

There are famous cases in which a severe deprivation relatively late in life had led to furious concentration upon power. Joseph II of Austria, "the revolutionary emperor," as Saul K. Padover has called him, was transformed into the grim figure of his later days not only by the untimely death of his beloved wife but also by the shattering humiliation of the discovery that his wife had not loved him.[8] A turning point in the hitherto somewhat unfocused career of John Bright was the critical experience of losing his first wife. Three days after her death Richard Cobden after offering words of condolence said: "There are thousands of homes in England at this moment where the wives, mothers and children are dying of hunger. Now, when the first paroxysm of your grief is spent, I would advise you to come with me, and we will never rest until the Corn Laws are repealed." And he did.

The same principle of using power for compensatory purposes is exemplified in the undeniably important role of real or fancied physical limitations.[9] We remember the "withered arm" of William II of Germany, attributed to a fall when he slipped out of the hands of an English governess. And there was the short stature of Napoleon. We think, too, of the rapacious ambition of the palace eunuchs in the history of both China and the Near East. The fact or the fear of sexual inadequacy has been a bitter spur to the accentuation of power. Queen Elizabeth was plagued by persisting doubts as to her attractiveness and capacity as a woman. The smallpox that scarred Mirabeau turned him into an object of distaste to

[8] Specific studies are: Gerth (1940); Nomad (1932); Benda (1955); and Gooch (1952).

[9] Alfred Adler (1924) put heavy stress on compensations against organic inferiority as a major dynamism of personality. Eduard C. Lindeman phrased the hypothesis with his customary skill in *The Meaning of Adult Education:* "We are slowly coming to see that all 'power-grabbers' and dictators who reach out for unusual power are in reality compensating for inner deficiencies of their personalities."

his father. The ugliness of the famous political orators, Lord Brougham and John Randolph of Roanoke, was undoubtedly a factor in their political intensity. The infantile paralysis that Franklin D. Roosevelt overcame left him a better disciplined and more power-centered personality than when it struck him down. Like many men who escape death, he achieved the inner self-confidence and perspective of one who lives "on borrowed time."

An early illness or enforced period of inactivity has sometimes played a more important role in the development of personality than even the determination to overcome handicaps. Delicate children have gained knowledge from reading that aided in the consolidation of political aims. Mazzini, for instance, and William Pitt, Jr., appear to have made productive use of early invalidism.

The intensive study of infancy and childhood, conducted by modern methods of careful record taking, has underlined the decisive importance of the early years in shaping the structure of personality. These data have prodigiously documented and refined ancient maxims about the crucial significance of the early years. The data go in the direction toward which we have been pointing. The accentuation of power is to be understood as a compensatory reaction against low estimates of the self (especially when coexisting with high self-estimates); and the reaction occurs when opportunities exist both for the displacement of ungratified cravings from the primary circle to public targets and for the rationalization of these displacements in the public interest; and, finally, when skills are acquired appropriate to the effective operation of the power-balancing process.[10]

The factors that accentuate power in the person likewise operate in molding the response of the group. In general, according to our theory of power, we expect that power will be accented by groups when they expect it to protect them against deprivation or to restore and expand their influence. At the same time adverse estimates of the self must not be overwhelming, or the resort to power will be blocked by sentiments of utter hopelessness, such as have demoralized

[10] For a compendious review of research, see Breckenridge and Vincent (1965); and Murphy (1947).

certain folk cultures after exposure to the deprivations inflicted by the carriers of modern industrial civilization. Expectations favorable to the use of power in the future are strengthened by the recollection of successful applications of power in the past under similar circumstances. The paradigm case is Prussia in particular and Germany in general. To Prussians it was power in the disciplined form of military violence and, to a lesser extent, diplomacy that brought the group from the sandy barrens of the North Prussian plain to the startling eminence of a middle-sized and then a great power. Was Germany crushed by the Entente in 1918? Prussia had revived after being crushed to the earth by Napoleon and the French, and in the more distant past by the trauma of the Thirty Years' War and the depopulation and partition of the German people. The self of the representative German incorporated the symbol "German" and with it the entire myth of German history, character and destiny. The extremes of self-admiration and self-debasement present in this mythology provided a potent determiner for the accentuation of power in the name of the collective self throughout the group, and for the service of the central myth by the power-seeking personality.[11]

In reviewing the theory of political personality outlined in this chapter it may be useful to match it with the *homo politicus* of much popular and scientific tradition.[12] The image I refer to is that of the power-hungry man, the person wholly absorbed in getting and holding power, utterly ruthless in his insatiable lust to impose his will upon all men everywhere. Suppose that we refine this traditional conception into a speculative model of the political man comparable with the economic man of the older economic science.

The following postulates can be laid down (the numbering is arbitrary):

1. He demands power and seeks other values only as a basis for power.
2. He is insatiable in his demand for power.

[11] The detailed study of comparative politics has barely begun. Beginnings are made in Benedict (1946a); Kecskemeti and Leites (1945); Gorer (1943); La Barre (1945); and Gorer (1948).
[12] Catlin (1964) undertook to formulate a general theory.

3. He demands power for himself only, conceived as an ego separate from others.

4. His expectations are focused upon the past history and future possibilities affecting power.

5. He is sufficiently capable to acquire and supply the skills appropriate to his demands.

It is evident that the model, thus constructed, can only be completely satisfied by a world ruler, since the fifth postulate includes the idea of success. Since there have been no world rulers, this model can be used to investigate no known cases. (However, there have been universal states, if we take the expression to mean that the "known world" was under the domination of a single power of overwhelming strength.) Therefore, we can profitably begin to revise the postulates for the purpose of fitting the model to illuminate a broader range of concrete circumstances.

We can, for example, withdraw the success postulate, which makes the political man omnipotent, and simply make him omniscient, in the sense that he always foresees correctly the power consequences of the moves open to him in any given situation. This makes it possible for the political man to remain less than a world ruler, if he is counter-balanced by other power operators who similarly exploit to the full their power potential on the basis of correct calculation. But to postulate omniscience excludes the very features of reality that most require investigation if we are to build up a body of knowledge related to human behavior. One of the most rewarding questions to raise about decision making is this: on what expectations are wars declared, treaties signed, diplomatic intercourse resumed, international organizations launched or other measures used? Unless we can understand the interaction of expectations upon demand (and identification) we are not far along in comprehending anything worth knowing about the decision process. The examination of such perspectives calls for knowledge about how they interact not only in the person but also in the group; and how a given set of expectations or demands or identifications is affected by other perspectives and by other factors in the sociopolitical process.

The third postulate prescribes a wholly egocentric personality, since all demands are made solely for the expected enhancement of the primary ego. Hence the *homo politicus* is not permitted to have a self (by which is meant a symbol structure included with the primary ego and given equal treatment). According to our speculative model, the perfect power type is wholly absorbed with advancing the value position of the "sacred me" (not "us"). Hence he sacrifices anyone and everyone at convenience for his power, and does not conceive of power as a means of advancing the value position of family, neighborhood, nation or any other group. If we allow unconscious as well as conscious demands to be included in our model, the psychiatrist at least is likely to say that this *homo politicus* is never found in nature, and is most closely approximated by a few paranoid psychotics or psychopaths. It must be admitted, however, that these are met in history in positions of power, as in the notable instance of "mad King Ludwig" of Bavaria who liked a bit of human blood in his hunting bag.[13]

Let us conclude by saying that while everyone is compelled to agree that this model of the political man of tradition does, in fact, perform a certain scientific purpose by highlighting some historical and contemporary figures, such as the "mad Caesars," the model is unsuitable for the most comprehensive inquiries into the decision-making process. The conception is far out of line with many known cultures, social structures and even crisis facts. The emendations and elaborations called for in relation to such circumstances are almost literally "too numerous to mention."

There is the danger, often exemplified in economic analysis, of choosing a speculative model, which applies to a few extreme instances, and becoming absorbed with the refined restatement of the postulates, rather than with exploring the varied phenomena of society. As one economist wrote when criticizing a book on economic theory by a colleague,[14] "On pp. 76–77 his marionettes start as 'normal human beings . . . familiar in a modern Western nation . . . acting with ordinary human motives . . . knowing what they want and

---

[13] A guide to "pathographies" is provided by Lange-Eichbaum (1935).
[14] Hutchinson (1938:124), referring to Knight (1921).

seeking it intelligently.' But by p. 268 they have become 'mechanical automata.'" "Institutional economists" have attempted to absorb themselves in the context of concrete cultures and specific circumstances. But they have been rather slow in spinning a web of useful theory between the classical models of the perfect market and the many-colored tapestries of everyday life. In more recent times there are signs of a deliberate quest for speculative models of sufficient richness to further the interests of science and policy.[15]

Warned by this example, we use a theory of the political type that can be directly implemented with data of observation stemming from any concrete situation. Our political man:

1. accentuates power
2. demands power (and other values) for the self (the primary ego plus incorporated symbols of other egos)
3. accentuates expectations concerning power
4. acquires at least a minimum proficiency in the skills of power

The man who accentuates power is doing so *relative* to others, and therefore power personalities can be detected, by comparing them with standard expectancies for a culture, a social layer, a crisis or some other specified frame of reference. Besides accentuating power, it is recognized that the political type is not fully described until we know whether he is accentuating power in relation to one part of the self or all. We know that some identifications with the nation, for instance, guide and indeed swallow up the energies of the person. So far as the acquiring and exercise of skills is concerned, we provide only for some minimum degree of mastery which permits some measure of survival in the arena of power.

Our central picture of the political man, therefore, reduces the wolf man, the *homo lupus,* to a special pigeon hole. He is but one of the entire process by which primary motives are displaced onto public targets and rationalized in the name of public good.

[15] A clear instance: Friedman (1946).

Power as a Compensatory Value
for Political Leaders
Alexander L. George

Some years ago, Harold D. Lasswell drew upon the findings
and theories of various schools of dynamic psychology in
formulating a general hypothesis about the "power seeker"
as a person who "pursues power as a means of compensation
against deprivation. *Power is expected to overcome low
estimates of the self,* by changing either the traits of the self
or the environment in which it functions" (Lasswell, 1948:
39 and 53). The pervasiveness of power strivings as compensation for organic or imagined defects was given early emphasis by Alfred Adler. The fruitfulness of Adler's theories
for subsequent social psychological approaches to personality
is now widely recognized (Murphy, 1947: ch. 24).

LASSWELL'S POWER SEEKER

Lasswell deliberately formulated the hypothesis about the
"power seeker" in such general terms in order to encompass
a great variety of more detailed findings and hypotheses
about such matters. As a result, his hypothesis provides a
relatively "shallow" account of the origins of a need for
power, foregoing explanations have greater depth. There are

Reprinted by permission of the author and publisher from the
Journal of Social Issues, Volume 24, 1968, pp. 29–49.

resulting advantages, however, that should not be minimized. The hypothesis provides an alternative explanation of the need for power in terms (i.e., compensation for low self-estimates) that are easier to establish than a more detailed account of its earlier and deeper origins. The problems of interest to the political scientist generally do not require the same level of explanation in matters of this kind that the psychoanalyst is interested in. Moreover, the political scientist lacks the data, observational opportunities and diagnostic skills for making fuller in-depth reconstructions. Under these circumstances, attempts to do so are likely to be difficult, frustrating and unduly speculative—as well as often being unnecessary.

By linking the emergence of an individual's high valuation of, or need for power to low self-estimates, Lasswell's hypothesis usefully orients research on "power-oriented" political leaders to findings emerging from research on childhood development and socialization and to ego psychology. Attention is directed to the development of the "self" component of the ego, beliefs about the self, the extent and quality of self-esteem and its implications for behavior. In this context, attention is also directed to the emergence of the individual's personal values. Thus, the hypothesis holds that some individuals develop an unusually strong need or striving for power (and/or for other personal values such as affection, deference, rectitude) as a means of seeking compensation for damaged or inadequate self-esteem. Personal "values" or needs of this kind—which may be regarded as "ego motives" since they are part of the ego subsystem of the personality—are an important part of the individual's motivational structure. The operation of these "values" in the individual's behavior can be related not merely to deeper unconscious motives but also to the sphere of the "autonomous" functioning of the ego. In addition to utilizing various devices for dealing with unconscious motives (the classical ego defenses), the ego is also capable of employing various adjustive and constructive strategies in efforts to secure satisfaction for personal "values" such as the need for power, affection, deference, etc., thereby maintaining personality equilibrium. The emergence of these adjustive and constructive strategies, and their operation in the individual's choice, definition and performance of political roles constitute a useful focus for studying the interaction of personality and political behavior in political leaders.

The "shallowness" of Lasswell's hypothesis—i.e., the fact that it refers only to that layer of unconscious needs present in the ego self-system (i.e., the personal "values" referred to), does not rule out the possibility of exploring deeper levels of motivation and psychodynamic processes. Rather, far from cutting off this possibility, assessment of an individual's personal needs or values can provide a useful stepping stone to efforts to probe deeper, more complex dimensions of motivational structure and dynamics. Inferences can be made from the strength and operation of these personal needs to deeper levels of motivation. Psychoanalytic and related theories provide hypotheses linking personal needs that are part of the ego's self-system with the arcane recesses of motivation and its psychodynamics. These "ego motives" also have a linkage with psychogenetic, developmental hypotheses; many hypotheses of this kind are available concerning the origins of damaged self-esteem which, in turn, creates strong needs for power or other values.[1]

Another merit of Lasswell's general hypothesis about the "power-seeker", or *homo politicus,* is that it encourages the political scientist to move beyond the question of the detailed psychogenetic origins of the need for power to focus on fuller study of the development of the power seeker's interest in politics. How does the individual who emerges from childhood and into adolescence with this kind of subjective need for power go about developing a knowledge of politics, selecting one or another political role, acquiring relevant political skills, creating or utilizing opportunities to become a leader of organized groups? There are central questions concerning the socialization of political leaders, and they have important linkages with the emphasis in Lasswell's hypothesis on the compensatory character of some leaders' interest in power.

[1] I plan to develop these observations more fully in work in progress.

LASSWELL'S HYPOTHESIS IN POLITICAL
BIOGRAPHY

This paper attempts to broaden the theoretical framework of Lasswell's general hypothesis and suggests a method for employing it in research on political leaders. It is hoped that this will encourage those who want to use Lasswell's hypothesis in psychological biography to pay greater attention to the data requirements implicit in the hypothesis and to employ more explicit standards of inference in such studies.

Additional research in this direction seems highly desirable. While it is by no means the case that all political leaders are "power seekers", those whose interest in politics is of the kind postulated in Lasswell's hypothesis are of particular interest to political scientists and historians. As in the case of Woodrow Wilson, political personalities of this kind often emerge as reformers and innovators if successful in obtaining political office. Once in power, they often attempt to recast political institutions, reinterpret and expand the functions of existing political roles or create new ones which fit their needs, political style and aspirations. A better understanding of this kind of political personality, therefore, may throw light on the nature and psychodynamics of "role-determining" as against "role-determined" political leadership. Of course, the creation or reinterpretation of leadership roles can only be understood in the context of social-historical dynamics and the institutional setting. However, as Gerth and Mills observe (1953: ch. 14), the "great leader" has often been a man who successfully managed such institutional dynamics and created new roles of leadership.

Lasswell's general hypothesis has had some influence on subsequent studies of political leadership and political behavior more generally (Barber, 1965; Edinger, 1965; Hargrove, 1966; Lane, 1959). Some years ago I found it particularly valuable for understanding the development of Woodrow Wilson's interest in political power and some of the dynamics of his political behavior. In the belief that Lasswell's hypothesis is of wider application in the study of political leadership, I will try to show how it can be utilized in a relatively systematic manner for purposes of data collection and data interpretation. This requires that meaningful operational definitions be given to the key terms in the hypothesis: "low self-estimates", "power", "compensation". I will indicate some of the problems encountered in doing so, present a set of provisional operational definitions, and illustrate their application with materials available to the biographer on Woodrow Wilson.[2]

LOW SELF-ESTEEM

Let us begin with that portion of the hypothesis that postulates the presence of low self-estimates in the subject of study. Many life experiences can produce damaged self-esteem in the basic personality. We need not delve deeply here into the question of the psychogenesis of low self-estimates, either generally or for a specific person or the origins of other related personality dynamisms.[3]

[2] I will necessarily have to be selective in citing illustrative materials from Woodrow Wilson's career. Fuller documentation will be found in George and George (1956b: particularly 114–121). In preparing the biography, published in 1956, we learned of the existence of the Freud-Bullitt study of Wilson but it was unavailable to us.

[3] In 1948 Lasswell drew upon studies of personality development available at that time to present a generalized account of the causal conditions and psychodynamic processes whereby extreme cravings for power, respect and related deference values or needs come into being (Lasswell, 1948:44–54). It may be noted that Lasswell's earlier treatment of this question is quite compatible with Erik Erikson's more recent and somewhat more specific tracing of the origins of such personality dynamisms to special characteristics of the child's conflict relationship with his father and the way in which it is eventually resolved. In this respect, Erikson (1964:202–203) finds important common features in the childhood and adolescent development experiences of a number of reformers and innovators who have been studied: Luther, Gandhi, Kierkegaard, Woodrow Wilson, Eleanor Roosevelt. Of particular interest to our discussion of Lasswell's general hypothesis is Erikson's observation that in their early years all of these five reformers and ideological innovators exhibited low self-estimates, a

For our purposes an answer to the causal question—on which there are a variety of theories—is not essential; we can draw upon and utilize descriptions of the dynamics of such behavior, about which there tends to be less disagreement in the literature of dynamic psychology. Whatever creates a given personality dynamism in a particular individual, such as low self-estimates, it is the presence of that dynamism itself that is directly relevant to most of the questions we want to ask about his interest in leadership, his behavior in seeking political office and his performance in office.

The existence and operation of a dynamism such as low self-estimates often can be readily identified in the kinds of historical materials about a political leader (or aspirant to leadership) that are usually available to biographers. In addition, materials of this kind can sometimes be elicited by the investigator from the subject himself or from others who have known him.[4]

THE CASE OF WILSON

In Wilson's case, the importance of childhood experiences in this respect is richly suggested in materials collected by the official biographer (Baker, 1927). These suggest that some of the critical experiences leading to damaged self-esteem lay in the character of Wilson's relations with his father, a Presbyterian minister.

Dr. Joseph Wilson, a man of handsome and distinguished appearance, was an accomplished preacher. He was also a strict disciplinarian. He placed on young "Tommy", his first son, the burden of living up to his very high expectations for

---

strong conscience, precocious attention to "ultimate concerns" and a sense of responsibility for a segment of mankind. (In recent years Wolfenstein (1967) has explored in detail and on a comparative basis the question of psychogenetic origins in developing a model of the revolutionary personality.)

[4] Edinger (1965:275–281) reports that he found useful for structuring his interviews and search for data on Kurt Schumacher the earlier version of the operational definition of this hypothesis presented in our unpublished 1956 paper.

moral and intellectual attainments. Dr. Wilson undertook to
supervise the boy's early schooling. A harder taskmaster it
would be difficult to find. To illustrate: Dr. Wilson, who had
at one time been a professor of rhetoric, had a passion for
the correct use of the English language. "Tommy" was not
permitted the use of an incorrect word or an unpolished
phrase. His compositions had to be rewritten, sometimes four
or five times, before the elder Wilson was satisfied. This instruction, continued over a period of years, was of the most
intensive, exacting kind and demanded severe and conscientious application.

The father dealt with his son's imperfections with that
caustic wit for which he was noted among all who knew him.
In this tension-producing situation the child never openly re-
belled. It is significant, however, that he was slow in achieving the usual intellectual skills. He did not learn his letters
until he was nine. He could not read until he was eleven.[5]

"Low self-estimates" can be given detailed operational content for purposes of data collection by specifying some of the
subjective feelings of which it may be comprised. For example: (a) feelings of unimportance; (b) feelings of moral inferiority; (c) feelings of weakness; (d) feelings of mediocrity;
(e) feelings of intellectual inadequacy. Many of these, and
others, were present in Wilson's case. He felt eternally inferior to his father, in appearance as well as in accomplishment. His own recollections of his youth indicate early fears
that he was stupid, ugly, worthless and unlovable. These
feelings apparently had rich opportunities for elaboration in
his religious convictions concerning the fundamental wickedness of human nature. Data on subjective feelings of this
kind, of course, may not always be available to the investigator. It would be useful, therefore, to supplement this
operational definition of low self-estimates with items of behavior that are perhaps more easily observed.

[5] For a fuller account of this and other materials on Wilson, see
George and George (1956b: ch. 1), which also indicates some of
the father's positive contributions to the development of his son.

THE POWER MOTIVE

We turn now to the term "power" in Lasswell's general hypothesis. Several difficulties arise in attempting to give it a relevant operational definition. We must remind ourselves that "power" here is a value or need for the possession or exercise of sanctions or the means for influencing others. Accordingly, we do not seek to define "power" in order to measure objectively its presence or use. Rather, we define "power need" as the desire for and enjoyment of power, the high valuation or cathexis of power. And we want to find ways of identifying the presence of such a power need.

The character and content of an individual's "power" motive may be shaped by the conditions that gave rise to low self-estimates and its accompanying psychodynamics. One possibility is that the ensuing demand for power may be re-active-formative against the fear of passivity, of weakness, of being dominated. Another possibility is that the demand for power may be aggressive or destructive. Power, then, may be desired for various reasons in different power-demanding persons and perhaps at different times in the same individual. That is, power may be desired for one or more of these reasons: (a) so as to dominate and/or deprive others; (b) so as not to be dominated, or interfered with, by other political actors; (c) so as to produce political achievements. (It may be useful on future occasions to specify additional variants of the power need, or to restate these differently.)

As the third of these possible components of a "power need" implies, it may be *instrumental* at times rather than primary in persons who seek compensation thereby. Thus power may be desired and exercised in order to satisfy other personal needs, such as a need for achievement, for respect, for security, for rectitude. In some instances, one of the components of a power motive we have postulated—the desire not to be dominated by others—may seem to be an end in itself, more highly valued than other needs. In other cases, the desire for, pursuit and exercise of power may be clearly or predominantly instrumental for gaining satisfaction of other needs and values.

Two other conclusions about the status of the "power" motive have emerged from our effort to apply Lasswell's general hypothesis to Wilson. First, the demand or need for "power" in compensation-seeking political types does not operate uniformly in the subject's political motivation under all conditions. Rather, the presence and/or strength of the "power demand" (or of some components of it) in the individual's motivation varies, being subject to special arousal conditions. A second conclusion is that an individual's striving for "power" in the context of compensation may either be reinforced by, or in conflict with other strong needs—such as the need for affection, approval, respect, achievement, rectitude, etc.—that he may also be pursuing in the political arena.

In the case of a *multi*-valued political personality like Wilson, it is a complex task to establish the underlying motivational structure of different needs, and especially, to gauge the shifting interrelationship and priority of these needs. In attempting to determine the role of personality in the subject's political behavior it becomes necessary, therefore, to assess not merely the relative strength of individual needs or motives in the personality system generally but, more important, the ways in which the subject reconciles competing or conflicting needs in choosing his goals, and the conditions under which one or another need or pattern of needs has primacy in his behavior. For the importance and operative role of different needs in specific situations depends not only on their relative strength but may vary with the subject's shifting expectations as to the possibility of satisfying them in each situation. As the above suggests, I recognize that damaged self-esteem can create unusually strong needs for several values, not merely for power or another single value. In Wilson's case, we inferred a strong need also for affection, respect, rectitude and enlightenment. The interrelationship of these strong, at times competing, values in Wilson's motivation and political behavior is depicted in *Woodrow Wilson and Colonel House* (George and George, 1956b; for a brief summary see 319–322). I should add that in my initial study of Wilson (unpublished paper, 1941), I attempted to estimate from available historical data Wilson's high or low demand for most of the eight values the Harold Lasswell has listed and described on a number of occasions, including his contribution to the present volume. I do indeed agree with his emphasis on the importance of characterizing the subject's position with respect to all eight values. In the present paper, however, I have focused more narrowly than in the full-length study on the need for power and the problems of operationalizing it.

POWER-STRIVING FOR COMPENSATION

Let us turn now to the compensatory process mentioned in Lasswell's formulation about the "power seeking" type. If this hypothesis is correct and applicable to political leaders like Wilson, we would expect that in acquiring and exercising power the subject experiences not merely reduction of tension but also euphoric feelings of a kind that serve to counter some of the low self-estimates from which he suffers. The problem of establishing and tracing such a compensatory process empirically requires close examination of the relationship between (a) low self-estimates, (b) specific items of behavior that express the individual's power demand and satisfy it to some extent, and (c) the substantive content of the ensuing compensatory gratifications, if any. In this respect, however, it is well to heed the warning of clinical psychologists who have observed that uniform regularities cannot be expected between particular items of manifest behavior and their tension-reducing, equilibrium-restoring functions for the personality. The complexity of the dynamics of behavior in this respect adds to the difficulty of devising operational indicators of manifest behavior that can be taken as giving expression to the demand for "power" in persons striving thereby for compensation. For, evidently, the same item of manifest behavior may fulfill different functions for different personalities and, at different times, for the same individual.

We must be satisfied for the time being, therefore, with cataloguing various items of political behavior that may or may not express an individual's striving to gratify one or another component of his power need. In constructing such a catalogue we have drawn upon the syndrome of behavior associated with the so-called "compulsive" character in Freudian psychoanalytic accounts (Freud, 1950:45–50; and Fenichel, 1945:278–284). We list six items of behavior that serve as possible indicators of a striving for power gratification on the part of a compensation-seeking personality:

. . . *Unwillingness to permit others to share* in his actual or assumed field of power.[6]
. . . *Unwillingness to take advice* regarding his proper functioning in his actual or assumed field of power.
. . . *Unwillingness to delegate* to others tasks that are believed to belong to his regularly constituted field of power.
. . . *Unwillingness to consult* with others, who have a claim to share power, regarding his functioning in the actual or assumed field of power.
. . . *Unwillingness to inform* others with respect to his functioning in his actual or assumed field of power.
. . . *Desire to devise and impose orderly systems* upon others in the political arena.

Before leaving this topic, we remind ourselves that these items are only *possible* indicators of a power need in the personality. Depending on the context, behavior of this kind may serve other functions for the personality as well as its power need; or it may be entirely divorced from the individual's striving for power gratification.

Occurrences of these items of behavior in the leader's political activity may indeed be solely role-determined, being called for by his assessment of the way in which role expectations should be interpreted in the light of the requirements of the situation. On the other hand, personality needs may reinforce or conflict with role requirements and may either improve or distort his assessment of the situation and his choice of action alternatives.

In more general terms we are asserting the possibility that personality needs and motives of an unconscious character

[6] What is meant by "actual or assumed field of power" will be clarified shortly.

may influence an individual's *selection* and *definition* of political roles for himself; further, these needs may infuse themselves into his *performance* of these roles and help account either for unusually skillful or inexpedient behavior on behalf of the policy objectives to which he has ostensibly committed himself in the political arena. The fact that a person's behavior *can* be interpreted in terms of role demands, therefore, does not relieve the investigator from considering the possibility that aspects of basic personality are also expressing themselves and shaping such behavior. It is incorrect, therefore, to define the problem as some proponents of role theory tend to do in terms of "role versus personality". Rather, the interplay of role and personality needs to be considered.[7]

THE PRESENCE OF CONFLICTING EVIDENCE

There are many striking instances of these six items of behavior in Wilson's career. But, at the same time, there are also numerous examples and testimonials to the fact that in exercising the powers of his office Wilson did consult and inform others, took advice and delegated authority. Faced with apparently conflicting evidence of this kind, we found it fruitful to examine the behavior in question more closely. We found that different observers reporting on this aspect of his political behavior seemed to mean different things when asserting that he did or did not "consult". Some of the disagreement among observers on this score could be reduced to a language problem—that is, the absence of a rigorous standard language used scrupulously by all observers reporting on his behavior. (This can be dealt with by defining terms like "consultation" more precisely and translating reports by participant observers accordingly.)

The apparently conflicting evidence was reconciled also

[7] A particularly useful statement of this is provided by Levinson, (1959). A fuller discussion of these points with reference to Wilson's interest in writing constitutions (interpreted as manifesting and satisfying a desire to devise and impose orderly systems on others) appears in my unpublished paper (1960).

by analyzing the *conditions* under which Wilson did and did not consult, etc. This led to the formulation of a more selective statement of Lasswell's general hypothesis that has already been implied by including the phrase "in his actual or assumed field of power" in listing above the possible behavioral indicators of a power need. Let us clarify the phrase.

In order to overcome or compensate for low self-estimates, the power-seeking personality attempts to carve out a sphere of activity in which he can demonstrate his competence and worth. The importance of such a developmental process to a personality suffering from damaged self-esteem is obvious.[8] Achievement of competence in a given sphere of activity, however narrow or specialized it may be, provides the personality with a "field" in which it can function productively, possibly with considerable autonomy (freedom from "interference" from others), perhaps aggressively and self-righteously on occasion and more generally in a manner as to reach a personality equilibrium otherwise lacking for someone who suffers from low self-estimates.

Lasswell's general hypothesis is transformed in this way into a more selective one which helps to resolve the apparent inconsistency or contradictory behavior of the subject with regard to some of the six behavioral indicators listed above. Thus, the selective version of the hypothesis holds that manifestations of power-striving are not encountered throughout the entire range of the subject's political behavior but operate more selectively, that is, only when he is performing in his actual or assumed field of power. Even this formulation, we shall note shortly, does not sufficiently identify and restrict for a particular individual the conditions under which his power need manifests itself directly.

We may recall that Lasswell's general hypothesis about *homo politicus* confines itself to explaining a need for power

---

[8] The present discussion of "compensation" as emerging from a developmental process in which the individual suffering from low self-estimates carves out a "sphere of competence" and a "field of power" can be usefully related to Eric Erikson's concept of the adolescent identity crisis. The fruitfulness of a synthesis of Lasswell's hypothesis about power as compensatory for low self-estimates with Erikson's model of adolescent identity crisis is demonstrated, I believe for the first time, in Barber (1968).

in terms of compensation for low self-estimates, without venturing to push the explanation further in order to account also for the origins of low self-estimates. While the study of a power-oriented leader's career and political behavior may benefit from hypotheses as to the origins of his low self-estimates, the investigator need not feel hobbled by an inability to provide more specific, in-depth hypotheses of this kind (or to demonstrate such hypotheses). Rather, if he can demonstrate the applicability of Lasswell's general hypothesis to his subject, this should suffice by way of explaining his need for power. The investigator can then proceed to the essential, and more rewarding task of relating the subject's compensatory interest in power to his emerging expectations and orientations to the future, i.e., what he wants the state of affairs to be like in the near and more distant future, and how he proposes to help bring about these desired changes.

IN WILSON'S CASE

In Wilson's case, we find him engaged from early adolescence to early maturity in carving out or creating what we here have called a "field aim" and a "sphere of competence". An interest in politics manifested itself early. In his fourteenth year, Wilson organized a group of boys into a club and composed a constitution for it. Two years later his political interests had become more sharply defined. We find him sitting at his desk under a picture of Gladstone. When his little cousin asked who it was, Wilson replied: "That is Gladstone, the greatest statesman that ever lived. I intend to be a statesman, too". He settled his ambition upon a political career in his sophomore year in college. Thereafter, we find him defining his political ambition in terms of available political roles and striving to acquire knowledge and skills relevant to successful performance of the preferred political roles selected for himself. Thus, in his sophomore year at Princeton, Wilson read a series of articles on the relationship between oratory and political leadership. These articles, the official biographer notes, were "the precipitate that clarified the mind of the eager youth. They discovered to him the field which he loved. They made him suddenly aware of his own powers. . . . *He* could debate, he could lead"! Wilson sat down at once to write his father that he had discovered he had a mind. It is clear that oratory recommended itself to him as a means of achieving influence and control over others. At the close of his sophomore year, he wrote an article for the *Princetonian* which reveals his own ambitions: "What is the object of oratory? Its object is persuasion and conviction—the control of other minds by a strange personal influence and power".

Even before he became a teacher, Wilson had a clear idea of the use to which he would put his talent for oratory and a clear conception of the political role which he wished to play, should the opportunity arise. After the publication of his first book, *Congressional Government,* in 1885, he wrote his fiancée confessing that his heart's first ambition lay elsewhere:

> . . . I have a strong instinct of leadership, an unmistakably oratorical temperament, and the keenest possible delight in affairs; and it has required very constant and stringent schooling to content me with the sober methods of the scholar and the man of letters. I have no patience for the tedious toil of what is known as 'research'; *I have a passion for interpreting great thoughts to the world; I should be complete if I could inspire a great movement of opinion,* if I could read the experiences of the past into the practical life of the men of today and so communicate the thought to the minds of the great mass of the people as to impel them to great political achievements . . . . My feeling has been . . . . that *my power to write was meant to be a handmaiden to my power to speak and to organize action* . . . (italics supplied)[9]

WHEN WILSON CONSULTED

Even within his "actual or assumed field of power" a leader who pursues power as a compensatory value does not

[9] For documentation and elaboration see George and George (1956b:23).

invariably refuse to consult and take advice, to inform others and to delegate, etc. I will briefly summarize some of the more discriminating observations regarding Wilson's willingness or unwillingness to permit others to share in the powers of his office that emerged from an analysis of the conditions in which he acted one way or the other: (a) He typically consulted more readily in order to obtain facts rather than opinions; (b) he consulted and took advice more readily from those whose approval and affection he could count on;[10] (c) he could delegate power in matters in which he was little interested, matters which did not engage his aspiration for great achievement.[11]

WHEN WILSON COOPERATED

Wilson's expressed willingness to consult and cooperate with legislators was always a complicated matter. We found it necessary to distinguish two types of situations in analyzing Wilson's relationship with legislative bodies.

First, as long as the possibility existed of getting what he wanted from the legislature, Wilson could operate with considerable skill in order to mobilize potential support. He could be, as in the first year of the Governorship and in the "honeymoon" period of the Presidency, extremely cordial, if firm; gracious, if determined; and generally willing to go

[10] Persons like Senator Glass, Joseph Tumulty (his secretary), and especially Colonel House could serve Wilson as advisers either because they would not push their disagreements with him once they saw that his mind was made up, or because they were so deferential to him that they would accept his point of view when he finally formulated a position.

[11] Thus the official biographer, Baker (1927), could correctly observe that it was difficult for Wilson to delegate authority, "especially in matters which profoundly engaged his interest or awakened his emotions". And at the same time, Josephus Daniels, Wilson's Secretary of the Navy, could remark also with justice that "From the inception Mr. Wilson gave the members of his Cabinet free rein in the management of the affairs of their department. No President refrained so much from hampering them by naming their subordinates. Holding them responsible, he gave them liberty, confidence and cooperation".

through the motions of consulting and granting deference to legislators whose support he needed. It is this phase of his "party leadership" that excited the admiration of contemporaries and historians alike. However, these skillful tactics of leadership were predicated on the expectation that he would be able to push through his proposed legislation in essentially unadulterated form. As Wilson often put it, he was willing to accept alterations of "detail", but not of the "principles" of his legislative proposals.

Second, once opposition crystallized sufficiently to threaten the defeat or marked alteration of his legislative proposals, Wilson was faced with a different type of situation. Skillful political behavior—the logic of the situation—now demanded genuine consultation with opponents to explore the basis of disagreement and to arrive at mutual concessions, bargains and formulas to assure passage of needed legislation. In this type of situation Wilson was unable to function expediently and proved singularly gauche as a politician. Once faced with strong opposition to a legislative proposal to which he had committed his leadership aspirations, Wilson became rigidly stubborn and tried to force through his proposal without compromising it.

In these situations, the desire to succeed in achieving a worthwhile political objective, in part or in essence if not fully and exactly as he preferred, became of less importance than to maintain the equilibrium of his personality system. He seems to have experienced opposition to his will in such situations as an unbearable threat to his self-esteem. The ensuing struggle for his self-esteem led, on the political level, to stubborn self-defeating behavior on his part. For to compromise in such situations was to submit to domination in the very sphere of power which he had carved out for himself to repair his damaged self-esteem. Opposition to his will, therefore, set into motion disruptive anxieties and brought to the surface long-smouldering aggressive feelings which, as a child, he had not dared to express.

Thus, for example, when the possibility of rejection of the Treaty by the Senate was mentioned to him, Wilson snapped: "Anyone who opposes me in that, I'll crush"! When the

French Ambassador told Wilson that the Allies would be glad to accept American membership in the League even with a set of reservations that would satisfy influential Republican Senators, Wilson curtly replied: "Mr. Ambassador, I shall consent to nothing. The Senate must take its medicine". When the acting Senate Democratic minority leader, Hitchcock, suggested concessions to win over enough Republican Senators, Wilson replied: "Let Lodge hold out the olive branch". Earlier, upon returning from the Paris Peace Conference in February 1919 Wilson publicly announced his determination to strike back at Senatorial critics of the Treaty: "I have fighting blood in me," he boasted, "and it is sometimes a delight to let it have scope. . . ." (George and George, 1956b:235, 289, 301, 311).

We have noted a cyclical pattern of this kind in Wilson's career, a repetition of this maladaptive self-defeating behavior as President of Princeton, Governor of New Jersey and as President of the United States. This was not an area in which he was able to learn from his earlier difficulties and failures, a fact which testifies indirectly to the presence and operation of strong unconscious motives.

EVIDENCE OF COMPENSATION

Let us take up now another problem encountered in attempting to make relatively systematic applications of Lasswell's general hypothesis. The hypothesis requires evidence that the exercise of power over others does indeed yield the individual compensatory gratifications. For the hypothesis to hold, and to be applicable to a given individual, it is not sufficient that he find it generally pleasant to exercise power; its exercise must provide him with satisfactions of a special kind appropriate to his low self-estimates.

The prospect for obtaining systematic evidence of subjective feelings of this kind from materials conventionally available to the biographer or to the student of political leadership must be viewed soberly. Yet, even episodic and fragmentary evidence of this kind—and perhaps that is all that can be realistically expected—will serve to give insight into the compensatory dynamics of the subject's involvement in various areas of his political behavior.

The next step in operationalizing the general hypothesis is to formulate a catalogue, however tentative or incomplete, of the *types of euphoric feelings* a personality of this kind might be expected to experience if, indeed, the hypothesis is correct regarding the compensatory character of his interest in power.

A first approximation of this kind was derived from psychoanalytic literature in which several types of euphoric feelings associated with power-striving and gratification are described. The listing of these feelings was then elaborated and structured more systematically by identifying the logical counterparts to the low self-estimates identified and listed above. From this emerged the following list of five low self-estimates and the corresponding euphoric feelings to be expected in cases when power was exercised in a manner that the subject could represent to himself as being successful:

Low Estimates of Self	*Euphoric Feeling*
	(from successful functioning in actual or assumed sphere or power)
Feelings of unimportance:	*Sense of uniqueness,* the subjective experiencing of which may be paraphrased as follows: "If what should be done is to be accomplished, I must do it since no one else will undertake it or is in a position to do it". (Note the relation to the feeling that one is the "chosen instrument", the feeling of being "indispensable" for a certain task, the feeling of having a "mission".)
Feelings of moral inferiority:	*Sense of superior virtue:* "I know best what is right (moral) in this matter".

Low Estimates of Self	*Euphoric Feeling*
Feelings of weakness:	*Sense of superior strength:* "No one can tell *me* what to do in this sphere; others, not I, must yield".
Feelings of mediocrity:	*Sense of superior ability:* "No one else can do this (whatever the subject is doing in his field of power) so well".
Feelings of intellectual inadequacy:	*Sense of intellectual superiority* (in sphere of competence and power functioning): "My judgment is infallible; I never make mistakes; I can rely upon my own reasoning".

WILSON'S EUPHORIC FEELINGS

We did not expect that euphoric feelings of the kind listed above would be explicitly and fully articulated very often in the kinds of historical materials available for the study. Perhaps the most that could be expected were occasional hints or expressions of such feelings. In the end, however, a surprising amount of relevant data of this kind was turned up indicating that Wilson had experienced many of these euphoric feelings from the exercise of his power. Some of this material has already been presented. A few additional examples of the kind of historical material we have regarded as evidence in this respect will be cited here.

After rewriting the constitution of the Johns Hopkins debating society, thereby transforming it into a "House of Commons", Wilson reported to his fiancée the great pleasure he had derived from the project:

It is characteristic of my whole self that I take so much pleasure in these proceedings of this society . . . I have a sense of power in dealing with men collectively which I do not feel always in dealing with them singly.

Indeed, all his life long, Wilson was rewriting constitutions, deriving satisfaction from reordering the relations of men along what he considered to be more fruitful lines. That constitution-writing had a deep personal meaning for Wilson is further suggested by the fact that such activities were always also instrumental to his desire to exercise strong leadership.

As a youth, he revamped the constitution of every club and organization to which he belonged in order to transform it into a miniature House of Commons. Indeed, he often renamed it thus. In these model Houses of Common in which Wilson, as the outstanding debater, usually became Prime Minister, independent leadership was possible and the orator could make his will prevail. Thus, rewriting constitutions was for Wilson a means of restructuring those institutional environments in which he wanted to exercise strong leadership by means of oratory, a skill in which he was already adept as an adolescent and to the perfection of which he assiduously labored for years. From an early age Wilson's scholarly interest in the workings of American political institutions was an adjunct of his ambition to become a great statesman.

When Wilson's career is studied from this standpoint considerable light is thrown on the intriguing question of the role of personal motivations in political inventiveness and creativity. (George and George, 1956b:144–148, 321–322.) Political psychologists have hypothesized that a compulsive interest in order and power is often to be found in strong political leaders who were great institution-builders and who made it their task to transform society. The case study of Wilson lends support to his hypothesis.[12]

---

[12] It should be noted, as Barber has emphasized (1965, and in a personal communication), that political institutions also "compensate". In order to survive and to act, institutions also develop adaptive strategies and ways of handling conflict. It is the interplay of these institutional adaptive strategies and habits with those of individual incumbents that has important implications for the stability and effectiveness of government.

WHEN CARVING OUT A SPHERE OF COMPETENCE

The process of carving out a sphere of competence, already referred to, is marked by a tendency to shift from one extreme of subjective feelings to the other: that is, from lack of self-confidence to high self-estimates and self-assurance in the actual or assumed field of power. Wilson could establish a sphere of competence for himself only by meeting very high standards. He went through painstaking, conscientious study and practice in order to acquire the necessary knowledge and skills, and in order to legitimize in his own eyes his right to a sphere of competence in which to function autonomously and as a leader of other men. But once having established it, he could not permit himself or others to question it. Within this sphere of competence, he felt free—almost defiantly—to assert a sense of intellectual superiority.

One of his friends, Mrs. Edith G. Reid, cites a letter he wrote at the age of thirty to a former classmate:

Hiram, I have—as I hope you have not discovered, but as you doubtless have—an intellectual self-confidence, possibly out of all proportion to my intellectual strength, which has made me feel that in matters in which I have qualified myself to speak I could never be any man's follower. . . .

To this Mrs. Reid comments:

Such confidence in himself might at this time seem merely youth's bravado, but it was part of the essence of his nature—the quality which made people so often exclaim, 'Do you never think yourself wrong'? And the answer would always be the same. 'Not in matters where I have qualified myself to speak'.

This type of see-saw process, from great uncertainty to extreme certainty, can be noted not only in Wilson's development but also in his decision process in specific situations. Many of his decisions reflect the characteristics of the compulsively conscientious person who passes from pronounced subjective doubt to extreme subjective certainty. Once Wilson emerged with a decision on an issue, especially one which mobilized his aspirations for high achievement, his mind snapped shut. He felt his decision was the only possible one morally as well as intellectually. Having conscientiously put himself through a laborious examination of relevant facts, he categorically identified his view of the matter with righteousness and would not permit himself or anyone else to question it. Thus, a dogmatic insistence on a particular viewpoint frequently followed a protracted period of indecision on the question. Once he had evolved his own position, he was typically impatient of any delay on the part of others, even those who might still be committed to ideas which he himself only shortly before had held with equal tenacity.

For years, for example, he opposed federal action to establish women's suffrage. When at last, during the war, he was converted to the cause, he began at once to deride Senators who did not instantly respond to his plea that the Senate concur in a constitutional amendment to enfranchise women:

'When my conversion to this idea came' he told a group of suffragettes on October 3, 1918, 'it came with an overwhelming command that made it necessary that I should omit nothing and use the position I occupied to enforce it, if I could possibly do so. I pride myself on only one feature of it, that I did understand when circumstances instructed me. There are some men who, I am sorry to say, have recently illustrated the fact that they would not learn. Their minds are provincial. They do not know a great influence when it is abroad . . . . I have to restrain myself sometimes from intellectual contempt.'

Unfortunately, this was a typical attitude, often openly expressed, toward those who also shared in the power of decision and who disagreed with him.

Again, after a period of agonized uncertainty about whether or not to lead the nation into World War I, he convinced himself of its necessity and ever afterwards vehemently denounced those whose doubts persisted. For, as he wrote Arthur Brisbane on September 4, 1917, the issues had assumed in his mind "a great simplicity". (George and George, 1956b:120–121.)

IN CONCLUSION

The provisional operationalization of the key terms in Lasswell's hypothesis that has been presented and illustrated in this paper with reference to Wilson may have to be revised or supplemented if other leaders are also studied in some detail. Hopefully, these operational definitions and lists of possible indicators will be useful even for those leaders who, as I would expect, express their power need in ways different from Wilson's. From this standpoint, the question is: Are the operational definitions sufficiently general and comprehensive to permit somewhat different findings for different leaders, i.e., different results expressed within the framework of a standardized set of operational definitions of "low self-estimates", "power need", "power striving", "compensation"?

It will be seen that I distinguish between the question of the "generality" of the operational definitions (which I hope can be obtained) and the question of the "generality" or uniformity of the *behavioral manifestations* of power-as-a-compensatory value (where I expect to find interesting variations among different leaders who fall under Lasswell's general hypothesis about the power-seeker but possess different kinds of multi-valued personalities and/or operate in different political contexts).

Another problem can be anticipated if Lasswell's hypothesis is applied to a larger sample of political leaders. This concerns the matter of the observational approach the investigator needs to take in order to establish whether adult political leaders who apparently possess high self-esteem suffered earlier in life from low self-estimates and, hence, whether their self-esteem is importantly "compensatory". To employ or test Lasswell's hypothesis does require a *developmental* study of the individual. Cross-sectional observations and measurements of the self-esteem status of an adult political leader may, if of a superficial character, fail to turn up indicators of the earlier low self-estimates problem experienced by the personality; hence, that individual may be incorrectly placed outside of Lasswell's hypothesis.

Operationalization of Lasswell's general hypothesis is, in any case, necessary if it is to be applied systematically in empirical research on political personality and behavior. These operational definitions must be valid, of course, from the standpoint of the findings and theory of dynamic psychology; but at the same time, they have been selected and formulated so as to provide links to the kind of empirical data about political behavior that is available to political scientists.

We are, as a result, in a better position to organize collection of relevant and critical data for application and assessment of the hypothesis. If these operational definitions are adequate and defensible, they provide specific links to relevant empirical data that is already available about the subject or that, possibly, can be acquired from him or from others who know him. The presence of behavioral data of this kind, properly analyzed and interpreted, provides a demonstrable basis for inferring the applicability of the general hypothesis to the political personality of the subject in question—i.e., his interest in power as a means of compensation for low self-estimates—and, of course, for additional analysis of the role this dynamism plays in his political behavior: in his choice of political roles, the character and skillfulness of his performance of those roles. Conversely, the absence of such behavioral data on low self-estimates, on a subjective interest in power, and on compensatory gratifications from its exercise can be taken as an empirical basis for rejecting the applicability of the general hypothesis to a given political leader.

The effort to apply Lasswell's hypothesis to Woodrow Wilson, it should be noted, led to the formulation of a more selective version of the hypothesis, one which identified the special conditions under which the kind of personal need for power postulated by the hypothesis was present in Wilson's political behavior. This highlights the importance in such studies of identifying the "field of power" within which the individual will strive for compensation and the types of situations in which the individual's power-need will be aroused.

If we may generalize provisionally from this one case, the demand or need for power in compensation-seeking personalities does not operate uniformly in the individual's political motivation under all conditions. The presence or strength of the power demand (or of some components of it) may be expected to vary, being subject to special arousal conditions. Finally, our study calls attention to the fact that *homo politicus* is likely to be a multi-valued personality; his striving for power as compensation may be reinforced by, or conflict with strong personal needs for other values that he may also pursue in the political arena. It is a complex but necessary task to establish not only general motivational patterns in multi-valued leaders but also the conditions under which one or another need or pattern of needs has primacy in the subject's political behavior.

Power Motivation and the Political Personality
Rufus P. Browning and Herbert Jacob

How important is the desire for power in the quest for political office? To what extent does it dominate the acts of politicians, of political leaders? The common assumption, reflected in many political biographies and in popular writing, is that the quest for power propels many into politics and is a most likely explanation for much of the politician's activity. Political scientists—especially in recent years—have been a bit more cautious. Harold D. Lasswell (1948:229–230) wrote fifteen years ago that political man accentuates power, demands power for the self, accentuates expectations concerning power, and acquires at least a minimum proficiency in the skills of power. Yet a few years later, speaking of democratic political man, Lasswell noted that the power-hungry individual may be too compulsive and rigid to win power; he is more likely to be found at the fringes of the political system than at its center (Lasswell, 1954). In reviewing what little evidence existed on the motivations of politicians, Robert Lane (1959:128) suggested that "among the leaders of a democracy there is little tendency for a higher-than-average concentration of persons with needs to exercise power over others."

Little empirical work has been done in the field, for valid

Reprinted by permission of the authors and publisher from *The Public Opinion Quarterly*, Volume 28, 1964, pp. 75–90.

measures of power motivation have not been available.[1] In recent years, however, psychologists have developed a projective test that taps power motivation as well as achievement and affiliative motivation. They have given the test to experimental groups, students, businessmen, and armed forces personnel, and to a nationwide sample. One of the developers of the test has used it to expound a unique psychological theory of economic development (McClelland, 1961a). This paper applies the test for the first time to politicians. We examine the intensity of power motivation (as measured by the test) displayed by politicians in two widely separated locales. The questions we ask are: (1) How strongly are politicians motivated to seek power, achievement, and friendship (affiliation) as compared with non-politicians? (2) To what extent do characteristics of the political system—specifically, the kinds of positions available and the opportunity structure of the community—make a difference in the motivations of the individuals attracted to politics?

THE TEST OF MOTIVATION[2]

The test we used is an outgrowth of the Thematic Apperception Test. Like the TAT, it assumes that respondents will reveal deeply rooted impulses in their imaginative responses to pictures. The form we used consisted of six pictures: an older man talking to a younger one in a rather old-fashioned office; a man sitting at what is apparently a drafting table with a picture of a woman and children in front of him; seven younger men around a table; a man working at a desk in an otherwise dark office, hat and coat piled at the side; a man in city clothes talking to a boy sitting on a farm fence; and a man leaning back in what many people interpret as a seat in an airplane with papers or a book on his lap.

[1] Still unique in its effort to test such hypotheses is McConaughy (1950).
[2] The main sources of information and theory about the test are McClelland et al. (1953), McClelland (1961a), and Atkinson (1958).

These pictures sometimes evoke stories with clear political content, such as this one:

> [This man] is organizing, no doubt, or joined an organization, giving his points or giving his political—giving out what he thinks is so, giving out his orders, or forming an organization. He's a leader. I have no doubt that he wants good government. If this is the same man in this picture, he has one thing in mind and that is to bring out the picture for generations to come. These people will go out, no doubt, this man is going out now to campaign. You've got four interested parties listening to him and they're going to bring charges against him.

The main character is an influential person, he is engaged in influencing activity, and he wants to be influential—all signs of concern about power. Power-oriented stories may also be present in an entirely non-political context:

> It looks like a group of young fellows in a club. One is pointing up some decision, trying to get the others to go along. One is not interested at all, and one is undecided. The man sitting down, pointing, is the one who is very strong with his thoughts. He is going to win out and get his point across.

The scoring system does not depend on the context of the plot but rather on the actions or feelings depicted. When a story involves attempts to control others, it is scored for power motivation. Additional points are scored if someone in the story is actually influencing others, anticipates doing so, shows joy or anguish about influencing others, states a need to influence, or overcomes obstacles in influencing others. The stories are scored in a like manner for achievement motivation when stories concern individuals trying to do well in any activity and for affiliative motivation when stories involve attempts to win or maintain friendly relationships with others.

The scoring system has been standardized to allow self-training with the use of a manual, so that a novice can quickly score stories expertly.[3] Each story is scored separately for each of the motives. A maximum possible score on the six-story test is 60 for power and affiliative motivation and 66 for achievement, but these are never attained; almost all of our scores lie in the 0 to 20 range.

The test is well validated, in several ways.[4] Versions of it have been experimentally validated (mainly with students), in that the test has been shown to measure individual responses to experimental situations that are presumed to arouse motivation. For instance, men who were told the test was a measure of ability and might affect their career chances scored higher in achievement motivation than men who were told it was just a graduate student's experiment. Candidates for campus office had higher power motivation scores while waiting for ballots to be counted than other students showed during an ordinary classroom session. Students who had just been rated for popularity by their fra-

---

[3] See the scoring manuals in Atkinson et al. A score-rescore rank-order correlation of .90 indicates sufficient skill to use the results of the test for research purposes. Both authors attained this standard.

[4] See McClelland (1953) and Atkinson (1958: Chapters 3–6). The particular advantage of a validated psychological test in this research (in contrast, for example, to data from interviews) is that it provides an assurance that the same motives are being measured in many separate studies of a wide range of important dependent variables, ranging from class-related differences in child-raising practices to patterns of decision making. The network of theoretically meaningful empirical associations that attach to the test as the result of extensive research, and the repeated experimental validations, far outweigh in our opinion an unsuccessful attempt by Reitman to arouse achievement motivation in student subjects after the method of the original experimental validation studies. See Reitman (1960). In addition, it should be noted that projective measures of motivation are subject to special limitations vis-à-vis test-retest reliability. However, "it would not appear wise to insist on high test-retest reliability before using such measures because it is so hard to replicate testing conditions—to put the subject back in the condition he was in before he made the first response. Instead, one can rely on other criteria, such as validity, for inferring stability of motivational dispositions indirectly" (McClelland, in Atkinson 1958:20). Test-retest checks have in fact yielded low correlations (about .4) (Birney, 1959).

ternity brothers scored higher in affiliative motivation than a fraternity group that took the test routinely along with a food-rating test.

More substantial and theoretically much more interesting validations than these, however, stem from dozens of studies exploring relationships between motivation, on the one hand, and features of behavior, role, status, upbringing, and other variables, on the other hand.[5] Studies have shown that men with strong achievement motivation perform well in a variety of tasks, tend to persist longer, choose moderate, realistic risks rather than very safe or very doubtful ones, and perform better as the chances of success drop, apparently stimulated by the challenge of a difficult task. Achievement motivation in men is the result of quite specific patterns of relationships with the boy's father and mother, and these characteristic child-raising practices are related to the socio-economic class of the parents.

Somewhat fragmentary evidence indicates that men with strong power motivation are more argumentative and try to influence others more frequently (Verkoff, 1956 and 1958: 105–116).

Studies of the behavioral correlates of affiliative motivation suggest that those who score high tend to seek approval more than others, but their peers rate them as relatively unpopular; they are also rated as overcautious and dependent on others for decisions. In contrast, men high in achievement motivation but low in affiliative motivation are rated as socially poised and adept, self-possessed, and consistent; this group is strong in such qualities as conversational facility and ability to communicate ideas effectively. Furthermore, this group (*low* in affiliative motivation) states a preference for working with people rather than with things.[6] Note that affiliative motivation—concern with warm, friendly relationships—is not necessarily an approach motive and apparently may often be a real barrier to dealing with people.

[5] McClelland very briefly cites and summarizes conclusions from studies of the behavioral correlates of achievement motivation, and much more extensively in 1961a: Chapters 6–8.
[6] Shipley and Verkoff (1958:83–94); Atkinson, Heyns and Verkoff (1958:95–104); and Groesbeck (1958:383–399).

It seems that strong concern for friendly personal relationships, perhaps accompanied by anxieties that interfere with attempts to relieve such concern, manifests itself in part in behavior that is usually not admired or liked—approval seeking, excessive caution, vacillation, etc. It is apparent that motive-generated acts may not lead to goal attainment and motive satisfaction. Affiliative motivation is not the same thing as sociability or liking to be with people. We should not expect the stereotype of the glad-handing politician to score high on this motive.

In short, these measures of motivation are associated with a large range of variables prominent in leadership recruitment and other behavior of leaders—e.g., risk taking, class background, dependence, consistency, sensitivity to opportunities to influence others. For instance, it would be surprising if the ability to assess risks and a willingness to take moderate, realistic ones were not important ingredients in the rise to high office and in the making of public policy decisions. As another obvious example, we are very often concerned about the degree of dependence of political executives on the people with whom they deal. It seems plausible that motivational factors are important in cases like these.

ADMINISTRATION OF THE TEST

In the present application, the authors gave the test to politicians at the beginning of an hour-long interview on their political careers. It was introduced as a test of imagination, with no hint given that the purpose was to measure motivation. Stories respondents told were recorded in one case by shorthand (Browning) and in the other by tape recorder (Jacob), with respondents' consent. When the stories were scored, the identity of the respondent was effectively hidden.

We tested politicians in two places: a middle-sized Eastern city (Browning) and two parishes (counties) in Louisiana (Jacob). In Louisiana, the sample consisted of 50 elected local officials who represented 67 per cent of all elected officials in their parishes.[7] In Eastern City, respondents were a random sample of 23 businessmen (not retired) who had been or were ward chairmen, had run for or held elective office (both local and state) in the city, or had held appointive patronage positions, usually only part-time in conjunction with political activity at the ward level.[8] In addition, the test was given in Eastern City to a sample of 18 politically inactive businessmen who matched 18 of the businessmen-politicians with respect to type and size of business, career level and specific occupation, religion, ethnic background, urban residence, average education, and age.

MOTIVATIONS OF POLITICIANS

In the literature of political science, one can find almost as many reasons for expecting politicians to exhibit moderate power motivation as high power motivation. Although politics is frequently concerned with power, blatantly power-hungry individuals are distrusted in a democratic system. It is common, nevertheless, to suppose that all politicians have at least some basic traits in common, among them concern for power (Jacobs, 1962).

Our evidence does nothing to support this image. In Table 1, Eastern City politicians have only slightly higher mean power motive scores than the matched non-politicians, and the variation within both groups is large. Indeed, in Louisiana, 12 of the 50 politicians scored zero on the test. In short, politicians we tested did not uniformly have any particular level of power motivation, and are not clearly different in

[7] The remainder of the officials in the two parishes were accounted for as follows: 5.4 per cent were located in remote fishing communities quite different from the rest of the parishes; 2.7 per cent were women, for whom the test was not appropriate; 12.1 per cent were respondents who took the test but for whom the tape recordings were defective; and 12.1 per cent were officials who could not be contacted.

[8] Of a population of 32 businessmen-politicians, 27 were selected by a random process, 23 were interviewed. Of the 4 dropouts, 2 were out of town during the interviewing period, 2 refused to be interviewed.

power motivation from non-politicians of similar occupation and status.

The sociability of politicians has often been noted. The test permits us to assess concern for warm personal relationships. We hypothesized that politicians would score low on this trait, for much of politics is inimical to this kind of relationship. In contrast to sociability, i.e. a friendly manner, the real need for friendship and approval that characterizes a high level of affiliative motivation is probably incompatible with political activity. Politicking often requires single-minded attention to winning over others or manipulating them; it may also entail hurting some friends and helping others if one tends to regard political acquaintances and associates as potential friends.

TABLE 1

MEAN MOTIVE SCORES OF POLITICALLY ACTIVE AND
INACTIVE BUSINESSMEN IN EASTERN CITY
(18 MATCHED PAIRS)

Motive*	Politicians	Non-politicians	Diff.	p of Diff.†
Power	6.5	5.2	1.3	.13‡
Affiliation	4.2	2.9	1.3	.28§
Achievement	7.4	6.1	1.3	.20‡

* Differences within groups between power, achievement, and affiliative motive scores do not signify that a group has, for instance, on the average "more" achievement than affiliative motivation; the evocation of motive-related imagery of various sorts is heavily dependent on the cues in the particular pictures used. Hence scores for each motive are comparable between individuals or groups, but not between motives in the same individual or group.

† From Wilcoxon matched-pairs signed-ranks test on ranked motive scores; hence the different p-values in spite of identical differences between means.

‡ One-tailed.

§ Two-tailed (difference not in predicted direction).

The data in Table 1 show that this line of reasoning is apparently wrong—in Eastern City, businessmen-politicians as a group are *more* concerned with friendship than businessmen who are not politicians. In Louisiana, the degree of dispersion on this measure was about the same as in Eastern City. As with power, politicians apparently do not possess a uniform level of affiliative motivation and are not clearly different from non-politicians.

Familiar characterizations of politics as involving risk taking and persistence led us to hypothesize that politicians would score high on achievement motivation. But the Eastern City politicians did not in any sense score significantly higher than non-politicians (Table 1). In Louisiana, 10 of the 50 had zero scores, while others scored quite high.

In sum, our data indicate that none of the three motives are peculiarly characteristic of the total samples of politicians tested. When compared with a control group, politicians did not differ markedly from non-politicians. Moreover, in both Eastern City and Louisiana, all three sets of motive scores showed considerable dispersion, indicating a lack of homogeneity in our samples with respect to motivation.

MOTIVATION IN THE CONTEXT OF THE POLITICAL SYSTEM

This variation in scores encourages us to look for factors that would lead individuals with different motives to enter or remain in politics. Two obvious sets of factors involve the characteristics of the political system and within the system, the characteristics of the specific offices available. We believe that these characteristics engage the motivations of politicians in identifiable patterns that can help us explain the recruitment of certain individuals into politics.

Motivated behavior—for example, the choice of one activity over another less preferred—is the product of (1) the individual's underlying motivation, or need for a certain kind of satisfaction, and (2) his expectations or perception of motive satisfaction in the alternative activities.[9] A person highly motivated for power may choose to concentrate on

[9] We are following here the suggestions of Atkinson (1958: Chapter 20).

business (or take it out on his wife) rather than get into politics. In some cases, this is the result of other motives—for instance, a desire to make a great deal of money, or a desire for prestige in a group in which business occupations are highly valued. But the choice is in part also the result of the individual's perceptions of business and politics. He may be quite ignorant of politics and expect opportunities for influence only in business. He may perceive opportunities in politics but expect, rightly or wrongly, that they are out of his reach. He may perceive political power but see politics as a dirty game in which one must deal with and accept as associates lower-class and perhaps even dishonest people. Choice depends on expectations or perceptions as well as on motives.

Many of the ingredients of the possible combinations of perceptions and motives are the consequence of the political system in which the individual finds himself. Is it easy or difficult to enter? Is accession to power closed to all outside a particular social, racial, or economic group? Are important decisions tightly controlled by a small, durable elite? Does political activity in the system involve considerable financial sacrifice? Is politics an arena where important decisions are in fact being made? Is politics a bitterly competitive activity in the community, or is it relaxed, easygoing, and friendly? The answers to this sort of question will help determine the kinds of satisfactions and dissatisfactions perceived in politics by individuals of varying socio-economic status who are motivated in varying degrees for power, achievement, and affiliation. Men who are strongly power-motivated, for instance, are likely to be attracted only to certain kinds of political systems, and then only to certain offices or roles within the system. Men intensely motivated for achievement will get into politics and seek office only when they perceive opportunities for achieving, with effort, whatever it is they define as achievement—perhaps getting a new school or new streets built, or initiating a redevelopment program, or perhaps simply running a businesslike city government. Where such opportunities are seemingly not available, strongly achievement-motivated men are not likely to enter politics on their own initiative.[10]

We shall consider relationships, first, between motivation and kind of office held or run for and, second, between motivation and characteristics of the political systems.

Motivational differences among offices. We made no systematic direct measurement of perceptions of power, achievement, and affiliative opportunities in the offices that appear in our samples, but we felt justified in dichotomizing the offices into positions with high and low potential for achievement and power (see Table 2). The division was carried out on the basis of our own impressions and of the impressions of others, including some of the respondents intimately familiar with the communities. For this purpose, we defined positions with high power potential as those from which any occupant would be perceived to have relatively plentiful opportunities for advancement to more influential positions or for influence over matters of public policy, party affairs, or the enforcement of laws, where enforcement was in practice a matter of discretion for the officeholder.[11] Not all occupants of these positions were influential, but the positions were generally regarded as ones from which one *could* exercise influence, and all the men who we knew were influential were occupants of positions of this sort.

To classify the offices according to achievement potential, we defined achievement potential as opportunity to attain policy objectives or to advance to higher offices. The definitions of achievement and power potential are largely over-

[10] Inferring from high motive scores of certain officeholders that they sought office because of their motivation depends on the assumption that they initiated their own political activity rather than being recruited by their party. Our impression of the kind of men who are recruited by the parties for local and state offices is that they are likely to be less strongly power- and achievement-motivated than those who initiate their own activity; if so, motive scores of all those in office underestimate the role of motivation in self-recruitment.

[11] This last subcategory arises only in the case of some Louisiana justices of the peace and constables who exercised discretion over enforcement of gambling laws.

TABLE 2

POSITIONS WITH HIGH AND LOW POWER AND ACHIEVEMENT
POTENTIAL IN EASTERN CITY AND IN CASINO AND CHRISTIAN
PARISHES, LA.

| | Power Potential | | Achievement Potential | |
	High	Low	High	Low
Eastern City	City Council State Representative State Senator	City Clerk Registrars of Voters, Vital Statistics Patronage, sinecure positions Ward chairmen	Same as for Power Potential	Same as for Power Potential
Casino Parish	Justice of the Peace Constable Parish Council Parish School Board State Representative Parish-wide (Sheriff, Assessor, etc.)	None	Parish Council Parish School Board State Representative Parish-wide	Justice of the Peace Constable
Christian Parish	Parish School Board Parish Council Parish-wide (Sheriff, Assessor, etc.)	Justice of the Peace Constable	Parish School Board Parish Council Parish-wide	Justice of the Peace Constable

lapping, in practice—attaining policy objectives is, in our dictionary, equivalent to influencing matters of public policy. Consequently, positions high in achievement potential are also high in power potential. The converse is *not true,* however. Positions high in power potential may not be high in achievement potential. For example, if some of the ward chairmen in Eastern City had been party leaders who were influential with respect to party nominations but not with respect to public policy, they would have been classified high in power potential but low in achievement potential. Similarly in Christian Parish, where gambling is non-existent and justices of the peace have little control over anything, they are rated as low in both respects; in Casino Parish, we have classified them as high in power but low in achievement potential, for they made decisions that affected gambling but could not hope to rise to higher office.

It must be understood that our categorizations depend not on formal characteristics of the offices but on an estimate of the prevailing expectations about the offices. Moreover, the distinctions were drawn without reference to the motive score of the incumbents. The discussion and data which follow must be interpreted within the limitations of these operational definitions, but we believe that they are accurate both in terms of the meaning of the test of motivation and, roughly, in terms of perceptions of political offices in the communities studied.

As Table 3 indicates, men in positions with high power and achievement potential in Eastern City had considerably higher power-motive scores and perhaps higher achievement-motive scores than those in low-potential positions. In Louisiana, the direction of differences in power and achievement motivation is the same as in Eastern City, but the difference in achievement motivation between high- and low-potential offices is relatively large, in power motivation, slight.

Since we have a non-political control sample for the Eastern City politicians, we can check the implications of these data by comparing Eastern City politicians in high- and low-potential offices separately with their samples of matched political inactives. The hypothesis relating motivation of

TABLE 3

MEAN MOTIVE SCORES OF NON-SCHOOL BOARD
POLITICIANS IN POSITIONS WITH HIGH AND LOW
POWER AND ACHIEVEMENT POTENTIAL

Motive	Position Potential		Diff.	p of Diff.
	High (N)	Low (N)		
Eastern City:				
Power	7.9 ⎫ (10)	4.7 ⎫ (13)	3.2	.02
Achievement	8.3 ⎭	6.5 ⎭	1.8	.13
Louisiana parishes:				
Power	5.9 (26)	4.9 (10)	1.0	.26
Achievement	5.9 (14)	3.5 (22)	2.4	.06

NOTE: Combining Eastern City and Louisiana parishes and hold-ing *place* constant, *p*-values of partial linear regression coefficients (*motive* on *position potential*) are: for power, .01; for achieve-ment, .03. Other *p*-values from Mann-Whitney U test on ranked scores.

officeholders to the opportunities of the offices is strongly corroborated. Politicians in high-potential positions scored much higher in both achievement and power motivation than their matched sample ($N=9$ pairs).[12] With each motive, only one non-politician scored higher than the politician he was matched to. In contrast, politicians in low-potential positions scored insignificantly lower in both motives than their matched inactives. In short, politicians in offices with high power and achievement potential are more strongly motivated for power and achievement than politically in-active men from the same occupational and socio-economic strata. The implication is that high-potential offices attract men with relatively strong achievement and power motiva-tion.

A role-theory explanation—that holders of high-potential offices have developed strong power and achievement motiva-

[12] These are the mean scores: power motive—politicians 8.3, non-politicians 5.2, $p=.03$; achievement motive—politicians 8.6, non-politicians 4.7, $p=.03$ (by Wilcoxon matched-pairs signed-ranks tests; see Siegel 1956).

tion over a period of years because of long exposure to power and achievement opportunities—does not account for these results. In Eastern City, where data were gathered on candidates as well as on officeholders, candidates for high-potential positions have the same distinctive motivational characteristics as long-time officeholders. Moreover, politicians in high-potential positions in spite of weak power and achievement motivation are more likely to drop out of politics than strongly motivated officeholders, according to our data. Apparently, motivation affects entry into the political arena and willingness to remain in office, but officeholding does not determine underlying motivation (though it may serve to arouse existing motives). Some motive change may take place because of role learning, but these data do not support such a hypothesis.[13]

Fourteen school board members in the Louisiana parishes are excluded from Table 3 in order to make the data comparable to Eastern City figures, where school board members

TABLE 4

MEAN MOTIVE SCORES OF LOUISIANA SCHOOL BOARD MEMBERS AND
OTHER LOUISIANA POLITICIANS IN POSITIONS WITH HIGH
POWER AND ACHIEVEMENT POTENTIAL

Motive	School Board (N=14)	Other High Potential	(N)	Diff.	p of Diff.
Power	4.7	5.9	(26)	1.2	.13
Achievement	6.5	5.9	(14)	0.6	.34
Affiliation	3.0	1.7	(26)	1.3	.05

NOTE: Affiliative motive scores are for men in high-power-potential positions; p-values from Mann-Whitney U test.

[13] Still another explanation might attribute motive differences to differences in social class or class background: relatively high-status men are elected to high-potential offices, and their motivational characteristics are associated with their class rather than with the way they attain their political positions. In both localities, men in high-potential positions do come from somewhat higher-class families; they have somewhat more education (Louisiana only) and higher incomes. But those who rank highest with respect to these social characteristics do not account for the differences in motivation between men in high- and low-potential positions. Motivational differences remain when social class and class origin are held constant.

were not sampled. When school board members are examined separately, as in Table 4, we find that they score somewhat lower on power motivation and somewhat higher on achievement and affiliative motivation than other officials. The data are not conclusive, but they are suggestive. What might make school board members different from others who hold high-potential positions?

In many localities, school board elections are not considered to be part of the ordinary political game. Elections to the board are often non-partisan. The board usually does not serve organization maintenance functions for local parties in the sense that mayoralty office or the city council often do through their control over patronage and over a range of policies. School board politics usually seems less "political" in the sense that there is (or appears to be) less open competition for leadership and less clearly power-oriented behavior. Serving on the school board has more of the flavor of civic duty, in which one is expected to do what is best for all, than of political career.

In Louisiana, only a few of these considerations hold true. The elections are as partisan as those for parish council; school boards control important sources of patronage through the dispensation of custodial and bus-driving positions, through the award of contracts, and through the purchase of land. It is true that there is more public comment when the school board is used for partisan purposes than when power politics are played on the parish council; candidates for the board make some effort to dissociate themselves from partisan politics, whereas other officials do not. Nevertheless, there are grounds for suspecting that motivational differences between school board members and other officials are smaller in the Louisiana parishes than in many other localities. In cities that have both vigorous party or factional politics and a non-partisan school board, we expect motivational differences between the two sets of officeholders to be greater.

Motivational differences between political systems. Opportunities for exercising power and for achieving—hence for satisfying relevant motives—vary not only among offices within local political systems but also from one system to another. What are the distinctive features of the two political systems we studied? Eastern City's parties compete vigorously, and alernation between them occurs even though each has dominated the scene for several terms at a time in recent decades. At the same time, each party is tightly controlled by a small and only slowly changing set of leaders, so that mobility within the local party structure is somewhat limited. This is not necessarily a sharp restriction on achievement and power opportunities, however, since expectations are prevalent that it is possible to go on to state legislative office or higher from the position of councilman or mayor. Recent city administrations have been vigorous, initiating very important new policies, such as large-scale urban redevelopment. The city government is the focus of demands from diverse groups, and the consensus, in a relatively stagnant economy, is that the city's future depends heavily on the initiative and ability of its political leaders. Opportunity in the economic arena is further restricted by the exclusion of several immigrant minority groups from the highest positions in industry and finance.

The Louisiana parishes, in contrast, have witnessed immense growth and industrialization in recent years. There is no consensus that the most important decisions are to be made in the political process; rather, opportunities for power and achievement abound in the commercial and industrial life of the area. Parish politics is factional, fragmented, shifting, personal. There are no parties competing on the basis of issues, defining important public problems, and mobilizing support for their stands. Factions and individuals compete, but there is little focus on matters of general interest or on public problems that might appear as a challenge to men who otherwise would be attracted to business or professional careers. Furthermore, political mobility upward to state or national offices from a background of parish officeholding is practically unheard of.

In sum, opportunity for power and achievement in local politics is smaller in the parishes than in Eastern City; opportunity for movement up to higher office is much smaller; opportunity for power and achievement in the economic arena is relatively greater. These quite striking differences between Eastern City, on the one hand, and the two parishes, on the other, suggest that Eastern City politics will attract more strongly power- and achievement-motivated men than will the politics of Christian and Casino Parishes. If, as we suggested above in relation to school board politics, concern for policy is likely to stem from at least moderate

TABLE 5

MEAN MOTIVE SCORES OF BUSINESSMEN-POLITICIANS IN HIGH- AND
LOW-POTENTIAL POSITIONS IN LOUISIANA AND EASTERN CITY*

Position Potential	La. Parishes	(N)	Eastern City	(N)	Diff.	p of Diff. between Communities
	Power Motive					
For Power:						
High	5.8	(13)	7.9	(10)	2.1	
						.04
Low	2.0	(2)	4.7	(13)	2.7	
	Achievement Motive					
For Achievement:						
High	6.3	(9)	8.3	(10)	2.0	
						.04
Low	3.8	(6)	6.5	(13)	2.7	
	Affiliative Motive					
For Power:						
High	1.5	(13)	3.0	(10)	1.5	
						.05
Low	3.5	(2)	4.3	(13)	0.8	

* School board men excluded.
NOTE: Affiliative motive scores are for men in high- and low-power-potential positions. The data in this table differ from those in Table 3 in that Louisiana politicians who are not businessmen are omitted to assure comparability with Eastern City data. All p-values are 1-tailed for partial linear regression coefficients for *motive* on *place* with *position potential* held constant as the second independent variable. Although 1-tailed significance levels of α =.05 are reached or nearly reached for all six coefficients (*place* and *position potential* for each of three motives), it is of interest to note that these two variables together account for only between 7.5 and 20 per cent of the variance in motive scores.

levels of affiliative motivation, Eastern City politicians may also be somewhat more motivated in this direction.

The hypothesis is supported by data in Table 5, in which Eastern City businessmen-politicians are compared with those Louisiana politicians who are also businessmen, with power and achievement potential of their offices held constant. The Eastern City politicians show substantially higher power, achievement, and affiliative motivation than their counterparts in Louisiana.[14]

SUMMARY AND CONCLUSIONS

Simply being a politician does not entail a distinctive concern for power, or for achievement or affiliation. For the communities studied our data show that businessmen in local politics do not differ in motivation from politically inactive businessmen. However, patterns of political and non-political opportunities in different communities, and the distribution of opportunities among political offices, are related to the motivational make-up of officeholders. The data for Eastern City and the Louisiana parishes are consistent with the propositions that relatively plentiful opportunities for power and achievement in the economic arena channel strongly motivated men into economic rather than political activity; that in communities where politics and political issues are at the center of attention and interest, men attracted to politics are likely to be more strongly power- and achievement-motivated than in communities where politics commands only peripheral interest; that political systems that offer upward political mobility attract men with relatively strong achievement and power motivation; and that concentration in a political system on matters of strictly party or factional organization and power, to the near exclusion of public policy concerns, tends to keep men with strong affiliative needs out

[14] We recognize that the data may also be interpreted as supporting either or both of two other hypotheses: (a) interviewer effects are responsible for the differences; (b) the relatively low motive scores of the Louisiana politicians simply mirror differences in the general populations of the two locales. Since there is no way of excluding these possibilities, our interpretation is only suggestive.

of politics. Similar relationships hold for specific offices within the communities studied. Offices with high potential for power and achievement are occupied by men who are more strongly power- and achievement-motivated than politicians in low-potential offices.

The implications of data of this sort are not trivial, as a glance back to our summary of the behavioral correlates of these motives reminds. Groups of men who differ with respect to these traits will run a government in sharply different ways, we suspect. Furthermore, the pool of local politicians available for advancement to higher office is a major input to the pool of state and national leaders. Patterns of motivation in local politicians will determine in part what kinds of political leadership we experience in the future. What kind of political system is likely to recruit authoritarian leaders, men whose strong power motivation is untempered by affiliative concern? What sort of politics will produce leaders with high achievement motivation and the characteristics of high levels of performance, response to challenge, and a propensity for moderate risk that go with it?

It is here that the significance of data on personality is apparent, in the decisions of political leaders, in their yielding to certain pressures rather than to others, in their acceptance of some decision premises over others. Information on the motives of politicians provides us with links between complex social, economic, and political variables, on the one hand, and patterns of the recruitment and behavior of leaders, on the other.

PART THREE
POLITICAL MAN AND PERSONALITY TYPES

Introduction

If political recruitment is characterized by specific types of psychological motivation, this would suggest that individuals attracted to specific kinds of political activity and statuses might constitute specific types in broader psychological terms —such as distinctive personality types—as well as raise the question of whether or not it would be possible to distinguish, in terms of personality, among different kinds or types of political actors.

Aristotle notwithstanding, human beings are not by nature political animals. Man, of course, is by nature a social being, but not a political animal on the same grounds. *Homo politicus* is created out of the apolitical *homo civicus*. As Dahl (1961:59–60) points out, ". . . though human beings must and do live in political systems and share the benefits of political life, they do not necessarily participate in political life; they are not necessarily interested in politics, nor do they always care what happens in politics, know about political events, or share in making decisions." In most political systems, in fact, the political stratum constitutes only a minimum of the adult population.

This situation of political apathy and indifference seems to be universal—at least in democratic political systems. The active political stratum constitutes a very small portion of the citizenry: only about one to two percent of the population either (1) hold public or party office, or (2) are candidates for political office.

Milbrath (1965) has offered a typology of political "actors" which corresponds to (1) "Gladiatorial activities" (political warriors), (2) "Transitional activities" (support activities, such as making financial contributions, attending political rallies, campaigning), (3) "Spectator activities" (those passively interested in politics), and (4) "Apathetics" (those disinterested in politics). The two latter categories, it is estimated, account for ninety-five percent of the population.[1]

One of the questions for this section, then, is whether or not categories, or social types, such as these, of political man can be distinguished in terms of modal personality. Our specific concern is to explore the thesis that distinct personality types characterize the various sorts of political man. The empirical data are again inconsistent, but one cannot ignore the overwhelming evidence deriving from the many studies which have revealed distinct personality profiles for various forms of political behavior.

Mussen and Wyszynski (1952), for example, in a study of some of the psychological correlates of political interest and disinterest, conclude that political apathy and political activity are specific manifestations of more deep-lying and more pervasive active and passive orientations. Utilizing a number of items from the various scales developed in *The Authoritarian Personality* study, these researchers present distinct profiles for both ideal types of "political" individual: the political and the apolitical. Manheim (1959) similarly found that politically active people exhibit personality profiles which differ significantly from those of the general population. More specifically, Sanford (1951) and Levinson (1964) make similar observations that authoritarians are among the most apathetic political personalities; while, on the other hand, Barker (1963), as we shall see in Part Four, contends that there are equal numbers of authoritarians among political passives as there are among political actives and militants.

In our first selection for this section, considering a very

---

[1] Dahl (1961) offers a parallel, and somewhat similar, typology, when he speaks of (1) the powerful, (2) the power-seekers, (3) the political stratum, and (4) the apolitical stratum.

specific type of political activist, Milbrath and Klein report on a study of Washington lobbyists. Their subjects were administered shortened subscales from the Dominance, Self-control, Social Presence, Sociability, and Self-acceptance scales of the Gough California Psychological Inventory, as well as a version of the F scale. Milbrath and Klein conclude that a sociality-dominance-esteem syndrome is a facilitating, but not sufficient, condition for participation in politics, while authoritarianism seems to be a barrier that applies across the board to all types of partisan political activity.

Elsewhere Milbrath (1965) argues that authoritarians are not apt to succeed in politics because they lack necessary psychological qualities; in particular, (1) they cannot tolerate ambiguity (which apparently he inordinately imputes to politics), and (2) they lack the necessary psychological skills for the job. Success in politics, of course, is a more specific question than attraction to, and entry into, political roles; and success in politics undoubtedly is dependent on, among other things, the possession of the right set of skills.

Louise Harned, in our second selection for this section, in a study of chairmen of committees of political wards, discusses the relationship of personality to political leadership, and explores the question of what attracts people to active participation in the organization of political parties. Focusing her work on the central cluster-variables of power and submission in the authoritarian personality, Harned hypothesizes that this kind of political party activity might have special appeal to the authoritarian individual, owing to the hierarchical structure of political parties and to their relationship to the agencies of political power in the community.

Harned's research shows that people who work for political parties are likely to be neither authoritarian nor non-authoritarian, but that authoritarianism does seem to be associated differentially with the way in which the political role is performed, as well as with some political attitudes and opinions that appear relevant to the gratification that political leaders may derive from party activity. For authoritarian personalities, the formal organization of the party hierarchy and their own position in it are of primary importance, and they seem to derive special satisfaction from a dominant role in the organization, as well as from a submissive status in relationship to party superiors.

Harned's findings seem at first glance to be inconsistent with the observations and conclusions of Milbrath and Klein; however, she submits that authoritarians may be more active in political parties, while comparatively apathetic in other types of organizations, because the nature and structure of social statuses and roles within political parties are such as to permit the authoritarian to find therein adequate gratification for the specific psychological needs of his personality.

But what about the "active elite" of politics? Can the lawmakers, for example, be distinguished from other species of political man? There are only two pieces of research that are directly relevant to this question. McConaughy (1950), in a work frequently cited in this respect, administered a number of projective personality tests to a small sample of state legislators in South Carolina, and to a control group. He found no statistically significant differences between the two groups; and, although his sample of only eighteen men was indeed too small to permit any substantial projections, he observed that the political leaders were more self-sufficient, decidedly more extroverted, slightly more dominant, more self-confident, more masculine, less fascistic, less irritable, less tense, less neurotic, and had fewer feelings of inferiority than the general male population of his control group of non-politicians.

In our third selection, DiRenzo reports on a comparative study of parliamentarians and non-politicians which was done in Italy. This work is particularly interesting, because, among other things such as its cultural context, it involves subjects representing a number of major political parties of an ideological nature. Utilizing the Dogmatism scale, DiRenzo's work suggests that distinct types of dogmatic personality are attracted and/or recruited to the parliamentary role in a differential and modal manner rather than in a random or unsystematic fashion.

DiRenzo's findings substantiate the research hypothesis that professional politicians are characterized by personality structures which are more dogmatic than those of non-politicians, and suggest further that distinctions in terms of such personality structures can be made even more precisely on the basis of political party affiliation and ideology, a question to which we shall address ourselves in more detail in Part Four. His work shows that parliamentarians are character- ized by being dogmatic and authoritarian in fundamental per- sonality structure, and that they can be distinguished from non-politicians on the basis of general personality structure.

Despite these interesting and supportive findings for the thesis which constitutes the focus of our concern in this sec- tion, the problem of further specification is with us again in this question of political types. We need to realize that poli- tics is not a homogeneous activity—not even for the so- called political elite, and hence we need to avoid the dilemma of having millions of people constituting "political man" by trying to fit them all into one common category. Lasswell spoke to this question by suggesting that: "Political types may be distinguished according to the specialized or the com- posite character of the functions which they perform and which they are desirous of performing. There are political agitators, administrators, theorists, and various combinations thereof. There are significant differences in the developmental history of each political type" (1930:262).

A number of specifications of the *homo politicus* need to be considered in future research. First of all, in terms of politically active and inactive types, we need to distinguish among the kinds and degrees of political involvement, from such things as voting versus making financial contributions to political parties and/or active campaigning for them.[2] Secondly, one of the keys to political action lies in the way in which the political actor defines his situation, and personality, as we shall see in Harned's selection, can be a major element for differential definitions of political situations. Relevant in this regard are such things as self-images, conceptions of the political role, and role orientations. Thirdly, we need to ex- plore the style and forms of political activity.[3] For example,

[2] See Milbrath (1965) for suggestions along these lines.
[3] A work which has received much attention in this regard, at least among political scientists, is that of Barber (1965). While he presents interesting descriptions and social profiles for ad hoc classifications of legislative style, Barber's work suffers from being

in terms of political representation, we need to specify the focus of representation in terms of whose interests are being represented.[4] Fourthly, attention needs to be given to different types (e.g., mayor, alderman, judge) and status levels (e.g., municipal, state, federal) of political office, part-time versus full-time activity, and kinds of social routes and recruitment (e.g., election or appointment) to office.[5] Fifthly, successful and unsuccessful politicians may be distinguishable on personality grounds. And, sixthly, we need to determine the extent to which particular types of personality within a given political role are selected and/or modified by various kinds of legislative and/or ideological systems. Recognizing these sorts of conceptual and functional distinctions, further research is needed, and the selections in this section are designed to put these questions in the proper perspective.

Quite useful too, as regards the refinement of certain dimensions of the interaction of personality and politics, would be knowledge about the developmental history of the distinct personality types associated with various modes of political activity. It would be interesting to determine, for example, whether or not particular sets of socialization experiences culminate in different kinds of politically oriented types of personality.[6]

Ultimately, of course, the significance of the question of distinctive personality types relates to the consequences which such situations have for the quality and the functioning of political roles and systems. This question will be one of our principal concerns in Part Six. There we shall explore the question of whether or not the structures and processes of political organization are related in any way to the kinds of personality types which are attracted into political statuses and systems.

---

atheoretical and devoid of any conceptual dimensions related to the existing body of personality theory and methodology. Of related interest is Hargrove (1966).

[4] See Wahlke (1962) for one typology along these lines.

[5] On this point, see DiRenzo (1967a:154–162).

[6] For a recent statement on these issues, see Froman (1961), who attempts to tie the social environment to political behavior by means of the intermediary of personality.

Personality Correlates of
Political Participation
Lester W. Milbrath and Walter W. Klein

What induces people to participate in politics? This question
has fascinated students of political behavior for many years.
Studies of voting behavior and other forms of political participation have provided a good deal of suggestive evidence
leading toward an answer.[1] The variables that correlate with
political participation can be categorized in a number of
ways. A distinction is often made between environmental
variables and personality variables. The two kinds of variables
are readily distinguished by the different methods used to
measure them; it is not quite so obvious that they are analytically distinct. Personality is to a considerable extent the
product of environment; in fact, one can argue that environment affects behavior primarily through its impact on
personality. On the other hand, personality often affects environment; persons may purposely approach, or avoid, or
significantly alter particular environments or environmental
elements. There is a circularity of cause and effect between
personality and environment which confounds attempts to
treat them as separate factors correlating with political behavior.

Reprinted by permission of the publisher from *Acta Sociologica*,
Volume 6, 1962, pp. 53–66.
[1] For a very comprehensive review of the literature and findings on
political participation, see Lane (1959).

On this basis, it is sometimes argued that it is unnecessary to collect personality data, which are difficult to measure, since environmental variables suffice to account for political behavior. Socio-economic status (SES), for example, has repeatedly been found to correlate with personality measures which, in turn, correlate with certain types of political participation.[2] Why not drop out the personality link and use only SES to account for political participation? The difficulty with this tactic is that SES measures alone do not account for enough of the variance; too many deviant cases are left unexplained. When statistical controls are applied so that one's sample is confined to a single SES stratum one still finds significant correlations between personality traits and political participation. For example, the studies cited in note 2 show that, with the SES factor controlled, traits like effectiveness and sociability are still significantly correlated with political participation. It is our conclusion that both environmental and personality measures must be utilized in any attempt to account for the variance in political participation.

Personality traits, like effectiveness or sociability, should be conceived as important but not sufficient conditions for participation. A barrier concept is useful here. A person who does not feel personally effective or who is not sociable has a barrier to participation in politics; in exceptional circumstances he may jump the barrier and join the political fray, but ordinarily he will sit on the sidelines. The mere possession of these traits, however, does not insure participation in politics; it merely means there is a smaller barrier to surmount.

These personality factors, and environmental factors as well, that have been shown to correlate with political participation seem to correlate also with participation in other types of community activities. In other words, political participation seems to be a special case of a general social participation pattern. Personality factors requisite for general social participation are also requisite for political participation, but their presence does not necessarily produce political activity. We are not aware of any study which has isolated a person-

[2] The "efficacy," "duty," and "personal effectiveness" syndrome used in the SRC voting studies is one example. Campbell (1960: chp. 18). "Sociability" is another example, see Milbrath (1960).

ality trait which drives people specifically into politics; even the much discussed "drive for power" finds many alternative modes of expression. The types of persons discussed in Lasswell's writings on political personality (Lasswell, 1951a) might be examples of persons driven into politics by overall personality needs.

We cited some studies in note 2 which use statistical controls of SES while relating personality traits to political participation; it might be reassuring to examine such relationships using a sample in which the usual SES factors and some additional environmental characteristics are constant within the sample itself. Although it was not originally designed to test the relationships discussed in this paper, a study of Washington lobbyists being conducted by the senior author provides such a sample. A random sample of 114 respondents was drawn from a total population of 614 officially registered Washington lobbyists; 101 of the 114 were interviewed. At the conclusion of the interview each respondent was given a short personality test and was asked to fill it out and mail it back to the interviewer; 88 of the 101 did so,[3] and it is from this group that the data reported in this paper are derived.

The lobbyists in this sample, by self-identification of social class and by interviewer rating, are almost uniformly in the upper-middle SES stratum. All have the same occupation; they are almost uniformly well educated (only 12 had not attended college); nearly all have high incomes (all but 2 over $5,000 and all but 16 over $10,000). The income differences that exist do not seem to reflect class differences; income does not correlate significantly with any of the personality traits or types of participation discussed in this paper. The sample provides additional environmental controls not included in most other studies. All respondents live and work in the same city, they all plug into the same overall communication network, they interact with the same set of governmental decision-makers as well as one another. The only major environmental characteristic that varies from lobbyist to lobbyist is the type of association or group which he represents; we will present some evidence later which suggests that

---

[3] Some respondents failed to answer all the items on the test thus the N for some scales may be as low as 80.

this factor, as well, does not significantly affect the correlations reported in this paper.

In terms of occupation, education, and income, lobbyists are the kind of person that we would expect to be active in politics.[4] It is relevant also that lobbyists are required by their job to have the training, experience, and skills that facilitate entry into politics; they do not have a skill barrier to political participation. It is curious, then, to discover that they are not uniformly active in partisan politics (Milbrath, 1958). To be sure, lobbying itself is a type of political activity, but it is activity required by a job or role and the definition of this job for most lobbyists does not include participation in partisan politics. After reviewing considerable evidence (a major hypothesis of the study was that lobbyists would be active in partisan politics), it is our conclusion that whether or not a lobbyist is active in partisan politics depends mainly on his pre-lobbying experience rather than upon his role as a lobbyist.

Just as the job does not require political activity, it does not forbid such activity. A few respondents felt that their role would not allow partisan political activity, but this interpretation was not widely held either by lobbyists or by those with whom they normally interact. There was no evidence that members of Congress, or other role players in the Washington political system, expected lobbyists to be political neutrals. In summary, we have a group of people who have the requisite skills for political activity, who live and work in the same socio-economic strata, who are subjected to many of the same environmental stimuli related to participation, and who are free to participate or not as they are personally inclined. If personality traits do correlate significantly with political participation in this sample, we can be reasonably confident that normal measures of environmenal variables alone could not account for variance in political participation. This would support our contention that personality must be

[4] In the SRC 1956 electoral study sample, joining a political club correlated .38 with an occupational index, .36 with education, and .22 with income. A campaign activity index correlated .17 with occupation, .31 with education, and .23 with income. All of these correlations are statistically significant.

studied as well if one hopes to account adequately for political behavior.

The reader might dissent that even though current environment is held constant for our respondents (as well as can be expected anyway at this stage of social science development), their pre-lobbying environment certainly must have varied. This is undoubtedly true, but the only way that pre-lobbying environment could affect current behavior is through the retention of environmental effects in respondents' personalities. Analytically, we are still caught up in the circularity of cause and effect between environment and personality. Our only claim to analytical clarity in this study is that the effect of current environment is largely held constant in this sample; therefore, any differences found in political participation very likely stem from personality as it embodies the effects of past experience. It is quite another question to inquire how the different personalities developed, a task beyond the scope of this paper.

The short test instrument administered to the lobbyists contained shortened sub-scales from the Dominance, Self-Control, Social Presence, Sociability, and Self-Acceptance scales of Gough's California Psychological Inventory (CPI).[5] It also contained Christie's version (1958) of the F scale with half the items reversed to compensate for possible response set.

In order to ascertain how closely the shortened sub-scales measured the same things as Gough's full scales, part-whole correlations were computed on samples of professional males, college males, and high school males. These part-whole correlations were sufficiently high to assure us that the sub-scales were measuring substantially the same thing as the full scales. The data shown in Table 1 for the Dominance scale are typical of all the scales used.

The Gough sub-scales, however, were so highly intercorrelated that we began to suspect that they measured the same general syndrome. Reliability coefficients were computed for each scale using Horst's correction (1953) for the Kuder

[5] Permission to do this was granted by Professor Gough and the Consulting Psychologist's Press Inc., Palo Alto, California which owns the 1956 copyright on the CPI.

TABLE 1

DOMINANCE SCORES ON FOUR POPULATIONS

	Professional males N-45	College males N-210	High school males N-40	Lobbyists N-80
Part-whole r's	.78	.91	.92	
Mean	12.82	10.37	9.57	14.75
Standard deviation	2.98	3.72	4.03	3.10

Richardson formula. We then applied a correction for attenuation to estimate the correlation between the true variance components of the respective scales.[6] The resulting correlation matrix is shown in Table 2.

The exceptionally high intercorrelations shown in Table 2 lead us to believe that reliability coefficients of the various scales are underestimated, even after the application of Horst's correction to the K-R formula.[7] (In some cases, application of the correction for the attenuation formula resulted in estimated correlations greater than unity.) Despite the probable underestimation, the matrix clearly suggests that, at least in this sample, the Sociability, Social Presence, and Self-Acceptance sub-scales measure the same thing and that the Self-Control sub-scale measures the same thing in a reverse direction. The Dominance sub-scale has something in common with the other scales, but there is sufficient differ-

[6] Correction for attention, Guilford (1954:400–402):

"Intercorrelations of tests, and of tests with criteria, are restricted in size because of the amount of error variance in each, where error variances are uncorrelated. This is as it should be if we want the coefficient of correlations to indicate how well one fallible measure can be predicted from another fallible measure. If, however, we want to know how much the true variances are related and how well they can be predicted, we must take into account the reliabilities of the measures.

"If complete correction for attenuation gives a coefficient close to 1.0 (within sampling error), one should conclude that one has in X and Y essentially two forms of the same test. Their entire true-variance components are in common."

[7] The following are the reliability coefficients for the various scales: Dominance, .73; Sociability, .56; Social Presence, .56; Self-Acceptance, .38; Self-Control, .67.

TABLE 2

CORRELATIONS BETWEEN TRUE-VARIANCE COMPONENTS
OF THE FIVE GOUGH SUB-SCALES.

	Dominance	Sociability	Social Presence	Self-Acceptance
Sociability	.80			
Social Presence	.83	1.00		
Self-Acceptance	.92	1.00	1.00	
Self-Control	−.53	−.90	−.100	−.100

ence shown to suggest that it should be treated as a separate scale.

It seemed wise, analytically, to combine the Sociability, Social Presence, Self-Acceptance, and Self-Control items into a new scale which, for lack of a better term, we have called *"Sociality."* This scale contains 22 items (several items appeared in more than one of the previous sub-scales) and has a corrected Kuder-Richardson reliability coefficient of .67 (see Table 3). It is our belief that this new scale measures five qualities grouped around the general syndrome we have called Sociality. First of all, it measures social skill, the knowledge and skill required to do the right thing at the right time. Second, it measures social ease, the ability to feel comfortable and to take the initiative in social interaction. Third, it measures ego strength, the feeling that one's qualities and actions are equal to that of persons encountered socially. Fourth, it measures self-liking or self-acceptance which is the ability to like oneself even in the face of evidence that one is not perfect. Finally, it measures a propensity to be active, to try and get a lot accomplished. Although these assumed factors are related, we do not believe that this scale measures a unidimensional characteristic; we prefer to call it a syndrome.

The Dominance scale contains 19 items and has a corrected K-R reliability of .73 (see Table 3). Gough describes it this way:

> To assess factors of leadership ability, dominance, persistence, and social initiative. *High scorers:* aggressive, confident, outgoing, planful, having initiative; verbally fluent, self-reliant. *Low scorers:* retiring, inhibited, commonplace, indifferent, silent, slow in thought and action; avoiding situations of tension and decision; lacking in self-confidence.[8]

One would expect the Dominance scale to discriminate well between persons who participate in politics and those who do not. Table 3 shows the correlation of Dominance, and several other scales, with various types of political activity. The correlations reported in this table are Phi coefficients which are a conservative estimate of the Pearson r. We have used this metric because some of the variables are dichotomous and because some of the variables also do not have the parametric qualities assumed for use of the Pearson r. Although dominant persons, as measured by this scale, tend to be more active than non-dominant persons, only one of the correlations (that with campaigning) achieves significance. The Sociality scale described above, does a better job of distinguishing participants from non-participants. Persons ranking high on Sociality were significantly more likely to have been active in a political party, to have given 25 hours or more to a political campaign, to have given 3 or more monetary contributions to a political party or candidate in the past 5 years, and to have solicited political funds than were persons ranking low on Sociality.[9] (The failure of all the scales to correlate significantly with officeholding will be discussed later.)

The pattern of results with the Sociality scale confirms some

[8] For a more complete description and the presentation of validating data consult: Gough (1957) and Gough, McClosky, and Meehl (1951).

[9] A study of South Carolina legislators (McConaughy, 1950) showed them to be decidedly more extroverted and only slightly more dominant than adult males in the state. They were also decidedly more masculine and decidedly more self confident than the average person.

TABLE 3
CORRELATION OF SCALES WITH POLITICAL ACTIVITY

	Dominance 19 items Corrected K-R reliability .73	Sociality 22 items Corrected K-R reliability .67	Sociality + Dominance 41 items Corrected K-R reliability .80	Esteem 5 items Corrected K-R reliability .92	F Scale † K-R reliability .55
Party Activity	.18	.22*	.24*	.25*	−.31**
Campaigning	.31**	.28**	.44**	.38**	−.23*
Contribute Political Funds	.09	.19*	.20*	.15	−.24*
Solicit Political Funds	.18	.35**	.25*	.39**	−.29**
Holding Elective Public Office	.14	.14	.20	.14	−.08
Activity Score in Non-Political Groups	.35**	.43**	.37**	.30**	−.05
Dominance	—	.31**	—	.55**	−.16
Esteem	.55**	.64**	.62**	—	−.13
F Scale	−.16	−.19*	−.22*	−.13	—

* Correlation significant for this size sample, at .05 with one-tailed test.
** Correlation significant for this size sample, at .01 with one-tailed test.
† Split-half reliability on F+ was .54 (projects to .67 on 10 items), and on F— it is .41 (projects to .64 on 10 items). The K-R reliability shown is not corrected as the F scale items have five response categories.

findings of the senior author from a study of monetary contributors [to politics] and non-contributors in North Carolina (Milbrath, 1960). Respondents ranking high on sociability (as measured by a 5 item scale, some of the same items in the Sociality scale) were significantly more likely to contact a politician, campaign, solicit funds, and be consulted on policy. These results were obtained while SES statistical controls were applied. It is theoretically significant that the four behaviors achieving significance, even when SES is controlled, all require social interaction.

Since lobbyists contact politicians and are consulted on policy as a matter of course in their jobs, correlations between these behaviors and Sociality were not computed on the lobbyist sample (as they were on the North Carolina sample). For the lobbyists, the Sociality scale correlates most highly with campaigning and soliciting funds (both significant on the North Carolina sample). Being active in a party, contributing funds, and holding office (none of which achieve statistical significance in the North Carolina study) also show the lowest correlations for the lobbyists. It seems clear, then, that sociability operates selectively. Persons who do not possess sociability have a barrier inhibiting their participation in political activities that require a high level of social interaction.

The correlation between Dominance and Sociality is .31, suggesting that there is some commonality between the two factors (the matrix in Table 2 also shows this), but also some differences. We were curious to see if combining the two measures in one long scale would increase the ability to discriminate participants from non-participants. The combined scale has 41 items and has a corrected K-R reliability of .80. Only for campaigning (where Dominance shows its only significant correlation) does the combined scale show a strikingly higher correlation than the Sociality scale. For party activity and political contributing the correlations are approximately the same as the Sociality scale, and for soliciting funds it is much lower than Sociality. We conclude that the combined scale is not appreciably better than the Sociality scale or the much shorter "Esteem" scale about to be discussed.

In our general exploration of personality variables and lobbying behavior we applied Guttman scaling techniques to several sets of items that seemed, intuitively, to relate to certain lobbying activities. One of these short scales, which we shall call *"Esteem"*, worked remarkably well in discriminating between political participants and non-participants. It is made up of these 5 items: "As long as the job gets done I do not mind if someone else gets the credit." "I like to be the center of attention." "I tend to dramatize a story I am telling." "It makes me uncomfortable to put on a stunt at a party even when others are doing the same sort of thing." "It is hard for me to tell anyone about myself." Three of the 5 items appear in the Sociality scale and, not surprisingly, it correlates .64 with that scale. It also correlates .55 with the Dominance scale where there is no item overlap. Guttman's criteria for scalability seem to fit this scale nicely; it has a coefficient of reproducibility of .92, marginal frequencies are not extreme, and respondents are well spread out over the length of the scale. The corrected K-R reliability coefficient for the Esteem scale is .92. Our data do not allow us to infer reliabilities of this scale on other populations, but we believe it to be a very stable unidimensional scale.

The Esteem scale seems to measure self-esteem as well as a desire for receiving esteem from others. We have a hunch it measures something very much like the dominance-sociality syndrome that we have been talking about, although it should be tried out on different populations before we can be very certain. Esteem performed much better than Dominance and slightly better than Sociality in separating participants from non-participants; except for campaigning and contributing funds, it performed about as well as the combined Sociality-Dominance scale which has 8 times as many items. We consider it the best short measurement of the general sociality-dominance syndrome shown here to be facilitating or predisposing factor for certain types of political participation.

Table 3 shows the correlations of the various scales with a score for activity in non-political groups. This measure was introduced as a validating criterion for the scales. Group activity correlated quite well with Sociality (43), as we would expect, and also significantly with Dominance (.35); the correlation with Esteem was lower (.30), but not strikingly so.

Why do these scales not correlate significantly with holding public office? First one must distinguish between elective and appointive officeholding. Elective officeholding would probably have shown a significant correlation with these personality variables in a larger sample, but only 5 persons in this small sample had held elective office. Four out of the 5 scored high on Dominance, Sociality, and Esteem; but 5 cases are simply not enough to draw a significant correlation. We have little doubt that the sociality-dominance-esteem syndrome is important in determining whether people run for elective office or not. This syndrome is not important, however, for holding appointive office. Many lobbyists had held appointive office but this behavior shows no correlation with the personality variables discussed in Table 3. The North Carolina study showed very similar results.

This finding suggests some implications for the political system. We have just seen that elective officeholders rank higher on dominance-sociality-esteem than appointive officeholders. Another cross-tabulation from the larger lobbyist study shows that persons coming to lobbying from working on the Hill, as Member of Congress or staff assistant, rank higher on dominance-sociality-esteem than persons coming from the executive branch. We also learned that persons working in the legislative branch are more active in politics and have more strongly partisan attitudes than persons working in the executive branch. This suggests that personality factors enter into the selection of decision-makers in the executive branch and decision-makers in the legislative branch. Recent history has shown that power is shifting from the legislative to the executive branch. Perhaps it is time for comparative research on the characteristics and quality of decisions, especially as they may be affected by personality factors, between officers in the executive branch and officers in the legislative branch.

Authoritarianism, as measured by the F scale, seems to be a different variable from the dominance-sociality-esteem syndrome even though it is slightly negatively correlated with those measures. The correlation with the group activity score is only —.05 which is another bit of evidence that it is not just a reverse measure of the sociality syndrome. A high score on the F scale correlates negatively with all the types of political participation considered in this study. In the case of party activity and political contributing, the negative correlation is higher than the positive correlation of these activities with the sociality syndrome. The Kuder-Richardson reliability of the F scale is .55, somewhat less than the reliabilities for the other scales. Christie, who computed split-half reliabilities on this sample for both the positive and negative F scale items reports that lobbyists show greater internal consistency than is exhibited by most samples of college students; lobbyists, incidentally, also rank higher on F than college students.[10]

The F scale used here is relatively free of response-set bias and is probably as good a short measure of authoritarianism or F as is available.[11] On the other hand, we are not quite sure what authoritarianism or F actually means in terms of behavior. The scale may only predict willingness to follow authoritarian leadership, although we cannot even be sure of this. We cite our data in the hope that it will help interpret what a high score on F does mean. Our data indicate that persons scoring high on F do have a barrier to partisan political activity. The barrier is not absolute, a few high scorers are active, but the tendency for high scorers to shun political activity is clear. Furthermore, it seems to hold true across the board for all the types of political activity included in this study. The original work on the authoritarian personality by Adorno and associates has been criticized

[10] Personal letter from Christie dated May 28, 1957.
[11] The F scale has had a particularly troubled history because of its proneness to response-set bias. This difficulty has also muddled the interpretive waters so that it is really difficult to state precisely what the F scale does measure. To review all that has been written on authoritarianism, the F scale, and response set would take us far afield. The landmark study is T. W. Adorno (1950). A major critique is Cristie and Jahoda (1954). An article by Cristie and Cook (1958) pulls together references on authoritarianism to that date. Several recent articles on response-set not only report the latest stages in that debate but contain fairly complete references to the literature: Chapman and Campbell (1959); Gage, Leavitt, and Stone (1957); Small and Campbell (1960).

for not showing the behavioral impact, especially on politics, of authoritarianism. Lasswell has suggested that authoritarians will tend to be relegated to minor political roles (Lasswell, 1954). Our data suggest that they will shun the rough and tumble of partisan politics. Persons scoring high on F have repeatedly been shown to be prejudiced and to have anti-democratic attitudes; if these beliefs are seldom implemented through ordinary political channels, as our data suggest, such persons may be less dangerous to a democratic political system than might be supposed. They might, of course, choose extraordinary political channels, but there is little encouragement in the American political system for such ventures.

We have been alert to the possibility of response-set bias and, to the best of our knowledge, the findings reported in this paper are not affected by that factor. All of the scales contain both negative and positive items; thus, positive or negative response-set bias will show up as contradictions in content and will have the effect of lowering correlations. In addition to this, a response-set score was derived for each lobbyist from response patterns to the various scales; only 11 respondents showed extreme response-set tendencies whereas 46 had neutral (content sensitive) response patterns (the remainder were at an intermediate range). This score was used as a statistical control for several of the correlations shown in Table 3; in no case did the resulting tables show a lower correlation than the original table. The response-set controlled tables have so few cases per cell, however, that we have reported only non-response-set controlled correlations in Table 3.

Lobbyists are not very typical of the general population; can our results be generalized to a larger population (adult American citizens, for example)? We cannot be completely confident, but we believe that our findings for the sociality-dominance-esteem syndrome would be confirmed if a similar study were conducted on American adults. Variables similar to these have been found to correlate with political participation in studies of several other populations (political contributors, legislators, law students, adult citizens). We are somewhat less confident that the findings with the F scale can be generalized to the population at large. To our knowledge, this is the first clear-cut finding that a high score on F reflects a barrier to political participation.[12] If the same relationship does, in fact, hold in the general population, then former studies have not used fine enough methods to reveal the correlation[13]; but it is also possible that our finding is characteristic only of lobbyists. We have no data for resolving this dilemma at this time.

It is a major contention of this paper that the correlations shown between personality traits and political participation cannot be traced to current environment. One environmental factor which is not naturally controlled on this sample is the type of organization for which each lobbyist works. When these organizations are categorized by the subject matter with which they deal (farm, labor, business, etc.), these categories do not correlate with political participation nor does the application of these categories as a control affect the correlation of personality traits with participation. These organizations might, however, be grouped according to their "power at the polls." To do this, the various organizations were first rated as high, medium, or low on size of membership, financial resources, and concern with electoral outcome. These three ratings were then combined into an overall "power at the polls index." It turns out that representatives of organizations with high power at the polls are more likely to be active in politics than representatives of organizations with low power at the polls. Power at the polls correlates .31 with party activity, .15 with campaigning, .33 with contributing, and .38 with soliciting. If any environmental variable might destroy the correlation between personality traits and partic-

---

[12] Fillmore Sanford (1950) found that authoritarians were less likely to participate in politics and other community activities. His finding, however, was not obtained with SES or other environmental controls. This is a serious omission since F has repeatedly been shown to correlate with SES.

[13] The F scale is not related to political participation on the SRC's 1956 election study sample. Response-set controls or SES controls do not bring out a relationship either. They report some correlations of F with other variables for college graduates only, but even here there is no significant correlation between F and political participation.

ipation on the lobbyist sample, power at the polls would be the most severe test.

Power at the polls was run as a control on all the correlations shown in Table 3. The overall effect was minor or negligible. Table 4 shows the results when Esteem is correlated with four political activities, first for the representatives of organizations with power at the polls and then for the representatives of organizations with low power at the polls. This table is typical of the results shown for the other personality measures. It is our conclusion that the organizations lobbyists work for have no appreciable effect on the correlations between personality traits and political activities.

TABLE 4

CORRELATION OF ESTEEM WITH POLITICAL ACTIVITY: SAMPLE
CONTROLLED FOR POWER AT THE POLLS

| | *Uncontrolled sample* | *Representatives of organizations with* | |
		high power at the polls	*low power at the polls*
Party activity	.25	.21	.27
Campaigning	.38	.42	.37
Contributing money	.15	.22	.18
Soliciting funds	.39	.45	.33

SUMMARY

A sample of Washington lobbyists provides relatively tight environmental controls for testing correlations between personality traits and political participation. Several scales drawn from Gough's California Psychological Inventory showed such high intercorrelations that they were combined into an overall Sociality scale. This scale does a much better job of separating political participants from non-participants than Gough's Dominance scale; this was especially true for those types of political behavior which require social interaction. In spite of increased reliability, a combined Sociality-Dominance scale performs only slightly better than Sociality alone in separating participants from non-participants. A short 5 item Esteem scale is highly correlated with the so-ciality-dominance syndrome and is just as effective in sep-arating participants from non-participants as the longer scales. As an external validating criterion, all of these scales correlate significantly with a score showing depth of involve-ment in non-political groups.

We conceive of the sociality-dominance-esteem syndrome as a facilitating but not sufficient condition for participation in politics. A person with low sociality-dominance-esteem is not likely to participate, but those with high sociality-domi-nance-esteem will not necessarily participate. Persons who are low on these qualities have a greater barrier to participation in those activities which require a high degree of social inter-action such as campaigning and soliciting political funds. These results closely confirm results obtained earlier on a sample of political contributors and non-contributors in North Carolina. The sociality-dominance-esteem syndrome is prob-ably just as facilitative of activity in community groups as it is of political activity. In a sense, political activity can be conceived as a special case of general group activity.

Authoritarianism as measured by the F scale seems to be a barrier to participation. It is a barrier that seems to apply across the board to all types of partisan political activity (and possibly all community activity) instead of correlating more highly with some specific activities than with others as did the sociality syndrome. This evidence of low participation by people who score high on F suggests that authoritarians may be slow to implement any anti-democratic prejudices they may possess, insofar as they shun the means of political expression commonly employed in the United States.

Authoritarian Attitudes and Party Activity
Louise Harned

If the essence of an organization is partly determined by the motives and aspirations of its members the question of why men and women participate actively in political parties, even in modest positions, has meaning for the nature of the party system. Both fiction and factual analyses have noted that local party organizations are often staffed by people who join in search of such rewards as social outlets, jobs, or increased clientele. Obviously, the essentially non-political nature of these motives has profoundly shaped the operation of parties and political life in the American local community by extending the functions of parties into realms theoretically unconnected with government.

These categories of reward for participation by no means exhaust the possible attractions of party activity, even for people who have no particular ambition for elected office or a policy-making role in government. The significance of different specific rewards may vary for people of differing personality structures. Although no single component can be considered as the sole, or most important, psychological influence upon political action, the California study on authoritarianism has provided a method for the analysis of the effects of at least one aspect of personality (Adorno, 1950). Moreover, the authoritarian syndrome analyzed by the Cal-

Reprinted by permission of the author and publisher from *The Public Opinion Quarterly*, Volume 25, 1961, pp. 393–399.

ifornia investigators seems particularly relevant to an inquiry into participation in hierarchical organizations, such as parties. In brief, the constellation of attitudes considered to characterize an authoritarian personality are as follows: the tendency to conform, to adhere rigidly to conventional values, complemented by a tendency to condemn others who violate such values (this can be related to general hostility toward out-groups and positive attitudes toward in-groups); the tendency to submit uncritically to, to identify with, the strong leaders of in-groups, accompanied by a desire to dominate those considered weaker than oneself (this involves a general preoccupation with power relationships); the tendency to concentrate on externals, to be "anti-intraceptive" in relation to one's own experience, to blame one's troubles on a hostile and threatening environment; the tendencies to think in terms of stereotypes and superstitions, to be cynical about other people's motives; and the tendency to be fearful and suspicious of sexual impulses (Adorno, 1950:222–279). Of particular relevance to the present analysis are those characteristics pertaining to power and submission. Activity in political parties may have special appeal to those with authoritarian traits, owing both to the parties' hierarchical structure and to their relationship to the agencies of political power in the community.

THE STUDY

The present paper is a report on some data relating authoritarian attitudes to rewards and satisfactions gained by party work. It is based on material gathered in 1953–1954 by interviews of a random sample of forty-one ward committee chairmen in New Haven, Connecticut. A control group of twenty-seven men and women inactive in politics was also interviewed. This group paired with politicians in terms of sex, education, occupation, income, religion, race, and ethnic background.

The examination of authoritarian characteristics of New Haven committeemen was based on their responses to three of the projective questions devised by Daniel J. Levinson as part of the California study[1]:

1. We all have impulses and desires which are at times hard to control but which we try to keep in check. What desires do you have difficulty in controlling?
2. We all have times when we feel below par. What moods or feelings are the most unpleasant or disturbing to you?
3. What great people living or dead do you admire most?

In selecting these questions, care was taken to see that the responses to them would represent most of the psychological qualities found by Levinson to characterize ethnocentric (authoritarian) and anti-ethnocentric (equalitarian) subjects.

The method of categorizing the responses was the same as that described in Levinson's chapter on projective questions in *The Authoritarian Personality*. Each politician was given an authoritarianism score based on assigning one point for each response with a low authoritarian content, two points for a neutral answer, and three points for a response high in authoritarian content.

In general, there is no evidence that more people of high than of low authoritarian tendencies are likely to work for political parties, but authoritarianism does seem to be associated with some political attitudes and opinions that appear relevant to the satisfactions certain ward leaders may derive from party work.[2]

[1] Adorno (1950:545–600). In Levinson's terminology these particular questions were specifically designed as a measure of ethnocentrism. However, since the responses to them can be interpreted as revealing most of the authoritarian (or equalitarian) attributes, it is feasible to use them for that purpose here.

[2] Of the 27 matched committeemen, 55.5 per cent had authoritarian scores of 8 to 9, as compared to 62.9 per cent of the 27 matched non-politicians. This percentage difference is not of statistical significance.

EMPHASIS ON PARTY ORGANIZATION

The committeemen with the highest authoritarian scores appear to place more emphasis on the importance of party organization per se. Table 1 compares high authoritarianism scores with scores on the "organizational emphasis scale," based on responses to the following questions:

1. If you wanted to ask someone for information about political affairs, to whom would you turn?
2. What do you think is the most important aspect of your job as committeeman?
3. Why do you think letters to Congressmen are effective?

One point was added to each committeeman's organizational emphasis score if he would seek information or advice from a member of the party hierarchy who was not his friend, whose importance to him was based on rank in the party; if he thought that the most important aspect of his job was limited to its organizational side (e.g., involving his position of leadership in the ward apparatus); and if he thought that Congressmen took cognizance of letters because of his official position and not because of his personal and friendly experience with his elected representative.

It appears that for those with relatively substantial author-

TABLE 1

PERCENTAGE OF WARD CHAIRMEN WITH HIGH AND LOW
ORGANIZATIONAL EMPHASIS SCORES WHO RATE HIGH
OR LOW IN AUTHORITARIANISM

| Organizational Emphasis Score | Authoritarianism Score | | | |
	Low (3–7)	High (8–9)	Total	(N)
Low (0–1)	60	40	100	(20)
High (2–3)	28.6	71.4	100	(21)
Total group of ward chairmen	43.9	56.1	100	(41)

$\chi^2 = 4.06$; $.02 < p < .05$

itarian tendencies the formal organization of the party hierarchy and their own position in it are of primary importance.
Authoritarian ward leaders seem to derive special satisfaction
from a dominant role in their ward organization and from a
submissive status in relation to party superiors, to whom they
turn for information and help not because they know them
personally but in frank acknowledgment of their sanctified
position. This is fully consistent with the general conception
of authoritarian attitudes toward dominance and submission.

NUMBER OF ORGANIZATIONS PARTICIPATED IN

The material also suggests that political activity may play a
more important role for authoritarian ward leaders than it
does for equalitarians. Although there is no difference between the two groups with respect to the number or types of
organization other than parties to which they belong, there is
a definite tendency on the part of chairmen with lower authoritarian ratings to consider themselves active participants
in more associations. Only 26.1 per cent of the committeemen
with high authoritarian scores, in contrast to 72.2 per cent
of those with lower ratings, stated that they were active in two
or more organizations other than parties ($x^2=8.6$; $p < 1\%$).
This difference is in partial conflict with the observations of
Robert E. Lane (1955:179), who found that authoritarians
tend to belong to more organizations than do equalitarians,
but it appears to be in harmony with some of Fillmore Sanford's conclusions. The New Haven data can be interpreted to
reflect Sanford's findings that authoritarians "do not get
themselves involved in group activities nor readily accept responsibility" (Sanford, 1950:178). In his concluding analysis,
Sanford hypothesizes that authoritarians "will be found in
leadership positions where appointment has come from above
and where . . . responsibility is primarily to . . . superiors
rather than to followers" (Sanford, 1950:181). While this is
not strictly true of the position of ward chairman, those aspects of the job to which this description applies may be
particularly important to authoritarian politicians. Although

there is machinery for the election of chairmen, in fact there is rarely a contest and the practice of co-option seems to be frequent. Second, the responsibility of a ward leader to "deliver the vote" to his superiors is the most obvious duty he has to perform. His obligation to his followers as chairman of the ward committee and representative of his district is a relatively minor one and certainly can be interpreted as such if the chairman feels so inclined. Thus, the nature of the job can at least partially explain why authoritarian men and women may be active in political parties while comparatively apathetic in other types of organization.

IDEOLOGICAL PARTISANSHIP

One characteristic of parties which clearly distinguishes them from other community organizations appears to be particularly unimportant to committeemen with authoritarian tendencies. Except for a limited number of independent political associations, parties are the community organizations most directly concerned with the issues of the day. Without overemphasizing the importance of ideology as a factor precipitating participation in party work, it is nevertheless reasonable to assume that people gain satisfaction from belonging to an organization which represents an ideological position similar to their own.[3] However, the New Haven data suggest that such ideological partisanship is not of paramount importance to authoritarian men and women. One section of the study involved a detailed examination of some of the ideological attitudes of ward workers. In connection with this, an ideological partisanship scale was devised based on whether or not the responses to questions of policy favored the position of the chairman's own party.

[3] Whether the ward chairmen's ideological positions were developed before they became active in politics or whether they were "created" by their party work is a question that will not be considered here. It should be noted, however, that the investigation showed a relationship between number of years of party activity and degree of ideological partisanship, indicating that party work itself tends to generate such attitudes.

The scale was based on the following questions:

1. Some people think the national government should do more in trying to deal with such problems as unemployment, education, housing and so on. Others think that the government is already doing too much. On the whole would you say that what the government has done has been about right, too much, or not enough?

2. Some people think that since the end of the last world war this country has gone too far in concerning itself with problems in other parts of the world. How do you feel about this?

3. Some people feel that it was our government's fault that China went communist—others say there was nothing that we could do to stop it. How do you feel about this?

TABLE 2

PERCENTAGE OF WARD CHAIRMEN WITH HIGH AND LOW
AUTHORITARIANISM SCORES WHO SCORE HIGH OR LOW
ON THE IDEOLOGICAL PARTISANSHIP SCALE

Authoritarianism Score	Ideological Partisanship Score			
	Low (0–3)	High (4–6)	Total	(N)
Low (3–7)	27.8	72.2	100	(18)
High (8–9)	65.2	34.8	100	(23)
Total group of ward chairmen	48.8	51.2	100	(41)

$\chi^2 = 5.72$; $.01 < p < .02$

4. Do you think we did the right thing in getting into the fighting in Korea three years ago or should we have stayed out?

5. Some people think that the national government can reduce taxes now and still keep up an adequate military defense. Others say it would be impossible. How do you feel about this?

6. Some people think that the constitution of Connecticut is too clumsy and that therefore the state government is in-

efficient. Others think that the constitution is all right as it is. How do you feel about this?[4]

As can be seen from the data in Table 2, there appears to be a definite association between high authoritarian ratings and low scores on the ideological partisanship scale. Only 34.8 per cent of the twenty-three chairmen with authoritarian scores of 8 to 9 had partisanship ratings of 4 or over, as opposed to 72.2 per cent of the ward leaders with authoritarian scores of 7 and under.[5]

DISCUSSION

The significance of these findings in terms of the wider context of the American party system may basically be that the presence of people with authoritarian attributes within the organizations' ranks tends to accentuate those familiar aspects

[4] The general approach and four of the questions used were devised by the Michigan Survey Research Center in its study of the 1952 elections. See Campbell, Gurin, and Miller (1954:116–123); and Campbell, Gurin and Miller (1953). The responses of the New Haven sample were categorized in the same way as those of the Michigan survey. One point was added to the "ideological partisanship" score of each respondent if his position on a given issue represented that generally taken by his party. For further details on methodology, see Harned (1957:102–105).

[5] Space does not permit detailed examination; however, it should be noted that this relationship persists despite pressures tending to its modification. What relationship there is between authoritarianism and opinions on any of the specific issues on which the partisanship score was based appears in an association between pro-Democratic opinion on internationalism and intervention in Korea and a low authoritarianism score. Significantly, the relationship between intervention and equalitarianism was due to Republican, not Democratic, ward chairmen. The latter, with only two authoritarian exceptions, took the party line. This suggests that, in a situation where party position was easily perceived, authoritarian Democrats showed no hesitation in conforming. This display of loyalty may be allied less with fundamental beliefs than with a tendency on the part of more authoritarian people to submit to the established leadership of their party as an in-group with which they are identified. For further details on this point, see Harned (1957:153–155).

of the system that involve well-oiled, disciplined hierarchies and action largely devoid of ideological content. It is true that these characteristics of the "game of politics" as played in the United States are accepted as inevitable facts of life. Nevertheless, ward chairmen operate on a strategic level in American cities, for they represent a group that can serve as a transmission point between the party superstructure and the ordinary citizen. To the degree the democracy is based on the necessity for an informed electorate, ideally such ward politicians could perform a useful job as opinion leaders on issues in their neighborhoods. If local chairmen are uninterested in issues, as those with authoritarian tendencies appear to be, it goes without saying that they will not effectively fulfill this function. Moreover, if parties organized on a democratic basis are desirable, it would seem regrettable to have the lower echelons staffed with men and women more concerned with approval from above and their personal control over well-organized ward committees than with communicating their own desires to their leaders and in turn responding to the ideas of their followers. That there are a substantial number of chairmen whose participation in party activity is largely limited to these concerns is certainly not surprising to anyone familiar with the literature on city politics. The data discussed in this report would seem to indicate that those who are so restricted and who therefore may themselves limit the role and shape the operation of parties tend to be people with psychological characteristics that can be labeled "authoritarian."

Professional Politicians
and Personality Structures
Gordon J. DiRenzo

Behavioral scientists have described many of the roles involved in political activity, but the study of political roles
has extended only limitedly to the consideration of the total
personality structure of the political actor. Our fundamental
concern here is to distinguish a general personality type that
characterizes the professional politician and to consider in
some respects its consequences for political participation.

The general proposition of this study is that any occupation[1] is apt to be marked by a relative concentration of certain kinds of personalities.[2] This assertion is based upon the
hypothesis that certain personality types tend to be attracted
and/or recruited to particular occupations in a differential
rather than in a random or unsystematic fashion, and seemingly so disproportionately as to constitute modal personality
types for these occupations. There is some empirical evidence
to substantiate this position.[3] The tentatively plausible ex-

Reprinted by permission of the publisher from the *American
Journal of Sociology*, Volume 73, 1967, pp. 217–225.
[1] The term "occupation" is used generically for such designations
as profession, vocation, career, job, work, etc.
[2] The significance of this issue perhaps was captured initially by
Everett C. Hughes, who posed the question: "To what extent do
persons of a given occupation 'live together' and develop a culture
which has its subjective aspects in personality?" (Hughes, 1928:
768).
[3] See Inkeles (1959).

planation for this situation is that there is a congruent relationship between the personality and the occupation which is functional for the occupational system and psychologically gratifying for the individual.

METHOD

The professional politician—in fact, political man in general—has been presented rather extensively as a fundamentally authoritarian personality who is motivated basically by the search for personal power.[4] Our methodological approach focuses upon the conceptual orientation of dogmatism which has been offered by Rokeach (1960) as an alternative to that of *The Authoritarian Personality* (Adorno, 1950). Rokeach has made a conceptual distinction that allows for different kinds of authoritarianism by avoiding reference to the specific or *substantive content* of authoritarian ideologies and concentrating instead on *formal content*—that is, what they seem to share in common—and, even more particularly, by concentrating on the *structural properties* common to various authoritarian ideologies. Dogmatism is defined as "a relatively closed cognitive organization of beliefs and disbeliefs about reality, organized around a central set of beliefs about absolute authority which, in turn, provides a framework for patterns of intolerance and qualified tolerance towards others" (Rokeach, 1954:195). It is thus not so much *what* as *how* one believes that distinguishes the dogmatic personality structure.

[4] Spranger (1928:104); Lasswell (1930:52, 1948:22); Michels (1962:205); Gottfried (1955); Heberle (1959); Matthews (1954: 57, 1960:48); Lane (1959:123–124); Downs (1957:27–36); Schumpeter (1950:282). Empirical evidence for this position is inconsistent. See McConaughy (1950); Hennessy (1959); Harned (1961); Browning and Jacob (1964); Lane (1955); Sanford (1951); Mussen and Wyszynski (1952); and Milbrath and Klein (1962).

Instrument

The operational measurement for dogmatism is the Dogmatism Scale. Since we felt that the length of a personality inventory would be a crucial consideration with political subjects, we adopted an abbreviated version of the Dogmatism Scale, known as the D-10 Scale.[5] Its coefficient of reproducibility in the scalogram analysis is .83, which leaves some question about the unidimensionality of this instrument.

The D-10 Scale was standardized for Italian usage by the author with the assistance of Italian psychologists. Validation for the discerning power of the Italian instrument was performed by using a modification of the "Method of Known Groups."[6] Favorable statistical results were obtained in several applications of this procedure. Directions for answering the D-10 Scale were basically the same as those used by Rokeach in his original work with the exception of one modification. The usual six alternative answers of the Likert form were modified to four (agree-disagree partially, agree-disagree completely) which are more standard in Italian psy-

[5] This shortened form was developed by Schulze, who utilized Guttman's scalogram analysis to select those items from the Dogmatism Scale which best meet the various criteria of unidimensionality, item consistency, and reproducibility, and which are most representative of the single factor of dogmatism. The D-10 Scale was tested for validity with two samples. The coefficients of correlation between the final forty-item version of the Dogmatism Scale (D-40) and the D-10 Scale were .76 and .73, respectively. These are somewhat inflated, of course, since identical elements appear in both scales. Coefficients of correlation similar to those of the parent scale were obtained when the shortened version was associated with instruments measuring other elements in the dogmatism syndrome (Schulze, 1962).

[6] Details on this procedure may be found in my "A Social Psychological Analysis of Personality Structures of Members of the Italian Chamber of Deputies" (doctoral dissertation, University of Notre Dame, 1963; Ann Arbor: University Microfilms, Inc., #63-7323); also in my "Standardizzazione Italiana della Scala di Dogmatismo di Rokeach," *Orientamenti Pedagogici*, XII (1965), 926–939.

chological terminology and usage. No "neutral attitude" response was used in order to force a selection on the abbreviated instrument. The dogmatism score was computed on a positive or negative basis within a possible score range of -20 to $+20$.

Political Sample

The universe of subjects for this research constitutes the male membership of the Chamber of Deputies of the Italian Parliament for the year 1961 (Third Republican Parliament). The established sample was to include all of the members of the smaller parties, and a 20 per cent selection of the larger parties which was drawn by means of a table of random numbers. We managed to make direct contact with 145 deputies out of the potential sample of 193 (32 per cent of 596 Chamber members). Of this number, six had to be deleted from our analysis due to the lack of responses on key questions, seven accepted instruments for self-completion but failed to return them, and only three openly refused to be interviewed. On this basis, we feel that the sample is free from self-selection.

The final number of subjects that entered into the study is 129, which constitutes about 22 per cent of the universe for Chamber membership. While our sample represents about one-fifth of the total membership of the Chamber, the percentage of the individual parties represented in the sample is much greater in many cases, particularly those of the smaller parties. Table 1 contains the relevant data for the universe and sample selections. The political sample is adequately representative of the membership of the Chamber of Deputies. Approximate frequency distributions have been obtained for the following factors: age, education, occupation, parliamentary experience, and regional constituencies represented.

The D-10 Scale was administered to the political sample in schedule form as part of a private interview which was conducted with each subject. All of these data were collected during the months of May–August, 1961.

TABLE 1

DISTRIBUTION OF POLITICAL AND NON-POLITICAL SAMPLES
BY POLITICAL PARTY AFFILIATION

Party	Percentage Universe*	Percentage Political Sample	Percentage Non-political Sample
Christian Democracy (DC)	45.8	24.0	31.8
Italian Social Movement (MSI)	4.0	13.9	13.7
Italian Communist party (PCI)	23.6	19.3	8.0
Italian Democratic party (PDI)	3.1	2.3	6.4
Italian Liberal party (PLI)	3.0	8.5	10.0
Italian Social Democratic party (PSDI)	2.8	6.2	8.4
Italian Socialist party (PSI)	14.5	16.2	9.1
Miscellaneous†	2.8	9.1	7.0
Total	99.6	99.5	94.4‡

* Represents composition of the Chamber of Deputies and may be taken as a reflection of the popular strength of these parties.
† Includes representatives and supporters of the Italian Republican party (PRI).
‡ Five per cent had unknown political preferences.

Control Group

In order to relate the findings for the political sample to non-politicians, a control group was drawn from the Italian population. A simple quota sample was established of about five hundred individuals who were administered a brief schedule consisting of the D-10 Scale and several questions relating to social and political backgrounds. Each of twenty-five freshmen students at the University of Rome who were taking courses in public opinion was instructed to select twenty respondents for this purpose. Specific directions were given to approximate proportional distributions of the political sample in terms of sex, age, education, and professional backgrounds. The choice of individual subjects beyond these requirements was left to the student pollsters. Well over five hundred respondents were obtained. From this number was extracted a usable sample of 436 "non-political" individuals who neither had been elected to political office nor had been political candidates.

Since professional politicians at the parliamentary level are seldom representative of the total general population which they represent, the non-political sample as selected should not be expected to be a precisely matched control in terms of frequency distributions for political party affiliation and social background factors, such as religion, occupation, and education. It is, in fact, somewhat skewed in terms of religion toward Catholicism and in terms of education toward the upper levels. Moreover, supporters of the Christian Democratic party are represented disproportionately.

The control group in some respects is apt to be more representative of the general Italian population. In drawing this control, however, we were confined to the geographic locality of metropolitan Rome. Regional and provincial residence in Italy seems to be a social and psychological variable of considerable importance. Perhaps, in this regard, the control is not truly representative of the Italian population and is apt to be predominantly southern in mentality. Nevertheless, in spite of these handicaps, the non-political sample, which we use as suggestive rather than probative, appears to be a suitable control for our purposes, particularly since the critical variables are more likely to be skewed antithetically to the hypothetical directions.

HYPOTHESIS

The specific hypothesis that constitutes the focus of this study is simply that professional politicians are characterized by personality structures which are more dogmatic than those of non-politicians. The test of this hypothesis will be made by comparing our dogmatism data for the political sample to those of the non-political control group.

FINDINGS

Our data show that professional politicians appear to be generally dogmatic in personality structure. Seventy-six per cent of the sample scored positively (dogmatic) on the D-10 instrument, and 21 per cent negatively (non-dogmatic), within the possible range of −20 to +20. The mean dogmatism score for this sample is 5.51, with a standard deviation of 6.75.

For the non-political control group, we found that, of the total of 436 individuals, 74 per cent scored positively and 20 per cent negatively, as determined along the possible score range of −20 to +20. The remaining 6 per cent obtained neutral scores. The mean dogmatism score for the entire control group was 3.66, with a standard deviation value of 5.36.

Proportionately, in terms of personality type and absolute measure, there is no substantial difference between the two samples. In terms of valence, however, there is a crucial difference. The statistical application of Student's method to the means of these two samples yielded a t-value of 3.245, which is statistically significant at the .01 level. This evidence substantiates the research hypothesis and suggests that politicians and non-politicians can be distinguished in terms of the dogmatic personality structure.[7]

TABLE 2

MEAN DOGMATISM SCORE COMPARISONS OF POLITICAL AND NON-POLITICAL SAMPLES FOR INDIVIDUAL PARTIES

Party	Political Sample			Non-political Sample			t-Value	α
	N	$\overline{X}$	S.D.	N	$\overline{X}$	S.D.		
DC	31	7.96	6.48	139	3.91	4.58	4.069	.001
MSI	18	9.55	3.90	60	3.91	5.58	3.949	.001
PCI	25	.92	5.49	35	2.88	5.01	1.425	n.s.
PDI	3	9.33	4.64	28	3.07	4.86	2.059	.05
PLI	11	4.00	5.29	44	4.52	5.36	.285	n.s.
PRI	5	8.00	3.52	28	4.10	5.09	1.590	n.s.
PSDI	8	9.00	3.39	37	1.41	7.30	2.804	.01
PSI	21	2.23	7.70	40	5.20	5.57	1.692	.1
Total*	129	5.51	6.75	436	3.66	5.36	3.245	.01
	$F=4.368$; $p<.01$;			$F=1.729$; $p>.05$;				
	dfb, 7; dfw, 114			dfb, 7; dfw, 403				

* Includes minor party affiliates.

This consideration of the dogmatic political personality may be pursued with an analysis of the comparative political and non-political findings for each of the major political parties. Using Student's *t*, a test of difference was applied to the mean D-10 scores for each party. As may be seen in an inspection of Table 2, the political sample mean is greater than that of the non-political sample for all except three parties: Communists (PCI), Socialists (PSI), and Liberals (PLI). No statistically significant differences were found, however, between the respective means in these three parties.

Statistically significant differences were derived for all other parties with the exception of the Republicans (PRI): for Christian Democrats (DC) and the neo-Fascists (MSI) at the .001 level; for the Social Democrats (PSDI) at the .01 level; and for the Monarchists (PDI) at the .05 level. Significant perhaps is the fact that politicians and non-politicians of the political center and the political right tend to differ in per-

[7] The term "dogmatic personality" has never been used by Rokeach. It should be understood, therefore, as an innovation of the present writer.

sonality structure, whereas similarities in personality structure tend to be found for parties on the political left. The respective exceptions are the PRI and the PLI; however, the latter showed only a slight difference.

Significant relationships are found between various degrees of religious practice and dogmatism. As may be seen in Table 3, the lowest dogmatism means (1.73) in the political sample was derived for non-believers, whereas respondents professing Catholicism yielded means in the various categories of religious practice that average 7.33—clearly a marked discrepancy. Again, the findings for the religious variable are not consistent between the political sample and the non-political control group. An analysis of variance applied to the categories of religious practice for the political sample yielded an F-ratio of 4.510, which is statistically significant at the .01 level. No statistical significance on the basis of the same procedure was found for the non-political control group ($F=1.137$); there is, however, a pattern of response similar to that for the political sample.

TABLE 3

MEAN DOGMATISM SCORES OF POLITICAL AND NON-POLITICAL SAMPLES FOR RELIGIOUS PRACTICE

Religion	Political Sample			Non-political Sample			t-Value	α
	N	$\overline{X}$	S.D.	N	$\overline{X}$	S.D.		
None	41	1.73	6.38	20	2.80	5.34	.637	n.s.
Catholic (1)*	38	7.55	6.64	144	3.82	6.01	3.309	.001
Catholic (2)	11	9.18	3.48	95	4.18	4.90	3.258	.01
Catholic (3)	5	6.80	4.87	66	3.39	4.87	1.489	.20
Catholic (4)	17	8.35	6.07	64	3.75	4.81	3.264	.01
Catholic (5)	13	4.76	5.88	20	2.80	6.11	.885	n.s.
	$F=4.510$; dfb, 5;			$F=1.37$; dfb, 8+;				
	dfw, 119; $p<.01$			dfw, 426; $p>.05$				

* Catholic categories indicated here refer to the intensity of religious practice: (1) attends church at least once a week, (2) nearly every week, (3) about once a month, (4) only for the major festivities, and (5) never attends church.

† This test involves three other categories of religious practice which are omitted here because there are no corresponding affiliations for the political sample with which to make a comparison.

With the exception of religious practice, our data show no relationships between dogmatism and social background factors. These include age, educational level, parliamentary experience, and the geographic region of constituency. No statistically significant differences were obtained on the basis of analyses of variance applied to the means of all the subcategories for each of the factors. Moreover, a precise inspection was made for differences between individual combinations of the categorical means. Utilizing Student's *t*, with statistical significance acceptable minimally at the .001 level under these conditions, none of the derived *t*-values is statistically significant.

DISCUSSION

We offer two explanations to account for the outcome of the parties which show higher (but not statistically significantly different) dogmatism means than the corresponding non-political samples. One includes a question of fundamental ideology, and the other involves the processes of political recruitment.

Our data reveal parallel associations among political ideology, religious practice, and dogmatism which make for theoretical consistency. No religious tenet is explicit in some political ideologies, although in platform all tend to be either anticlerical or quite respectful to the church. The "pro-church" parties—the more dogmatic ones—are found on the conservative right, while the "anti-church" and less dogmatic ones are on the liberal left. Specifically, there are marked correlations between membership in the PCI and the PSI and the lack of adherence to any religious ideology. This finding is consistent with the political ideology of these two socialist parties.

Politicians should be expected to be more committed to party ideology than the non-political followers, for whom party affiliation in this study is merely a matter of expressed preference. Moreover, given the popular followings of the PCI and PSI, one could question the intellectual receptivity of the populace for Marxism on the grounds of educational and literacy levels. Italian people—that is, the general population—are not ideologically oriented, except in terms of religion, in their political behavior (Kogan, 1964:5). Therefore, in the cases of the PCI and the PSI, we would expect to find more atheists among the political sample and more Catholics among the non-political sample, given the religious orientation of the nation. Ninety-two per cent of the PCI representatives professed no religion; whereas, in the non-political control group for the PCI, 61 per cent claimed to profess Catholicism. For the PSI political sample, 62 per cent, as opposed to 8 per cent of the non-political control group, claimed to be non-believers. The element of commitment to political ideology would seem to account for the lesser degree of dogmatism in the non-political sample of these two parties.

The second, and perhaps more crucial, element for explaining the pattern of findings for personality structure along the lines of political parties is that of recruitment procedures. Under the election system used in Italy, the political parties are able to exercise considerable control over the candidates who are offered to the voters, and to a great extent actually determine the results of the popular elections and those who will be recruited into the system.[8] Methods of recruitment are not consistent in the individual parties. There is some evidence that the parties of the political left—the PCI and the PSI—are the least democratic in the selection of candidates, or the recruitment of representatives. About one-fourth of our political sample—and these came almost exclusively from the two parties in question—stated that the

[8] The method of voting in Italy is known as the *scrutinio di lista* or list vote. Although there are many variants of this method which has been adopted by several countries on the European continent, the basic principle is that the elector votes not for an individual candidate or candidates but, rather, for a party list of candidates. Strictly speaking, therefore, the competition is not among individual candidates but, rather, among the political parties. Thus, the electors determine how many seats each party shall receive, but it is the party organization that decides who shall occupy them. The *cursus honorum* in this system may be more in the nature of an ascribed rather than an achieved social status. This is an important fact to bear in mind for the analysis of our data.

decision to place their candidacies for the Chamber was not their own, but that of their party.

We contend that the difference in dogmatism scores for the individual political parties may be influenced strongly by the various methods of recruitment. There may be a selective bias operating, in that party leaders apparently choose—knowingly or unknowingly—individuals with particular kinds of personalities. Kogan, in speaking of the Italian situation particularly, states: "The party leaders are more likely to choose candidates who will be reliable followers rather than independent and individual thinkers" (1964:9). And we suggest that they do so for the purpose that these particular kinds of personalities are functionally necessary for the party and its political system. This situation, then, raises the question of whether such political representatives should be considered as recruited (appointive) or self-recruited (elective) politicians. Our hypothesis is directed exclusively to the latter type, but apparently both types of political man are present in our sample. The evidence suggests that where self-recruitment is allowed to operate politicians are more likely to be dogmatic and authoritarian personalities, but that where the recruitment process is controlled a differential selection of personalities may be operating according to the needs of the system. Thus, in this latter case, the hypothetical conception of the dogmatic political personality may or may not obtain. On the other hand, this element of differential recruitment, in terms of our findings, should serve to substantiate further our research hypothesis that the self-recruited (elective) professional politician is dogmatically closed-minded in personality structure.

Not all of the subjects in our political sample manifest the political personality in the conception presented here. We have hypothesized the existence of only a modal type, which has been confirmed by our methodological procedures. There may be a host of sociological and psychological factors at work in individual cases to account for higher or lower scores on the dogmatism measure.

A more specific delineation of the politician in terms of the degree of one's professionalization to political life is apt to reveal significant differences of a more precise nature in the political personality structure.[9] Other factors involved in a more precise analysis of such data on the political personality would include (1) the status level of political office within the system,[10] (2) the function of the particular political office (including the overlapping executive branch or other political functions), (3) the type of social routes that are used to reach political office, (4) political opportunism, (5) fundamental differences in political parties in terms of ideology and structural organization, (6) the element of party factions, and (7) self-images and conceptions of the political (parliamentary) role.[11] The delineation of the professional politician in terms of more precise considerations, such as these, may reveal an association of differential personality structures.

The significance of these findings for explaining political behavior may be noted in a consideration of the functional congruence between personality systems and the political systems in which they operate. In order for social systems to function as they have been structured to function, the personality systems involved have to operate in harmony with the social system. The problematic situation is that social systems may recruit personalities that, by and large, do

[9] Sartori, in his study of the Italian parliamentarian, distinguishes three categories of "professionalization to political life." These are the non-politician (the gentleman politician), the semi-professional politician (one who has another occupation and is not interested in politics primarily for party interests), and the professional politician (Sartori, 1961).

[10] We are suggesting that party representatives be distinguished in terms of "leaders" and "representatives." Lasswell speaks on this question when he offers this hypothesis: "Intensely power-centered persons tend to be relegated to comparatively minor roles." That is, he claims this to be true more likely of dogmatic personalities (Lasswell, 1954:222).

[11] One of the focal aspects of the relationship of personality to occupational structures should concern the conceptions of the social roles involved, and the specific role behavior which takes place. Our data suggest that among the parliamentarian subjects there is by no means a homogeneous conception of their political role—in terms of either what it is or what it ought to be. Relevant in this regard would be a delineation in terms of such role-taking conceptions as (1) parliamentarian, (2) representative, and (3) clientelistic, which have been proposed by Wahlke, Eulau, Buchanan, and Ferguson (1962: Part IV).

not or cannot function effectively within particular social systems.

Our argument implies that the form of government in a particular social system is related to the kind of personalities that are recruited into the polity, or who are potential recruits for that system. Specifically, in reference to our data, the dogmatic and authoritarian personality contains those psychological elements which are considered to be pathological to such an extent that they inhibit one's contribution to the democratic process.[12] Yet, we would not contend that all agents of a particular system need to be either democratic or authoritarian in personality structure, as the case may be, but only that the active co-operation of a sufficient number of the respective type is required for the system to function in either a democratic or authoritarian manner. In fact, it is possible that all decision-making cannot be—from a functional perspective—the result of an exclusively democratic or authoritarian process, as the case may be. Both types of roles may be required in any system. The crucial factor is the modality of the personality structures that characterizes the system. Any political system—of whatever form—needs the functional support of a sufficient number of congruent personalities. There is some empirical substantiation that this situation obtains.[13]

Any situation that does not maintain an effective degree of congruence between the two systems is apt to result in dysfunctional consequences for either the personality systems or the social systems—or both. Stability and change in social organization (social systems) is, to an extent, a function of the respective congruity or incongruity which they share with the personality systems involved therein. The greater the congruity, the more stable the organization and the more minimal the social change. We should suggest, for example, that political consensus and cleavage—exemplified in such forms as alliances, coalitions, factions, and changes in party affiliation—may be a function of the composition of the total personality structures within any given political system.[14]

[12] For a treatment of this question, see Lane (1962b:401–412).
[13] See Dicks (1950) and Inkeles et al. (1958).
[14] See my volume, *Personality, Power, and Politics* (1967).

PART FOUR

PERSONALITY AND POLITICAL IDEOLOGY

Introduction

Do "radicals" and "conservatives" differ in personality? Given that personality reveals significant relationships with political activity and political roles—what people do—it should follow that similar associations exist as well in regard to political ideology—what people think and believe. In fact, in the matter of ideology,[1] we have one of the few areas of politics in which there is considerable belief, among the otherwise skeptical crowd, that distinct modes of personality are differentially and intimately related. This view is particularly true in regard to political extremism; but while the premise of the argument appears justified, the substance, as we shall see, does not always square with the evidence.

One prevalent belief is that political extremism, of whatever type, is an accompaniment—even a product—of a general syndrome of authoritarianism, dogmatism, and/or alienation. The empirical evidence, however, shows that this particular interaction of personality and political behavior is more likely to be limited to extremist ideologies of the political right. While the relationship between authoritarianism and ideology is far from simple, Rokeach (1960) and DiRenzo (1967a) provide similar arguments that, given the content and structural nature of rightist ideologies, such findings are theoretically consistent.

[1] We define "ideology" as a system of opinions, beliefs, attitudes, and values regarding man and society, or any part thereof.

Our first selection for this section offers a documentation for extreme politics of the political right. Dicks, working with a sample of German prisoners during and after World War II, demonstrates, in a psychoanalytic perspective, the relationship between personality dispositions and orientations toward Nazism. Dicks's fundamental hypothesis is that, in terms of specific patterns of psychoanalytic variables, there is a distinct Nazi personality—a hard, fanatical type, holding Nazi beliefs and ideology with conviction—as opposed to the non-Nazi or anti-Nazi German.[2] It is this type, Dicks contends, that constituted the Nazi elite.

Communism is usually the topic of conversation when the political pendulum swings to the extreme left. A great deal has been written regarding the psychological bases of Communist ideology and party membership, but little empirical evidence has been collected on this question. In our second selection for this section, Inkeles and his associates report on a study of the Soviet sociopolitical system in terms of its political ideology and political methodology.

These researchers studied a highly selective sample from the population of the Soviet Union, namely, former citizens of Great Russia who "defected" during or after World War II, and focused their investigation on the participation of the subjects in, and adjustment to, the new Communist sociopolitical order.

The Inkeles group shows that the modal personality type within their sample was incongruent with the demands made upon the Russian people by the new Stalinist sociopolitical system, and that socioeconomic mobility within this system is positively correlated with a particular personality structure[3] in terms of its congruent relationship with the structure of the Communist sociopolitical system.

[2] For more on the anti-Nazi type, see Fromm (1941), Schaffner (1948), and Levy (1948). Jaensch (1938), the Nazi psychologist, also was concerned with the "antitype," that is, the one thought to be incongruent with National Socialism. He described a personality type with remarkable similarities to the typology of *The Authoritarian Personality,* and saw this personality type as exemplifying the best virtues of National Socialist manhood.

[3] For a discussion, with case studies, of the personality type that the Soviets are trying to develop, see Bauer (1956).

Almond (1954) has observed that there are wide variations in the "appeals of communism" between countries, between social classes, between transient and long-term members, and between other kinds of social categories. He suggests, nonetheless, that, in many instances, neurotic needs make Communism an attractive political movement as a dignified outlet for hostility, as a source for strong authority, as a shelter for loneliness, and as a compromise for feelings of inadequacy. In these respects, Almond finds that individuals in the higher echelons of Communist organizations are much less neurotic and much more ideological about their membership in Communist establishments. DiRenzo (1967a), in his study of the Italian parliament, offers some support for these contentions. His data show that Communist members of the Italian parliament are remarkably antithetical types as regards the dogmatic/authoritarian or fascist/Nazi personalities.

Communism and Soviet Russian society often are equated to each other, and such a myopic perception is not fair to either in terms of their substantial differences. Adequate study of the multiple relationships between personality and Communist ideology, as indeed all political ideologies, will need to consider the marked variations in the sociocultural contexts in which it is found.[4]

Within a political system there may be a variety of political ideologies, but each of them is in some way modified by the national or cultural ethos. Communism is one of the more demonstrative examples of this principle. Americans, partly as a consequence of their lack of any personal or direct experience with Communism, think of this ideology as a fundament of a monolithic world movement. Yet, for a proper understanding of this ideology, we need to distinguish among the many Communist parties and organizations around the world: Russian, Yugoslavian, Bulgarian, Chinese, Cuban, Italian, even American, and so forth. Each of these Communist organizations is fundamentally Marxist, but much less perceptible to the unsophisticated observer are the subtle variations in their political methodology. A Communist

[4] For other studies that explore the relationship of personality to Communism, see Mead (1951) and Dicks (1952).

party "in power" may not, from the perspective of its political methodology, be the same kind of political organization as one working to subvert a democratic or autocratic regime. The Italian Communist party, for example, is not a Bolshevist party, although some factions within it, and others which on occasion have splintered off into new parties, are fundamentally Bolshevistic. These kinds of social and cultural distinctions, we believe, are similarly true for all other varieties of political ideologies which exist around the world today.

One of the most systematic efforts to relate personality to ideological orientations is the work of Herbert McClosky. Although he has sought to define the personality characteristics of individuals holding positions at all points along the continuum of liberal to conservative politics, his work has dealt primarily with conservatism—partly as a vehicle, and partly as a function of the time of his research. McClosky's work, however, has become a classic contribution to the field of personality and politics and it has relevant application today.[5]

McClosky, in our third selection for this section, shows that the "extreme conservative" is differentiated sharply from both the "liberal" and the "moderate liberal" by a pattern of personality traits that very closely resembles those of the authoritarian personality.[6] Other well-known studies (Adorno, 1950; Rokeach, 1960; Barker, 1963; and DiRenzo, 1967a) support this thesis that conservatives tend to be authoritarian. On the other hand, Schoenberger (1968), in more recent research, challenges these findings, and McClosky's conclusions in particular, and contends that most conservatives do not fit the mold of psychic maladjustment, anomy, alienation, and outgroup hostility. Schoenberger suggests that these

[5] The outlooks on conservatism and liberalism, as McClosky points out, have remained fairly constant throughout the recent centuries, and the data which he presents show that there is a considerable regularity and coherence in the body of norms which are preferred in either political orientation.
[6] McClosky does not identify conservatism with "right-wing authoritarianism" and contends that there are significant differences between the two types, with the latter being a more extreme version of the former in some respects.

discrepancies may be due to (1) different ways of defining conservatism, and (2) different ways of measuring conservatism; and he hypothesizes that these variations may be distinguished on the basis of (1) political grounds (those concerned primarily with questions of economic and social policy on the one hand, and with powerful and conspiratorial domestic threat on the other), and (2) social differences (one, a segment of the young, educated, technologically competent, and economically successful middle to upper-middle class; the other, less competent and less "successful" on these dimensions).[7]

On the whole, however, the available studies on the interaction of personality and political ideology—particularly in terms of authoritarianism—have shown more significant and consistent results with ideologies of the political right. This situation may be a function, at least in some cases, of the bias of the particular personality instruments that have been used in much of the past research along these lines. In one of the major criticisms of the now classic study of *The Authoritarian Personality*, particularly in terms of its well-known F scale, which has been the principal tool for measuring authoritarianism, Shils contends that the Berkeley investigators ". . . have failed to observe that at the Left pole of their continuum there is to be found an authoritarianism impressively like the Authoritarianism of the Right" (1954:38). He argues, in short, that Communists and fascists are alike in personality structure. In support of this view, Kornhauser and his associates (1956), in their study of American automobile workers, discovered, among a number of other interesting associations between personality and political participation, that authoritarianism is related to political extremism whether of the political right or the political left.

That authoritarianism is not limited to any one extreme of the political continuum is demonstrated in a methodological analysis by Barker, which we present as our fourth selection for this section. Barker discerns similarities and differences

---

[7] For a rejoinder, see McClosky (1969). For a methodological statement on how to improve the definition and categorization of political ideology of various kinds, particularly in terms of its relationship to personality, see Levinson (1968).

among authoritarianism of the political left, center, and right. In comparing the F scale and the D scale, along with other instruments, in terms of their discriminatory functions, he demonstrates, as alleged (see Christie and Jahoda, 1954), that the research of *The Authoritarian Personality* was guided by an ideological bias which also entered into the construction of the F scale, and that, as a consequence, it does not measure leftist authoritarianism at all. He argues that it is possible to discriminate authoritarianism at any point on the political continuum. This contention, however, often leads to the erroneous belief that *all* individuals holding extremist ideologies, regardless of content, and whether of the political left or the political right, are psychologically similar, if not identical, in being basically authoritarian personalities.[8] Such a view implies that, while extremists among themselves are seemingly oriented in different ideological directions, they are all fundamentally identical, which means being equated to authoritarianism in personality and to violence in method.

We believe that one of the major reasons for this false belief is that more frequently than not exclusive concern in the analysis of political extremism is placed on what its advocates *do* rather than, or as well as, on what they ideologically believe or propagandistically profess. Herein lies the failure to distinguish between political ideology and political methodology (see DiRenzo, 1967a and Rokeach, 1960) in the analysis of political belief systems and political parties. For example, Communism, as an ideological movement in a monolithic perspective, invariably is equated to Leninism or Stalinism, which actually are but two specific, however dominant, at least in the recent past, methodological variations of Marxism.

Evidence (see Rokeach, 1960 and DiRenzo, 1967a) indicates that significant differences in personality types exist in

---

[8] Eysenck (1954), for example, on the basis of his research in England, argues that Communists and fascists have in common a high degree of "tough-mindedness," a syndrome closely related to that of dogmatism and authoritarianism. His conceptual and theoretical formulations have been strongly criticized by Christie (1956) and Rokeach and Hanley (1956) for serious deficiencies in sampling, data analysis, and data interpretation. For a rejoinder defending his work, see Eysenck (1956).

regard to differences in both ideology and methodology, and that the two political dimensions are not necessarily structurally consistent on the *de facto* level of politics. Hence, however paradoxical, one can find authoritarian ideology implemented with non-authoritarian methodology, and conversely, democratic ideology with authoritarian methodology. In fact, we believe that within this distinction between political ideology and political methodology lies one of the fundamental areas of reconciliation between the seemingly competitive explanations offered by sociologists and psychologists for much political behavior.

As Inkeles (1961:193) suggests, the formal or explicit "content" of a political ideology, and general political orientations, such as left or right, conservative or radical, as well as political party preference, may be related more to, and determined mainly by, "extrinsic" social characteristics, such as social class and other social background variables; but the form or style of political ideology—favoring force or persuasion, compromise or arbitrary dictation, being tolerant or narrowly prejudiced, flexible or highly dogmatic in policy— is determined largely by personality considerations.[9] Indeed, as we shall see in the next section, it is personality which shows a more intimate relationship to concrete political

---

[9] A more sociological view in this regard is that, as proposed by Lipset (1960) for example, all political ideologies, as well as the political parties which espouse them, more likely can be distinguished by leftist, centrist, and rightist orientations or factions— and the implication is methodological orientations or factions— which in turn can be distinguished in terms of different bases of social classes. For a contrary view, i.e., that "social class has little relation to basic political ideology," see Selznick and Steinberg (1964), who contend that social class is significant only because it modifies the relationship between political ideology and opinions regarding concrete political issues, such as economic questions, e.g., welfare programs. To reconcile these views of Inkeles and Lipset, it would need to be demonstrated that different social classes are characterized by different types of personality, but the available evidence does not support such a hypothesis. See DiRenzo (1967a: Chapter 8). Moreover, as McClosky points out in his selection, social class has little effect on conservatism which cuts through the social class fabric and, as he says, ". . . personality factors seem to exercise a fairly uniform influence on the formation of conservative or liberal outlooks at all social levels."

ideology and methodology, such as are embodied in particular parties and in the styles and forms manifested and utilized by particular factions or candidates.[10]

The interactions between personality and political ideology should hold just as true for political parties, considered as ideological systems, and indeed it does for ideological parties at least (see DiRenzo, 1967b). The evidence available for American political parties, however, is inconsistent, and it appears that personality is not likely to reveal any invariably significant relationship in these instances.[11]

Major political parties in the United States are ideologically more amorphous and less differentiated than those in other countries. These parties, hoping to attract support from almost every segment of the electorate, have functioned more as brokerage organizations and less as ideological movements. Hence party preference in America frequently tells little about the precise nature of one's ideological orientation, and the corresponding relationship of this to personality. Political affiliations in these cases may be due more directly to historical, sociocultural, and even situational variables. It appears that for American political parties, as will be shown in

[10] Levinson (1964) advances the thesis that the diversity of political ideologies in a given situation, wherever this is true, such as in a multiparty political system, e.g., in Italy, is related to the diversity of personality structure which exists in the corresponding population. It is in this respect that we can appreciate his contention that personality not only facilitates the acceptance of options that are personally meaningful—and, of course, the rejection of those options which are not similarly compatible—but that it also facilitates the creation, wherever possible, of personally meaningful options.
[11] Campbell et al. (1954) and Berelson et al. (1954), in studies of the 1948 national elections, one thought to be fought primarily along economic lines, found no systematic differences in authoritarian scores between Republicans and Democrats. Lane (1955), on the other hand, in both the 1948 and 1952 elections, found that Republicans tended to be predominantly authoritarian. Manheim (1959), on the basis of several factors, found personality differences between Republicans and Democrats that could be distinguished further on the basis of sex. Our own research (DiRenzo, 1968, 1971) suggests that the dogmatic/authoritarian personality syndrome is modally associated, more frequently, but not always, with the political right, and in particular with the Republican party.

the next section, differences in personality may be related more significantly to concrete forms of "ideology," such as that represented by particular factions, and/or espoused by particular candidates, rather than in terms of general party preferences or affiliations.

The relationship between political ideology and personality, however, can be expected only when the political actor is provided with a sufficiently diversified ideological situation which—offering political and psychological stimuli which are sufficiently different—permits the significant interaction of personality. The sociopolitical system may constrict the range of ideological and party choices which are available, by such methods as legitimizing some alternatives and not others. Examples of this situation in the United States would include Communism and monarchism. When provided with minimal options, which, or which in effect, offer little or no ideological—or even methodological—diversity, a political selection or preference more likely will be made on the basis of non-personality variables. In this kind of a political situation, the role of sociological factors, such as social backgrounds, is more likely to be dominant, perhaps even relatively exclusive, in whatever choice is made.

These extended and more complex considerations on the interaction of personality and political ideology, hopefully, will serve to underscore our concern that the conjoint perspectives of political theory, sociological theory, and personality theory are required for more comprehensive explanations of political behavior.[12]

[12] More recent developments in the analysis of personality and ideology have included the following: Hofstadter's work (1965) on the "conspiratorial" view of politics (the fantasies, ego defenses, and modes of thought that give coherence, meaning, and emotional appeal to the conspiratorial interpretation of political affairs); Bittner's (1963) attempts, in a historical and phenomenological approach, to delineate, in terms of psychological properties and themes, a genotypic conception of radicalism; Lane's (1962a) analysis of political orientations in terms of "cabalist" identification; and Talmon's (1962) description of various psychological properties of millenaristic ideology. For more extended, and interesting, discussion, including a number of propositions for further research and analysis, on the relationship of personality to political ideology, see Levinson (1964b, 1968) and Lane (1973).

Personality Traits and National Socialist Ideology
Henry V. Dicks

INTRODUCTION

The object of this paper is to report, rather belatedly, a war-time study on German prisoners of war which served to throw some light on the connections which exist between character structure and political ideology, and to illustrate the methods used in investigating both these sets of data. In this way it may contribute by way of example or prototype to future work in the integration of clinical psychiatry, social anthropology, and political science. In brief, the study consisted in contacting a random sample of German Prisoners of War passing through a certain British Collecting Centre, and subjecting them to prolonged interviews according to a schedule presently to be described in detail, drawing up a "personality profile" which was then compared with the political ideology of the same man as ascertained (in the greater part of the sample) by another interviewer, and finally, subjecting this comparison to a test of statistical significance. Concurrently a much larger random sample was being subjected to a political interrogation alone, from which a general distribution of political attitudes among the German Prisoner of War population could be derived.

The writer happens to be bi-lingual and partly educated in German schools. On being posted to the Directorate of

Reprinted by permission of the publisher from *Human Relations*, Volume 3, 1960, pp. 111–153.

Military Intelligence he was instructed to undertake any suitable studies which might help in the understanding of the enemies' mind and intentions and in the conduct of psychological warfare. The study which is about to be described was a by-product of other work, more directly relevant to the war, which the writer was briefed to do between 1942 and 1946. The main effort during the period in question was directed to a running survey of enemy morale which enabled us to plot fluctuations in the expectations and preoccupations of German prisoners during various phases of the war for purposes of propaganda. It was from this part of the work that we derived, amongst other things, our data on the distribution of political attitudes in the sample population.

The second piece of work consisted in the description and evaluation of the human relations and morale structure within the German Armed Forces as seen through the eyes of a British Army psychiatrist (Dicks, 1944a, 1944b). It seemed of some practical importance to devise, if possible, a psychological technique by which selectors in the future Allied Administration of Germany might be helped to distinguish Nazis from non-Nazis without recourse to the very crude and fallacious criteria of reference to formal membership of the Party and the like. It also occurred to the writer at that stage, that here might be a method which, if further refined, could find general application in that branch of Social Science concerned with the study of the relation between culture and personality. Some practical use was in fact made of the correlations of personality and political attitudes obtained and presented in this paper, when, early in the organisation of the Control Commission for the British zone of Germany, a Selection Centre was set up for potential high-level German personnel in which both the technical and the general frame of reference of this study formed part of the criteria used in the screening procedure.

During many informal conversations with some two thousand German prisoners of various ranks and arms, and as a result of the study of captured documents both of an official and of a purely private character, a broad picture of the general recurring regularities of German mental behaviour became gradually apparent.

It is not the intention in these pages to pillory the German people. The study required concentration on the origins of their recent mass behaviour. Many aspects have not been covered. When speaking of "national character" we mean only the broad, frequently recurring regularities of certain prominent behaviour traits and motivations of a given ethnic or cultural group. We do not assert that such traits are found in equal degree, or at all, in all members of that group, or that they are so conjoined that the extreme is also the norm. Neither do we assert that the traits are found singly or in combination in that group alone.

It should also be emphasised that this study was not concerned with the historical, political, or economic conditions which might have brought about the emergence of what we have called the "national character" or its manifestations in German Nationalism, Militarism, and National Socialism. It confined itself to psychiatric findings in present living individuals and endeavoured to test certain hypotheses concerning their mental make-up in relation to their political beliefs and convictions at the time of the interview. Nothing in this paper must be taken to imply that the economic and historico-political field forces are in any way under-rated by the writer.

HYPOTHESES

This paper then will be limited to that part of the work which consisted in an attempt to compare and show the interdependence of personality structure and political ideology in the population studied. Before proceeding to the detail of the method and its results, a statement of the assumptions and preliminary hypotheses which underlay it is called for.

The basic assumption made was that a political ideology was only in part a function of intellectual indoctrination or automatic group-conformity and that the sincerity with which men held various views on social and political matters was part of a Gestalt in which their personality structure was more or less deeply involved. Hence, for the adequate appreciation of a social or political movement it was essential to appraise the psychological structure of its participants, grading them in some way in terms of intensity of identification with the ideology and aims of the movement, and of consequent dynamism as carriers or infective agents. It was thought that the more an ideology fitted unconscious need systems of an individual, the greater would be the cathexis given to it by him.

The second assumption was, in brief, that the child is father to the man, and that the life history of individuals provides a clue to later character structure and to the ways in which the main infantile conflicts and emotional vicissitudes had been transformed into what have been called character traits, seeking expression in social behaviour.

The third assumption was that a national culture was likely to produce certain recurring regularities in the pattern of meeting the frustrated need systems consequent upon the socialisation of children through educational influences. It might, therefore, be possible to describe and define more precisely a configuration of personality traits which was shared by a large number of representatives of a given cultural group over and above regional, social-economic, educational, or other sub-group differences. Then, any desired sub-group of the culture could be subjected to comparison with the "norm" in respect of the presence and intensity of the traits or variables by which the main group had been described.

The processes of arriving at a working hypothesis to be tested grew slowly out of impressions left by previous participation in German life, which was not at that youthful time subjected to any critical or scientific evaluation, but which nevertheless formed an important part of one's experiences. In 1941 the writer was detailed to take over for some six weeks the psychiatric care of Rudolf Hess, then recently arrived in Britain. The description and evaluation of Hess' personally appears elsewhere (see Rees, 1957). Here it is mentioned only as one of the factors contributing to the selection of certain psychological variables to be looked for in the German and in particular in the Nazi personality. (It will later be seen that some of the traits looked for on strength of contact with Hess did not in fact prove to be significant in distinguishing one kind of German from another). A third important preliminary to the setting up of a working hypothesis was the unrivalled opportunity for informal conversations with a heterogeneous group of German Prisoners, together with "mass observation" of their behaviour amongst themselves, and the study of a great variety of documents already alluded to. Some six weeks or more after this process of steeping oneself in the current German idiom, a series of pilot interviews was begun, branching out from a routine political interrogation already practised at the camp before the writer's arrival. During these pilot interviews both ideology and something of a personality assay were attempted together, and the conviction grew that the following hypotheses would repay more careful study.

1. That the German prisoners who held Nazi or near Nazi beliefs and ideology with conviction and fanaticism, had a personality structure which differed from the norm of German national character in the sense that they embodied this structure in more exaggerated or concentrated form.

2. That Nazis or near Nazis were likely to be men of markedly pre-genital or immature personality structure in which libido organisation followed a sado-masochistic[1] pattern, based on a repression of the tender tie with the mother and resulting typically in a homo-sexual paranoid (extra-punitive) relation to a harsh and ambivalently loved and hated father figure, with its attendant sadism towards symbols of the displaced bad portion of this figure; in increased secondary ("defensive") narcissism; in libido splitting *vis-à-vis* female love objects; and in tendencies towards hypochondriacal (internal persecutor) and schizoid or hypomanic (guilt denial) features.

[1] Cf. Fromm (1942). This book and Fromm's views were not at that period known to the writer.

DESCRIPTION OF THE STUDY

Distribution of Political Attitudes

To test these hypotheses, it was necessary to turn on, as it were, a higher power of the microscope on a statistically adequate sample of the prisoner population passing through our hands and to devise a method of examination of these selected men by which their personality structure on the one hand, and their political attitudes on the other, could be as clearly as possible examined in parallel. Ideally, a team of at least three should have been required for doing the job thoroughly. There should have been a psychiatric interviewer, his clinical observations and inferences should have been supplemented and corrected by the use of projection tests and other quasi-normative personality evaluations by a clinical psychologist, whilst political attitudes should have been examined by a third interviewer, working blind in relation to personality factors, but skilled in interviewing and in the appreciation of German social and political outlook.

This would, however, have turned the study into a formal laboratory set piece of very doubtful value, considering the setting. Few of the subjects would have reacted as spontaneously as in fact they did. Only one of these desiderata could in practice be obtained; very soon the work was divided between the writer covering the entire aspect of personality study and a number of "lay" interviewers who conducted almost all the political interrogation after a period of tuition and supervision by the writer in accordance with the schedule reproduced as Table 1. Naturally, political ideas and emotions were often expressed in the course of the psychological interview, and personal life stories were equally frequently given to the political interrogators. This was a limitation on the "purity" of the "experiment" which is hard to remedy in what is essentially a piece of "fieldwork."

TABLE 1

Name of P/W   Age   Rank
Unit   Domicile   Education
Profession   Parents' Religion   Own Religion
Class

A. OUTCOME OF THE WAR

Germany wins   Compromise Peace   Doubtful
                 Germany loses

Germany wins:—
   Within one year   Within two years   In over two years
*Notes on views (e.g. (i) World Dominion, (ii) "United Europe",
(iii) Restoration of Independence to Occupied Territories (which?)
(iv) How Germany will win).*
Compromise Peace:—
   With Western Powers   With Russia   "All round"
Doubtful:—
Notes:—
Germany loses:—
   Western Powers invade first   Russia invades first
Where will Germany stabilise her defence line in (*a*) France,
   (*b*) Italy?

B. ATTITUDE TO REGIME

Complete loyalty   (*FI*) Believer with reservations   (*FII*)
   Divided   (*FIV*) Anti-Nazi   (*FV*) Unpolitical   (*FIII*)
Believer with reservations:—   Doubtful:—
Notes:—   *Notes:—*
Anti-Nazi:—   Unpolitical:—
Notes:—   *Notes:—*
Attitude to Hitler personally:—
Notes (e.g. Worship, Acceptance, Doubt, Hostility, Any substitutes?)

C. HOME FRONT

Confident   Doubtful   Pessimistic
Doubtful and Pessimistic:—
*Notes on topics discussed (e.g. Food, Clothing, Sabotage, Foreign
   Workers, Effect of Losses, Women's Call-up)*
Effect of Air Raids:—
   Very dangerous   Dangerous   Ineffective
   Notes:—

TABLE 1 (contd.)

D. ATTITUDE TO UNITED NATIONS

(i) BRITAIN

Hostile   Divided   Admiring
Notes:—

(ii) U.S.A.

Hostile   Divided   Admiring
Notes:—

(iii) RUSSIA

Hostile   Divided   Admiring
Notes:—

German defeat of Russia:—	Yes	Doubtful	No
Russian occupation	Feared	Indifferent	Welcomed
Western Powers preferred:—	Yes	Indifferent	No

Notes:—

E. PROPAGANDA

(i) GERMAN

Hostile   Divided   Admiring
Notes:—

(ii) B.B.C

Listened to:—   Yes   Heard quoted   No
Notes on opinions:—

(iii) SCHWARZSENDER (Freedom Stations)

Listened to:—   Yes   Heard quoted   No
Notes on opinions:—

(iv) MOSCOW

Listened to:—   Yes   Heard quoted   No

(v) LEAFLETS

Read   Seen, not read   Heard quoted   No knowledge

F. POST-WAR EXPECTATIONS IF GERMANY LOSES

German people exterminated   Square deal and reconciliation
Germany will rise in new war   Other

TABLE 1 (contd.)

G. SERVICE CONDITIONS

Satisfied: G.A.   Dissatisfied: G.A.
             G.N.   G.N.
             G.A.F.   G.A.F.
Notes (*Subject matter of grouses: e.g. awards, Officers, rations, etc.*)

H. FIGHTING QUALITIES

High   Fair   Poor
   Notes:—

A few words of explanation as to the way in which the
above schedule was employed may be useful. It will be seen
that there are certain items which were simply checked, but
that for each item there were spaces for notes (larger than
the reproduction here shown) in which the interrogator would
write qualitative observations on his subject's responses, noting especially striking phrases, clichés culled from Nazi propaganda, fervid declarations of faith, accusations against the
Allied Powers, all manner of expressions of opinions or doubt
on the political side, which influenced the interviewers' judge-
ment. Some of the headings and material had of course more
value to psychological warfare and morale themes than to the
mere assessment of these men's political attitudes. That was
especially true of our recording of the numbers who listened
to, or were familiar with Allied radio transmission and later
with Allied leaflets, and of conditions inside Germany. Even
in the responses to such enquiries, however, the political
temper of a man was laid open or substantiated.

The schedule was never filled in in the presence of the subject, but was completed later. Any data from other sources
were added to the notes, and finally the man was placed by
the observer, frequently after case discussion between several
interrogators who knew the subject well, in one of five
categories as follows:—

F.I. Fanatical, whole-hearted Nazis (*the hard core*); people
   who had thoroughly identified themselves with the ideology,
   aims, and attitudes of the Nazi leadership, as stated and
   propagated in the written and spoken pronouncements of
   the N.S.D.A.P. and its affiliated organizations.

F.II. Believers with reservations (camp followers and near Nazis); a fraction which was more nearly identical with former German Nationalists, and not infrequently better educated than the fanatics; who were ready to admit certain shortcomings of the Nazi regime and its methods of waging war, but usually on the grounds of inefficiency rather than on ethical or political grounds. The veneer of Western culture was usually somewhat thicker than in the zealots.

F.III. Unpolitical men; the group composed of men essentially concerned with private motives such as subsistence and security, who usually also passively accepted the current social and political conditions. The repetition of a number of Nazi-political clichés without emotional conviction was discounted.

F.IV. "The divided" (later called passive anti-Nazis by Norman Brangham); were men in conflict, disillusioned, not knowing where they stood. They had often supported Hitler in the past because of the promise of economic benefits and political order, but they had a general bias against Nazism and war. They were often recruited from former believers with reservations, and were mostly loyal patriots.

F.V. Active convinced anti-Nazis; men who had maintained opposition in feeling, thought and sometimes in deed to the regime on religious, ethical, political, or individualist grounds.

It must be stressed that these were classifications which had been made on empirical grounds before the beginning of the study here described. In practice it was a useful division which corresponded to the realities of political interviews and attitudes of the German forces towards the war and it was accordingly retained as the basis for political classification of the population studied. It must be emphasized also that at this stage the *F* rating stood merely as a code for a set of political attitudes and had as yet no connotations as to personality structure. It was precisely these connotations which the subsequent study set out to discover.

Taking the main items in the political schedule, the *F.I.* group tended to expect German victory usually in a short time and to be followed by world dominion, or at least dominion over a united Europe from which all non-Germanic influence would be excluded. They expressed complete loyalty to their regime and its leaders, and were ready to testify dramatically to the rightness of their beliefs. They usually equally readily minimised difficulties on the home front; regarded even our later air-raids as ineffective; professed unwavering hostility to and contempt for the three major Allied nations, and in particular expressed what came to be called the "Bolshevik Bogey." It followed that they usually dismissed with contempt our radio transmissions, or staunchly professed never to have heard them. Under "post-war expectations" they most readily thought that in the "purely hypothetical" event of an Allied victory the German people would be exterminated, or alternatively that Germany would rise in a little while to try world conquest once more. Their opinions were expressed with emotional fervour and in Goebbels' language.

The believers with reservations (F.II.) tended in general towards similar scores and the difference between them and the fanatics was usually one of emphasis, degree, or conviction; but sometimes such men would admit criticism of one or more Nazi leaders or their policies; would tend to grant the seriousness of the threat from Allied bombing, and would find something to admire or be ambivalent about in their enemies.

The unpolitical group (F.III.) would tend in the main to give replies of the "don't know" type. Characteristic of what the unpolitical subject might say is the following—'First we had the Kaiser, then Mr. Ebert and Mr. Hindenburg, and now that Hitler, but we still have to milk our cows'. Such men were readily worried about the home front and their dear ones and were usually indifferent as to the outcome of the war or the resulting political situation, provided that they retained some security, property and means of keeping themselves and their families alive. Their attitude was summed up in a recurrent sentence: 'All this is far too difficult for me, I am only a small man'.

The passive anti-Nazis (F.IV.) tended to score in the doubtful headings much more often than not, but sometimes made gallant attempts to profess their loyalty and belief in victory and a great future for Germany, in order to cover up their lack of faith. Their remarks on Nazi leaders usually tried to stress the constructive and beneficial aspects of the regime, while regretfully admitting that all was not well. Their doubts were often shown in gestures, hesitancies and modes of expression rather than by the substance of their remarks.

The anti-Nazis (*F.V.*) tended to favour German defeat, from which alone they hoped a better world could be reconstructed. They wished to make amends all round. They would express freely, although sometimes with anxiety, their hostility to the regime, its ideas, and it leading personalities. They would tend in general to be admiring either towards Britain or the U.S.A. or Russia, not always towards all three, but would tend to have more objective political views about the comparative merits of Germans and non-Germans than other German prisoners, except when they were doctrinaire Marxists or "anti-German" renegades. They would equally reject German propaganda and admire the truthfulness or efficacy of ours. They would expect a square deal from the Allies and discount German atrocity propaganda of the "strength-through-fear" type.

Such, briefly, were the ways in which these five categories tended to score and answer the schedule. The interview was by no means stereotyped, but was conducted in an informal manner.

The sociological data of all men undergoing the questionnaire were carefully recorded under such headings as age, regional affiliations, urban or rural, bombed or non-bombed area, occupational and economic status, educational level, arm of service, service rank, and parents' and man's own religious beliefs or affiliations. These data were incorporated in current reports to Psychological Warfare agencies, together with the assessment of and reasons for the men's satisfaction or dissatisfaction with their service conditions and with subjective assessments on the part of the interrogator of their fighting qualities and with a note of the type of military unit from which they stemmed. For purposes of correlating such social data with political and military morale, preparations were made in 1944, with the collaboration of Edward Shils, Hazel Gaudet, Elmo Wilson and others of the SHAEF

Psychological Warfare Division, to review these data and make them capable of being compiled and worked over on a large scale. This was, however, not completed at the time and the records passed out of the writer's hands.[2] Some impressions might, however, be worth giving. The fanatical Nazis were usually under 35 and of lower-middle class origin, with an admixture of intellectuals and working-class youths, the latter often of the tough bully type. The believers with reservations tended to be of better education than the fanatics and were drawn from the class of regular soldiers, more solid intellectuals and business men, but contained a considerable sprinkling of working-class men in the upper income brackets. The unpolitical group was mostly composed of small town artisans, country folk, unskilled workers, enlisted regular service personnel and minor civil servants. The divided or passive anti-Nazi category contained much the same population as the *F.II.s*, with whom there was two-way traffic. The anti-Nazis (*F.V.*) comprised many sorts of men, from working-class Trade-Unionists and Marxists to convinced Catholics and Protestants, intellectual liberals, men with an international outlook, and not a few aristocratic conservatives of the "good old" sort. The young sons of these types of people were a not inconsiderable ingredient. In short the *F.V.s* contained the same kind of collection of persons and types as would have formed any continental Resistance movement. In no case was formal membership of this or that Nazi party branch made the basis of classification. To many professions such membership was a condition of employment and signified little.

In all some four hundred unselected prisoners were subjected to the political interrogation at the centre where this study was carried out. In addition, from the summer of 1944 onwards the field interrogation teams and the Psychological Warfare Division of SHAEF and its Army representatives were conducting analagous interrogations based on this method on a large scale. Some of these teams passed through an intensive course of instruction and role playing given by the writer and by his now experienced colleagues. The con-

[2] Some details of these studies may be found in Shils and Janowitz (1948).

TABLE 2

AVERAGE DISTRIBUTION OF POLITICAL ATTITUDES

In a Sample of *ca* 1,000 German P.O.W.s

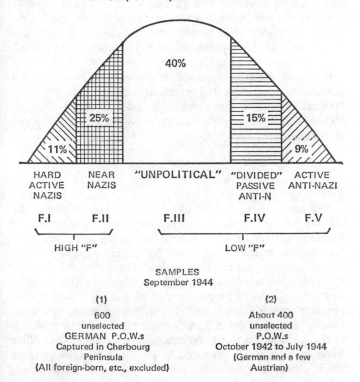

HARD ACTIVE NAZIS	NEAR NAZIS	"UNPOLITICAL"	"DIVIDED" PASSIVE ANTI-N	ACTIVE ANTI-NAZI
F.I	F.II	F.III	F.IV	F.V

HIGH "F"   LOW "F"

SAMPLES
September 1944

(1)	(2)
600 unselected GERMAN P.O.W.s Captured in Cherbourg Peninsula (All foreign-born, etc., excluded)	About 400 unselected P.O.W.s October 1942 to July 1944 (German and a few Austrian)

solidated figures may be conveniently expressed as a graph sufficiently accurate over the period September 1942 to July 1944 to bring out the salient distribution of the five types of political attitude. These are shown in Table 2.

It will be noted that during most of the period in question a large proportion of German soldiers, sailors, and airmen did not yet feel that the war was lost. It should be noted that all foreign-born levies were excluded, and only citizens of the German Reich and a few Sudeten Germans and Austrians were admitted into these samples. It should also be noted that the *F.I.*, *F.III.* and *F.V.* figures remained practically constant up to the very end of these opinion checks, whereas the *F.II.* category tended to change towards the *F.IV.* as the outcome of the war became more certain. Naturally the *F.III.s* tended to colour their statements in accordance with the fluctuations of the fortunes of war, but essentially retained their dominant preoccupation with private aims.

It is against this background of our acquaintance with the distribution of political convictions and attitudes towards National Socialism of a considerable sample of German P.O.W. that the second part of the study here dealt with must be considered.[3]

Personality Studies

THE SAMPLE

The sample consisted of 138 men, examined between the autumn of 1942 and the spring of 1944. They were unselected—that is to say we had to rely on what prisoners happened to be recently captured by sea, air, or land and sent to the collecting centre in question. The period of the war accounts for the relative shortage of "Army" in the sample, and for the relative preponderance of the upper educational brackets among aviators and skilled U-boat crews, and later, among the *élite* of the Afrika Corps. From the list of prisoners in the camp names would be selected by the camp duty office because the subjects happened to have a few hours to spare from other interviews or prior to removal from camp, which was small and had a large turnover. General treatment and living conditions in the camp were good, and a welfare service in accordance with the provisions of the Geneva Convention was in being.

In no sense could the sample be described as accurately reflecting the composition of the German male population or even of the Wehrmacht. One had to do the best one could. The group in fact included people from 18 to 55 years old at

[3] A full treatment of the morale and political attitude studies during the SHAEF period in World War II will be found in Lerner (1949).

various socio-economic levels, and from private to Lt. Colonel in rank; from farm labourer to University lecturer in the educational scale, with a high proportion of regular soliders especially among the naval fraction of the sample.

The composition of the sample is shown in Table 3.

THE METHOD OF EXAMINATION

The method of examination consisted of prolonged, personal, non-directed interviews in a quiet room, an informal atmosphere being maintained; in not a few instances several interviews, the average time per man being about two hours. It was an essential condition that the subject was willing and

TABLE 3

SERVICES		OCCUPATIONAL	
Navy	60	1. Professional, Higher Executives, land owners and University students	17
Army	48		
Air Force	32		
		2. Managers, business clerks, "White collar" workers	20
RANK			
Officers	26		
Non Officers	112	3a. Big factory skilled workers	6
AGE GROUPS*		3b. Small factory skilled workers	16
17–21	44		
22–28	43	4. Unskilled laborers	4
29–35	25	5. Independent tradesmen (tailor, cobbler, small shopkeeper, etc.)	19
36+	26		
		6. Small farmers, etc.	6
* These groupings were decided on by reference to ages of subjects at the beginning of the Nazi regime.		7. Merchant seamen, fishermen	2
		8. Regular services (Many ex-skilled operatives among these e.g., electricians and mechanics).	48
EDUCATION			
Primary	9		
Post-Primary (Secondary and Tech.)	50		
"Higher" (University and Technological graduates)	79	REGIONS OF ORIGIN	
		Seaboard	40
		Berlin	16
		Rest of Prussia	46
		"Rhineland"	16
		Bavaria	8
		Wurttemberg	6
		Thuringia (Saxon)	5

ready to converse. No kind of pressure was used, as it would have been fatal to the whole spirit of the study. No psychiatric or medical status was disclosed, the interviewer merely representing himself as an officer privately interested in the prisoners as men. The main skill consisted in preserving a heart-to-heart rapport, so that formal test procedures, filling up of schedules in the men's presence and similar evidences of special investigation had to be avoided. Rough notes were sometimes taken at the interview, but the case record was written or dictated immediately afterwards, from memory.

At times it was possible to obtain a Matrix Intelligence Test on the grounds of the man's wish to know how he should use his period in captivity to fit himself for post-war life, but this added little to the kind of data interesting for the purpose in hand. Murray's Thematic Apperception Test came into the writer's hands too late to make it worthwhile using without experience.

The aim of therapeutic closure was achieved with scarcely any exceptions. It was possible to verify that the individuals so interviewed had enjoyed their talk, and were at worst left slightly non-plussed by the purpose of such a prolonged "chance encounter". In the main they felt helped by someone taking time to interest himself in them as human beings.

THE SCHEDULE OF PERSONALITY VARIABLES

Though the conduct of the interview was non-directive, the data it sought to obtain were arranged in a schedule previously worked out, to test the hypothesis above defined, by reference to a *personality profile*. The Schedule was divided into (a) Social background data, consisting of the details already listed under Table 3; (b) psychological background data and (c) present personality traits.

The two latter will now be delineated, as originally conceived and defined. Their choice and the use that was made of them represents the crucial point of the whole study. They are based on the psycho-analytic hypothesis of personality development. The variables represented by the categories used are, of course, open to challenge by other schools of thought, while the skill or accuracy with which they were assessed at interview and in the light of additional data about each subject remains unverifiable, like any clinical psychiatric diagnosis not tested by long observation and by the criterion of therapy.

PSYCHOLOGICAL BACKGROUND DATA

These data are selected items of the early personal history of the individual. The time factor and the reality situation, which forbade more than a certain degree of contact with each subject, imposed necessary limitations on what could be ascertained. This part of the examination restricted itself to getting a general picture of the life history, emphasizing the parent-child relationships as recalled by the subject or as readily inferred from the account given by the subject. No attempt was made, for example, to collect systematically feeding and toilet-training data. It was felt to be practicable only to record the following as variables:

(I) PARENTAL PREDOMINANCE IN CHILDHOOD
   (a) Father dominated
   (b) Mother dominated
   (c) Equal harmonious influence of both parents
   (d) Equal conflicting influence of both parents
   (e) Broken homes: deaths, divorce, orphanages, foster-homes, etc.
   (f) No inference made[4]

The criteria for the above were defined by data on the description given by the subject to such questions as: Tell me about your people—which of them do you resemble—who had most influence? Who made the major decisions? Who had the money bags? Who wore the trousers? Who did the punishing? In more tricky cases these enquiries might be phrased as general questions referring to what the man felt was typical of a good German home, and how he would behave if he had such a home. The data under this head were recorded without attempt at evaluating intensity.

Much qualitative detail, in varying degree of depth and

[4] The score "No inference made" was provided for every variable, but will not be repeated in the text.

clarity was naturally obtained, but this did not lend itself readily to coding.

(II) RELIGIOUS ATTITUDES

A simple set of alternatives, without finer discrimination, but subsuming obvious major differences in parental cultural and social value systems to which the subject would have been exposed. Scored separately for each parent.

(a) Observing, sincere Catholic.

(b) Observing, since Protestant.

(c) Easy-going, tolerant indifference or nominal adherence.

(d) Consistent atheism, rationalism, secularism, materialism.

(e) *Gottgläubig*—This last category represents the peculiar Germanic-Nazi deism, hostile equally to traditional Christianity and to the attitudes under (d) above.

The same categories were also used to differentiate the subject's own current religious attitude under "Traits" (below), and will not be repeated in the description.

(III) SOLUTIONS OF THE OEDIPAL PHASE

This was the heading under which information concerning the course of emotional development from the infantile Oedipus phase was recorded. The inferences were drawn both from the history and from present attitudes. This category is to be considered as transitional between historical background and present character structure. From it several other variables are derived, as will appear below.

Under this heading Father and Mother cathexes were dealt with separately as follows:

Mother Cathexis

Intended to record whether a man's love bonds with the infantile mother-figure were judged

(a) to be still attached to his actual Mother or to a mother surrogate of his childhood, or

(b) to have been transferred to a female love-object of the man's own generation in the manner considered the "normal" state of affairs, i.e., to his wife, sweetheart, or mistress.

Against these scores there were three sub-categories provided for cases in which the Mother cathexis was judged to be predominantly transferred to symbolic objects:—

(c) the *Führer* (or similar male authority figure) as the protecting, nourishing figure loving all his children. This heading was introduced on empirical grounds after pilot interviews.

(d) The State or the man's service (e.g. his unit), or other "secular" institution fulfilling a similar substitutive nurtural, maternal role, it having been found on pilot interviews that a number of German P.O.W. felt their service *milieu* to function as a mother which protected, clothed, fed, and paid them.

(e) A church, or similar "spiritual" institution. (Mother Church, etc.) The five alternatives so derived were scored, but not rated quantitatively.

Father Cathexis

Through this variable it was tried to get a supplementary picture of libido vicissitudes, and classify the major possible outcomes of the tie to the father. It was assumed that the relationship to male leader figures is modelled on, and draws the subject's libido from the Oedipal, father relationship. Evidence related to these secondary figures was included in the total appraisal, in addition to expressed and inferred attitudes towards the actual father or childhood father surrogates. The following categories were drawn up as alternatives to be scored about each man.

(a) Mature Object Choice: This score was intended to show that the personality had largely overcome infantile attachments to the father symbol and was regulated by a mature ego-structure, free from major influences of an introjected father-image in the super-ego. This information, and that for the subsequent sub-variables, was obtained both from evidence in regard to relationship with paternal figures and by probing of attitudes relating to guilt, authority, submissiveness, and towards the upbringing of sons.

(b) Persistent Father Identification: This heading records the direct form of immature "fixation", in itself a normal transition phase in the male child, from which a boy derives a certain continuity of male cultural traits ultimately absorbed into his own ego-structure. The theory underlying this variable as here used is that a boy, faced with his ambivalent feelings towards his father, normally introjects the father and comes to identify himself with him, behaving towards his super-ego as if it were the punishing and rewarding father, and towards the environment with a mixture of omnipotence phantasy resulting from having his father as his ego ideal, and of inferiority and submissiveness due to reprojection of the super-ego into other authority figures. The quality of this identification is important. In so far as it is wholly benign it tends to its own supersession by maturity, and to the disappearance of ambivalence towards authority figures—cf. score (a) above. Its persistence is therefore always a symptom of some degree of guilt, ambivalence, and unresolved conflict over the Oedipus situation. This situation is conceived as the nucleus of subsequent attitudes towards freedom and authority; of guilt; of inhibitions on spontaneous tenderness, and on full maturation in heterosexual relationships; consequently of homosexual trends, inferiority feelings, and various mechanisms expressive of defences against castration threats from within and without.

(c) Equivocal or Partial Identifications: This score, as the name implies, is a form of divided Oedipus solution, where the individual has incorporated contradictory ("heteronymous") elements from both parents into his super-ego, has an unstable, split ego-ideal, with consequent contradictions in character, as for example in a man who followed his father into a military career but really always hankered after being a painter like his mother, uneasy in all social relationships involving these antagonistic inner forces.

(d) Rebel Attitude: This self-explanatory score represents a persistent immature rejection of paternal (or perhaps parental) authority. It might be termed a negative Oedipus solution, in which the subject clings to an attitude of defiance, covering a deeper castration anxiety and need for submission and dependence. It is the opposite of (*b*) above, in so far as it displays the hate aspect of the ambivalence towards authority, whereas in (*b*) the loving aspect of the ambivalence is uppermost.

(*e*) Mother Identification: This score records the result in an evasion of the father situation in that the child adopts the mother's attitude towards the father in dealing with the threat from a severe father figure. When the mother tie has to be surrendered, it is dealt with by introjection. It involves the personality in a passive, feminine alignment to love problems and often in overt behaviour, the extreme of which would be passive homosexuality and feminism. There is overlap, but not identity, with "Mother-fixation" under the heading of *Mother Cathexis* above. In the latter, the mother is still the overt love object; in the present case no such tie is manifested in conscious behaviour, though at a deep level this is the case. In Mother identification the Mother may be devaluated, and females regarded as rivals to the love of father-figures. As compared with identification, the simple persistence of attachment to the mother is a more naive and uncomplicated thing, implying different ways of dealing with Oedipus guilt. In "Mother fixation" (Score (*a*) under *Mother Cathexis* above) it is permissible to postulate a father tolerant of a boy tied to his mother's apron strings.

Guilt Inculcation

This category in contrast to the mere classificatory and qualitative scoring used above was rated on a three-point scale.

(*a*) Overt, grossly obvious guilt (Persecutory or depressive anxiety)

(*b*) Heightened guilt shown by inner drive, over-precision, obsequiousness, self-justification (Murray's "blame-avoidance")

(*c*) Normal limits.

This was intended to rate super-ego pressure as shown up in the life history. It is the weakest part of the study. There was lack of clarity in the original formulation, which did not for example differentiate between shame and guilt patterns or between felt ego-ideal pressures and defended, unrecognized super-ego pressures (such as manic denial). For this reason it was found to be non-discriminating. It failed to differentiate, say, between a projection and an acceptance of personal or group responsibility, both being lumped together as evidence of "guilt." In fact, varieties and levels of guilt are better brought out directly by the other variables employed.

Tenderness Taboo

This "background" category is based on Ian Suttie's ideas on the importance of tender love, especially in the maternal relationship, for the development of security and the integration of the personality of the child. It was scored as present or absent. Since we were primarily concerned with a delineation of the harsh, sadistic Nazi personality, we set up the quality in its negative aspect, i.e., a taboo, or prohibition on tender relations in the family culture of the subject. It will be seen that this also is closely bound up with the Oedipus situation, i.e., the degree to which the subject felt free or forbidden to have a tender mother-baby relationship. No attempt was made to seek out different possible antecedents for tenderness taboo, e.g., whether it was related chiefly to fear of the father or to a rejection by the mother on strength of the latter's acceptance of the harsh, "masculine" patterns of child upbringing. The assumption made was that a tenderness taboo signified repression of the internal loving mother in the personality, both as "need" and as "object."

This variable was looked for in the same topics as the general atmosphere and quality of parent-relationships, supplemented by data relating to present attitudes towards babies, young animals, artistic and humanitarian values and religious formulations. So much for what was recorded under "Background". The rest of the data were grouped under "Traits".

TRAITS

These were defined as aspects of personality and behaviour discernible as major themes to the psychiatrist at the time of examination, and less dependent on an exploration of early history. They were listed on empirical grounds after pilot interviews and from general discussion and contemplation of the German character. They are all to some extent overlapping or complementary and, psychologically, dependent on such nuclear experiences as the Oedipus situation. In contrast to background data, an attempt was made to rate most of the traits on a three point scale on clinical grounds. The following were the traits looked for as variables together with the scores, or other values, assigned to them:—

Ambivalence

The presence of irrational contradictory affects of love and hate towards one and the same object—in practice and under the circumstances of our enquiry often a "political" object, e.g., the *Führer* or The British. Another criterion of ambivalence was the need to balance overt or unrecognised hated objects with a good object, e.g., the dramatic transference of good qualities to one, and bad qualities to another of two British officers at the camp.

Three point scale:
  1. Gross, obvious
  2. Perceptibly heightened (or "clinically observable")
  3. Normal limits or absent.

EXAMPLE:
Score 1. *Gross:* Case 106, Age 32

'I am a German and cannot be a traitor,' while offering to do propaganda against the Germans.
'My sole happiness is my children,' when in fact he was always away.

Always belonged to two camps—Jesuits and Nazi party; later Nazi party and an opposition group. A conspirator who looked both ways at once.

Score 2. *Perceptibly heightened:* Case 107, Age 20

Considerable pull in two directions: 'When one is at home one thinks what a good place school is: one always wants to be somewhere different.' Went into Air Force because Father was veteran Pilot of World War I, but he hates discipline and military life. At school he wanted to join in the fun but also keep people at arm's length.

Score 3. *Normal:* Case 110, Age 22 (citation of record)

Father was just and not very stern. 'Everybody admired my Mother. She was loved by us all.' Tolerant towards all the farm hands, Polish and Russian: 'I love my own land and feel animosity to nobody.'

Split Libido

This concept is used to describe the dichotomy of tender and of sensuous love in relation to heterosexual love objects. The extreme case would be the man who marries an idealised frigid mother-figure with whom he is impotent, but who has repeated promiscuous relations with prostitutes or similar "debased" women.

The connections of this trait with the oedipal conflicts over mother-cathexis are obvious. There is also evidence from analytic practice that this trait is the outcome of a defence against homosexual impulses. Its conclusion was suggested by the personal histories of several Germans, and by perusal of German novels. Three point scale as previously.

EXAMPLES OF SCORING:

Score 1. *Gross:* Case 128, Age 22 (excerpt from Diary)

'I cried like a child for I' (his fiancée). 'Why is everything in life so double-edged? . . . I's picture looks so strange.' 'It was a lovely night with that little girl in barracks . . . but don't lower class women seem ugly? . . .' 'I can't do without some erotic experience . . . a whore-monger after all!' (gives list of casual pick-ups and dates during a fortnight's absence) etc.

Score 2. *Perceptibly heightened:* Case 201, Age 20

Note reads: Frequent allusions, with interested disapproval, to morals of Hitler Maidens, naked dancers, etc. Yet his idea of a wife is dull and demure. Cannot see full comradeship of sexes. 'Women must be kept out of politics' too.

Score 3. *Normal limits:* Case 110, Age 22

Note reads: He took a very sane view of the wife he wants. Not interested in getting mixed up with some glamorous, expensive, useless film star type . . .

Sadism

This trait was intended to describe the presence or absence in the personality of direct primitive aggressive traits derived from what is called the "pre-genital phase". It was taken for practical purposes to imply the impulses to dominate, bully, hurt or kill. It was felt from the beginning that rating such a quality would be almost impossible, as no man, except an occasional fool, would admit to an enemy officer such impulses even if he were conscious of them. Reliance was placed on circumstantial or indirect evidence (cf. known record of Kramer at Belsen) and on the impression made by the subject on the psychiatrist in the light of the latter's insight into psychological mechanisms. Means of confirming this evidence were at hand owing to the set-up of the centre.

There was no rating, only scoring under one of the following:

1. Overt, gleeful, apparently guilt free—the tough killer sort, i.e. (no intropunitiveness).
2. Stern, incisive, aggressive personality.
3. Indifference—calm acceptance of sadism in other ("impunitive").

The above three were classed together as anti-social forms of sadism.

4. Averagely aggressive, "normal" by British standards. (Loves a fight, but essentially kindly, tolerant, without need to kow-tow).
5. Gentle, submissive, over-conciliatory, smooth.
6. Horror, condemnation or guilt over sadism in others, squeamishness over atrocities, blood-phobias, etc.

These latter three were classed as social sublimations or reaction formations to sadism, No. 4 being regarded as the most mature disposal of initial aggressive trends, in an ascending degree of intro-punitiveness.

EXAMPLES OF SCORING SADISM: (Excerpts of notes)
Score 1. Case 90. Bomber Pilot, Age 25

Thrusting, prognathous face and manners. Bites his nails as he says: 'When we have liquidated Russia—then mercy on this Island! . . . Coventry will be child's play.' 'We had to break out, a nation of 100 million will not be ground down . . .' (thumps fist on table) 'We have not yet avenged ourselves for the way the French treated us in the Ruhr . . .' (About resistance men): 'If these fools will cut our cables they must go against the wall . . .' Further conversation discloses his delight at the fate of Jews . . . talks about 'draconic hardness.' Picks his spots on face and says 'I won't let them heal.' Gives impression of whipping one with his stream of bitter words.

Score 2. Case 89. Quartermaster, U-boat, Age 26

Hard, depressed eyes. 'I grew up in misery' . . . 'No time to laugh' . . . 'I gladly went to the service and my mother laughed when she saw me off—one is schooled there' . . . 'you should see our little boys march, heart and soul' . . . 'The German *must*—Frederick the Great's "damned duty and obligation" rules everything' . . . 'Those who differ are outsiders and do not count . . .' etc.

Score 3(*a*). Case 105. Midshipman, Navy, Age 21

The outstanding feature is the almost incredible indifference when he describes the drowning of his own shipmates before his eyes only a few days earlier.

Score 3(*b*). Case 84. W/T rating, U-boat, Age 22

Calmly relates how he has put a girl in trouble. Has watched his mother being 'sat on' by Father and approves. 'Can't help what the S.S. do—not my affair.'

Score 4. Case 82. U-boat, Stoker, Age 20

Fresh, friendly boy, full of stories of boyish pranks, skiing and fisticuffs. Father beat him when he was too cheeky. 'Can't understand why we have to have a war—always the decent fellows who belongs to sports clubs are killed' (said to a comrade).

Score 5. Case 91. Leading stoker, U-boat, Age 23

A simple, innocent fellow who excites protectiveness in all who deal with him. Exfeather-weight boxing champion. Early responsible for his young brothers, because mother was weakly. Hopes war will be over soon because it is so silly. At first timidly, but with growing confidence, criticises atrocities against Jews, and fears as result Germany will be terribly dealt with. Is polite, meek and agrees with all the kind officers who have had the interesting 'technical talks' with him.

Score 6(a) Case 81. Bomber crew W/T operator, Age 24

'I was never athletic and was over-protected, but joined because friends' taunts stung me.' Objects to stupid bombing raids. Can see only chaos and destruction resulting from war. Dreads reprisals for all the bad things done.

Score 6(b). Case 107. Sgt. Pilot, Age 20

Shut-in, thoughtful person, keen on philosophy and art. Hates uniform. Hates it when people quarrel, hates rough horse play and isolated himself from his comrades in the unit. Condemns any but the most chivalrous conduct, and winces at German and Russian barbarism.

It should be noted that the trait of "submissiveness," which has loomed so large in all discussions of the general pattern of German behaviour, appears in this schedule only as a sub-variant of the ratings for sadism. Psychologically this is justifiable in view of the close association of sadism and masochism. It was decided not to give submissiveness the status of a variable in this study. The aim was to distinguish Nazi types from others, and the trait of submission was held to be so widely distributed in the culture that it would fail in its purpose as a discriminating factor. (The omission has been rectified in later refinements of technique when we were able to invent suitable criteria for rating and distinguishing types of submissiveness separately, but this was achieved by team work after 1945 and cannot be included in the present paper).

Homosexual Trends

Under this trait were classified not only the comparatively rare perverts, but, more importantly, marked tendencies in the direction of male preference: depreciation of women, idealisation of male anatomy and beauty, advocacy and interest in male dominance and male associations, the cult of hardness and "manliness", hence the prizing of such obvious "phallic" virtues as male prowess, erectness, thrusting and daring, and condemnation of softness, yieldingness and laxity, the contempt for tender, feminine interests and objects, preference for sons, etc. The usual three point scale was used.

EXAMPLES OF SCORING:

Score 1. *Gross and obvious.* Case 108. L.A.C., Age 21

Father a neurotic who drank and deserted Mother when P.W. was aged 1. Mother out at work. Lonely childhood. 'Terribly fond of young people'. 'All my feelings are in the comradeship of the Unit and of Hitler youth'. (Asked about women in public life) says vehemently 'No—their place is in the kitchen!' Incontrovertible evidence of passive homosexual episode with another prisoner, six weeks only after capture. No interest in girls.

Score 2(*a*). *Perceptibly heightened.* Case 77. Lt. Fighter-Pilot, Age 21

'A father must train his son to his own liking and rescue him from his mother's apron strings'. 'If I have children, I could of course devote myself to my son—but a daughter, no, unless she was beautiful'. 'I love being an officer because it is beautiful to educate young men'. Uncritical worship of Hitler. Was 'his mother's all.'

Score 2(*b*). *Perceptibly heightened.* Case 126. Lt. Observer, Age 20

'My father shaped my education'. 'I have to thank his firmness that I was pulled out of the bad state (pampering owing to childhood illness, etc.)'.

Submission to stern discipline and bullying regarded as his salvation. Idealization of taking charge of young men, as youth leader and officer. He saw his greatest reward in their love and trust. 'But not as schoolmaster—only in the living emotional comradeship of the Hitler Youth or the Service'.

Score 3. *Normal limits:* Case 112. Lieut., Infantry, Age 22

This man has straightforward self-valuation, deprecates all this nonsense about good comradeship. Though experienced campaigner, was warm in his feeling about going to marry his girl.

Narcissism

The criteria for this trait were self-centredness, touchiness in self-esteem (Murray's "infavoidance"), preoccupation with own bodily prowess, appearance and self-adornment, pride, vanity, etc. It included concern about personal status (rank, exhibition of war decorations) as well as the displacement of personal narcissism to the military or national group. The derivation of his sort of narcissism is held to be a reaction to insecurity feelings—the result of not feeling loved and of feeling rejected, hence having to withdraw libido from outer objects and bestow an undue proportion on the Self (secondary narcissism). Three point rating scale.

EXAMPLES:

Score 1(a). *Gross:* Case 56. Major, Paratroops, Age 35

Aloof, conceited, pleased with himself, under which is great fear of showing his despair and emptiness. His recipe for living (abridged): 'A woman always looks first whether a man is polite, correct and properly dressed . . . Every woman gets angry if a good-looking man does not show her attention . . . You must play tennis well—correctly, surely— let the girl do the running about . . . and dance well—but miss a beat in a quick step if it maintains your dignity . . . 'I have never been completely in love or drunk—never let your blood get the better of you'.

Score 1(b). *Gross:* Case 87. C.P.O., U-boat, Age 25

Revolted from 'unhealthy' life in a bakery where he might contract lung trouble. Spent all his spare time in open air swimming pools and gymnasia, and became an 'ace' among his admiring club-mates. No time for serious relationships. Found all the girls wanting—he sees through people so quickly. Kept himself aloof—how could anyone lower himself to get drunk like a swine! Touchy to 'insults' by interrogators. Fastidious, manicured, conceited. Defensive head mannerism when talking.

Score 2(a). *Perceptibly heightened:* Case 109. Lt. Artillery, Age 22

Cocky, conceited. Despises the common herd. Boasts of his feats of strength and toughness. Intolerant of criticism or differing opinions.

Score 2(b). *Perceptibly heightened:* Case 83. Captain-Pilot, Age 30

A swell. Enquires rank of interviewer. Asking for better face cream and bothers welfare officer daily for nail-file. Apologetic he has not shaved when visited unexpectedly.

Contempt for all inferior races. Personal charm, very open to flattery by remarks about his chestful of medals.

Inferiority Feelings

This trait overlapped with narcissism of which it is an aspect. It was listed separately in an attempt to rate evidence of disturbed narcissism, as expressed in the gap between level of aspiration ('a person like me ought to be capable of so much') and subjective self-valuation. Personal inferiority and its displacements to the group are both included as evidence. Unequivocal over-compensations are rated as part of the symptoms. Three point scale:

EXAMPLES:

Score 1. *Gross:* Case 81. Wireless Operator, Air Force, Age 24

Anxious, and touchy about only having elementary schooling. Feels unwanted by his stepfather. Weak and delicate, decided to become a flyer and hero. (Covered with combat medals). 'As a soldier one does not feel fear'. Deeply hurt by a 'high British Officer' who offended his soldierly honour. 'I must not be thought a cad'. 'I could not survive the disgrace of defeat, I would commit suicide rather than become a Russian serf'.

Score 2(*a*). *Perceptibly heightened:* Case 93. Stoker Petty Officer (Reserve), Age 42

'I am only a small man'. 'I did my duty, nobody can blame me'. 'We are desperate, poor little Germany' (marked personal identification).

Score 2(*b*). *Perceptibly heightened:* Case 123. Sgt. Flak, Age 29

Felt a weakling, owing to games prohibition—outgrew his strength. Refused a commission as not 'fitted enough'. Very defensive about the superiority of German institutions, but also said 'The German is so silly and impressionable, he cannot be allowed to think for himself'.

Projection

This trait category included paranoid mechanisms, from the upper limit of gross clinical systematised persecution

symptoms and suspicion to emotionally charged, extra-punitive scapegoat devices, self-exculpation, bitterness, innu-
endo, and touchiness. Rating took into consideration the degree of insight present. An attempt was always made to
allow for social stereotypes and for recent experiences. Three
point scale:

EXAMPLES:

Score 1. *Gross:* Case 205. Lt. Cdr., Engineer, Age 34

Father always felt to be an overpowering man. Felt he
was his weak mother's most difficult child, different from
the siblings. Always shy. As a boy felt others were laughing
at him. Felt unappreciated as a human being and only valued
for his technical ability. Had acute terror episode when he
felt he was being influenced by British secret rays to become
a traitor. Also felt sure the British were bent on annihilating
Germany. Reacts to political interrogation with *tu quoque*
arguments, and is on defensive before he is even attacked
by argument.

Score 2. *Perceptibly heightened:* Case 106. Lt. "Special duties" (German Propaganda Service), Age 33

Scents division, intrigue and secret plotting everywhere.
Felt he was envied his post at the Ministry of Propaganda.
An undermining, intriguing type who offered his services to
British psychological warfare, he is full of specious rationalizations of his conduct and blames his duplicity 'on the way
they have treated me'. He felt 'there was a spirit of revolution abroad' among the German people (1943), which was
unfounded and clearly a projection of his own renegade,
anti-father feelings. A hint of messianic flavour in his intention to found a new movement of national regeneration.

Score 3. *Normal limits:* Case 110. W/T operator, Air Crew,
Age 22

Even standard propaganda displacements (e.g., to Jews
and Slavs) are much reduced as compared with many POW's.
He carefully distinguishes between 'the man who looks much
like himself' and economic theory, and recognised that Slav
and German could live well together. No personal animosities
or suspicions. Optimistic about his personal future.

Hypochondria

This term denoted morbid preoccupation with minor complaints, fear of disease or of the serious nature of trivial ailments; fads and anxieties about the purity and wholesomeness of food and drink, about vitamins, etc., but excluded any fears of being poisoned, etc., by the captors. Anxiety states, hysterical symptoms and true "somatic paranoid" hypochondriases were included. The rating, on a three point scale, was in terms of the severity of clinical picture and of the depth of etiology.

The postulated psychological basis for including this variable is the interplay between projection and introjection mechanisms found in relation to a "bad object", in Klein's sense. This bad object introjected may become an "internal persecutor" (like a cancer or T.B. phobia)—or projected, when it is phantasied as an "external persecutor"—as under "Projection" above.

In view of the purely clinical nature of this well-known symptom, examples are scarcely required.

Psychoneurotic Anxiety

This trait category was used as a "blunderbuss" term to cover a variety of more than transient, overt neurotic symptoms, short of projection or hypochondria above, such as free-floating anxiety, psychosomatic conversions and phobic or compulsive states including stammers and tics. No attempt at exact clinical differentiation was made in the scoring, but a three point scale rated degree of severity and involvement of the personality in the symptoms.

Examples would cover the familiar syndromes and are omitted.

Depression

This variable includes the usual sense of that term in psychiatry, to denote the presence of any degree of affective disorder characterized by hopelessness, morose introspection, self-blame and self-destructive trends, associated with observable physical and behaviour symptoms such as "flexion" and retardation. A three point scale was used. Examples are scarcely required.

Unfortunately, the complementary trait of mania was omitted. Neither were of any significance as it turned out. Only one distinctly hypomaniac individual was observed.

Schizoid Tendencies

This heading covered only those cases in which a clinically morbid degree of personality split or thought disorder was observed. It overlaps to some extent with ambivalence and split libido, which also represent some degree of dissociation or instinct defusion, and of course with paranoid trends. Here we included such phenomena as loss of reality sense, depersonalisation; increase in the phantasy content of thinking; extreme shyness; asocial withdrawal tendencies; stereotypy; and "simplicity" and immaturity not warranted by level of general intelligence, especially when associated with the classical bodily configuration. It was found possible to score this category only in terms of presence or absence. The point was to try and differentiate between a personal psychopathy and the almost endemic German cultural split between affective and thought processes and between private and collective standards of value.

Apart from the social data recorded under Table 3, there were thus 17 main variables, with a provision for sixty different scores under their heads, either as qualitative distinctions or intensity ratings. In addition there was provision under each main variable for the "No inference made" score.

RECORDING OF DATA

As stated, Case histories were recorded at first by hand, later by dictation, immediately after the interview(s). Looking through these records after a lapse of some five to seven years, it is clear that in this respect technique varied a good deal from bad to good. Scores were assigned immediately, and reviewed in the light of other known data (documents, testimony of campmates, ex-shipmates, other interrogators, and special modes of observation). In most cases the record was a long narrative, but in some of the later cases the relevant material was recorded under the "17 variables", with a general rounding off of the personality history and description at the beginning and end of the record. In four cases it was possible to obtain near-verbatim records (in German) of the interviews: these were in addition written up as above with relevant passages of the verbatim notes marked and referenced for the relevant variable.

There was, of course, no way of keeping the men off political topics, and some of this necessarily formed part of the evidence. In such events an attempt was made to gauge the personal emotional involvement in the political or military views expressed. The F rating was copied from the Political Schedule Item B (See Table 1).

Next, a set of "hand Hollerith" cards of standard format were obtained, round the margins of which all scorable items of the social data, political variables (including F rating) and psychological variables were represented by a coded box. The scores were marked in the appropriate box on a separate card for each subject and rechecked for accuracy.

TREATMENT OF DATA

Mr. Edward A. Shils, then serving in the United Kingdom with a branch of the U. S. War Organisation, was acting as unofficial adviser to the writer during this investigation, and the coding and statistical treatment of the data were his contribution. In view of pressure of other work we decided that 138 was a sample just adequate for the chi square (χ^2) technique.

For purposes of testing the significance of our data against the F ratings, the scores were grouped in conformity with the preliminary hypothesis.

The political scores were divided into a Nazi and near-Nazi group comprising the $F.I.$ and $F.II.$, and a non-Nazi group composed of the $F.III.$, $IV.$ and $V.$

The Mother Cathexis data were divided into those where the mother-bond was given to an actual real female love object (scores (a) and (b)), and those in whom it was transferred to an ideal figure, human or institutional (scores (c)

and (d)). Score (e), the religious displacement, was not included as it was felt to belong to the "religion" variable. The Father Cathexis data were divided so as to include all scores indicating an alignment with the father on one side, and the alignment against the father on the other. Therefore scores (a), (b), and (c) were lumped together, and (d) and (e) formed the countergrouping.

Under Sadism the three so-called "anti-social" scores (1, 2, 3) were grouped together, and the three "social" scores were joined (4, 5, 6).

The "man's own religious attitude" category scores were so grouped as to contrast Church-adherence (a), (b) with militant non-church adherence (anti-Christianity) (d), (e) and both these with easy-going indifference (c).

The remainder of the scores under each main variable were divided into groups in whom the characteristic studied was absent or present. In the case of three-point scale ratings the "gross" and "perceptibly heightened" data were joined against the "normal limits" scores in respect of each variable.

It will be seen that this enabled us to recast the question of our hypothesis into a statistical form. The original question, it will be recalled, might have run: 'Is the Nazi a person who has had to reject his good mother-object in favour of submitting to a threatening father to whom he is fixated, so that he remains to a clinically distinguishable degree ambivalent, split in his libido, unconsciously homosexual, guilt-laden and unable to let his sadism mature into socially acceptable (loving or restitution-making) form, defensively narcissistic in order to protect himself from his guilt and inferiority which nevertheless betray themselves in heightened tendencies to project and to suffer neurotic anxiety, with special liability to hypochondriacal preoccupation with bad internal objects, and does he show any marked psychotic personality traits? And does he in this sense differ markedly from his non-Nazi compatriots?' The statistical expression of these two questions was cast into the tetrachoric formula, and calculated as shown in Table 4. By good fortune, there were, as it turned out, roughly equal numbers of High Fs (I and II) and low Fs (III, IV and V).

TABLE 4

	F rating			F %			X^2	Probability
	High (I+II)	Low (III, IV, V)	Total	High (I, II)	Low (III, IV, V)	Total		
Parent dominance								
1 Equal	31	41	72	.43	.57	1.00		
2 Mother +	23	26	49	.47	.53	1.00		Unreliable
3 Father +	54	67	121	.45	.55	1.00		
Man's religious adherence								
1 Roman Cath. (strict)	17	26	43	.40	.60	1.00		
2 Protestant (strict)	30	5	35	.86	.14	1.00	27.8	Between 0.01 and 0.001 Statistically significant
3 Nazi (Gottgl)	18	40	58	.31	.69	1.00		
4 Atheist etc.				.48	.52			
5 Indifferent	65	71	136			1.00		
Father Cathexis								
Father								
1 Mature object choice	58	52	110	.53	.47	1.00	10.3	0.00137 approx. Statistically significant
2 Persisting father identification								
3 Partial identification								

							Significance
Anti-Father							Less than 0.001 Statistically significant
4 Rebel	4	20	24	.17	.83	1.00	
5 Mother identification	62	72	134	.46	.54	1.00	21.5
Mother Cathexis							0.22067 Unreliable
1 Still attached to Mother	32	62	94	.34	.66	1.00	
2 Transf. to female partner	33	10	43	.78	.22	1.00	
3 Transf. to Fuhrer							
4 Transf. to State or Service	65	72	137	.47	.53	1.00	1.5
Guilt Feelings							0.00964 Statistically significant
1 Gross	44	42	86	.51	.49	1.00	
2 Perceptibly heightened	21	31	52	.40	.60	1.00	
3 Normal limits	65	73	138	.47	.53	1.00	6.7
Tenderness Taboo							0.12134 Unreliable
Present	37	25	62	.60	.40	1.00	
Absent	23	40	63	.37	.63	1.00	
	60	65	125	.48	.52	1.00	2.4
Ambivalence							
1 Gross, obvious amb.	51	49	100	.51	.49	1.00	
2 Perceptibly heightened	13	23	36	.36	.64	1.00	
3 Normal or absent	64	72	136	.47	.53	1.00	

TABLE 4 (cont.)

	F rating High (I+II)	F rating Low (III, IV, V)	F rating Total	F % High (I, II)	F % Low (III, IV, V)	F % Total	X^2	Probability
Sadism * Anti-Social (1, 2, 3)	42	26	68	.62	.38	1.00	12.63	Less than 0.01 Statistically significant
Social (4, 5, 6)	21	46	67	.32	.68	1.00		
	63	72	135	.47	.53	1.00		
Homosexual trends 1 Gross	46	39	85	.54	.46	1.00	4.1	0.04288 Statistically significant
2 Perceptibly heightened	18	32	50	.36	.64	1.00		
3 Normal	64	71	135	.47	.53	1.00		
Narcissism 1 Gross	49	46	95	.52	.48	1.00	1.7	0.19229 Unreliable
2 Perceptibly heightened	17	26	43	.40	.60	1.00		
3 Normal	66	72	138	.48	.52	1.00		
Inferiority feelings 1 Gross	41	39	80	.51	.49	1.00	1.3	0.2541 Unreliable
2 Perceptibly heightened	24	34	58	.41	.59	1.00		
3 Normal	65	73	138	.47	.53	1.00		

Projection								
1 Gross	45	30	75	.60	.40	1.00	.88	0.00301 Statistically significant
2 Perceptibly heightened	21	40	61	.34	.66	1.00		
3 Normal	66	70	136	.49	.51	1.00		
Anxiety								
1 Gross symptoms	49	43	92	.53	.47	1.00	4.2	0.04042 Statistically significant
2 Perceptible symptoms	16	30	46	.35	.65	1.00		
3 Normal	65	73	138	.47	.53	1.00		
Depression								
1 Gross symptoms	23	28	51	.45	.55	1.00	0.24	0.6242 Unreliable
2 Milder symptoms	42	43	85	.49	.51	1.00		
3 Normal	65	71	136	.48	.52	1.00		
Schizoid features								
1 Present	4	7	11	.36	.64	1.00	.050	0.4463 Unreliable
2 Absent	61	65	126	.48	.52	1.00		
	65	72	137	.47	.53	1.00		

Notes:
(1) Any distribution—probability of 0.05 or less is statistically significant.
(2) Split libido and Hypochondria were omitted from the table as unreliable.
(3) Where numbers in the first total column add to less than 138, the difference shows the number of cases in whom "No inference made" was scored for a given variable.

* Kindly recalculated as above by Mr. J. L. Boreham.

DISCUSSION

These statistical tables show that under the conditions and
with the method of study used the following variables showed
significant relationship to the political attitude or F factor:—

(i) A man's religious alignment; the solution of the Oedipus
situation in respect both to (ii) the Mother and (iii) the Father cathexes; (iv) Tenderness Taboo; (v) Sadism; (vi)
Homosexuality; (vii) Projection; (viii) Neurotic anxiety.

Within the limits of a paper in a periodical the discussion
of these correlations will have to be confined to the narrow
context of the study here described, and the temptation to
enter fully into the relationship of German culture, institutions
and character with the Nazi movement resisted.

It must be remembered that *in this study* it was only proposed to test the hypothesis that certain variables, abstracted
from a Gestalt which for short could be termed "German
national character" would be found in greater amount or
concentration in more Nazi personalities than in other Germans. The scoring was designed for this purpose and is otherwise meaningless in that it includes major characteristics of
the entire human race as viewed from the psycho-analytic
position. Its meaningfulness arises from the conjunction or
cluster of variables to form a syndrome which emerges as
having significance from the statistical assay.

The German Character

For the sake of readers not familiar with this field, a very
brief abstract of the formulation of the basic adult male
German character (disregarding finer shades due to sub-group
variation) must therefore precede the main argument. This
outline is culled from the writer's *Psychological Foundations
of the Wehrmacht* (1944b) supplemented by references to
Kecskemeti and Leites's (1945) study. There are several
studies on the German character written from the psycho-

dynamic angle which should be consulted,[5] and which are borne out by the findings of this report.

The "average" member of the Wehrmacht can be described as tense, earnest, industrious, meticulous, over-respectful to authority and anxious to impress. He is a martinet in his dealings with his social inferiors and his subordinates. He is very touchy about status. He requires uniformity and order, and is uneasy in unforeseen situations. He suffers from the *sentiment d'incomplétude*. In contrast to his striving for clarity and efficiency is his tendency to value, and search for, the depths of experience, that richness of emotional satisfaction he feels to be unattainable except by flinging away bourgeois restraints and fetters. He idealises his women in their role as mothers and as objects towards whom libidinal aim-inhibition is demanded; but he also depreciates them socially and sexually on the plane of reality: the typical German home is patriarchally structured.

Conformity and "loyalty", as of a servant to his master, are rated among the highest virtues, and demonstratively stressed in home and institutional life, almost as synonymous with "honour" on the one hand and with unquestioning obedience on the other. The emphasis on persevering toil as the goal of a burdensome life patiently if ostentatiously borne, is part of this pattern. Of a dominant person severity, imposingness, and hardness are expected, and love and admiration reactions towards it vary directly with the severity and punitiveness of the authority figure. A weak authority is despised, and hostile feelings towards it break surface. This associates the typically weaker, yielding mother with contempt, as one of those under paternal domination.

The mother-seeking tendencies, whether of sadistic or of passive colouring, are banned from personal awareness and form the background of guilt which the ready acceptance of "manly" father-submissive attitudes covers. The German mother, indulgent and over-protective especially to the favoured male baby in his early years, yet also connives at this "masculine" build-up of her son. She provides no adequate

[5] See, e.g., Brickner (1943); Dicks (1944a, 1944c, 1947b); Erickson (1948); Kecskemeti and Leites (1945); Rodnick (1948); and Schaffner (1948).

counter-weight to the father, but by culturally imposed inconsistency increases her son's guilt and confusion by furtive rewards behind the father's back.

Allegiance to paternal authority is furthered by the projection of the German's own repressed aggressive feelings to the authority itself, thereby increasing the estimate of that figure's punitiveness. Typically, non-conforming aggressive trends against authority are dealt with by identification with the authority and by counter-cathexis or reaction formation against the offending impulses. This leads to a kind of "surrender of the ego" in favour of authority, with the result of "externalising the super-ego". This is demonstrated in a reliance on social norms and clearly defined duties rather than on inner conduct regulation. Ego deficiency creates a sense of weakness or emptiness with consequent craving for depth and completeness.

The widespread impairment of personal autonomy leads to over-compensatory stress on secondary narcissism. This is shown on the personal level not only in status anxiety but also in brooding concern over individual "problems", in attempts to preserve areas of strict "privacy" in the personality, and in the cultivation of a "distinctive character" façade. On the group level we see the well-known national self-inflation of "Germanism" as much richer and "Kultur"-giving than lesser, shallower, un-understanding breeds of men, hence as entitled to lead and to gain the lead by any means.

The uncertainty of self-valuation leads Germans to the need to define status *vis-à-vis* all persons and groups and to violent fluctuation in "total" omnipotence and "total" impotence feelings; between the magical powers of their will and their self-assumed "efficiency" and sudden caving-in when confronted with "overwhelming facts" against which even titanic, "colossal" efforts are vain. While it is manly to struggle with hard "fate", it is useless to defy "inscrutable, inexorable destiny".

Direct return of repressed aggression is manifested in the handling of weaker persons, as, for example, children or inferiors in rank. In this situation the identification with a stern authority is given full play accompanied by a sense of moral rectitude. It is also frequently shown as touchiness, quarrelsomeness, and more importantly as an expectation of aggression on the part of others (individuals or outgroups) against whom one must be on guard. Germans seem to be readily insulted. This reaction is likely to be a mixture of id projections and displaced super-ego (authority) re-projections.

Displaced or vicarious satisfaction for aggressive needs which had undergone early repression is found in collective power symbols, or in support of projects for group aggrandisement, which promise fulfilment of forgone instinct gratifications in a millennium of plenty and of harmony.

A revalued return of masochistic longings is also typically exhibited in the stereotyped idealisation of "loyalty-conformity" (*Treue*) as the acme of "manliness"; the image being that of an obstinate, unruly boy who is hammered into shape and "tempered" into dogged virility by a strong father-figure represented for example by military induction. Repressed anti-paternal tendencies used also to have some degree of sanctioned outlet in the "adolescent revolt", when the young German would go "wandering" in search of "freedom", pseudo-adventurously, communing with Nature, flinging away sexual and urban restraint, but in reality evading rather than facing the conflict with authority. Fathers often secretly connived at this adolescent procedure, in the knowledge that it was the prelude to later conformity. It is in this wanderlust stage that conformity itself is often shown in the formation of gangs with "older brother" leaders, the whole group then defying "senile" authority without tears.

For the rest, "freedom" needs have mostly been transferred to the national group which, characteristically, should have no restraints or limits to its omnipotence, precisely because the personal ego is experienced as weak, helpless and the sport of inner and outer forces. Here an id projection is clearly at work. Against this infantile greed and omnipotence, now displaced to the needs of the group and moralistically rationalised as *Lebensraum* or as the inescapable consequences of *Machtpolitik* inherent in the struggle for existence, there militate the sated, rich, or covetous older rivals who want to keep the poor little German from his rightful heritage ("a place in the sun" as Kaiser Wilhelm put it). The German oscillated between virtuous, meek acceptance of deprivations inflicted by his own authority and the impatient rejection of the sense of inferior status in the eyes of sibling-nations.

The picture is thus mainly one of an ambivalent, compulsive character structure with the emphasis on submissive/ dominant conformity, a strong counter-cathexis of the virtues of duty, of "control" by the self, especially buttressed by reprojected "external" super-ego symbols. In this norm bound, burdened pattern there occur episodic "release" symptoms. Individually they are—attacks of rage, as when "unauthorised" encroachments are made on the jealously guarded ego-core. The release symptoms on the group level we have witnessed between 1864 and 1945. Both are often rationalised as "the end of the tether". Group "outbursts" are exculpated chiefly by projective mechanisms either as defensive wars justified by the danger threatening from dangerous (potency or status-menacing) external forces, or else as leading to "rewards" or "dues" for patiently borne deprivations implicit in excessive intra-group and personal self-control. Courage is drawn for these aggressive outbursts from group sanctions in joint loyalty to a good super-ego leader figure (Bismarck, Kaiser, Hitler) who takes responsibility and so incidentally shoulders the guilt of failure.

Hierarchical pyramidal patterns for social institutions with the Army as the model and apex were created as the most appropriate to meet the needs of such a character structure.

The Significant Variables

Returning now to an attempt to evaluate the data obtained from the personality studies in more detail it will be convenient to change slightly the order of the variables which were found to be significant as differentiating high-F-scoring German soldiers from their low-F-scoring compatriots.

Father Cathexis

By definition of this variable, and from the general outline of the German character in Section 1, it was expected that the type of person active in promoting the Nazi regime would show a high degree of identification with a harsh, authoritarian father-object, with all that this implies in the way of defence against feelings of "weakness" i.e., against making demands for indulgences on the mother. The successful maintenance of the father figure as good demanded the sternest counter-cathexis against doubt or criticism, and led to fanaticism or dogmatism, "total" conformity and "obedience" exalted as "loyalty" (*Treue*). The emergence of the militant Nazis in leadership roles favoured their assuming the characteristics of *successful* father or older brother behaviour in relation to less-ranking people towards whom the exercise of command and power was expected by the culture pattern. It was remarkable that even in cases where the real father was described as indulgent, the culture, through various secondary father figures, managed by the time adolescence was reached to turn the balance towards the identification with (or incorporation of) the collective stern, male super-ego norm, through which authoritarian, aggressive behaviour receives its group sanction. Aggression could operate without conscious guilt by this direct, super-ego permitted path. Part of the aggression connected to the bad fraction of the father-object was utilized in wielding stepped-down *Führer* power over subordinates. The rest of the "bad father" complex was displaced to various outgroup symbols, especially "rich old men" images such as the British (John Bull) or the Americans ("Jewish financiers").

Untransformed id aggression against the parents is persecuted partly in "weaker" people who become the bearers of repressed needs, such as the "greediness", "secret plotting" or "dirtiness" of Jews, Russians, and other scapegoat figures who "contaminate" the purity or ferment disunity by their "hypercritical" liberal ideas. German civilians fared hardly better than nationals of occupied countries in these men's esteem. The allied leaders were felt to share fully the destructive punitive characteristics of bad fathers, and this was taken as a matter of course. Another part of id aggression found outlet through the "revolutionary" *élan* of National Socialism, purporting to be the uprising of the young, iconoclastic builders of the millennium of the blond supermen against the weakening corrupt Christian-bourgeois rule of "arterio-sclerotic" (*verkalkte*) elders. In this phantasy-system Hitler played the role of the ever-young rebel older brother, himself a self-avowed oppressed "little man", and received the full positive father cathexis.

Those who scored "equivocal Oedipus solutions" had histories of suppressing their regressive longings for indulgence or their artistic natures associated with mother values.

Mother Cathexis

The chief inference from the prevalence in the high F class of scores indicating gross transfer of mother-significance to political or institutional symbols is this: passivity and affection can only be expressed in relation to objects sanctioned by the Nazi sub-culture. To be tied to a female was the equivalent of being feminine or weak oneself. One could be married, but this bond counted for less than the State, the Party or the Service. The possibility of a false skew in the high F results under this variable exists in that the sample contained an undue proportion of naval personnel serving regular engagements, sometimes motivated by bad home background. It is not unusual for men in any country to "go to sea" under the deeper pressure of "prodigal son" restless, security-seeking impulses and to attach maternal values to the ship in which they serve. Even Germans call their ships "She". Even so, the withdrawal of libido from real women, and the co-existence of father identifications in the same group shows the nature of the process at work, laying the subject open to acceptance of Nazi authoritarianism.

Equally significant in this variable is the correlation between low F ratings and the capacity for frank loving relationship to female objects. German prisoners with good object relations to a loved, and presumably loving, woman were less prone to libidinize military or political institutions with excessive cathexis, in disregard of other human values and relationships. It is well known how anxious the Nazi leaders were to win more citizens over to a "We" consciousness, away from private allegiances, towards investing most of their love in the metaphysical "National community" with strongly emphasised "Mother Earth" attributes.

Religious Adherence

The table supplements what has just been said. The Churches, more especially the Catholic Church, formed the one remaining counter-weight to state totalitarianism in Germany, opposing it with their own claims on the individual. "Mother cathexis" (and it usually was the mother of the subject who had had the religious influence) transferred to a religious body was less likely also to flow towards Party or other "man-made" groups. This is not the place to go into the details of the interesting differences between German Catholic and Protestant attitudes in respect of the demands of the State on the individual or of the influence on individual or group structure.

What is perhaps even more significant in the table is the high correlation between high F and the vague deistic mumbo-jumbo which was professed by the $F.I.$ and $II.$ Essentially this was a creed of fatalistic belief in a Higher Providence modelled on the German Super-ego, a tribal deity which had placed Germany in the centre of the Universe and had sent trials of strength to this unique nation, destined for leadership. The *gottgläubig,* or God-believer, was at one and the same time rejecting "effeminate" pacifist Judaeo-Christianity and "godless" Marxist materialism. A number of the latter with some of the toughest nihilistic Nazis made up the "Atheist" scores.

It was not unexpected that the "easy-going indifferent" group correlated on the whole with low F scores as here defined. In other contexts religious puritanism and secular political fanaticism might well form a joint group to be contrasted with this category.

Tenderness Taboo

The result throws additional light on the fate of dependent and passive love needs in men who have remained identified with a punitive father image, in which hardness was a virtue and softness a failure. Softness was equated with impotence, surrender and femininity; hardness with steely nerves, potency and manliness in crudest metaphor of childish evaluation of parental roles. To behave like a poor frightened, soft-hearted mother would also be to give way to tender, passive desires towards the father. Any awareness of such tendencies becomes tabooed, together with those activities, objects, and interests which associate with feminine values: love of the arts, protective tenderness to weaker things, expressions of sensitivity, affection or *finesse* in relation to life. Expressions of tenderness would also be unconsciously equated with regression towards a favoured state of infancy in which sphincter-control was not yet demanded, nor an ascetic check placed on the enjoyment of the maternal body and caresses. To betray such a weakness would thus signify a treason against the father and a preference for the mother. The picture is that of the "affectionless character", with affinities to the tough delinquent personality.

Sadism

The results of the correlations are in keeping with expectations. It was interesting that the people scoring under "overt, gleeful" were of three kinds: the "elegant pansies" who demanded hair-nets and face cream from their captors; the innocent "baby-face" boys; and the thin-lipped film villains. We may see in the sadistic attitudes of the first two the operation of reaction formations against passive, tenderness-seeking trends in "spoilt-boys", who have turned their frustration and rage resulting from deprivation into a pattern of revenge. One also gained the impression that the need to recoup oneself for a sense of weakness by exerting power over something had a kind of therapeutic value to the subject—e.g., as in discharging machine-guns at distant victims or kicking elderly Jewesses, de-humanized symbols of repressed primary good objects that had to become bad. The slight displacement of sadistic power-needs to phallically or anally-invested weapons ensured conformity with the militaristic norm of the "100 per cent, thorough-going soldier". The lack of permitted good objects in the world of the over-sternly educated, wooden-faced disciplinarians makes other people either objects of abject devotion if they are in dominance over them, or else into unreal, faecal part-objects to mould, destroy, attack or bully as the sole means of feeling reality and "emotion". The Nazi-German tendency to speak of people as "human material", as "racial groups" or as "flocks of sheep" was of a piece with this depreciation of human values. Here is another aspect of the affectionless character who has been forced to repress his good objects and gain the approval of the sadistic super-ego by compulsively "going one better" in the persecution of bad objects.

By contrast the so called "social" transformations of aggressiveness by maturation or by reaction-formation of a restitutive or "depressive" pattern (accepting inner control and responsibility) betoken a much less disturbed even if embivalent, relation to early objects which is reflected in the concern shown to preserve them.

As a curious antinomy to the prevalence of aggression, there is in Germans of all types a squeamishness and dislike of avowing or of facing aggression, as shown by their submissiveness in the face of strong or imposing behaviour, and in their avoidance of direct reference to aggressive acts. No military vocabulary has such a wealth of circumlocution to express brutality; few armies have taken greater pains to make war impersonal and out of sight of the enemy's face. Germany took the utmost pains to keep the enemy at arm's length and away from the homeland. This would seem to be an effort at warding off assault and castration fears from the self. The "Sadists" (as herein defined) had identified themselves with a castrating authority expected to do terrible things to one if he got within range, and did these horrible things themselves. If results on oppressed victims were not as they expected, they would say, "we have not been hard enough."

The non-sadists felt the "enemy" to be placatable by "good" behaviour on their part, and in any case sufficiently potent for good to preserve and cherish, mostly by typical compulsive reaction formations. Their ambivalence was less and not so rigorously polarized into "Black" and "White".

Homosexuality

The scores in this variable confirm the expectation that passive subordination to a severe, punitive father whom it is necessary to love, should result in the heightening of unconscious homosexuality. Its significance for the subject tended to be disguised or countered by the already mentioned revaluation of such submissive feelings as "manly", if they concerned authority or leader figures. Being beaten in childhood, being drilled and bullied during military training were socially and individually valued as pleasant and fortifying experiences. Such experiences held in common cemented the typical "adolescent gang" comradeship of the Armed Forces and especially its *élite* units filled with Nazis, their bonds strengthened by common devotion to a leader (Hitler especially but also many subordinate heroes of the "ace" type). Such leader worship was often expressed in highly lyrical, barely desexualised terms.

Homosexual traits, as signifying a "masculine protest" defence, have already been related to the depreciation of "feminine" values and interests, and to the glorification of manly strength. It is a well-established psychoanalytic finding that the homosexual's fear of women is at bottom the dread of being like them. The trait thus links up with tenderness taboo and its antecedents. It is one way in which ambivalent love needs of affectionless characters can be expressed in clumsy, adolescent fashion as an institutionalised "cult of manliness" akin to Spartan practice. This way was institutionalised by German militarism.

Projection

The finding indicates that the high *F* scorers had typically managed to reproject their super-ego, i.e., their father image highly charged with punitive and destructive qualities. In so far as the culture norm and indeed individual situations demanded an emphasis on the positive or love aspect towards such an authority, the negative or hate aspect of the ambivalence had to be displaced away from the personal and the in-group authority in order to preserve these as good. In these people both primary hate and later criticism or rebellion against the super-ego-authority had to be warded off. In this way the self and the authority could remain blameless and loveworthy. The attribution of hostility to any stranger, common enough in German culture, becomes a necessity for sadistic individuals, so that they can justify their aggression as counter-aggression and self-defence. Nazi propaganda has shown many examples of this tendency and has provided the group with images for this purpose. The scapegoats were split further into Id-images (the greedy Jew or the bloodthirsty Bolshevik), and "disappointing" near in-group images, such as the treacherous British "Nordic" brothers who had created the Versailles treaty and now further betrayed Aryan solidarity by fighting on the "Id" side. The reader is referred to the remarks made in this connection under *Father Cathexis* above.

In a written record it is not easy to convey the difference between those who were merely believing the Nazi version of recent history in a country with a controlled press, and those to whom guilt projection, self-justification and narcissistic, touchy bitterness about the necessity to be brutal in order to make the world safe from "inferior vermin" was a dire need of preserving their personality. Perhaps the most stereotyped attitude ran like this: "all these scheming sophisticated enemies around us have abused our notorious unsuspecting simplicity, goodness, and softness. But if they think us such fools as to submit to their will to destroy us, we will know how to defeat their evil intent with the greatest ruthlessness; now we shall act without mercy or scruple . . ." Lack of insight into the effect on their neighbours of prior aggressions committed by the Germans themselves followed the pattern of *"Cet animal est très méchant; quand on l'attaque il se defend"*, whereas this very same idea was also often used by high *F* Germans in self-justification. The cognate stereotype was: 'I cannot understand why we nice Germans, of all people, should be hated by everybody.' The frequent expectations of annihilation, castration, etc., at the hands of the Allies in case of their victory has already been referred to as the responses of high *F* scorers in the political interview.

Neurotic Anxiety

That high *F* scorers should have reacted with neurotic symptoms twice as frequently as their compatriots was at first sight a surprising result. So far as combatant stress was concerned, the risks and experiences of the high and the low *F* scorers had been similar. Most of the P.O.W.'s belonged to service units where both physiological and personality screening might have been expected to weed out predisposed men, such as flying personnel, U-boat crews and armoured corps. In this respect the high *Fs* tended to be "better" specimens. On reflection, however, the finding was consistent with that conception of the outbreak of neurotic symptoms which stresses the importance of social factors on the integration of personality. The difference between the high and low *F* scorers must have been in the meaning of capture and of the loss of their combatant status and service *milieu* to them. We already know that the high F personality is strongly extra-punitive, heteronomously regulated and supported in his morale by the combination of leader and comrades. The very fact of capture not only arouses paranoid fears about his captors' intentions. In doing so it also activates the deeper ambivalency conflicts which give rise to this persecutory anxiety. Passive impulses of surrender and admitting submission to the now proven stronger enemy (see above under German character) are no longer counteracted by the inner effects of all the forces of the Nazi-military brotherhood and leadership, but have to be fought off by the poor little ego alone, suddenly faced with a change from an armed potency role to a disarmed impotence role.

Looking over the case histories, somatic conversions of a hysterical type predominated in the clinical pictures. This accorded with the general impression by the writer and other observers that German soldiers in general tended to be terrified of admitting to "nervousness": 'the German soldier has no nerves' ordained Hitler, whom himself suffered from what was almost certainly hysterical blindness in World War I. The favourite alibi for moral weakness or "collapse" was physical, i.e., projected to the somatic sphere. The genesis of these neurotic symptoms was thus a way of canalizing guilt at capture ("weakness") and anxiety at being abandoned by supporting authorities and faced by hostile authorities whom they now wanted to be loving authorities. Self-punishment, quasi-medical self-justification and a veiled but demonstrative appeal for sympathy and succour were expressed in these terms.

By contrast the less tensely super-ego-ruled and less internally persecuted characters of the low Fs were able to adjust more easily. In some cases psycho-somatic disorder was present in them before capture when it signified anti-service protest. For the rest it occurred chiefly in the conflict-torn "good-soldier but-not-a-Nazi" *F.III.* personalities whom it was decided, as will be recalled, to class with non-Nazis for statistical stringency.

The Non-Significant Variables

Despite the fact that some of the selected variables, which were included on the strength of the preliminary hypothesis, did not discriminate between the high and low F scorers, a few words about these are in place. No more need be said about *guilt* which was sufficiently criticized in the section on Psychological Background Data.

Parent Dominance was too crude and superficial a concept, and invited such descriptions as 'When I was small it was Mother but later it was Father', or 'each in their proper sphere', etc. The observation by field workers, or else the inferences from other data among our material would have been more informative on this point. Most observers are in fact agreed on the regularity of father dominance in the great majority of German homes. Even the partially dissentient Rodnick (1948) brings much evidence in favour of this situation, though he is apparently not fully aware of the ambivalent depreciation-idealization split governing the status of women in German society.

Ambivalence was evidently too generalised a trait in the culture to use as a discriminating variable in this study. The numbers were too small to justify re-combinations. By definition the most divided men were the *F.III.* rated as non-Nazis. Even so, it is the writer's impression that the pattern of ambivalence was different in the high F scorers and the low F group. Whereas the low Fs tended to be torn between the good and bad qualities of their own authorities (Nazi regime, trust in their propaganda) and hence also to be partly disloyal and favouring the Allies, democracy, etc., the high Fs had polarized their good and bad objects rigidly: divine Hitler-Germany versus satanic enemies. The split was more extreme, there was no shades of grey.

Libido Split failed completely as a discriminating factor. There were many unmarried men, the majority of the sample had spent three or more years in service conditions and so on. The impression remains that the attitude to the mother which brings about this phenomenon is widely dispersed in German culture. The psychological factor really tested for was affectionless sensuality and this emerged more clearly in the data about tenderness taboo, sadism and homosexuality.

Narcissism and its closely co-varying inferiority feelings were a "disappointment", as can be seen by referring back to the formulation of the working hypotheses. Possibly, by sub-dividing "Gross" scorers from "perceptibly heightened" and normal, a different result might have been achieved, but that may be true of the other variables. The prevalence of narcissistic features as shown especially by touchiness about status and evidences of vanity and conceit seemed as independent of political attitude as possible, though the transfer of inflated ego needs and claims to the national group tended to be more common in the high *Fs*. This possible differentiating factor, i.e., the displacement of secondary narcissism to group symbols was not followed up in this study.

The reason for the non-discriminatingness of *Inferiority Feelings* is easier to understand *a posteriori*. In this variable were recorded many such plaintive expressions as 'Who am I to judge such things? I am only a little man' or 'We Germans are everywhere disliked'. Some of these stereotyped statements by *F*. III, IV and V were of a simpler "humble-pie eating", submissive character than the boastful, over-compensatory assertions of superiority by the *F.I.* and *II.*, which could be easily "cracked" to reveal very similar doubts about worth and potency. It might have been better to discriminate "compensatory superiority" and straight "inferiority" as variables, than to lump them together.

Depression and Schizoid Tendencies were included without great expectations, but rather as a safeguard, especially as there was much talk of "madness" of the Nazis at that time. As regards depression, the table would seem to show merely that any loss of objects (through being captured) whether these be real people or symbolic substitutes, was liable to cause depressive reactions in a certain proportion of German prisoners of war.

The High F Syndrome

An attempt must now be made to formulate a coherent picture of the character structure of the high *F* scorer. Such a picture must be an abstraction, a genotype composed of the essential trends and behaviour patterns of a large number of individuals. To the writer such a delineation would have the reality of experience as a frequently recurring stereotype of life history, attitudes and views in persons he has known. To the reader not already familiar with German and Nazi mentality in living persons, a typical case is likely to be more acceptable, and will now be quoted exactly as noted within a few minutes after leaving his room seven years ago. Translations of German terms have been added in parentheses. The method of recording was that of grouping notes under the relevant variable headings. These are somewhat condensed since a magnificently revealing private diary formed a valuable source of detailed evidence, as well as the frank comments of a group of Non-Nazi fellow-P.O.W's whom the subject had managed to offend.

Case 128, Junior Lt. "W.", German Army Signal Corps,
    Age 21. Single. Captured Tunisia 15.3.43. Interview
    15.9.43. 2½ hours.

Although only in Tunisia for a short time, W. appears to have managed to be wounded twice and spent most of his service time in hospitals where he was eventually captured. He has a few mild grouses about treatment by French and Americans but not against the British.

Background. He is an *Auslandsdeutscher* (German domiciled abroad). His father was a business man in Belgium, where W. also went to a German *Oberschule* (High School) for six years. At the *Umsturz* (Hitler's accession) in 1933 the father transferred to a German State Service and W.'s home has been in various foreign cities. For two years he was at a N.S. *Politische Erziehungsanstalt* (National Socialist Political Training College). Then, for some reason, he was taken away and went to a private Internat (Boarding School) where he tried to do his *Abitur* (University Matriculation Examination), but, according to his diary, failed. After this he joined the Army. He does not yet know what he wants to do in after-life as he has not got a regular commission.

Parents. Father and Mother German. Father was always the head of the house. He compared this arrangement with the authoritarian state of which the family was the proto-type. It would not do for the husband to be *"unter dem Pantoffel"*—(henpecked). It was uncomprehensible to him that there could be equal partnership of the parents. He appears to have been somewhat spoilt and evinces no particular attachment to either parent. The impression received of both of them is dim. The mother is a staunch Lutheran churchwoman but when W. resigned from the Church on typical Nazi grounds she was not allowed to interfere and the father said: 'You must do as you think right, my boy'. He had one sister, whom he regards rather as a little toy (diary). Score: *F.+*

Guilt drive. As will be seen from the diary, he considers himself rather a roué and makes a frantic effort to appear as hard as nails. In his adventures with various girls there are emotional sentences of pseudo-remorse rather than genuine concern, e.g., *'Bin ich denn ein Schwein?'* (Am I really a heel?) and there is an elaborate façade of self-justification by the new Nazi "Darwinian" paganism and compensation can be seen in his taking the point of view that one has to be above reproach in one's conduct as an officer. The guilt sense is, however, repressed and on the surface it is absent. A certain self-justification is constantly in evidence during the interview. Score: *G.D. 2.*

T.T. His attitude towards the opposite sex is a somewhat hectic and forced one and he seems to depend very much on constant sexual adventures and makes a great show of yearning for kisses, etc. Essentially the tender element seems to be lacking in his personality. He was at pains to point out that no such nonsense as house matrons or feminine influence was tolerated at his Nazi school. His mother and sister were just brushed aside, although he admitted that the mother is the *Mittelpunkt* (centre) of the family. Score: *T.T.+*

Religion G.G. Although he admitted the existence of a higher Direction of the world, he emphatically rejected the

Christian ethic as being too soft and could not agree with the Sermon on the Mount as being un-German and unbiological. Consequently he had joined the majority of the "new" Germans who stood aside and preferred to work out their own salvation. He did not admit that religious philosophy should play any part in *Weltanschauung* which he interpreted as being merely the order of this world and nothing to do with the supernatural order, in which politics and the State were not concerned. It was a mistake to mix the two. Score: *G.G.*

Mother Cathexis. It is difficult to come to a definite conclusion. This is a case where some analysis would need to be done. The psycho-pathological picture as it presents itself is of a pathetic need for erotic reassurance, whilst the main allegiance is given to the State and the regime. It does not seem as if successive girl friends are fulfilling other than narcissistic reassurance functions, whereas his essential anchorage is in Germany itself as a conception. Score: *4.*

Father Cathexis. He is very much on the side of authority, and, in fact, considers it his duty as an officer to upbraid those who do not support authority and the established order (see his letter of complaint to a superior officer). There has been displacement from the actual father to the Nazi hierarchy which he accepts as the natural order, but he states also that his actual father was a very strong Nazi. Score: *2.*

Ambivalence. As appears from the diary, his relation to some of his girl friends is marked by duplicity and ambivalence. The same is true of his attitude towards his comrades whom he is ready to report and get into trouble if they do not agree with him. His attitude during the interview was one of exaggerated politeness and apology for the many uncomplimentary references to England and British policy. The attitude to England itself is one of envious and two-faced admiration. In this case the personality itself is thoroughly identified with this split. Score: *1.*

Split Libido. This is gross and the best evidence is his own diary which need hardly be amplified. He was quite pleased to convey the impression that he was a *roué,* a breaker of hearts, but that somewhere a girl worthy to marry him was awaiting him (he was engaged to an idealized girl), but that the series of naughty little adventures was part and parcel of a German gentleman's mode of living. (Cf. also section in this paper, Split Libido, for extracts from his diary). Score: *1*.

Sadism. M.C. (another informant) says: "A great bully, full of stories of life at school when he was delighted, with some assistance, to bully and kick those weaker than himself. Very proud of these stories."

He could not, of course, in an interview, be brought to relate such stories, but it was very clear that his attitude was one of naked use of power which he justified and considered as the right biological attitude. This applied in his whole-hearted approval of the means used by the State for dealing with inferior races. He is thoroughly and joyously identified with the view that might is right and that the need, i.e., achievement of power, justified the means which would be hallowed by success. Score: *1*.

H.S. He is quite consciously identified with the view of the predominance of the male. His attitude is devoid of tender aspects and rather of the conscienceless gang sort. At the same time, his complete subordination to authority and the voice of the master appears from his attitude towards his school. The relegation of woman to an inferior status is very marked. He is ambivalently devoted to a young man in the same P.O.W. party and has several sentimental entries about him. Score: *2*.

Narcissism. He is an entirely self-centered and pitiless young poseur in whom object relationships are of the nature of narcissistic identifications. He is conceited, preoccupied with his self-regard and "face" as an officer. His introspections reveal morbid preoccupation with his own reactions and his dependence on entirely autistic erotic gratification. The essential shallowness of feeling which has always got to be whipped up by erotic experience is expressed by *"Ich glaube ich könnte mit dem Mädchen glücklich werden"* (I think I could be happy with that girl). Another entry: *"Ein langer Tag zusammen; sie ist ja so verliebt"* (A long day together; she is so much in love). *"Wenn die Frau weint und mich anfleht muss ich lachen"* (When the woman weeps and implores me I have to laugh). There are a number of allusions in his diary to possible continuing masturbation which would be very likely. Fairly purrs when he thinks he is treated with due respect by the British. Score: *1*.

Projection. There is some evidence of projection apart from the customary Nazi foreign political views in which Jews and Freemasons play a big scapegoat part. Two personal traits that might be mentioned are his resentment at any rough treatment on the part of Transit camp authorities such as the remark in his diary: *"Behandelt wie Verbrecher und Gisindel"* (Treated like criminals and rabble), which is an accurate reflection of his own attitude, and further his undue suspicion of the motives of many of his fellow prisoners. He is very ready to pounce on critics of the Nazis with accusations of disloyalty and is up in arms over minor pilfering in the German-run camp kitchen, etc. Despite his own obvious police-dog attitude, rationalized as watching over "German honour", he remarks that the other officers are not comradely towards him. He is incapable of seeing that he himself has an essentially anti-social priggish, telltale attitude. Score: *2*.

Inferiority Feelings. The whole personality is full of over-compensations. He is a little, rather weedy youth who fancies himself as the paragon of soldierly virtue and obviously tries to hide behind a very thin façade of polite correctness to pose as the upholder of Nazism in the camp: *"Man kann manchmal zweiflen, aber wir glauben, weil wir Deutsche sind"* (One can sometimes have doubts, but we have faith because we are Germans). He is also very touchy where his own status is concerned and has a great feeling of satisfaction that the shame of his failure of the *Abitur* is compensated by his now being an officer. His national inferiority towards the British is openly expressed. His sexual life is also a compensation for an essential shallowness of feeling. Score: *1*.

Hypochondria. There is slight preoccupation with his health but in view of two wounds and dysentery this is not above normal. Score: *3*.

Anxiety. In the sense of neurotic symptoms enough evidence has already been adduced to show that this boy has a very profound anxiety state. He is restless, has an inner drive and a few days at a station are enough to make him enter in his diary that he has *Budenangst*, i.e., claustrophobic symptoms. He is dependent on constant distraction and change and the above mentioned erotic gratification, interspersed with occasional bouts of drunkenness. There are repeated entries about: *"Das Warten ist schrecklich—ein ulkiges Gefuhl im Bauch"* (This waiting is frightful—such a queer feeling in the stomach). He has, however, a capacity to tolerate some anxiety and speaks of a dread of flying; he refused to be flown again in an air ambulance. He appears to have little capacity for making friends. His bearing during the interview was nervous and over-deferential for a boy of good education. His clinging to his officer status and his extreme nationalism also have an anxious and compulsive character. Score: *1*.

Depression. Apart from a certain amount of military pessimism there is no evidence of true depression. Score: *3*.

Schizoid Split. The high degree of narcissism, the incapacity for deep affect and the almost frantic clinging to the reality of officer "face" and N.S. *Begeisterung* (fervour) betoken a schizoid personality which is further supported by his appearance and physique. He is a small man with a tight cynical mouth with an incongruous petulant protruding lower lip, hostile, questioning, suspicious eyes behind horn-rimmed spectacles, dark hair which grows low on his temples. The personality makes a most unpleasant impression and one cannot warm to him. In no direction was any warm human feeling discovered. He is full of *ad hoc* arguments and has a very ready intelligence. One feels that if his Nazi faith were taken away from him, the personality would break asunder as there is no other central integrating factor. In my opinion a schizoid psychopathy: "affectionless character"

F Rating. It is not necessary to describe his political views in detail as they are absolutely standard and marked by a cynical ferocity. The only deviant feature is that he thinks that Germany is still so immature that she needs to be bullied into a sense of unity. Score: *1*.

The rabid, compulsive quality in this young Nazi was perhaps that which made him the most typical embodiment of the high *F.* syndrome; he was selected as one kind of polar extreme of the species: the spoilt, insecure, restless type from a comfortable home, but not daring to love or be ordinary.

A sense of split and disunity, only held together by fanatical identification with symbols of group power, runs through the personality. It would not be true to say that other individuals rated as *F.I.* in the series could have been diagnosed as suffering from so marked a character disorder as to justify the term psychopathy; but the same elements were there.

It is the contention of the writer that the character disorder it is proposed to call the "High *F* syndrome" is a cultural artifact and not a genetic or constitutional affliction of the individual. It belongs rather into the same order of phenomena as "the Puritan character" or "the Public School Type". All these represent in their own time and place behavioural and motivational patterns easily derivable from the larger cultural area in which they are embedded. The derivation would seem, at least in the case of the Nazis, to be explained in terms of a selective reinforcement of behavioural traits, defence mechanisms, etc., typical of the German norm, brought together to form a logical extreme, almost a caricature of these norms. Each trait or variable was, in its way, a German virtue, inculcated and socially admired as attributes of a leader personality among them. The ideal of being a heroic, virile nation of soldiers has been held before German youth for at least a century. To be modelled on the pattern of the masterful commander who has learnt to subdue all weakness or "irrelevant" moral softness in others by first having it beaten out of himself by an "iron" authority was the proudest aspiration. Fathers would reinforce the trend in their sons in both directions—submission and need to dominate. The unrecognised damage to the personality had to be shored up by a number of culturally generalised defensive patterns which, because of their function of sustaining or containing the repressed, were themselves of the nature of reaction formations, rigidly held and socially highly valued.

Of such a character were some of the other constituent traits of the Gestalt we have called the High *F* syndrome. This is true of the stress on minimizing the influence of mothers and women, on the glorification of male dominance and friendship visualized as a dare-devil, but disciplined, camaraderie of front line soldiers. The brittleness and deeper vulnerability of the norm demands rigid definitions of status both in interpersonal and in inter-group relations, with prescribed or expected arrogant or submissive behaviour *vis-à-vis* status-inferiors and status-superiors in accordance with the hierarchical principle, jealousy guarded and enforced.

Even the adolescent revolt was patterned and condoned as a safety valve, channelled towards homosexual rivalry, combativeness and tests of strength, (duels, alcoholic tolerance, etc.), with concessions towards sexual licence, in the confident expectation that the powerful pressure of group norms would in due time bring the wheel full circle towards conformity. It was quite smart to be thought a young conscienceless rip.

In any culture there will be some more and some less complete representatives or active carriers of the pattern. Once the "Prussian authoritarian" pattern above outlined had become the dominant trend in Germany, those who were most efficiently displaying its characteristics were likely sooner or later to 'reap the social advantages of going furthest along the approved path of behaviour—group produces recognised example; recognised example influences group: group produces more extreme example——' (Brickner, 1943).

The case-history cited, and some of the extracts adduced as examples of scoring in the preceding section, support the view that in the case of Germany the bearers of the more extreme traits were those whose character development had most suffered the distortion implied in the process of personal assimilation to demanded norms. It is as if in their anxiety to placate their super-egos, the high Fs had fallen over backwards. In psychiatric terms this would imply a higher than average level of persecutory anxiety with more desperate need to dissociate, project, and even regress. There is surely a direct connection between the degree of felt harshness of internalized parent objects and the level of badness of the inner world, i.e., repressed aggression. It is likely that the relation between a harsh cultural ego-ideal and this repressed aggression is that of reciprocal aggravation, according to the formula 'character moulds institutions, institutions perpetuate character.' Thus the two inter-war generations, in an era of rapid social change, appear to have had the effect of accelerating the cumulative effect of this field relation:

personality $\longrightarrow$ culture.
$\longleftarrow$

The level of anxiety which the defeat in World War I and its consequences must have produced in characters of this kind can be imagined, economically threatened, socially displaced and with their influence reduced as they were. The records suggest maniac denial and regression to magical restitution and vengeance phantasies. The now weak and therefore despised nation had to be rescued from its shamers and traducers by the romantic hero-gang. Narcissistic identification with Germany demanded a sharpening of split in the ambivalence. Germany *must* be good and powerful—outgroups alone were evil and attackable. It only required Adolf Hitler's considerable gifts of verbalizing these phantasies and giving them coherence to bring many birds of a feather together round the hero-leader they required. In this sense many of the detailed responses and imagery of objects of love and hate in our sample were copied direct from Hitler and his chief lieutenants. But these in turn were really nothing more than the previously acclaimed *clichés* and symbols, adapted and formulated into a paranoid system: the narcissan megalomania and group solipsism, the guilt denial by rationalizing all aggression as counter-aggression sanctioned by group status and "survival" claims; the homosexual self-surrender by the sworn gang of brothers to the worshipped "Man of Destiny" who took all responsibility; and the persecutory projection of all infantile weakness, hate and greed impulses to the various outgroups who could thus become the target of total destructive attack. Maternal good object values, as represented for example by Christianity, were pushed aside and persecuted as "sissy". Though the activist Nazi felt himself in this as a member of the *élite*, he also acted as a mere passive agent of the now substituted "Higher Destiny", carrying out, automaton-like, the promptings of his id, coming to him as the Führer's doctrine, his super-ego safely in the care of those above him. It seems as if id and harsh super-ego had here achieved a fusion of direction or aim.

We have seen that in the section on the distribution of political attitudes towards National Socialism that there were, among the active male population of the *Wehrmacht*, never

less than 35 per cent of active carriers of this ideology with
verbal or implied support for its associated practices; with a
hard fanatical core of some 10 per cent. It is not therefore
surprising that National Socialism despite its internal irrationality and self-contradictions, already implied in its name,
had the success the world has witnessed. It was so close to
the personal dynamics and phantasy needs of a considerable
proportion of the cultural group and had formulated them in
such culture-syntonic terms that resistance was ineffective.
Even for those not sharing the high F syndrome personality,
there was something to assimilate from the models of successful high F behaviour held up before them by the *élite* of
German society preponderantly composed of the type we have
described here. The vast majority of those not classified as
F.I. and *II.* were submissive and apolitical. In other words
they possessed, at least, one set of the attitudes shown by the
more extreme types, namely that of subordination to strong
authorities, but they lacked the aggressive paranoid activism,
probably because their inner object world was of a kindlier
nature. The ideals which the Nazis claimed to incarnate were
however so widely and pervasively preached in German institutions that even persons of "non-authoritarian" personality
accepted them. Only the small group who might be called
compulsively anti-Authoritarian (as some sub-varieties of the
F.V. class) could bring themselves to real rejection of the
Nazi pattern, and then usually because they had cathected
some other system—e.g., Catholicism or Marxism.

CONCLUDING REFLECTIONS

The writer is aware that the publication of work seven years
old may strike his readers as now somewhat naive and elementary in a field which has since the end of the war been
much studied. It may, however, stand as a example of a
method of enquiry into the motivations in political ideology
and behaviour, just because it was carried out under field
conditions and without the refinements and rigours of a completely planned piece of research. Despite its length, this
paper has had to restrict its persuasive illustrative material to

a minimum. Nor is any *a posteriori* criticism attempted—this is left to the methodological trained reader with the object of eliminating errors in future work of this type.

Considerable refinements in method were, in fact, made in the subsequent applications of the method by the team responsible for the screening centre under British Control Commission auspices in 1945–6. It is to be hoped that at some future time the now scattered members of that team will be able to publish the sequel. Similar work in a U. S. Control Commission screening centre bears traces of having been influenced by the study here described (Levy, 1946; Schaffner, 1948).

It cannot be denied that political currents of recent years have tended to wash away a clear awareness of the deeper character structure possessed by the leading *élite* of one of the most cataclysmic movements in the history of Western Society. A reminder may not come amiss. What is being done in Germany or elsewhere to protect society from the dangers of the "High *F*" in places of power, and to ensure a change in the pattern of parent-child relations, educational policy, and social mores according to a more loving, tolerant code of human values to prevent his like being perpetuated in civilized communities? And what studies are going on, based on the psychodynamic concepts, to enquire into the host of politically significant group phenomena now challenging the wisdom of our epoch?[6]

[6] As if in answer to this concluding question, the writer has just received the large volume, *The Authoritarian Personality* (Adorno, 1950), which on first reading seems to embody nearly all the concepts of this present paper, and which describes just the kind of refinements of technique not available to the writer.

Modal Personality and Adjustment to the Soviet Socio-Political System
Alex Inkeles, Eugenia Hanfmann, and Helen Beier

Two main elements are encompassed in the study of national character.[1] The first step is to determine what modal personality patterns, if any, are to be found in a particular national population or in its major sub-groups. In so far as such modes exist one can go on to the second stage, studying the interrelations between the personality modes and various aspects of the social system. Even if the state of our theory warranted the drafting of an 'ideal' research design for studies in this field, they would require staggering sums and would probably be beyond our current methodological resources. We can, however, hope to make progress through more restricted efforts. In the investigation we report on here we studied a highly selected group from the population of the Soviet Union, namely, former citizens of Great Russian nationality who 'defected' during or after World War II. We deal, furthermore, mainly with only one aspect of the complex interrelations between system and personality, our subjects' participation in an adjustment to their Communist sociopolitical order.[2] We find that certain personality modes are outstanding in the group, and believe that we can trace

Reprinted by permission of the publisher from *Human Relations*, Volume 11, 1958, pp. 3–22.
[1] For a discussion of the basic issues and a review of research in this field see Inkeles and Levinson (1954).
[2] For analysis of another aspect of the psychological properties of this group, see Hanfmann (1957).

their significance for our subjects' adjustment to Soviet society.

SAMPLE AND METHOD

An intensive program of clinical psychological research was conducted as part of the work of the Harvard Project on the Soviet Social System.[3] The Project explored the attitudes and life experiences of former Soviet citizens who were displaced during World War II and its aftermath and then decided not to return to the U.S.S.R. Almost 3,000 completed a long written questionnaire, and 329 undertook a detailed general life history interview. The individuals studied clinically were selected from the latter group. Criteria of selection were that the interviewee seemed a normal, reasonably adjusted individual who was relatively young, had lived most of his life under Soviet conditions, and was willing to undertake further intensive interviewing and psychological testing.

The group studied clinically included 51 cases, forty-one of whom were men. With the exception of a few Ukrainians, all were Great Russians. Almost half were under 30, and only 8 were 40 or older at the time of interview in 1950, which meant that the overwhelming majority grew up mainly under Soviet conditions and were educated in Soviet schools. Eleven had had a minimum education of four years or less, 22 between four and eight years, and 18 advanced secondary or college training. In residence the group was predominantly urban but if those who had moved from the countryside to the city were included with the rural, then approximately half fell in each category. As might be expected from the education data, the group included a rather large proportion of those in high-status occupations, with 11 professionals and

[3] The research was carried out by the Russian Research Center under contract AF No. 33(038)-12909 with the former Human Resources Research Institute, Maxwell Air Force Base, Alabama. For a general account of the purposes and design of the study see: Bauer, Inkeles, and Kluckhohn (1956). The clinical study was conducted by E. Hanfmann and H. Beier. A detailed presentation is given in the unpublished report of the Project by Hanfmann and Beier (1954).

members of the intelligentsia, 7 regular army officers, and 9 white-collar workers. Sixteen were rank-and-file industrial and agricultural workers, and five rank-and-file army men. In keeping with the occupational pattern but running counter to popular expectations about Soviet refugees, a rather high proportion were in the Party (Erickson, 1950) or the Young Communist League (Hanfmann and Beier, 1954). Again running counter to popular expectations about refugees, the group was not characterized by a markedly high incidence of disadvantaged family background as reflected either in material deprivation, the experience of political arrest, or other forms of repression at the hands of the regime. Ten were classified as having been extremely disadvantaged, and 15 as having suffered minor disadvantage.

All of the Soviet refugees have in common their 'disaffection' with Soviet society. The clinical group included mainly the more 'active' defectors who left Soviet control on their own initiative, rather than the 'passive' who were removed by force of circumstance. Thirty-four had deserted from the military[4] or voluntarily departed with the retreating German occupation armies. In general, however, the clinical group was not more vigorously anti-Communist than the other refugees. They overwhelmingly supported the principles of the welfare state, including government ownership and state planning, and credited the regime with great achievements in foreign affairs and economic and cultural development. They refused to return for much the same reasons given by other refugees: fear of reprisal at the hands of the secret police, because of former oppression, opposition to institutions like the collective farm, or resentment of the low standard of living and the absence of political freedom. In psychological adjustment, finally, they seemed to reflect fairly well the tendency toward adequate adjustment which characterized the refugees as a whole.

With regard to the parent refugee population, then, the clinical group was disproportionately male, young, well edu-

---

[4] This was in part a result of our selection procedure. The larger project was particularly interested in post-war defectors, almost all of whom came from the Soviet military occupation forces in Germany. Half of the men fell in that category.

cated, well placed occupationally and politically, and 'active' in defecting.[5] In its internal composition, the sample was also unbalanced in being predominantly male, but otherwise gave about equal weight to those over and under 35, in manual vs. white-collar occupations, from urban or rural backgrounds, with education above or below the advanced secondary level.

Each respondent was interviewed with regard to his childhood experience, some aspects of his adult life, and his adjustment to conditions in a displaced persons' camp. Each took a battery of tests which included the Rorschach, TAT, a sentence-completion test of 60 items, a 'projective questions' test including eight of the questions utilized in the authoritarian personality study, and a specially constructed 'episodes' or problem-situations test. We regard the use of this battery of tests as a matter of special note, since most attempts to assess modal tendencies in small-scale societies have relied upon a single instrument, particularly the Rorschach. The various tests differ in their sensitivity to particular dimensions or levels of personality, and differentially reflect the impact of the immediate emotional state and environmental situation of the subject. By utilizing a series of tests, therefore, we hope that we have in significant degree reduced the chances that any particular finding mainly peculiar to the special combination of instrument, subject, and situation will have been mistakenly interpreted as distinctively Russian. In addition the use of this battery enables us to test our assumptions in some depth, by checking for consistency on several tests.

Each test was independently analysed according to fairly standard scoring methods, and the results were reported separately.[6] In reporting their results, however, each set of

[5] The young post-war defectors on the whole did prove to be less stable and more poorly adjusted. Apart from this issue of adjustment or 'integration', however, they shared with the rest of the sample much the same range of outstanding personality traits. Therefore, no further distinctions between that group and the rest are discussed in this paper. See E. Hanfmann and H. Beier (1954). [6] On the 'Episodes Test' a detailed report has been published, see Eugenia Hanfmann and J. G. Getzels (1955). A brief account of results on the Projective Questions has also been published in Helen Beier and Eugenia Hanfmann (1956). The other results

analysts made some observations on the character traits which seemed generally important to the group as a whole. Further, in drawing these conclusions the analysts made use of a criterion group of Americans matched with the Russian sample on age, sex, occupation, and education. The availability of such test results posed a challenge as to whether or not these general observations, when collated and analysed, would yield any consistent patterns for the group as a whole.

To make this assessment we selected the eight major headings used below as an organizing framework. We believe that they permit a fairly full description of the various dimensions and processes of the human personality, and at the same time facilitate making connections with aspects of the social system. These categories were, however, not part of the design of the original clinical research program,[7] and were not used by the analysts of the individual instruments. While this circumstance made for lesser comparability between the tests, it acted to forestall the slanting of conclusions to fit the analytic scheme. The statements in the conclusions drawn by the analysts of each instrument were written on duplicate cards, sorted, and grouped under all the categories to which they seemed relevant. The evidence with regard to each category was then sifted and weighed, and where there were ambiguous findings the original tables were re-examined for clarification. Relevant impressions based on the interviews were also drawn on. Similarities and differences between those in our sample and the matching Americans aided in grasping the distinctive features of the Russian pattern. On this basis a characterization of the group was developed under each heading of the analytic scheme.

It should be clear that the sketch of modal personality characteristics presented below is not a simple and direct

---

were described in the following as yet unpublished reports of the Project, which may be examined at the Russian Research Center: Beier (1954), Rosenblatt *et al.* (1953), Fried (1954), Fried and Held (1953), Rosenborough and Phillips (1953).

[7] The basic categories were suggested to Inkeles by Levinson in the course of a seminar on national character, and are in part discussed in Inkeles and Levinson (1954). They were somewhat modified for the purposes of this presentation.

translation of particular test scores into personality traits. Rather, it is an evaluative, summary statement, following from the collation and interpretation of conclusions drawn from each test, conclusions which were in turn based both on test scores and on supplementary qualitative material. The word modal should not be taken too literally in this context. We have relied on some tests scores when only a small proportion of the sample manifested the given response or pattern of responses, if this fits with other evidence in developing a larger picture. In stating our findings we have been freer with the evidence than some would permit, more strict than others would require. We attempted to keep to the canons of the exact method, without neglecting the clinical interpretations and insights. In this way we hoped to arrive at a rich and meaningful picture of the people studied, a picture that would provide an adequate basis for an analysis of their adjustment to the socio-political system.

BRIEF SKETCH OF RUSSIAN MODAL PERSONALITY CHARACTERISTICS

Central Needs[8]

Since all human beings manifest the same basic needs, we cannot assert that some need is unique to a given national population. Among these universal needs, however, some may achieve greater strength or central importance in the organization of the personality, and in this sense be typical of the majority of a given group.

Probably the strongest and most pervasive quality of the Russian personality that emerged from our data was a need for *affiliation*. By this we mean a need for intensive interaction with other people in immediate, direct, face-to-face relationships, coupled with a great capacity for having this need fulfilled through the establishment of warm and personal contact with others. Our subjects seemed to welcome others

[8] See Murray (1938a). We do not strictly follow Murray in our use of the 'need' terminology.

into their lives as an indispensable condition of their own existence, and generally felt neither isolated nor estranged from them. In contrast to the American subjects, the Russians were not too anxiously concerned about others' opinion of them and did not feel compelled to cling to a relationship or to defend themselves against it. Rather, they manifest a profound acceptance of group membership and relatedness. These orientations were especially prevalent in test situations dealing with relations between the individual and small face-to-face groups such as the family, the work team, and the friendship circle.

Closely linked with the need for affiliation is a need for *dependence* very much like what Dicks (1952) spoke of as the Russians' 'strong positive drive for enjoying loving protection and security', care and affection. This need shows not only in orientation towards parents and peers, but also in the relations with formal authority figures. We did not, however, find a strong need for submission linked with the need for dependence, although Dicks asserts it to be present. In addition there is substantial evidence for the relatively greater strength of *oral* needs, reflected in preoccupation with getting and consuming food and drink, in great volubility, and in emphasis on singing. These features are especially conspicuous by contrast with the relative weakness of the more typically compulsive puritanical concern for order, regularity, and self-control. However, our data do not permit us to stress this oral component as heavily as does Dicks, who regards it as 'typical' for the culture as a whole.

Several needs rather prominent in the records of the American control group did not appear to be of outstanding importance in the personality structure of the Russians. Most notable, the great emphasis on *achievement* found in the American records was absent from the Russian ones. Within the area of interpersonal relations our data lead us to posit a fairly sharp Russian-American contrast. Whereas *autonomy*, those needs were rather weakly manifested by the Russians. In approaching interpersonal relations our American subjects seemed to fear too close or intimate association with other individuals and groups. They often perceived such relations as potentially limiting freedom of individual action, and therefore inclined above all to insure their independence from or autonomy within the group. At the same time the Americans revealed a strong desire for recognition and at least formal acceptance or approval from the group. They are very eager to be 'liked', to be regarded as an 'all right' guy, and greatly fear isolation from the group. Finally we note that certain needs important in other national character studies were apparently not central in either the American or the Russian groups. Neither showed much need for dominance, for securing positions of superordination, or for controlling or manipulating others and enforcing authority over them. Nor did they seem markedly distinguished in the strength of hostile impulses, of desires to hurt, punish, or destroy.

Modes of Impulse Control

On the whole the Russians have relatively *high awareness* of their impulses or basic dispositions—such as for oral gratification, sex, aggression, or dependence—and, rather, *freely accept* them as something normal or 'natural' rather than as bad or offensive.[9] The Russians show evidence, furthermore, of *giving in* to these impulses quite readily and frequently, and of *living them out*. Although they tended afterwards to be penitent and admit that they should not have 'lived out' so freely, they were not really punitive towards themselves or others for failure to control impulses. Of course, this does not mean complete absence of impulse control, a condition that would render social life patently impossible. Indeed, the Russians viewed their own impulses and desires as forces that needed watching, and often professed the belief that the control of impulses was necessary and beneficial. The critical point is that the Russians seemed to rely much less than the Americans on impulse control to be generated and handled from within. Rather, they appear to feel a need for aid from without in the form of guidance and pressure exerted by

[9] Such a statement must of course always be one of degree. We do not mean to say that such threatening impulses as those toward incest are present in the awareness of Russians or are accepted by them more than by Americans.

higher authority and by the group to assist them in controlling their impulses. This is what Dicks referred to as the Russians' desire to have a 'moral corset' put on his impulses. The Americans, on the other hand, vigorously affirm their ability for *self*-control, and seem to assume that the possession of such ability and its exercise legitimates their desire to be free from the overt control of authority and the group.

In this connection we may note that the review of individual cases revealed a relative lack of well-developed *defensive structures* in many of the Russian subjects. Mechanisms that serve to counteract and to modify threatening feelings and impulses—including isolation, intellectualization, and reaction formation—seem to figure much less prominently among them than among the Americans. The Russians had fewer defenses of this type and those they had were less well established.

Typical Polarities and Dilemmas

Within certain areas of feelings and motives individuals may typically display attitudes and behavior that belong to one or the opposite poles of the given variable, or else display a preoccupation with the choice of alternatives posed by these poles. Such preoccupation may be taken to define the areas of typical dilemmas or conflicts, similar to the polarized issues, such as 'identity vs. role diffusion' and 'intimacy vs. isolation', which Erikson (1950) found so important in different stages of psychological maturation.

In our Russian subjects we found a conscious preoccupation with the problem of *trust vs. mistrust* in relation to others. They worried about the intentions of the other, expressing apprehension that people may not really be as they seem on the surface. There was always the danger that someone might entice you into revealing yourself, only then to turn around and punish you for what you have revealed. Another typical polarity of the Russians' behavior is that of *optimism vs. pessimism,* or of faith vs. despair. One of our projective test items posited the situation that tools and materials necessary for doing a job fail to arrive. In responding to this item our Russian subjects tended to focus on whether the outcome of the situation will be good or bad for the actor, while the Americans at once sprang into a plan of action for resolving the situation. Finally, we may include under the typical polarities of the Russians' attitude that of *activity vs. passivity*, although in the case of this variable we found little indication of a sense of a conscious conflict. However, the subjects' choice of alternatives in the projective tests tended to be distributed between the active and the passive ones, while the Americans' preference for the active instrumental response was as clear-cut and strong as was their generally optimistic orientation.

The pronounced polarities of the Russians' orientation lend support to Dicks's assertion that 'the outstanding trait of the Russian personality is its contradictoriness—its ambivalence' (Dicks, 1952). Two qualifications, however, must be kept in mind. First, the strength of our Russian subjects' dilemmas may have been greatly enhanced by the conditions of their lives, both in the Soviet Union and abroad. Second, the American subjects also show some involvement in problematic issues, though they were different from the Russian ones. Thus the problem of 'intimacy vs. isolation' or 'autonomy vs. belongingness', to which we have already alluded, seemed a major dilemma for Americans whereas it was not such an issue for the Russians.

Achieving and Maintaining Self-Esteem

In their orientations toward the self, the Russians displayed rather low and *unintense self-awareness* and little painful self-consciousness. They showed rather high and *secure self-esteem*, and were little given to self-examination and doubt of their inner selves. At the same time they were not made anxious by examination of their own motivation or that of others, but rather showed readiness to gain insight into psychological mechanisms. The American pattern reveals some contrasts here, with evidence of acute self-awareness, substantial self-examination, and doubting of one's inner qualities.

We were not able to discern any differences between Americans and Russians in the relative importance of *guilt* versus *shame* as sanctions. There were, however, some suggestive differences in what seemed to induce both guilt and shame. The Americans were more likely to feel guilty or ashamed if they failed to live up to clear-cut 'public' norms, as in matters of etiquette. They were also upset by any hint that they were inept, incompetent, or unable to meet production, sports, or similar performance standards. The Russians did not seem to be equally disturbed by such failures, and felt relatively more guilty or ashamed when they assumed that they had fallen behind with regard to moral or interpersonal behavior norms, as in matters involving personal honesty, sincerity, trust, or loyalty to a friend. These latter qualities they value most highly and they demand them from their friends.

Relation to Authority[10]

Our clinical instruments presented the subjects with only a limited range of situations involving relations with authority. These did not show pronounced differences in basic attitudes between Russians and Americans except that Russians appeared to have more fear of and much less optimistic expectations about authority figures. Both of these manifestations might, of course, have been mainly a reflection of their recent experiences rather than of deeper-lying dispositions. Fortunately, we can supplement the clinical materials by the life history interviews which dealt extensively with the individual's relations with authority. A definite picture emerges from these data. Above all else the Russians want their leaders—whether boss, district political hack, or national ruler —to be warm, nurturant, considerate, and interested in the individuals' problems and welfare. The authority is also expected to be the main source of initiative in the inauguration

[10] Relations to authority may be thought of as simply one aspect of a broader category—'conceptions of major figures'—which includes parents, friends, etc. We have included some comments on the Russians' perceptions of others under 'cognitive modes' below.

of general plans and programs and in the provision of guidance and organization for their attainment. The Russians do not seem to expect initiative, directedness, and organizedness from an average individual. They therefore expect that the authority will of necessity give detailed orders, demand obedience, keep checking up on performance, and use persuasion and coercion intensively to insure steady performance. A further major expectation with regard to the 'legitimate' authority is that it will institute and enforce sanctions designed to curb or control bad impulses in individuals, improper moral practices, heathen religious ideas, perverted political procedures, and extreme personal injustice. It is, then, the government that should provide that 'external moral corset' which Dicks says the Russian seeks.

An authority that meets these qualifications is 'good' and it does what it does with 'right'. Such an authority should be loved, honored, respected, and obeyed. Our Russian subjects seemed, however, to expect that authority figures would in fact frequently be stern, demanding, even scolding and nagging. This was not in and of itself viewed as bad or improper. Authority may be, perhaps ought to be, autocratic, so long as it is not harshly authoritarian and not totally demanding. Indeed, it is not a bad thing if such an authority makes one rather strongly afraid, make one 'quake' in expectation of punishment for trespassing or wrongdoing. Such an authority should not, however, be arbitrary, aloof, and unjust. It should not be unfeeling in the face of an open acknowledgment of one's guilt and of consequent self-castigation. Indeed, many of our subjects assumed that authority can in fact be manipulated through humbling the self and depicting oneself as a weak, helpless person who needs supportive guidance rather than harsh punishment. They also assumed that authority may be manipulated by praise or fawning, and seduced through the sharing of gratificatory experiences provided by the supplicant—as through the offer of a bottle of liquor and the subsequent sharing of some drinks. Russians also favor meeting the pressure of authority by evasive tactics, including such devices as apparently well-intentioned failure to comprehend and departures from the scene of action.

Throughout their discussions of authority our respondents

showed little concern for the preservation of precise forms, rules, regulations, exactly defined rights, regularity of procedure, formal and explicit limitation of powers, or the other aspects of the traditional constitutional Anglo-Saxon approach to law and government. For the Russians a government that has the characteristics of good government listed above justifies its right to rule by virtue of that performance. In that case, one need not fuss too much about the fine points of law. By contrast, if government is harsh, arbitrary, disinterested in public welfare—which it is apparently expected to be more often than not—then it loses its right to govern no matter how legal its position and no matter how close its observance of the letter of the law.

Modes of Affective Functioning

One of the most salient characteristics of the Russian personality was the high degree of their *expressiveness* and emotional aliveness. On most test items the Russian responses had a stronger emotional coloring, and they covered a wider range of emotions, than did the American responses. Their feelings were easily brought into play, and they showed them openly and freely both in speech and in facial expression, without much suppression or disguise. In particular they showed a noticeably greater *freedom and spontaneity in criticism* and in the expression of hostile feelings than was true for the Americans. There were, further, two emotions which the Russians showed with a frequency far exceeding that found in the Americans—*fear,* and *depression* or despair. Many of the ambiguous situations posited in the tests were viewed by them in terms of danger and threat, on the one hand, and of privation and loss, on the other. Undoubtedly this was in good part a reflection of the tense social situation which they had experienced in the Soviet Union, and of their depressed status as refugees, but we believe that in addition deeper-lying trends were here being tapped. These data provide some evidence in support of the oft-noted prevalence of depressive trends among the Russians.

Modes of Cognitive Functioning

In this area we include characteristic patterns of perception, memory, thought, and imagination, and the processes involved in forming and manipulating ideas about the world around one. Of all the modes of personality organization it is perhaps the most subtle, and certainly in the present state of theory and testing one of the most difficult to formulate. Our clinical materials do, however, permit a few comments.

In discussing people, the Russians show a keen *awareness of the 'other'* as a distinct entity as well as a rich and diversified recognition of his special characteristics. Other people are usually perceived by them not as social types but as concrete individuals with a variety of attributes distinctly their own. The Russians think of people and evaluate them for what they are rather than in terms of how they evaluate ego, the latter being a more typically American approach. The Russians also paid more attention to the 'others'' basic underlying attributes and attitudes than to their behavior as such or their performance on standards of achievement and accomplishment in the instrumental realm.

Similar patterns were evident in their perception of interpersonal situations. In reacting to the interpersonal relations 'problems' presented by one of the psychological tests they more fully elaborated the situation, cited more relevant incidents from folklore or their own experience, and offered many more illustrations of a point. In contrast, the Americans tended more to describe the formal, external, characteristics of people, apparently being less perceptive of the individual's motivational characteristics. The Americans also tended to discuss interpersonal problems on a rather generalized and abstract level. With regard to most other types of situation, however, especially problems involving social organization, the pattern was somewhat reversed. Russians tended to take a rather broad, sweeping view of the situation, *generalizing* at the expense of detail, about which they were often extremely vague and poorly informed. They seemed to feel their way through such situations rather than rigorously to think them through, tending to get into a spirit of grandiose planning but without attention to necessary details.

Modes of Conative Functioning

By conative functioning we mean the patterns, the particular behavioral forms, of the striving for any valued goals, including the rhythm or pace at which these goals are pursued and the way in which that rhythm is regulated. In this area our clinical data are not very rich. Nevertheless, we have the strong impression that the Russians do not match the Americans in the vigor of their striving to master all situations or problems put before them, and to do so primarily through adaptive instrumental orientations. Although by no means listless, they seem much more *passively accommodative* to the apparent hard facts of situations. In addition, they appeared less apt to persevere systematically in the adaptive courses of action they did undertake, tending to backslide into passive accommodation when the going proved rough. At the same time, the Russians do seem capable of great bursts of activity, which suggests the bi-modality of an *assertive-passive pattern* of strivings in contrast to the steadier, more even, and consistent pattern of strivings among the Americans.

To sum up, one of the most salient characteristics of the personality of our Russian subjects was their emotional aliveness and expressiveness. They felt their emotions keenly, and did not tend to disguise or to deny them to themselves, nor to suppress their outward expression to the same extent as the Americans. The Russians criticized themselves and others with greater freedom and spontaneity. Relatively more aware and tolerantly accepting of impulses for gratification in themselves and others, they relied less than the Americans on self-control from within and more on external socially imposed controls applied by the peer group or authority. A second outstanding characteristic of the Russians was their strong need for intensive interaction with others, coupled with a strong and secure feeling of relatedness to them, high positive evaluation of such belongingness, and great capacity to enjoy such relationships. The image of the 'good' authority was of a warm, nurturant, supportive figure. Yet our subjects seemed to assume that this paternalism might and indeed should include superordinate planning and firm guidance, as well as control or supervision of public and personal morality, and if necessary, of thought and belief. It is notable, in this connection, that in the realm of conative and cognitive functioning orderliness, precision of planning, and persistence in striving were not outstandingly present. Such qualities were rather overshadowed by tendencies toward over-generalizing, vagueness, imprecision, and passive accommodation. Countering the image of the good authority, there was an expectation that those with power would in fact often be harsh, aloof, and authoritarian. The effect of such behavior by authority is alienation of loyalty. This fits rather well with the finding that the main polarized issues or dilemmas were those of 'trust vs. mistrust' in relations with others, 'optimism vs. pessimism', and 'activity vs. passivity', whereas the more typically American dilemma of 'intimacy vs. isolation' was not a problem for many Russians. Though strongly motivated by needs for affiliation and dependence and wishes for oral gratification—in contrast to greater strength of needs for achievement, autonomy, and approval among the Americans —our Russian subjects seemed to have a characteristically sturdy ego. They were rather secure in their self-estimation, and unafraid to face up to their own motivation and that of others. In contrast to the Americans, the Russians seemed to feel shame and guilt for defects of 'character' in interpersonal relations rather than for failure to meet formal rules of etiquette or instrumental production norms. Compared with the Americans, however, they seemed relatively lacking in well-developed and stabilized defenses with which to counteract and modify threatening impulses and feelings. The organization of their personality depended for its coherence much more heavily on their intimate relatedness to those around them, their capacity to use others' support and to share with them their emotions.

RELATIONS OF MODAL PERSONALITY AND THE SOCIO-POLITICAL SYSTEM

In the following comments we are interpreting 'political participation' rather broadly, to cover the whole range of the individual's role as the citizen of a large-scale national state. We therefore include his major economic and social as well as his specifically political roles. This may extend the concept of political participation too far for most national states, but for the Soviet Union, where all aspects of social life have been politicized, it is the only meaningful approach. Specifically, the questions to which we address ourselves are as follows.

Assuming that the traits cited above were widespread among the group of Great Russians studied by our project, what implications would this have for their adjustment to the role demands made on them by the social system in which they participated? To what extent can the typical complaints of refugees against the system, and the typical complaints of the regime against its own people, be traced to the elements of non-congruence between these personality modes and Soviet social structure?

A full answer to these questions would involve us in a much more extensive presentation and a more complex analysis than is possible here. We wish to stress that our analysis is limited to the Soviet socio-political system as it typically functioned under Stalin's leadership (see Bauer, 1952; and Fainsod, 1953), since this was the form of the system in which our respondents lived and to which they had to adjust. To avoid any ambiguity on this score we have fairly consistently used the past tense. We sincerely hope that this will not lead to the mistaken assumption that we regard the post-Stalin era as massively discontinuous with the earlier system. However, to specify in any detail the elements of stability and change in post-Stalin Russia, and to indicate the probable effects of such changes on the adjustment of Soviet citizens to the system, is beyond the scope of this paper. As for the personality dimensions, we will discuss each in its relations to system participation separately, rather than in the complex combinations in which they operate in reality. Only those of the personality traits cited above are discussed that clearly have relevance for the individual's participation in the socio-political system.

Need Affiliation. Virtually all aspects of the Soviet regime's pattern of operation seem calculated to interfere with the satisfaction of the Russians' need for affiliation. The regime has placed great strains on friendship relations by its persistent programs of political surveillance, its encouragement and elaboration of the process of denunciation, and its assignment of mutual or 'collective' responsibility for the failings of particular individuals. The problem was further aggravated by the regime's insistence that its élite should maintain a substantial social distance between itself and the rank-and-file. In addition, the regime developed an institutional system that affected the individual's relations with others in a way that ran strongly counter to the basic propensities of the Russians as represented in our sample. The desire for involvement in the group, and the insistence on loyalty, sincerity, and general responsiveness from others, received but little opportunity for expression and gratification in the tightly controlled Soviet atmosphere. Many of the primary face-to-face organizations most important to the individual were infiltrated, attacked, or even destroyed by the regime. The break-up of the old village community and its replacement by the more formal, bureaucratic, and impersonal collective farm is perhaps the most outstanding example, but it is only one of many. The disruption and subordination to the state of the traditional family group, the Church, the independent professional associations, and the trade unions are other cases in point. The regime greatly feared the development of local autonomous centers of power. Every small group was seen as a potential conspiracy against the regime or its policies. The system of control required that each and all should constantly watch and report on each other. The top hierarchy conducted a constant war on what it scornfully called 'local patriotism', 'back-scratching', and 'mutual security associations', even though in reality it was attacking little more than the usual personalizing tendencies incidental to effective business and political management. The people strove hard to maintain their small group structures, and the regime persistently fought this trend through its war against 'familieness' and associated evils. At the same time it must be recognized that by its emphasis on broad group loyalties, the regime probably captured and harnessed somewhat the propensities of many Russians to give themselves up wholly to a group membership and to group activity and goals. This is most marked in the Young Communist League and in parts of the Party.

Need Orality. The scarcity element that predominated in Soviet society, the strict rationed economy of materials, men, and the physical requirements of daily life seem to have aroused intense anxieties about further oral deprivation that served greatly to increase the impact of the real shortages that have been chronic to the system. Indeed, the image of the system held by most in our sample is very much that of an orally depriving, niggardly, non-nurturant leadership. On the other hand, the regime can hope to find a quick road to better relations with the population by strategic dumping or glutting with goods, which was to some extent attempted during the period of Malenkov's ascendancy, although perhaps more in promise than reality.

Need Dependence. The regime took pride in following Lenin in 'pushing' the masses. It demanded that individuals be responsible and carry on 'on their own' with whatever resources were at hand, and clamored for will and self-determination (see Bauer, 1952). Clearly, this was not very congruent with the felt need for dependent relations. At the same time the regime had certain strengths relative to the need for dependence. The popular image of the regime as one possessed of a strong sense of direction fits in with this need. Similarly it gained support for its emphasis on a massive formal program of social-welfare measures, even if they were not too fully implemented. This directedness has a bearing also on the problem of submission. Although the regime had the quality of a firm authority able to give needed direction, it did not gain as much as it might because it was viewed as interested in the maximation of power *per se*. This appears to alienate the Russian as he is represented in our sample.

The Trust-Mistrust Dilemma. Everything we know about Soviet society makes it clear that it was extremely difficult for a Soviet citizen to be at all sure about the good intentions of his government leaders and his immediate supervisors. They seemed always to talk support and yet to mete out harsh treatment. This divided behavior pattern of the leadership seemed to aggravate the apparent Russian tendency to see the intentions of others as problematical and to intensify the dilemma of trust-mistrust. On the basis of our interviews one might describe this dilemma of whether or not to grant trust as very nearly *the* central problem in the relations of former Soviet citizens to their regime. The dilemma of optimism vs. pessimism, of whether outcomes will be favorable or unfavorable, presents a very similar situation.

The Handling of Shame. The regime tried exceedingly hard to utilize public shame to force or cajole Soviet citizens into greater production and strict observance of the established rules and regulations. Most of our available public documentary evidence indicates that the regime was not outstandingly successful in this respect. Our clinical findings throw some light on the reason. The regime tried to focus shame on non-performance, on failures to meet production obligations or to observe formal bureaucratic rules. To judge by the clinical sample, however, the Russian is little shamed by these kinds of performance failures, and is more likely to feel shame in the case of moral failures. Thus, the Soviet Russian might be expected to be fairly immune to the shaming pressures of the regime. Indeed, the reactions of those in our sample suggest the tables often get turned around, with the citizen concluding that it is the regime which should be ashamed because it has fallen down in these important moral qualities.

Affective Functioning. The general expansiveness of the Russians in our sample, their easily expressed feelings, the giving in to impulse, and the free expression of criticism, were likely to meet only the coldest reception from the regime. It emphasized and rewarded control, formality, and lack of feeling in relations. Discipline, orderliness, and strict observance of rules are what it expects. Thus, our Russian subjects could hope for little official reward in response to their normal modes of expression. In fact, they could be expected to run into trouble with the regime as a result of their proclivities in this regard. Their expansiveness and tendency freely to express their feelings, including hostile feelings, exposed them to retaliation from the punitive police organs of the state. And in so far as they did exercise the necessary control and avoided open expression of hostile feelings, they experienced a sense of uneasiness and resentment because of this unwarranted imposition, which did much to color their attitude to the regime.

Conative Functioning. The non-striving quality of our Russian subjects ties in with the previously mentioned characteristics of dependence and non-instrumentality. The regime, of course, constantly demanded greater effort and insisted on a more instrumental approach to problems. It emphasized long-range planning and deferred gratification. There was a continual call for efforts to 'storm bastions', to 'breach walls', 'to strive mightily'. With the Russian as he is represented in our sample, it does not appear likely that the regime could hope to meet too positive a response here; in fact it encountered a substantial amount of rejection for its insistence on modes of striving not particularly congenial to a substantial segment of the population. Indeed, the main influence may have been exerted by the people on the system, rather than by the system on them. Soviet official sources have for many years constantly complained of the uneven pace at which work proceeds, with the usual slack pace making it necessary to have great, often frenzied, bursts of activity to complete some part of the Plan on schedule, followed again by a slack period. It may well be that this pattern results not only from economic factors such as the uneven flow of raw material supplies, but that it also reflects the Russian tendency to work in spurts.

Relations to Authority. In many ways the difficulties of adjustment to the Soviet system experienced by our subjects revolved around the gap between what they *hoped* a 'good' government would be and what they *perceived* to be the behavior of the regime. Our respondents freely acknowledged that the Soviet leaders gave the country guidance and firm direction, which in some ways advanced the long-range power and prestige of the nation. They granted that the regime well understood the principles of the welfare state, and cited as evidence its provision of free education and health services. The general necessity of planning was also allowed, indeed often affirmed, and the regime was praised for taking into its own hands the regulation of public morality and the conscious task of 'raising the cultural level' through support of the arts and the encouragement of folk culture.

Despite these virtues, however, the whole psychological style of ruling and of administration adopted by the Bolsheviks seems to have had the effect of profoundly estranging our respondents. A great gulf seemed to separate the rulers and the ruled, reflected in our respondents' persistent use of a fundamental 'we'-'they' dichotomy. 'They' were the ones in power who do bad things to us, and 'we' were the poor, ordinary, suffering people who, despite internal differences in status or income, share the misfortune of being oppressed by 'them'. Most did not know that Stalin had once asserted that the Bolsheviks could not be a 'true' ruling party if they limited themselves 'to a mere registration of the sufferings and thoughts of the proletarian masses' (Stalin, 1933:95–96). Yet our respondents sensed this dictum behind the style of Soviet rule. They reacted to it in charging the leaders with being uninterested in individual welfare and with extraordinary callousness about the amount of human suffering they engender in carrying out their plans. Our subjects saw the regime as harsh and arbitrary. The leaders were characterized as cold, aloof, 'deaf' and unyielding to popular pleas, impersonal and distant from the people's problems and desires. The regime

was seen not as firmly guiding but as coercive, not as pater-
nally stern but as harshly demanding, not as nurturant and
supportive but as autocratic and rapaciously demanding, not
as chastening and then forgiving but as nagging and unyield-
ingly punitive.

The rejection of the regime was however by no means
total, and the Bolshevik pattern of leadership was in many
respects seen not as totally alien but rather as native yet
unfortunately exaggerated. This 'acceptance' did not extend
to the coldness, aloofness, formality, and maintenance of
social distance, which were usually rejected. It did, however,
apply to the pressures exerted by the regime, which were
felt to be proper but excessive. Coercion by government
was understandable, but that applied by the regime was not
legitimate because it was so harsh. The scolding about back-
sliding was recognized as necessary, but resented for being
naggingly persistent and caustic. And the surveillance was
expected, but condemned for being so pervasive, extending as it did even into the privacy of one's friendship and
home relations, so that a man could not even hope to live
'peacefully' and 'quietly'. The elements of acceptance within
this broader pattern of rejection have important implications
for the future of the post-Stalin leadership. They suggest
that the regime may win more positive support by changing
the mode of application of many of its authoritarian and
totalitarian policies without necessarily abandoning these policies and institutions as such. Indeed in watching the public
behavior of men like Khrushchev and Bulganin one cannot
help but feel that their style of leadership behavior is much
more congenial to Russians than was that of Stalin.

The preceding discussion strongly suggests that there was a
high degree of incongruence between the central personality
modes and dispositions of many Russians and some essential
aspects of the structure of Soviet society, in particular the behavior of the regime. Most of the popular grievances were
clearly based on real deprivations and frustrations, but the
dissatisfactions appear to be even more intensified and given a
more emotional tone because they were based also on the
poor 'fit' between the personality patterns of many Soviet
citizens and the 'personality' of the leaders as it expressed it-

self in the institutions they created, in their conduct of those institutions and the system at large, and in the resultant social climate in the U.S.S.R.

SOCIAL CLASS DIFFERENTIATION

Since personality traits found in the Russian sample are merely modal rather than common to the group at large, it follows that sub-groups can meaningfully be differentiated by the choice of appropriate cutting points on the relevant continua. As a way of placing the individuals in our sample on a common scale, three elements from the total range of characteristics previously described were selected. They were chosen on the grounds that they were most important in distinguishing the Russians as a group from the Americans, and also because they seemed meaningfully related to each other as elements in a personality syndrome. The three characteristics were: great strength of the drive for social relatedness, marked emotional aliveness, and general lack of well-developed, complex, and pervasive defenses. The two clinicians rated all cases for a combination of these traits on a three-point scale. Cases judged on the basis of a review of both interview and test material to have these characteristics *in a marked degree* were placed in a group designated as the 'primary set'. Individuals in whom these characteristics were clearly evident, but less strongly pronounced, were designated as belonging to a 'variant' set. The 'primary' and 'variant' sets together constitute a relatively homogeneous group of cases who clearly revealed the characteristics that we have described as 'modal'. All the remaining cases were placed in a 'residual' category, characterized by markedly stronger development of defenses, and in most instances also by lesser emotional expressiveness and lesser social relatedness. This group was relatively the least homogeneous of the three because its members tended to make use of rather different combinations of defenses without any typical pattern for the set as a whole. Subjects placed in the 'residual' group appeared to differ more from those in the 'variant' set than the 'primary' and the 'variant' sets differed from each other.

However, even the 'residual' pattern was not separated from the others by a very sharp break: emotional aliveness and relatedness to people were present also in some members of this group. Each of our 51 cases were assigned to one of four social-status categories on the basis of occupation and education. All those in group A were professionals and higher administrative personnel most of whom had university training, and all those in the D group were either peasants, or unskilled or semi-skilled workers with no more than five years of education. Placement in the two intermediary categories was also determined by the balance of occupation and education, group B consisting largely of white-collar workers and semi-professional and middle supervisory personnel, and group C of more skilled workers with better education.

Table 1 gives the distribution of cases among the three personality types within each of the four status groups. It is evident that the primary pattern has its greatest strength in the lower classes, becomes relatively less dominant in the middle layers, and plays virtually no role at all in the top group. The 'residual' pattern predominates at the top level and is very rare among peasants and ordinary workers.[11]

TABLE 1
STATUS DISTRIBUTION OF
PERSONALITY TYPES AMONG FORMER
SOVIET CITIZENS

| | Personality Type | | | |
Status	Primary	Variant	Residual	Total
A	—	1	12	13
B	2	8	6	16
C	3	4	2	9
D	8	3	2	13
Total	13	16	22	51

[11] The method of assigning the cases to the three psychological groups was holistic and impressionistic. It is of interest to note, therefore, that when more exact and objective techniques were used on the Sentence Completion Test to rate a similar but larger sample of refugees on some differently defined personality variables, the relationship between occupation and education and the personality measures was quite marked in three out of five variables. See Fried (1954).

Since the distinctive patterns of adjustment to the Soviet system by the various socio-economic groups will be the basis of extensive publications now in progress, we restrict ourselves here to a few general observations. First, we wish to stress that, as our interviews indicate, both the more favored and the rank-and-file share substantially the same range of complaints against the regime, find the same broad institutional features such as the political terror and the collective farm objectionable, and view the same welfare features such as the system of education and free medical care as desirable. In spite of these common attitudes our data suggest that personality may play a massive role with regard to the socio-political system. The educational-occupational level attained and/or maintained by an individual in an open-class society is one of the major dimensions of such participation. This is particularly the case in the Soviet Union, where professional and higher administrative personnel are inevitably more deeply implicated in the purposes and plans of the regime, are politically more active and involved, and are subjected to greater control and surveillance. It seems plausible that persons in whom the affiliative need was particularly strong, expressiveness marked and impulse control weak, and the defensive structures not well developed or well organized would be handicapped in competition for professional and administrative posts in any society; they certainly could not be expected to strive for or to hold on to positions of responsibility in the Soviet system.

The pattern of marked association between certain traits of personality and educational-occupational level clearly invites a question as to whether the personality really affected the level attained and held, or whether the appropriate personality traits were merely acquired along with the status. This question raises complex issues which we cannot enter into here. We do wish to point out, however, that the characteristics on which our psychological grouping was based belong to those that are usually formed at an early age and are relatively long enduring and resistant to change. At first glance this affirmation of the early origins of the patterns described seems to be inconsistent with their observed association with educational-occupational level. However, the contradiction exists only if one assumes that obtaining a higher education and a superior occupation in Soviet society is a matter either of pure chance or exclusively of ability, unrelated to family background and the person's own attitudes and strivings. The data on stratification and mobility in Soviet society show, however, that persons born into families of higher social and educational level have a much better chance than do others to obtain a higher education and professional training (Feldmesser, 1953; see also Inkeles, 1950). Consequently, many people of the professional and administrative class grew up in families of similar status, and in those families were apparently reared in a way different from that typical of the peasant and worker families.[12] Presumably this produced enduring effects on their personality formation, which were important prior to exposure to common educational experience.

In addition, mobility out of the lower classes may have been mainly by individuals whose personality was different, for whatever reason, from that of the majority of their class of origin. Such differences can easily express themselves in a stronger drive for education and for a position of status. We must also allow for the role played by the regime's deliberate selection of certain types as candidates for positions of responsibility. Finally, there is the less conscious 'natural selection' process based on the affinity between certain personality types and the opportunities offered by membership in the élite and near-élite categories. In this connection we are struck by the relative distinctness of the highest status level in our sample, since only one person with either of the two variants of the modal personality of the rank-and-file shows up among them. These results bear out the impression, reported by Dicks, of radical personality differences and resultant basic incompatibilities between the ruled population and the rulers. The latter, we assume, are still further removed from the 'modal pattern' than are our subjects in the élite group.

We have yet to deal with the question of how far our observations concerning a group of refugees can be general-

---

[12] For a detailed discussion of *class differences* in the child-rearing values of pre-Soviet and Soviet parents see Rossi (1954).

ized to the Soviet population and *its* adjustment to the Soviet system? The answer to this question depends in good part on whether personality was an important selective factor in determining propensity to defect among those in the larger group who had the opportunity to do so.[13] It is our impression that personality was not a prime determinant of the decision not to return to Soviet control after World War II. Rather, accidents of the individual's life history such as past experience with the regime's instruments of political repression, or fear of future repression because of acts which might be interpreted as collaboration with the Germans, seem to have been the prime selective factors. Furthermore, such experiences and fears, though they affected the loyalty of the Soviet citizen, were not prime determinants of his pattern of achievement or adjustment in the Soviet sociopolitical system.[14] The refugee population is not a collection of misfits or historical 'leftovers'. It includes representatives from all walks of life and actually seemed to have a disproportionately large number of the mobile and successful.

Though we are acutely aware of the smallness of our sample, we incline to assume that the personality modes found in it would be found within the Soviet Union in groups comparable in nationality and occupation. We are strengthened in this assumption by several considerations. First, the picture of Russian modal personality patterns which emerges from our study is highly congruent with the traditional or classic picture of the Russian character reported in history, literature, and current travellers' accounts.[15] Second, much

---

[13] It is impossible to estimate accurately how many former Soviet citizens had a real chance to choose not to remain under Soviet authority. The best available estimates suggest that at the close of hostilities in Europe in 1945 there were between two and a half and five million former Soviet citizens in territories outside Soviet control or occupation, and of these between 250,000 and 500,000 decided and managed to remain in the West. See Fischer (1952).

[14] Evidence in support of these contentions is currently being prepared for publication. A preliminary unpublished statement may be consulted at the Russian Research Center: Inkeles and Bauer (1954).

[15] After this article was completed we discovered a report based almost entirely on participant observation which yielded conclusions about modal personality patterns among Soviet Russians

of the criticism directed by the regime against the failings of the population strongly suggests that some of the traits we found modal to our sample and a source of strain in its adjustment to the system are widespread in the population and pose an obstacle to the attainment of the regime's purposes *within* the U.S.S.R. Third, the differences in personality between occupational levels are consistent with what we know both of the general selective processes in industrial occupational systems and of the deliberate selective procedures adopted by the Soviet regime. Because of the methodological limitations of our study, the generalization of our findings to the Soviet population must be considered as purely conjectural. Unfortunately we will be obliged to remain on this level of conjecture as long as Soviet citizens within the U.S.S.R. are not accessible to study under conditions of relative freedom. We feel, however, that, with all their limitations, the findings we have reported can be of essential aid in furthering our understanding of the adjustment of a large segment of the Soviet citizens to their socio-political system and of the policies adopted by the regime in response to the disposition of the population.

---

extraordinarily similar to those developed on the basis of our tests and interviews. See Pfister-Ammende (1949).

Conservatism and Personality
Herbert McClosky

If justification were needed for taking notice once again of the liberal-conservative distinction, it would be sufficient, I suppose, merely to observe that this division has been injected into the politics of Western nations for at least two centuries and, depending on the nature of one's criteria, perhaps longer.

INTRODUCTION

The distinction between the two camps has not always been sharply drawn, of course, for both have been compelled, as a condition for survival, to hold important beliefs in common. Moreover, each has reversed itself on certain issues, such as government regulation of the economy, casting off old views in favor of beliefs previously cherished by the other. Competing for popular support in elections, and succeeding one another in office, the two camps have, of necessity, taken on many values in common, tempering their programs and adjusting their courses to the practical requirements of political contest. In a system like ours, where the parties have functioned less as ideological movements than as brokerage organizations hoping to attract majority

Reprinted by permission of the author and publisher from the *American Political Science Review*, Volume 52, 1958, pp. 27–45.

support from almost every segment of the electorate, the distinction has tended to be dulled even further, until, at the actual scenes of daily political struggle, it has often faded entirely. Even in political systems abroad where doctrinal parties are more frequently in evidence, the differences between liberals and conservatives have become operationally more obscure as the parties have shared office, confronted the reality of common problems, and competed for the support of the waverers at the middle ranges of the ideological spectrum.

We would be mistaken, however, to infer from this that all distinctions between the liberal and conservative tendencies are spurious, or that they are mere inventions of office-seekers or publicists. Not only do our Minnesota studies find many of the differences to be genuine, but the two camps bear a remarkable continuity with the patrilineal doctrines from which they have descended. For example, the credo of the "New Conservatives" (as distinguished from the shifting programs of conservative parties) includes few notions not already expressed by Edmund Burke, whose writings, despite seeming inconsistencies, are generally considered the fountainhead of modern conservative thought. The political writings of Russell Kirk, Clinton Rossiter, John Hallowell, or Richard Weaver, of the refurbished Southern Agrarians like Donald Davidson, the poets of nostalgia like T. S. Eliot, or of magazines like *Measure*, the *National Review*, the *American Mercury*, and *Modern Age*—express with varying degrees of intensity and spiritual violence the principles and doctrines which have enjoyed currency among self-styled conservatives for generations. Thus, despite modifications imposed by political exigency and despite even the sharp reversals that have occasionally developed on specific issues, the outlook of conservatism has, like liberalism, remained fairly firm through recent centuries. This suggests that both conservatism and liberalism may be "natural" or polar positions around which individuals of certain habitual outlooks, temperaments, and sensibilities can comfortably come to rest and be united with others of like disposition.

Many people, of course, do not exhibit the patterns of mind and personality that are fully identified with either of the polar positions, but embrace elements of both, in varying proportions. Nevertheless, it is reasonable to believe that a characteristic conservative focus exists, not only because of the historical continuity already noted, but also because liberal and conservative values would not, in the absence of such focus, fall into pattern, but would instead be distributed randomly throughout all sections of the population; *i.e.,* even if one knew some of the beliefs a given individual possessed, one could not predict by better than chance what other beliefs or values he held.

The data I will present show, however, that there is considerable regularity and coherence not only in the body of norms professed but in the relation between certain casts of character and personality on the one side and the degree of conservatism or liberalism expressed on the other.

Before proceeding to the body of the paper bearing on this relation, I should point out that we have had less interest in the conservative-liberal distinction as such than in the example it offers for the further study of political preference, belief, and affiliation—the subjects with which we have been centrally concerned in our research. Hence we have not been occupied with many of the questions about conservatism which have commanded the attention of political scientists and essayists. It has not been our purpose, for example, to explore the historical unfolding of conservative thought; to describe conservative movements of the past; to present the case for embracing or rejecting conservatism as a doctrine; to estimate the truth of its essential propositions or the validity of its claims; to ascertain the excellence or shabbiness of its moral outlook; or to resolve the question of its "real" definition. It has not been our intention either to challenge or support its assumptions, to make policy recommendations, or to exhort anyone for or against its doctrines. Admittedly, we have opinions and biases on these matters, and we are not blind to the possibility that they may influence the interpretation of our findings. Indeed, we assume that they will, no matter how disinterested our original intention. We should be very disappointed, nevertheless, if the controversial nature of the subject matter or the heat that may be generated by the findings were to obscure the scientific validity we have worked so hard to achieve.

A prefatory note concerning our interest in personality may also be helpful. Although certain assumptions about the nature of man were implicit in the thought of many of the classic political writers (Plato, Machiavelli, Hobbes, Locke, and Bentham come immediately to mind), the relation of personality to politics has, I think, received less attention from contemporary political scientists than it deserves. Spurred, however, by the injunctions of Graham Wallas that we must "deal with politics in its relation to the nature of man," and stimulated by the progress of academic, as well as Freudian, psychology, attention has here and there begun to be focused upon personality as an important dimension for the study of politics. In recent years the work of Lasswell, Fromm, the authors of *The Authoritarian Personality*, Almond, and a few others offer cases in point, and these have stimulated others. For my own part, I should like to make it clear that while I believe the study of personality to be extremely valuable, it would be naive to suppose that it could possibly serve as a universal device for the study of every problem encountered in political research. It cannot be substituted for certain other types of investigation which have interested political scientists, such as the study of institutional and legal structures, descriptions of political process, or the formal analysis of normative propositions. Rather, the study of personality offers one more category of explanation to accompany those already familiar to us, thereby adding an important new dimension to our understanding of political phenomena, and helping us to clarify or correct certain propositions about politics that have never been put to adequate empirical test.

THE CONSERVATISM MEASURE: DEFINITION AND VALIDITY

Because it is a key term in the language of political conflict, choked with emotive connotations, "conservatism" has naturally evoked controversy over its meaning. The problem of defining it has, furthermore, been confused in recent decades by the already mentioned switch in the economic attitudes of both conservatives and liberals, and by the rise of movements of the "radical right" of which the fascist parties are the most extreme example but which are also represented in somewhat milder form by such groups as the Conservative Citizens' Committees. Some prefer to reserve the "conservative" label for the advocates of laissez-faire capitalism, for critics of the New Deal or for Republicans of whatever ideological persuasion; for some it mainly signifies intemperate right-wing values of the McCarthy or *Chicago Tribune* type; while for others, it recalls the somewhat romanticized image of a Boston Brahmin—genteel, cultivated, practical, a gentleman of exquisite sensibilities and manners, a critic of the vulgarities of mass society, saddened by, though resigned to, the heavy price of equalitarian democracy.

Arguments occur as well over more esoteric questions: whether conservatism is a full-blown ideology or only a state of mind; whether it is a social posture found among the defenders of every type of society or a clutch of prejudices appropriate to a specific social class at a given historical stage; whether it is a set of empirically settled propositions about man and society or a body of self-evident truths, intuitively prized by persons of sufficient character to grasp their significance; and so on.

In the face of these diverse opinions, we cannot hope that the definition employed in our research, and the measure or "scale" that we constructed from this definition, will satisfy everyone. We have made an earnest effort, however, to extract from the tradition of self-styled conservative thought, and especially from the writings of Edmund Burke, a set of principles representing that tradition as fairly as possible. We have concentrated upon those attitudes and values that continually recur among acknowledged conservative thinkers and that appear to comprise the invariant elements of the conservative outlook. By the same token, we have tried to avoid attitudes or opinions that seemed to us situationally determined and which, for that reason, appear to be secondary and unstable correlates of liberal or conservative tendencies.

Many attitudes that arise mainly from party or class affiliation fall into this category, *e.g.*, attitudes toward free enterprise, toward trade unions, toward expansion of government functions, toward the New Deal and its welfare measures, toward tariffs, farm supports, and a number of similar issues that have featured prominently in political campaigns.

In spite of the differences, there is astonishing agreement among the disciples, and among disinterested scholars as well, that the following are characteristic, if not quintessential elements of the conservative outlook[1]:

(1) Man is a creature of appetite and will, "governed more by emotion than by reason" (Kirk), in whom "wickedness, unreason, and the urge to violence lurk always behind the curtain of civilized behavior" (Rossiter). He is a fallen creature, doomed to imperfection, and inclined to license and anarchy.

(2) Society is ruled by "divine intent" (Kirk) and made legitimate by Providence and prescription. Religion "is the foundation of civil society" (Huntington) and is man's ultimate defense against his own evil impulses.

(3) Society is organic, plural, inordinately complex, the product of a long and painful evolution, embodying the accumulated wisdom of previous historical ages. There is a presumption in favor of whatever has survived the ordeal of history, and of any institution that has been tried and found to work.

(4) Man's traditional inheritance is rich, grand, endlessly proliferated and mysterious, deserving of veneration, and not to be cast away lightly in favor of the narrow uniformity preached by "sophisters and calculators" (Burke). Theory is to be distrusted since reason, which gives rise to theory, is a deceptive, shallow, and limited instrument.

(5) Change must therefore be resisted and the injunction heeded that "Unless it is necessary to change it is necessary not to change" (Hearnshaw). Innovation "is a devouring

---

[1] The doctrines expressed in these paragraphs have been drawn from the writings of such acknowledged conservative spokesmen as Burke (1963); Hearnshaw (1933); White (1950); Hogg (1947); Kirk (1953); Rossiter (1955); Wilson (1951); Viereck (1955); and others. In addition, books and articles by numerous commentators were consulted, including such recent articles as Huntington (1957).

conflagration more often than it is a torch of progress" (Kirk).

(6) Men are naturally unequal, and society requires "orders and classes" for the good of all. All efforts at levelling are futile and lead to despair (Kirk and Rossiter), for they violate the natural hierarchy and frustrate man's "longing for leadership." The superior classes must be allowed to differentiate themselves and to have a hand in the direction of the state, balancing the numerical superiority of the inferior classes.

(7) Order, authority, and community are the primary defense against the impulse to violence and anarchy. The superiority of duties over rights and the need to strengthen the stabilizing institutions of society, especially the church, the family, and, above all, private property.

Some of the points in the conservative creed are, unfortunately, distinguished more for their rhetoric than for the clarity and crispness of their content. Nevertheless, owing to the fact that they comprise an integrated outlook, we were able to construct a scale that makes it possible to measure the strength of conservative belief in individuals and groups, and thus to classify persons according to the degree of conservatism they exhibit.

In constructing this scale, we began with an initial pool of 43 items, the majority of which were fairly straightforward statements of the various conservative beliefs just discussed. Here, for example are some typical items from the original set of 43:

If something grows up over a long time there is bound to be much wisdom in it.

If you start trying to change things very much, you usually make them worse.

It's not really undemocratic to recognize that the world is divided into superior and inferior people.

All groups can live in harmony in this country without changing the system in any way.

You can usually depend more on a man if he owns property than if he does not.

Our society is so complicated that if you try to reform parts of it you're likely to upset the whole system.

I prefer the practical man anytime to the man of ideas.

A man doesn't really get to have much wisdom until he's well along in years.

I'd want to know that something would really work before I'd be willing to take a chance on it.

No matter how we like to talk about it, political authority comes not from us but from some higher power.

Private ownership of property is necessary if we are to have a strong nation.

It is never wise to introduce changes rapidly, in government or in the economic system.

It's better to stick by what you have than to be trying new things you don't really know about.

Together with the items from a number of other scales we were simultaneously trying to build, the 43 items in the conservatism pool were submitted, through survey methods, to a large general sample of persons in the vicinity of the Twin Cities who were asked to state, in relation to each item, whether they agreed or disagreed. The patterns of their responses were then analyzed, with a three-fold purpose in mind: 1) to select from each pool those items which, by reproducibility and other statistical tests, clustered sufficiently to convince us that they belonged to the same universe; 2) to reduce the number of items in each scale to manageable proportions (we began with more than 2300 items and over 80 pools of scale items); and 3) to ensure that every item selected for a given scale was in fact measuring some degree of the same attitude dimension or, in other words, that all the items in the final scale were consistent with each other.

Altogether, the responses of over 1200 persons were sampled and analyzed in this preliminary scale-construction stage, a procedure that took more than two years to complete. Some 539 items, comprising an inventory of 53 separate scales, survived this stage. The remaining thirty item pools failed to meet our scale standards and were dropped. Conservatism emerged as a twelve-item scale, tighter, more refined, and with greater internal consistency than was found in the original 43-item pool, with which, however, it correlated +.83. Although the twelve-item scale did not encompass as wide a range of values as were contained in the initial item pool, its ranking of people from extreme conservatism on the one end to liberalism on the other was very close to the rank order yielded by the original 43 items, as the high correlation attests. Empirically, then, the shorter scale may be taken as an adequate, if not actually a superior and more refined substitute for the initial set of "conservative" items. (The scale has subsequently been refined further in a succeeding study, and the items reduced in number to nine.)

The validation of a scale, *i.e.*, determining the degree to which it in fact measures the thing it purports to measure, is at best a difficult and frustrating affair. Although we have not yet exhausted all the validation procedures planned for this scale, several considerations bearing on its validity can be offered. For one thing, the scale possesses a certain amount of "face validity," which is to say that the items it includes express on their face the values which most knowledgeable people would designate as conservative. In one validation procedure employed, we submitted subsets of items from the twelve-item conservatism scale to an advanced senior-graduate class in political theory, whose members had no prior knowledge of the study or its purposes. Each student was asked to supply a name or label for the group of statements and to write a paragraph explaining or justifying the label he had chosen. Of 48 students participating, 39 volunteered the word *conservatism* as best describing the sentiments expressed in the statements, five offered names that were virtually synonymous with conservatism (*e.g.*, *traditionalism*), while two supplied other names and two did not answer.

Thus, over 90 per cent of an informed group recognized that the items expressed values characteristic of conservatism, and were able to supply explanations consistent with the labels they chose.

The conservatism scale also correlated highly, and in the predicted direction, with several related measures that were being tested at the same time. For example, persons who scored as strongly conservative in the preliminary runs also proved, by comparison with the low scorers, to hold extremely conventional social attitudes, to be more responsive to nationalistic symbols, and to place greater emphasis upon duty, conformity, and discipline.

We also checked a number of individual statements that were not included as part of the conservatism scale but which, nevertheless, express sentiments or opinions that would be widely recognized as related to conservatism. In all but a few instances, the persons who score as extreme conservatives agree with these statements far more frequently than do those who score as liberals. The following are a few examples. [See next page.]

By reason of such criteria, we believe that the conservatism scale possesses the properties of a valid measure, and that it can be used with confidence in group studies or in research involving large samples. Similar procedures were employed in the development of the 52 other scales used in the original study (referred to as the *PAR* study, the initials standing for political participation, awareness, and responsibility); and the process was repeated in the development of 18 additional scales employed in a subsequent study of persons with extreme or "marginal" political beliefs (the *Marginal Believer* study). In constructing and validating some of the personality and social attitude scales, we were able to build on a great deal of previous work by clinical and social psychologists interested in the classification and measurement of personality traits; while in the case of other scales, such as Dominance and Social Responsibility, we were compelled to start afresh and to undertake elaborate empirical procedures to develop measures that fitted these concepts.[2]

The *PAR* study was carried out on a sample of 1211 persons in the Twin City area (not to be confused with the 1200 subjects previously employed in developing and pretesting the inventory of scales). The *Marginal Believer* study drew upon a cross-section sample of 1082 persons from the entire state of Minnesota,[3] together with two special samples of extreme Right-Wing and Left-Wing be-

[2] We have described the procedures employed in the development of these scales elsewhere (Gough et al., 1951, 1952).
[3] I should like to acknowledge the generous assistance of the *Minnesota Poll* and of its director, Sidney Goldish, for assistance in selecting this sample and administering the questionnaire.

| | *Per Cent Agree* | |
	Liberals (N=258)	Extreme Conservatives (N=282)
Duties are more important than rights.	32%	63%
The world is too complicated to be understood by anyone but experts.	26%	51%
You can't change human nature.	30%	73%
People are getting soft and weak from so much coddling and babying.	31%	68%
The heart is as good a guide as the head.	22%	58%
We have to teach children that all men are created equal, but almost everyone knows that some are better than others.	35%	73%
No matter what the people think, a few people will always run things anyway.	33%	63%
Few people really know what is in their best interest in the long run.	43%	77%

lievers, numbering almost 300 each. The data from the cross-section sample of the *Marginal Believer* project have confirmed in virtually every detail the findings relative to conservatism yielded by the *PAR* study. Hence the results described below have been borne out by two separate studies, carried out six years apart, on entirely different samples of the adult population. Most of the findings presented in this paper are drawn from the general population data of the *Marginal Believer* study, although we have equivalent results that could as easily be reported from the *PAR* project.

In each study, we broke the entire sample into quartiles of several hundred persons each, assigning subjects to one quartile or another according to their scores on the conservatism scale. Subjects scoring 7–9 on the conservatism scale were thrown into the uppermost or Extreme Conservative quartile; those with scores of 5–6 were labelled Moderate Conservatives; with scores of 3–4, Moderate Liberals; and the lowest quartile, with scores of 0–2, were called Liberals.

With these classifications, we next computed the scores of the four groups on each of the remaining scales used in the two studies, as well as on a large number of personal background characteristics for which we had also collected data in the course of the two surveys. A variety of tabulating and statistical procedures were then employed to check hypotheses, to note differences and similarities between groups, and to ascertain patterned or prototypic responses. In addition, all major tabulations were re-run with controls introduced for such factors as education, occupation, socio-economic status, and possible response set bias,[4] in order to be certain that the findings were not the spurious product of some hidden or disguised factor which, conceivably, we

[4] Among the most important and interesting of such response sets is the tendency exhibited by some respondents to agree—or to disagree—with statements regardless of their content. This tendency obviously distorts the response scores of the individuals who possess it. A number of special procedures were introduced to correct for this phenomenon, and to eliminate, as far as possible, the spurious influence of this factor. The procedures and findings bearing upon this "unthinking," "uncritical," or "acquiescent" tendency will be described elsewhere in a forthcoming technical monograph.

had been failing to take into account. We discovered, however, that even with such factors partialled out or otherwise
accounted for, the tendency to affirm or to reject conservative doctrines was significantly related to social and personality characteristics.

RESULTS

In turning now to some of the outcomes of the research, I
will confine myself in the main to the data that bear most
immediately on personality and related attributes, omitting,
for reasons of space, the material on political and social attitudes with which both studies have been greatly concerned.

Intelligence. One of the clearest findings in both studies is
that; contrary to claim, conservatism is not the preferred
doctrine of the intellectual elite or of the more intelligent
segments of the population, but the reverse. By every measure available to us, conservative beliefs are found most
frequently among the uninformed, the poorly educated, and
so far as we can determine, the less intelligent. The following table sets out a few of these relationships. [See next page.]

The Awareness scale, referred to in the table, is a test not
only of actual knowledge but also of the clarity of one's
grasp of the social process, past and present. It serves, to
some extent, as a crude intelligence test. The same can be
said, though less authoritatively, for the Intellectuality scale,
which assesses the degree to which intellectual habits have
been formed and are perceived as attractive. The findings
on these measures make plain that there is a sharp decline in
the level of information and intellectual grasp as one moves
from the more liberal to the more conservative sections of
the population. Similarly, an increase in the level of knowledge is usually accompanied by a corresponding decrease in
the incidence of conservatism. Individual items correlated
with intelligence bear out the same general tendency. Thus,
the item "I was a slow learner in school" is answered yes by
34 per cent of the Extreme Conservatives but by only 14
per cent of the Liberals. These differences on Awareness and

TABLE 1
COMPARISON OF CONSERVATIVES AND LIBERALS BY EDUCATION AND KNOWLEDGE, MINNESOTA SAMPLE*

	Liberals (N=190)	Moderate Liberals (N=316)	Moderate Conservatives (N=331)	Extreme Conservatives (N=245)
Education				
% with grade school education	9	14	29	49
% with some college education	47	33	21	12
Awareness				
% scoring low	9	25	45	66
% scoring high	54	32	21	9
Intellectuality				
% scoring low	7	20	34	56
% scoring high	62	43	26	11

* In this and the following tables *high* always means a score in the upper third of the scale named; *low* always means a score in the lower third of the scale named. The middle third is omitted from these tables. The table should thus be read across, as follows: Whereas 54 per cent of the Liberals score among the upper (or "high") third of the distribution on the Awareness scale, 32 per cent of the Moderate Liberals, 21 per cent of the Moderate Conservatives and only 9 per cent of the Extreme Conservatives have "high" scores on Awareness. It should also be noted that the differences between the extreme groups in this table, and in all the subsequent data reported, are statistically significant beyond the 1 per cent level of significance, which is to say that the probability is less than one in 100 that differences of these magnitudes could be occurring by chance given the size of our samples.

Intellectuality remain large and statistically significant even when education and other status factors are controlled.

Of course, not all conservatives are uninformed, not all liberals are knowledgeable, and not all the unlearned are conservative. The data show clearly, nevertheless, that the most articulate and informed classes in our society are preponderantly liberal in their outlook. Procedures carried out with a special sample of civic and political leaders in the *PAR* study bear this out even further, regardless of party preference or of other affiliations that might ordinarily be expected to have an influence upon liberal-conservative tendencies.[5]

Social-Psychological Attributes. Related to status and intelligence are a set of traits that reflect the interrelation of personality and life-style, and especially the degree to which people feel themselves to be the masters or victims of their immediate environment and of themselves. These traits have to do with one's sense of security, with the sense of belonging, isolation, and social support, with feelings of worthlessness, submissiveness, inferiority, timidity self-assurance, personal strength, and the like. In the preceding table are some of the scales we developed to assess this universe of feelings and attitudes, together with the scores registered by liberals and conservatives for each of these traits.

As these figures make plain, the Conservatives tend to score at the more "undesirable" end of the distributions on every one of the above traits. Uniformly, every increase in the degree of conservatism shows a corresponding increase in submissiveness, anomie, sense of alienation, bewilderment, etc. To some extent, the vast differences appearing in this table are a function of the somewhat higher status and education of the liberals in the sample. But the differences remain almost as large even when we control for these factors. Conservatism, in our society at least, appears to be far more characteristic of social isolates, of people who think poorly of themselves, who suffer personal disgruntlement and

[5] This conclusion receives at least implicit support from the findings of Stouffer (1955), in which leadership groups were found to be uniformly more tolerant of diversity and non-conformity than the general population.

TABLE 2
COMPARISON OF CONSERVATIVES AND LIBERALS BY
PERSONALITY TRAITS—SOCIAL

	Liberals (N=190)	Moderate Liberals (N=316)	Moderate Con- servatives (N=331)	Extreme Con- servatives (N=245)
Dominance				
% low	9	19	37	51
% high	72	50	29	14
Anomie				
% low	71	48	32	10
% high	4	16	30	59
Alienation				
% low	57	47	35	18
% high	11	20	27	45
Bewilderment				
% low	61	40	33	10
% high	9	20	34	57
Pessimism				
% low	44	35	31	19
% high	25	35	42	53
Social Responsibility				
% low	12	25	36	62
% high	47	31	23	8
Self-Confidence				
% low	18	23	32	35
% high	46	38	24	20
Guilt				
% low	62	42	36	18
% high	16	18	28	47

frustration, who are submissive, timid, and wanting in confidence, who lack a clear sense of direction and purpose, who are uncertain about their values, and who are generally bewildered by the alarming task of having to thread their way through a society which seems to them too complex to fathom.

Readers of Eric Hoffer (1951) will recognize in these findings support for his brilliant, intuitive characterization of the conservative and of the conditions which give rise to him. Far from being the elite or the masters or the prime movers, conservatives tend on the whole to come from the more backward and frightened elements of the population, including the classes that are socially and psychologically depressed. The significance of this, and of other findings reported in this section, will be considered in the evaluation section shortly to follow.

Clinical-Personality Variables. Turning now to a set of traits that are more straightforwardly clinical and psychological, conservatives and liberals are found to be sharply distinguished from each other in many of these characteristics as well. The differences, furthermore, are consistent with those cited in the personality-life style group. Scores on the more important of the clinical variables are shown in the following table.

The figures demonstrate with overpowering effect that conservatives tend once more to score on the more "undesirable," poorly adapted side of these personality variables. Of the four liberal-conservative classifications, the extreme conservatives are easily the most hostile and suspicious, the most rigid and compulsive, the quickest to condemn others for their imperfections or weaknesses, the most intolerant, the most easily moved to scorn and disappointment in others, the most inflexible and unyielding in their perceptions and judgments. Although aggressively critical of the shortcomings of others, they are unusually defensive and armored in the protection of their own ego needs. Poorly integrated psychologically, anxious, often perceiving themselves as inadequate, and subject to excessive feelings of guilt, they seem inclined to project onto others the traits they most dislike or fear in themselves.

If space permitted, these data could be buttressed by numerous other related findings in our studies, and the relationships so briefly presented here could be elaborated in dozens of ways. We must, however, move on to evaluate the data just offered and to analyze, in particular, their relation to conservatism as a political and social outlook.

ANALYSIS

If we may trust the evidence just presented, there seems little doubt that support for conservative doctrines is highly correlated with certain distinct personality patterns. The

TABLE 3
COMPARISON OF CONSERVATIVES AND LIBERALS BY PERSONALITY TRAITS—CLINICAL

	Liberals (N=190)	Moderate Liberals (N=316)	Moderate Conservatives (N=331)	Extreme Conservatives (N=245)
Hostility				
% low	59	38	26	9
% high	18	37	46	71
Paranoid Tendencies				
% low	56	42	28	13
% high	16	27	37	62
Contempt for Weakness				
% low	61	33	21	5
% high	8	18	29	55
Need Inviolacy (Ego Defense)				
% low	68	58	36	17
% high	11	20	38	60
Rigidity				
% low	58	43	29	14
% high	18	32	41	60
Obsessive Traits				
% low	47	40	29	22
% high	24	31	43	55
Intolerance of Human Frailty				
% low	52	30	17	6
% high	8	16	23	54

quantitative data do not immediately make plain, however, the nature of the connection between the two or the reasons for the particular relationships found. These questions take us into realms that are somewhat more theoretical and speculative.

In the explanations that follow I have proceeded from the view that most of the propositions fundamental to the conservative creed (as well as to the liberal creed) are in reality normative rather than empirical statements. Hence, they can neither be demonstrated nor refuted by experience or observation of the external world. The universe to which conservative doctrines refer is so ambiguous that it is often possible to assert with equal validity a given proposition or its contrary. For example, which can we demonstrate more firmly, that men are naturally equal or unequal? Anarchic or law-abiding? Essentially wicked or essentially good? Which is it correct to believe, that man is governed more "by emotion than by reason," or the reverse? Which generalization can best be supported by evidence, that change is a "devouring conflagration," destructive of mankind, or a boon that prevents stagnation and the withering of the human spirit? As for statements which claim—or for that matter deny—that society is ruled by "divine intent" and that power is made legitimate by Providence, one would be hard put to decide what manner of data would be needed before one could rationally embrace or reject either view.

If the assertions contained in the conservative creed cannot be referred to the world of experience for proof or refutation, we may conclude that one is led to conservatism not by the facts as such, but only by the way one happens to perceive or "structure" the facts. There are, I think, three main ways in which such structures are developed:

First, one may impose structure on an ambiguous field of phenomena by logical procedures. Conservative doctrines might, for example, be formally derived from some set of postulates or from another system of beliefs or cognitions. Many of us like to think that our beliefs are carefully reasoned out in this way, and that our several outlooks and attitudes are internally consistent, dispassionately arrived at, and valid. The practice of reasoning out and forming attitudes on complex social questions in this purely disinterested way is, however, rare. It may occasionally be found in a few intellectuals of unusual philosophic inclination, but it is not likely to be the essential element in determining most people's convictions. As Graham Wallas observed, even the methods of reasoning about social affairs are fixed by habit and by subjective leanings. Numerous psychological studies have shown, moreover, that judgments thought to have been derived analytically, or sometimes even from observation, become notoriously more unreliable as the ambiguity of the stimulus field increases.

A second possibility is that one's views of man and society are learned through indoctrination and group influence, so that an individual reared in an environment of conservative belief absorbs its attitudes unconsciously and with no particular awareness of alternatives. While such learning is obviously important in the formation of opinions and doubtless accounts for a great number of conservative (and liberal) believers, it cannot by itself adequately explain the personality differences revealed in our research. One should also keep in mind that Americans appear mainly to have been exposed to a liberal rather than a conservative tradition.[6] Then, too, it is difficult for anyone in a society as mobile and as literate as ours to escape all contact with alternative doctrines; hence, individuals reared in an environment of conservative belief are likely to have had *some* contact with liberal sentiments as well. Some measure of choice has probably been exercised, therefore, even by those whose beliefs have been determined chiefly by indoctrination.

This brings us to a third process by which cognitions of the

[6] For a full scale development of this thesis, *cf.*, for example, Hartz (1955). Interestingly enough, a belief in the predominance of a liberal tradition in America has frequently been advanced by new conservative writers, who point to it as an obstacle to a victory for conservatism. For example, Rossiter (1955:68) asserts that: "The American political tradition is basically a liberal tradition, an avowedly optimistic idealistic way of thinking about man and government. It is stamped with the mighty name and spirit of Thomas Jefferson, and its articles of faith, an American Holy Writ, are perfectibility, progress, liberty, equality, democracy, and individualism."

external world may be structured, namely, through projection of the personality of the observer himself. In this way, an individual creates a set of perceptions that express, or that are consonant with, his own needs and impulses. The more ambiguous the thing observed, the greater the likelihood that he will fashion his perceptions of it to accord with his own inner feelings. In other words, conservatives believe what they do not because the world is the way it is but because they, the observers, are the way *they* are. Liberals, observing the same world, arrive at quite different judgments about it. Thus, conservative doctrines may tell us less about the nature of man and society than about the persons who believe these doctrines. Although we cannot explain all our findings by reference to these projective processes, they do, I think, provide a key to the explanation of a good many of the results.

Even the data on intellectuality, knowledge, and intelligence bear some relation to these processes. The conservative, as we have seen, is psychologically timid, distrustful of differences, and of whatever he cannot understand. He fears change, dreads disorder, and is intolerant of nonconformity. The tendency of the prototypic conservative to derogate reason and intellectuality, and to eschew theory, seems in some measure to be an outgrowth of these and related elements in his personality. He is inclined to regard pure intellectual activity as dangerous to established arrangements, for in his view of the world such activity often gives way to utopian "schemes" or unrealistic "plans." Intellectuals are likely to be impractical dreamers and potential radicals, unstable people whose theories may weaken the foundations of the social order. The conservative tends, furthermore, to perceive intellectuals as bohemians, as deviants and non-conformists who flaunt the requirements of convention and who lack respect for property or religion. Excessive intellectual activity is thought to lead to skepticism and rationalism and, consequently, to the destruction of faith. Like Cassius, the intellectual thinks too much and is therefore very dangerous.

It will be obvious that this manner of perceiving intellectuals has little to do with the characteristics of the class of people being observed and much to do with the anxieties and torments of the observer.

Related to this is the tendency for conservatives to be attracted to sentiments that would have to be described as mystical, and even obscuranist. One comes upon this not only in the writings of Russell Kirk, Eric Voegelin, or other spokesmen for the "New Conservatism," but also in the responses of conservatives throughout our samples. To cite but one illustration among dozens, over 67 per cent of the Extreme Conservatives score in the upper third of the Mysticism scale compared with only 15 per cent of the liberals. Similarly the conservatives show a far greater tendency to agree or to say yes to items that are sweeping in nature and somewhat obscure in meaning. To judge from their responses, they apparently set far less store upon rigor or precision of thought, and allow less scope to the critical faculties. They also tend to score higher on the more extreme religious items and on the Religiosity scale itself.

To some extent, the findings on intellectuality are the result of the lower average education of conservatives. In the United States, at least, education is likely to lead to liberal rather than conservative tendencies. For one thing, it exposes the student to the American inheritance which, as we have noted, is primarily liberal. For another, education trains people in some measure to demand greater precision in speech and thought, to be more open-minded and tolerant, to be intellectually flexible and receptive to scientific modes of discourse, to reject mystical or non-natural explanations, and so on. These are traits which we find to be negatively correlated with conservatism; or, put another way, we find that individuals who learn to think in the ways just described are, other things being equal, far more likely to become liberals than conservatives.

If we turn next to the connection between conservatism and the variables reflecting hostility and suspicion, the role of personality in the formation of social beliefs becomes even more striking. In many ways hostility is a principal component of the conservative personality, as it is a principal component of conservative doctrine. It does not seem accidental, considering the data on hostility, that conservatives prefer to believe in man's wickedness, that they choose to see man as fallen, untrustworthy, lawless, selfish, and weak. Expressed as political doctrine, these projections of aggressive personality tendencies take on the respectability of an old and honored philosophical position. These tendencies may also lie at the root of the conservative inclination to regulate and control man; to ensure that he will not violate the conditions necessary for order; to train him to value duty, obedience, and conformity; and to surround him with stabilizing influences, like property, church, and the family. The high values placed on authority, leadership, and natural hierarchy, and on an elite to guide and check the rest of mankind, apparently derive from the same set of psychological impulses.

These personality needs can also be discerned in the scores registered on several of our other social attitude measures, as well as on many individual items. It may be noted, for example, that only 11 per cent of the Liberals scored at the high end of our ethnocentric prejudice measure,[7] compared with 71 per cent of the Extreme Conservatives. Similarly, 45 per cent of the Liberals but only 12 per cent of the Extreme Conservatives were high on a measure of Faith in People. A scale dealing with Political Suspiciousness showed conservatives to be far more mistrustful of others in this respect as well (55 per cent of the Extreme Conservatives were high, but only 14 per cent of the Liberals). From whatever direction we approach him, the prototypic conservative seems far more impelled to contain, to reject, and to take precautions against his fellow creatures.

The data on psychological rigidity offer additional support for these interpretations. It will be recalled that conservatives showed up as relatively inflexible and far more inclined than the rest of the sample to exhibit compulsive-obsessive traits. Not only are they less able to tolerate human foibles or weaknesses, but they are less tolerant of any and all differences between themselves and others. On a Tolerance scale developed for these studies, 55 per cent of the Liberals fell into the highest third of the distribution, compared with only 25 per cent of the Extreme Conservatives. An item asserting that

[7] Adapted and revised from the California Ethnocentrism scale, the original version of which is reported in Adorno (1950).

"A man oughtn't to be allowed to speak if he doesn't know what he is talking about" was answered affirmatively by 55 per cent of the Extreme Conservatives, but by only 8 per cent of the Liberals. Seventy-seven per cent of the Conservatives say that "It is wrong ever to break a law," while only 38 per cent of the Liberals assert this. As we have seen, 32 per cent of the Liberals but 63 per cent of the Extreme Conservatives think that "Duties are more important than rights." In a measure of the ability to tolerate ambiguity—a scale which expresses a need for certainty and for having all matters neatly pegged and ordered—the Extreme Conservatives appear considerably less able than others to live with uncertainty or ambiguity (67 per cent of the conservatives, but only 12 per cent of the Liberals, score high on this measure).

These are a few of the many supplementary findings which lend support to the hypothesis that the inflexible and exacting features of conservative social doctrine are related to the prototypic personality attributes of conservative believers. The connection does not seem surprising, so soon as one thinks about it. The extreme emphasis on order and duty; the elaborate affection for the tried and familiar; the fear of change and the desire to forestall it; the strong attachments to the symbols and rituals of in-group culture; the hope for a society ordered and hierarchical in which each is aware of his station and its duties; the unusual concern for law, authority, and stability—all these can easily be understood as doctrinal expressions of a personality pattern that has strong need for order and tidiness; that adjusts only with difficulty to changes in the environment; that cannot bear the uncertainty of questions left open, and requires answers; that is made uncomfortable by the give-and-take of free inquiry and the open society; that yearns for consensus, harmony of values, unequivocal definitions of the norms, and conclusive specification of the sources of authority.

It may seem ironic, in light of these traits, that conservatives also tend to exhibit the submissive, indecisive, retiring, and somewhat spiritless demeanor noted in our discussion of the social-psychological variables. I cannot pretend to follow, if indeed anyone can, the complex threads by which these several personality configurations are somehow held together. One can, nevertheless, observe (without explaining it) that persons who feel inadequate and who for one reason or another dislike themselves are often the quickest to aggress against others and to demand perfection of them. Similarly, by a process which psychologists have labelled "reaction formation," the disgruntled often seem to venerate the very society which frustrates them. It is almost as though, disliking themselves, they seek solace and support in an over-defense of society and in the over-institutionalization of life. Conservatives make a fetish of community, although it is apparent that in many ways they are more alienated from the community than most. This conclusion is suggested not only by their scores on such measures as anomie, alienation, and social responsibility, but by their unusually high scores on political cynicism, feelings of political impotence, and status frustration. In the same vein, although the intensity of their patriotism exceeds that of any other group, their faith in democracy (American or otherwise), is lowest of the four groups, while their scores on the totalitarian, elitist, and authoritarian values (which for the most part, the American creed rejects) are the highest of the four.[8]

CAUTIONS AND QUALIFICATIONS

Impressive though the conservatism data may be, we must take note of several important qualifications and problems bearing upon their interpretation, to which fuller attention will eventually have to be given. Here, for reasons of space, I can only comment briefly upon a few of these points.

1. The findings refer to aggregates, not to specific individuals. Doubtless, many of us know individual conservatives whose personalities differ in key ways from the prototypic pattern described here. In our research, some conservatives have been turned up who, in personality and other attributes, essentially resemble liberals. These, however, are exceptions, since the probabilities are strong that a conservative selected

[8] For a fascinating set of data on *conformity* as measured in an experimental group situation that fit, even in detail, with the findings presented here on conservatism, see Crutchfield (1955).

at random from the general population will resemble the conservative profile that emerges from the preceding data.

2. A question might also be raised about the propriety of classifying highly informed, upper status conservatives in the same category with uneducated conservatives of low status. Conceivably, the "elite" and the "mass" conservatives are motivated by very dissimilar influences and could be scoring high on conservatism for quite different reasons. This possibility cannot be dismissed lightly, especially when one considers that status and education factors account, by themselves, for a significant share of the total variance found in our data. Subsequent analyses will make it possible, we hope, to settle this matter conclusively; but for the present, at least one important consideration can be noted: when education and other status factors are controlled, we find that informed, upper status conservatives differ from informed, upper status liberals in precisely the same ways that conservatives in general differ from liberals in general; or, for that matter, in the same ways that "mass" conservatives differ from "mass" liberals. While the *range* of the scores varies as occupation, education, or knowledge varies the *direction* and *magnitude* of the differences between liberals and conservatives remain very much the same for all status and education levels. In short, personality factors seem to exercise a fairly uniform influence on the formation of conservative or liberal outlooks at all social levels.

3. The association between conservatism and the traits outlined exists in the form of correlations, which only tell us that the two go together. *How* they go together, and which is antecedent to which, is a more difficult and more elusive problem. Conservative doctrines appear, in some measure, to arise from personality needs, but it is conceivable, at least, that both are the product of some third set of factors. Both, for example, may have been learned or acquired simultaneously, through family indoctrination, in which case the connection between the two would be more epiphenomenal than causal. I do not think that this explanation can account for most of our results, but it will need to be checked out further.

4. The terms employed in the description of traits must be seen as relative and as having been mainly defined by the

items in the scales themselves. Satisfactory external validation has not always been available. Also, although clinical terms have been employed that might be used in the diagnosis of psychotics, we have used the terms only as terms of tendency within the normal population. None of them is intended to signify the presence of a pathological mental state.

5. One must be careful to avoid the reductivist fallacy of assigning all significance in the problems considered to personality factors. Equally, one must avoid the temptation to "psychologize" problems to such an extent as to strip them of their significance as genuine political or philosophical problems.

6. The term liberalism has been inadequately defined in our study so far. We have tended to call someone liberal if he rejected the values of conservatism. While our findings suggest that most of these people would in fact meet the definition of a liberal, our present classification of liberals is crude and needs to be refined. All persons who reject conservatism may not be liberals, for, as in the case of the "authoritarian-democratic" dimension, liberalism-conservatism may not be variables, paired in such a way that a high score on one necessarily signifies a low score on the other.

7. The connections between classical conservatism (or liberalism) and such factors as party affiliation, attitude on economic issues, and liberal-conservative self-designation have been extensively explored in our research, but could not be reported in the present paper. The correlation between them tends, however, to be fairly low, suggesting that for the present, at least, many Americans divide in their party preferences, their support of candidates, their economic views, their stands on public issues, or their political self-identifications without reference to their beliefs in liberalism or conservatism. The latter have influence, of course, especially among some of the more articulate groups; for the general population, however, political divisions of the sort named appear to be more affected by group membership factors than by personality.

8. Some readers may be inclined to identify our "conservatives" with "right-wing authoritarians," in the belief that we are measuring the latter rather more than the former.

This view would be difficult to support, however, for not only have we defined conservatism by reference to its most frequently articulated values (which are by no means identical with right-wing values), but we have also found that while right-wing authoritarians are in some respects a more extreme version of our conservatives, there are also significant differences between the two.

9. Finally, our findings have so far been drawn entirely from Minnesota samples, and the degree to which the conclusions can be generalized to conservatives everywhere and at all times is open to debate. We shall soon have comparable data on a national cross-section sample, which I have reason to think will bear out the present results. In fact, I am inclined to believe that the connections between conservatism and the personality configurations presented in the foregoing would very likely prevail wherever, and whenever, the members of a society are free to choose between conservatism and alternative, liberal systems of belief. But this is a subject for future research.

Authoritarianism of the Political Right, Center, and Left
Edwin N. Barker

After the California studies of the late 1940's (Adorno, 1950) the belief became widespread that a personality syndrome called authoritarianism had been isolated and that it could be measured by the F scale. The California group initially studied anti-semitism and ethnocentrism. After considerable work on these subjects they decided to construct a scale which would measure prejudice without appearing to have this aim. Specifically, they wanted a scale which would correlate highly with their scales for anti-semitism and ethnocentrism. In addition, in line with their evolving theory of underlying personality characteristics of the anti-semitic and ethnocentric individual, they hoped that the new scale would yield a valid estimate of general antidemocratic tendencies at the personality level. The F scale resulted.

The appearance of *The Authoritarian Personality* in 1950 stimulated a tremendous amount of further research and discussion. The authors were quite open in admitting that they emphasized the study of pre-fascist tendencies primarily and general authoritarianism only secondarily. However, many researchers have used the F scale as though it were a measure of general authoritarianism rather than rightist authoritarianism—seemingly forgetting one of the original purposes of the scale (as an indirect measure of anti-semitism). Two studies

Reprinted by permission of the publisher from the *Journal of Social Issues,* Volume 19, 1963, pp. 63–74.

are reported here which attempt to clarify the relations between authoritarianism and the F (Fascism) scale, between authoritarianism and political militancy and political "extremeness."

THE NEW YORK STUDY[1]

In 1957, data were gathered from 160 graduate students in the New York City area. The large majority of the sample were in their second year of graduate work in psychology or education. The following instruments were administered: The California Politico-Economic Conservatism Scale (PEC) was used to group the subjects as politically leftish, rightish, or middle of the road (Adorno, 1950:163). High scores on the 15 item scale signify acceptance of rightist ideology. A second measure used to form experimental groups was Rokeach's Dogmatism Scale, Form E (Rokeach, 1960). There is some evidence that it is closer to the concept of general authoritarianism than the F scale. The Dogmatism scale, unlike F, is not obviously related to political ideology. With the Dogmatism scale and PEC it was possible to group the subjects by political position and by level of dogmatism. The groups could then be compared as to F scale scores and scores on measures of authoritarian qualities. Form 60A of the F scale was used—a thirty-item form first published by Gough (1951).

The criteria for authoritarianism were selected in accordance with several conditions. Scales were selected which appeared to measure variables accepted as central to the authoritarian syndrome. No scale was considered unless it was known to have a significant relationship with the F scale. An attempt was made to choose measures which were free from bias to the Right or Left. The following measures of authoritarian qualities were administered: The Stereotype Test, constructed by Siegel (1954) to measure tendencies toward oversimplification and over-generalization with respect to groups of people. The Test for Tolerance-Intolerance of Cognitive Ambiguity (TICA), constructed by Siegel (1954) to measure

[1] Based upon Barker (1958).

the need to structure even when inappropriate. The sentence completion test for Anti-Intraception constructed by Hanfmann and Getzels (1953) and modified by Dorris, Levinson, and Hanfmann (1954) to measure the tendency to deny the self-relevance of one's own completions. The sentence completion test of Attitude to Authority, constructed by Mishler (1953) to measure the extent to which authority figures and demands are submitted to or rejected. The Opinionation Scale, constructed by Rokeach (1960) to measure the tendency toward intolerance and rejection of persons holding different beliefs. The scale is scored for Left Opinionation and Right Opinionation as well as for Total Opinionation. The Toughminded Scale was also included. It had been described by Eysenck (1955) as being essentially a measure of general authoritarianism.

The scale for Censorship Tendency was constructed for this study. The scale consists of names of well-known public figures associated with the political left and right and a list of organizations easily identified by their titles as being leftist or rightist. The subjects were instructed to indicate any of the persons listed whose tape recorded speeches they thought would be unwise for presentation on the radio and to indicate any of the organizations whose leaders should not be allowed to appear on television. The scale is scored for Left Censorship (censoring rightists) and Right Censorship (censoring leftists) as well as for Total Censorship.

The hypotheses of the study were as follows:

1. The F scale is biased toward authoritarianism of the right.

2. Authoritarians of the political right, center, and left are similar on measures of general authoritarianism.

3. Authoritarians of the political right and left differ in the manner in which they express their authoritarian qualities, i.e., in the "direction" or content of their authoritarianism.

RESULTS

An intercorrelation matrix was computed for the ten instruments. It was evident from the matrix that Eysenck's Toughminded Scale had no relationship with authoritarianism within this sample. The only significant correlation between Tough-mindedness and the other nine scales was with PEC ($-.33$, indicating a negative relation between toughmindedness and conservatism). The results are at variance with Eysenck's findings. In a personal communication in 1958, Eysenck offered the hypothesis that the results may be accounted for by the difference in intelligence and education between these subjects and his. At any rate, the Toughminded Scale is clearly unrelated to the other scales and it is not included in the following analysis.

The matrix of correlations between the eight measures of authoritarianism is composed of 28 correlation coefficients. Sixteen of those coefficients are positive and significant beyond the .01 level. Even when correlations between all positively stated and similarly constructed questionnaires are ignored, 12 of the correlations are significant. The theory of an authoritarian syndrome is supported—the authoritarian measures do cluster.

After correlational analyses, the questionnaires were divided into six groups. The abbreviations in parentheses will be used to signify the experimental groups: Thirty dogmatic rightists, above the mean on Dogmatism and PEC (DR); twenty dogmatic middle of the roaders, above the mean on Dogmatism and within the semi-interquartile range on PEC (DM); thirty dogmatic leftists, above the mean on Dogmatism and below the mean on PEC (DL); thirty non-dogmatic rightists, below the mean on Dogmatism and above the mean on PEC (NDR); twenty non-dogmatic middle of the roaders, below the mean on Dogmatism and within the semi-interquartile range on PEC (NDM); thirty non-dogmatic leftists, below the mean on Dogmatism and below the mean on PEC (NDL).

As for the hypotheses, the first one was that the F scale is biased toward authoritarianism of the right. The F scale had the following correlations: with PEC, .41 (significant beyond the .001 level); with Right Censorship and Right Opinionation, .57 and .55 (significant beyond the .001 level); and with Left Censorship and Left Opinionation .15 and $-.22$ (not significant). In addition, if the F scale is biased, one would expect the dogmatic leftists to score much lower on the F scale than the dogmatic rightists. The respective mean F scores were 97 and 120 (t test significant beyond the .001 level). It is clear that the F scale measures rightist authoritarianism quite well but does not discriminate leftist authoritarianism.

The second hypothesis was that authoritarians of whatever political position would obtain similar scores on the authoritarian criteria. Table 1 presents the means of the six groups.

TABLE 1
GROUP MEANS ON AUTHORITARIAN CRITERIA

Scale	Mean of Groups					
	DR	DM	DL	NDR	NDM	NDL
Intolerance of Ambiguity	14.9	15.3	14.2	13.1	10.5	11.1
Anti-intraception	12.3	10.6	11.6	9.6	9.5	11.3
Censorship	12.3	9.9	13.9	9.3	10.5	8.7
Stereotype	9.1	9.5	7.6	6.1	4.1	3.6
Opinionation	146.6	158.8	151.1	133.2	123.3	120.2
Submissiveness	17.5	14.8	14.6	15.5	13.1	12.8

Except for the case of Submission (Attitude to Authority) there were no significant differences between the means of DR, DM, and DL on the authoritarian criteria. Submission was included in the analysis although it did not meet the expectation that it would be unrelated to PEC. Submission and PEC correlated .40 which is significant beyond the .001 level. On Submission, DR has a significantly higher mean than DL (.01 level). The second hypothesis is supported by five of the six predictions—the dogmatists of the left, center, and right are similar in their high scores on the authoritarian criteria. In addition, when all dogmatists are combined and all non-dogmatists are combined and the means on the authoritarian criteria are compared, the dogmatists receive higher scores in each case. See Table 2.

The third hypothesis was that authoritarians of the left and right would differ in the manner in which they express their authoritarian qualities. We have already seen that they differed on the conservatively slanted items of the F scale. In addition, t tests of mean differences on the subscales of the

Censorship and Opinionation scales revealed the following: The dogmatic leftists had significantly higher scores than the dogmatic rightists on Left Censorship (.01 level) and Left Opinionation (.001 level). The dogmatic rightists had significantly higher scores than the dogmatic leftists on Right Censorship (.03 level) and Right Opinionation (.001 level).

TABLE 2

MEANS AND STANDARD DEVIATIONS OF DOGMATISTS AND
NON-DOGMATISTS ON AUTHORITARIAN CRITERIA

Scale	Dogmatists		Non-dogmatists		t	Significance of difference
	Mean	SD	Mean	SD		
Intolerance of Ambiguity	14.7	6.4	11.7	8.0	2.59	.01
Anti-intraception	11.6	5.7	10.2	6.3	1.50	.07
Censorship	12.7	8.0	9.4	7.8	2.61	.01
Stereotype	8.6	7.4	4.7	5.9	3.62	.001
Opinionation	151.3	20.6	129.6	26.0	5.80	.001
Submissiveness	15.7	4.4	13.8	4.1	2.76	.01

Thus, while the authoritarians of the left and right are *similar* in being high an Opinionation and Censorship Tendency, they are *different* in the direction of their censoring and opinionation.

Unfortunately, most studies of authoritarianism, including the one reported above, have correlated paper and pencil tests with other paper and pencil tests. While such studies are useful, it is desirable to bring our concepts to a test in "real life" whenever possible—to find suitable criterion groups, to test our predictive ability for example with types of political action or lack of it. In 1963 at the Ohio State University, such an opportunity presented itself.

THE OHIO STUDY

Columbus, Ohio, is commonly known as a rather conservative city politically. In the recent past it has generally voted Republican, in the last election overwhelmingly supporting a Governor running on a "balance the budget" platform. On the other hand, the Ohio State University has numbers of outspoken liberals as well as conservatives on the faculty. Thus, the University and the city are prone to a great deal of political controversy. In the months preceding this study, several controversies were prominent, the most intense one concerning the University's rules for allowing outside speakers on the campus. Within the past year the administration had refused to allow several speakers to appear on the campus to speak against the House Un-American Activities Committee. These actions touched off a great deal of political activity on the part of both faculty and students.

A student organization I will call The Leftists, numbering about 30 juniors and seniors, was quite active in the controversy, inviting more speakers to test the administration's position, putting out a daily mimeographed newsletter, picketing the administration building, even attempting to hire a plane to fly over the commencement exercises dragging a banner saying "Free Speech Now." Another student organization I will call The Rightists, numbering about 30 juniors and seniors, was not quite as active in this particular controversy. However, the group was quite active on other issues, inviting conservative speakers to forums and publishing regular ads in the school newspaper extolling the virtues of free enterprise, with cartoons depicting Good Capitalism, Evil Communism, and Sneaky Socialism.

Data were gathered from 26 of the Rightists and 29 of the Leftists. The instruments were administered individually by an undergraduate who knew the members of the groups and could reassure them concerning the anonymity of their responses. For a comparison group of non-organized juniors and seniors, data were gathered from 61 other students. The following instruments were administered to all groups: The PEC, the F scale, the Dogmatism scale, a revised and shortened form of the Censorship scale, and a political self-labelling scale, scored as follows: "Extreme Leftist" (1); "Socialist" (2); "Liberal Democrat" (3); "Democrat" (4); "Republican" (5); "Conservative Republican" (6); "States Rights" (7); "Extreme Rightist" (8).

The hypotheses of the study were as follows:

1. There is a strong relationship between the F scale and political ideology.

2. There is no relationship between authoritarianism (Dogmatism and Censorship) and political ideology.

3. There is no relationship between authoritarianism and extremity of political position.

4. There is no relationship between authoritarianism and degree of political activity (organized vs. non-organized students).

RESULTS

Table 3 presents the means of the three groups on the scales as well as the significance of the differences between the means.

The organized Rightists had an item mean on PEC of 5.5. On the political self-labelling scale they primarily labelled themselves "Conservative Republican," and secondarily as "Extreme Rightist." The non-organized comparison group of students had an item mean on PEC of 4.4 and labelled themselves primarily as "Republican" or "Democrat." The organized Leftists had a PEC item mean of 2.6. They primarily labelled themselves "Socialist," and secondarily as "Liberal Democrat." The differentiation between the groups is striking. There is very little overlap between the groups on both PEC and the self-labelling scale. The PEC scale has a possible range of item means from 1.0 to 7.0. If we call subjects who have item means between 3.1 and 4.9, "moderates," and subjects scoring outside that range, political "extremists," we find the following: The organized Rightists and Leftists are 71 percent extremists and 29 percent moderates, while the non-organized students are 92 percent moderates and only 8 percent extremists!

This picture is even more pronounced on the self-labelling scale. The student political organizations seem to be composed mainly of students with highly crystallized and polarized political attitudes while the comparison group of students is strikingly low on deviants from the absolute center of the political scales. The comparison group of non-organized students was drawn from classes in the Education College. Their PEC mean (62.4) is comparable to those reported in

TABLE 3

OHIO STATE UNIVERSITY MEANS

Scales	Organized Rightists		Non-organized Students		Organized Leftists	
Conservatism (PEC)	82.7	(.0001)*	62.4	(.0001)*	39.9	
F Scale	107.5	(.001)	89.4	(.001)	64.3	
Dogmatism	150.9	(.02)	139.2	(N.S.)	135.8	
Left Censorship	2.17	(N.S.)	2.12	(N.S.)	1.00	
Right Censorshp	5.21	(.01)	2.68	(.001)	0.12	
Total Censorship	7.38	(N.S.)	4.84	(.01)	1.12	
Political Self-Label	6.12	(.001)	4.32	(.001)	2.23	

* The numbers in parentheses give the level of significance of the t tests computed between adjacent group means. Differences between Rightists and Leftists on Dogmatism reached the .01 level; on Left Censorship, not significant; and on Total Censorship, .001 level.

other studies of college students, however their standard
deviation (3.08) is smaller than any the author could find in
the literature. It is known that PEC means vary according to
college major and occupation. The present finding raises the
question as to whether standard deviations vary in a similar
manner. The finding may mean that Education students are
an unusually homogeneous and politically moderate population. On the other hand, it may mean that students who have
given no overt sign of political commitment by participating
in political action are so uninformed that they answer political
attitude scales inconsistently thereby receiving "middle of
the road" scores. If the latter is so, studies (such as the New
York Study reported above) which have used unselected college students for determining the correlates of political attitudes have less meaning than has been attributed to them.
Before we make statements about correlates of being a "liberal" or a "conservative," we need to ascertain whether we
actually have any such people in our sample.

The first hypothesis stated that the F scale is strongly related to political ideology. Table 3 indicates that the Rightists
have a very significantly higher mean on the F scale than
the Leftists. The Spearman rank order coefficient was computed for the F scale and PEC scores of the 61 non-organized
students. R equalled .50 which is significant beyond the .01
level. In addition, if the F scale is biased toward conservatism,
one would expect authoritarians of the right to score significantly higher on the F scale than authoritarians of the left.
Those Rightist and Leftist subjects who scored 150 on Dogmatism were compared as to their F scale means. The
dogmatic Rightists had a mean F scale score of 114 while
the dogmatic Leftists had a mean of 82. The difference is
significant beyond the .001 level. It is clear that the F scale
is measuring rightist authoritarianism—not general authoritarianism.

The second hypothesis stated that there is no relationship
between general authoritarianism and political ideology. The
findings in the New York Study appeared to justify using
Dogmatism and Censorship as indices of general authoritarianism. Spearman rank order coefficients were computed for
Dogmatism and PEC scores on the non-organized students.

R equalled .07, not significant. However, Table 3 indicates that the Rightists received significantly higher Dogmatism scores than the other two groups. In addition, on Total Censorship the Leftists received significantly lower scores than the other two groups. Thus, the second hypothesis is not supported. Although the differences are not as great as on the F scale, the Rightists do have significantly higher scores on general authoritarianism. How does one explain the contradiction between these findings and those of the New York Study? Or the contradiction between the insignificant R's of the unorganized students in this study and the significant differences between the groups?

It appears that when one is dealing with subjects who range only from mildly conservative to mildly liberal, one will find no apparent relation between authoritarianism and conservatism. However, when the range is extended—when one has some *committed* conservatives and leftists in the sample, the differences in general authoritarianism begin to show. On Dogmatism for example, extreme leftists, moderate leftists, and moderate rightists have approximately the same means. However, the Dogmatism mean of the extreme Rightists goes up considerable. Similarly, when moderate leftists and moderate rightists are compared on the scale for Censorship Tendency there is little difference. However, when extreme rightists and leftists are added, the difference becomes significant—primarily because the committed Rightists and Leftists censor rightists about equally, while only the committed Rightists censor leftists. (Table 3) General authoritarianism is more associated with rightist ideology than with leftist ideology, although not as significantly as is "pre-fascist tendency" (F scale).

The third hypothesis was that there is no relationship between authoritarianism and extremity of political position. Some writers (Alexander, 1951; Bonnard, 1954; Drake, 1955; Taylor, 1960) have postulated an identity of the extremists of the left and right, implying that rigid, intolerant, authoritarian attitudes would be more common among "radicals" of whatever political persuasion. The New York Study had shown no evidence in support of such an hypothesis. All of the Ohio State subjects who scored between 46 and 74 on

PEC were combined to test this hypothesis. There were 72 of these "moderates." The remaining 44 subjects were combined as the "extremists." The two groups were compared as to mean scores on all scales. There were *no* significant differences. The third hypothesis is supported. No relationship was found between authoritarianism *or* pre-fascist tendency and "political extremity" *per se*.

It is often implied in the press and popular literature that rigid, intolerant, authoritarian attitudes will be found more often among politically active, militant, committed persons than among less militant, presumably less emotionally involved and therefore more "rational" persons. The fourth hypothesis was that there is no relationship between authoritarianism and degree of political activity (organized vs. non-organized students). The Rightists and the Leftists in this study appear to merit the adjectives "active, militant, and committed," e.g., manning picket lines, planning elaborate programs to publicize their beliefs, turning out political handbills, fund raising, and lobbying both in the university and beyond. To test this hypothesis the combined Rightists and Leftists were compared to the non-organized students on all scales. There were no significant differences on any of the measures. The hypothesis is supported.

It has been established that in this study the political Right not only has many more high F's than the Left, as was expected, but also the Right has more general authoritarians as measured by Dogmatism. For a final analysis, the dogmatists and non-dogmatists in each political organization were compared. Taking a score of 150 as the cutting point on the Dogmatism scale, dogmatists comprised 17 percent of the Leftists, 28 percent of the non-organized students, had 35 percent of the Rightists. Due to the small numbers of subjects in this analysis, the following statements must be taken as suggestive only. The dogmatic Rightists do not differ from the non-dogmatic Rightists in the "extremeness" of their political position. The dogmatic Rightists censor more leftists than the non-dogmatic Rightists, and are higher on the F scale, especially those items indicating authoritarian aggression, tendency toward projectivity, and emphasis on power and toughness.

The dogmatic Leftists do not differ from the non-dogmatic Leftists in the "extremeness" of their political position. The dogmatic Leftists censor more rightists than the non-dogmatic Leftists, and are higher on the F scale, especially those items indicating authoritarian aggression, projectivity, and power and toughness (like the dogmatic Rightists).

The dogmatic Rightists score higher on the F scale than the dogmatic Leftists. On Censorship, an intriguing result was found here as well as in the New York study: Dogmatic Leftists censor only rightists, while dogmatic Rightists censor both leftists and rightists, thus receiving a higher total Censorship score.

DISCUSSION

Work in the area of the authoritarian personality has been going on now for about 15 years. Taking into account the material presented in Christie & Jahoda (1954), in the review of the F scale literature (Titus & Hollander, 1957), the work of Rokeach, and the studies reported here, let us consider what we have learned. The first thing we can say with confidence is that the concept of an authoritarian syndrome has proven to be viable and fruitful. The expected clustering of variables does occur across groups, across time, and across geographical areas. Despite the deserved criticism of the details of the original California study, their major concept has been confirmed. Let us examine seven broad questions as to what we have come to know about the concept. We will consider the questions in a descending order of certainty, i.e., about the first questions we have a great deal of evidence and relatively sure answers. About the later questions we know less and our answers must be more tentative.

1. What is the relation of general authoritarianism to the F scale? It appears to be clear now that the F scale measures rightist authoritarianism (implicit pre-fascist tendencies) primarily, general authoritarianism somewhat, and leftist authoritarianism not at all.

2. What is the relation of general authoritarianism to the

liberal-conservative continuum? Before answering this question a word needs to be said about the concept of a unitary left-right dimension. Despite the logically valid criticisms of the concept of such a continuum, the fact remains that such a continuum exists in the minds of the general public and they generally (with the exception of the highly sophisticated) place themselves on such a continuum quite easily and with certainty. As long as this is so, the dimension "exists," and not only *can* be used as a variable, but *should* be used as a variable. Now, to the question. It appears to be established that there is somewhat greater compatibility between authoritarian traits and rightist ideology than between authoritarianism and leftist ideology. However, the correlation of authoritarianism and conservatism is not nearly so strong as was thought immediately after the California studies when the only measure available was the F scale. We now can state with confidence that it is quite possible to discriminate authoritarians at any point on the political continuum.

3. What is the relation of general authoritarianism to extremity of political position? The evidence appears to be that there is no relation. One can find authoritarians equally among "moderates" and "radicals." However, this question needs to be checked with samples with more extreme political positions than we have yet studied.

4. What is the relation of general authoritarianism to degree of political militancy? The evidence so far is that there is no relationship. It looks as though one can find equal numbers of authoritarians among political "passives" and "actives." However, more study is needed on possible differences in authoritarianism between different kinds of militancy.

5. What similarities and differences are there between authoritarians of the right and left? They are similar in that both groups score relatively highly on all measures of authoritarian traits. They are different in several ways that we know of: First, the rightist authoritarians are a bit *more* authoritarian than the leftist authoritarians, and they compose a larger proportion of their political group. While the two groups are alike in being relatively intolerant of, and punitive toward, their perceived enemies, they differ, of course, in who they see as their enemies. The *direction* of their intolerance and

authoritarian aggression is different. Also, the authoritarian leftists appear to be more selective in their intolerance, e.g., they tend to censor only rightists. The rightists, on the other hand, tend to be less discriminating, e.g., they censor other rightists as well as leftists. In addition, the authoritarian rightists appear to be more submissive to authority, or at least to the usual authority in our society, than the authoritarian leftists.

6. What differences are there between leftist authoritarians and leftist non-authoritarians? There is very little evidence on this question. There is some indication that the authoritarian leftists are more intolerant and show more authoritarian aggression toward ideological opponents than the non-authoritarian leftists, e.g., tending to censor rightists whereas the non-authoritarian leftists do not.

7. What differences are there between rightist authoritarians and rightist non-authoritarians? As above, there is very little evidence on this question. It appears that the authoritarian rightists may be more motivated by generalized hostility than the non-authoritarian rightists, e.g., authoritarian rightists tend to censor more leftists *and* more rightists than the non-authoritarian rightists. These last two questions deserve far more study.

PART FIVE
PERSONALITY AND POLITICAL DYNAMICS

Introduction

So far we have been concerned with the relationship of personality to political roles and to political ideologies. Differences in roles and ideology often are related to a host of differences in political dynamics of various kind. Accordingly we now wish to extend our considerations of personality and politics to more concrete levels and dimensions of political behavior. We deal here primarily with overt action rather than with motives, norms, beliefs, and values—and we ask about the relationship of personality to various dynamics of political processes.

Much of the research on personality in terms of political dynamics has dealt with voting and electoral behavior, including in particular the role of personality in the preference and selection of candidates for political office. Lane (1955), for example, has shown that authoritarian personalities vote no more nor less than other people. On the other hand, Kornhauser and his associates (1956), in their study of American automobile workers, found that employees characterized by anomie showed little interest in politics, and that they were much less likely to vote than those not manifesting these characteristics. When these people did vote, moreover, they tended to do so in a manner that was contrary to the prevailing sentiment among their fellow workers.

In our first selection for this section, Janowitz and Marvick, reporting on two nationwide samples studied in terms of authoritarianism, show the link between authoritarianism and voting behavior, and other types of political action. Their findings reveal that authoritarian individuals, to a greater degree than their opposites, view themselves as politically inefficacious: they believe themselves to be powerless to effect, or to influence, governmental and other kinds of political action. Such self-conceptions on the part of the authoritarians undoubtedly explain the major finding of Janowitz and Marvick that authoritarian individuals participate in voting activities to a significantly less extent than their counterparts.[1]

Another kind of electoral dynamic which has received considerable attention in terms of its relationship to personality is the preference for, and selection of, political candidates, particularly in presidential elections. Several studies in this regard have been undertaken to assess the relationship of the personality of the voter to that of the candidates in various campaigns and elections.

The common thesis of these studies is that politicians differ in terms of the image which they present or project—however intentionally or unwittingly—to the public and that the voter selects his candidate in terms of the congruity of this projected personality with his own personality. Hence the conclusion is that voting behavior, as a fundamental political dynamic, may be, at least in part, a function of some measure of identification between the political elector and the political candidate.

The reports from several studies along these lines, however, have provided contradictory findings on the effects of "authoritarianism" on the choice of presidential candidates. In our second selection for this section, DiRenzo attempts to resolve some of the inconsistencies of these findings in terms of both theoretical specifications and methodological refinements.

---

[1] From a methodological perspective, Janowitz and Marvick show that measures of authoritarianism, specifically items from the F scale, are at least as good a single-factor explanation of political behavior as several non-personality variables that are frequently used for this purpose. For a study that confirms some of the observations which Janowitz and Marvick make in this regard, see Farris (1956).

One of the principal factors in regard to these theoretical improvements, especially one which relates to our repetitive contention that more analytically specific distinctions need to be made in research in the whole area of personality and politics, is that campaigns with different issues or themes, as advocated by different candidates, stimulate different elements in the personality of the voter, and that oftentimes there are little, if any, differences in the political and/or the psychological stimuli given off by the competing candidates. Hence crucial consideration needs to be given to the nature of the particular campaign and election, with their specific issues or themes, particularly in terms of the presence or absence of significant differences in these regards on the part of the various candidates.[2]

DiRenzo, reporting on an analysis of the 1964 presidential elections which involved a study of dogmatism, shows that voting behavior appears to be a function of some measure of personality congruity between the political electors and the political candidates, and that dogmatism has a much greater significant association with the choice of presidential candidates than with preferences for political parties, which themselves nonetheless show a highly significant association with the personality of the voter. Moreover, his work offers a new dimension, in terms of the principle of personality congruency, for the explanation of the political dynamics of "frontlash" (Republicans voting for the Democratic nominee) and "backlash" (Democrats voting for the Republican candidate). A replication of this study in the 1968 elections (see DiRenzo, 1971) offers further substantiation for the fundamental thesis which is advanced by DiRenzo, namely, that the acceptance and/or rejection of political candidates are, at least in part, functions of the congruence/incongruence between the personality structures of the political electorate and the implicit psychological image of the political candidate.[3]

[2] For an elaboration on the theoretical specification of the political situations and circumstances in which personality is and is not likely to play a significant role in electoral choice, see Lane (1955) and Christie and Nisbett (1965).

[3] For an alternative approach to this question of congruent relationship between the personality of the electorate and preferences

Variations in personality can be related to a host of other political dynamics, including decision-making on the specific level of concrete issues. In regard to this particular type of political dynamic, Mongar, in our third selection for this section, and one which is substantially biographical in nature, examines, "in purely hypothetical and impressionistic" terms, the impact of the imputed personality of John F. Kennedy on four crucial decisions during his presidential tenure: the Cuban missile crisis, the Bay of Pigs invasion, the Meredith integration case, and the steel pricing episode.

Mongar contends that in a situation that simultaneously challenges the will of a nation and the self-esteem of the decision-maker, the decision processes in the political system could easily become fused with the psychodynamic processes of the personality of the executive; and the resolution of a policy crisis under these circumstances could depend ultimately on the outcome of a personal, emotional crisis. In other words, political dynamics at the decision-making level could become fundamentally a matter of psychotherapy. For example, in reference to the Cuban missile crisis, Mongar argues—in terms somewhat reminiscent of Lasswell's thesis—that Kennedy's value choice was conceived as an attempt to restore his self-esteem rather than to correct an implausible disequilibrium in the nuclear balance of power.

Elsewhere (1967c) we have attempted to demonstrate the value that the relationships between personality structure and political parties and ideologies have for action within political systems in terms of fundamental questions of political consensus and political cleavage. Utilizing data on the Italian parliamentary system (DiRenzo, 1967a), we have attempted to demonstrate the role of personality congruence, on the basis of modal personality types, in the formation of political alliances and governmental coalitions within a given party system, and in defections or changes in political party membership or affiliation. These kinds of political dynamics, it appears, may be, at least in part, functions of similarities

---

for political candidates, see the work of Maccoby (1969) on "life-long orientation" versus "anti-life orientation" which provides a new dimension on authoritarian and democratic perspectives along the lines of the earlier work by Fromm (1941).

and differences in the underlying modal personality structures of the respective groups.

The crucial question in these kinds of political dynamics concerns the degree of variation and difference which may be tolerated without consensus giving way to cleavage. What is the tolerable level of variation within individual parties, and incongruence, on the basis of modal personality types, within political alliances and coalitions, that does not precipitate political cleavages in the forms of party defections or factions and unstable or dysfunctional coalitions or alliances?

Other political dynamics which, on the basis of our own work, reveal different patterns of association with variations in personality structure, and which appear to be predictable on the basis of the principle of personality congruence, are different orientations and involvements in sociopolitical change, and the use or advocacy of different techniques of political protest and varying methods of social reform (DiRenzo, 1970).

Much of what has been said, and implied here, as well as in the selections that follow, involves the fundamental thesis offered by Levinson (1959) that personality is instrumental in political behavior in that it facilitates the acceptance and/or the creation of political options that are personally meaningful, and the rejection of those political options which are similarly incompatible. When, however, a personally congenial mode of political activity is not readily available, and the individual cannot create one for himself, he may nominally accept an uncongenial form of political action without strong commitment or involvement. It is in this kind of political situation that the dynamics of personality and those of the political process are not likely to be engaged in any significantly congruent or mutually supportive interaction.

Once again, however, this assumption constitutes a hypothesis which, in the interests of enhancing the value of personality as at least a partial explanation for political behavior, requires extensive empirical investigation, designed to provide a greater delimitation, and more precise analysis, of the many different kinds of political dynamics and situations in which personality phenomena may be at work.

Authoritarianism and Political Behavior
Morris Janowitz and Dwaine Marvick

In common sense language, the authoritarian is the individual who is concerned with power and toughness and who is prone to resolve conflict in an arbitrary manner. He is seen as having strong and persistent desires that others submit to his outlook. Social psychology in recent years has added the observation that the authoritarian person has another powerful desire of which he is not fully aware. He himself desires to submit to other individuals whom he sees as more powerful.

The predisposition of the authoritarian individual to conform to an "authority" is directly relevant to the study of political behavior in a democratic society. The "F" scale developed by the "Berkeley group" was designed specifically as a personality scale to identify "anti-democratic" individuals in a population (Adorno, 1950). Any reliable and valid method of analysis of such personality variables is of crucial importance in the study of political propaganda impact, the effectiveness of campaign arguments and appeals, the conditions under which political protest movements are likely to attract support, and a host of similar problems.

This paper reports the findings of an attempt to investigate (a) the extent of the authoritarian predispositions in two nation-wide samples and (b) the link between such predisposi-

Reprinted by permission of the authors and the publisher from *The Public Opinion Quarterly*, Volume 17, 1953, pp. 185–201.

tions and certain types of political behavior and attitudes. In the light of our present knowledge and research techniques, it is neither necessary nor feasible to postulate that we are concerned with authoritarian "personality." To talk about personality implies a comprehensive understanding of the life development of an individual's emotions. Instead, authoritarianism can be seen as a characteristic psychological reaction pattern to a wide variety of social situations. Since it is a characteristic reaction pattern of which the individual is not completely aware, only indirect approaches serve to reveal its presence.

Research into political behavior need not concern itself with all of the nine key dimensions which the Berkeley group included in the concept of authoritarianism.[1] In fact, two dimensions seem most directly relevant to political behavior research. One is "authoritarian submission," a tendency in an individual to adopt an uncritical and submissive attitude toward the moral authorities that are idealized by his ingroup. The other dimension is "power and toughness," a preoccupation with considerations of strength and weakness, domination and subservience, superiority and inferiority. The authoritarian scale reported in this paper is designed especially to tap these two dimensions whereas the "F" scale of the Berkeley group sought to tap a fuller range.

It should be recalled that, in the population which they studied, the Berkeley group found significant correlations between high authoritarianism and both anti-semitism and ethnocentrism. At the same time, they found that the authoritarian syndrome had only a moderately close relation to political-economic conservatism. In part, this may have been due

---

[1] The other key dimensions in the authoritarian syndrome are: conventionalism, authoritarian aggression, anti-intraception, superstition and stereotypy, destructiveness and cynicism, projectivity, and exaggerated concern with sex. Cf. Adorno (1950:228–229).

Individuals displaying a number of these characteristics in pronounced fashion were defined as highly authoritarian. The anti-democratic "F" scale was constructed as an instrument for tapping these deep-seated responses. This was accomplished by a series of attitude questions involving moral values and interpersonal relationships but without any specific political content.

to the conception of politics on which they based their scale of liberalism-conservatism. Their scale did not permit a distinction between "conservatives" and "reactionaries," nor a distinction between "liberals" and "radicals."[2] The authoritarian predispositions would seem to be more closely linked with the reactionary and radical positions than with an overall ideological continuum from liberalism to conservatism.

However, the approach of this paper was based on the assumption that authoritarianism would be (a) more relevant for explaining political participation and feelings of self-confidence about politics, and (b) less relevant for explaining specific political attitudes and preferences. The hypothesis was investigated that high authoritarians would tend to participate less and have less political self-confidence than low authoritarians in politics as presently organized. In order to understand how authoritarianism might be related to specific political attitudes and preferences, however, it was necessary to assume that the social origins of authoritarianism would differ for specific social groupings in the total population. Only by analyzing these social groupings individually would it be possible to relate adequately authoritarianism to specific political preferences and attitudes.

RESEARCH DESIGN

In seeking to clarify the relationship between such authoritarian traits and political behavior, the methods used by those interested in spelling out the nature of authoritarianism cannot readily be employed. If the problem is how to gain intensive access to individuals in order to chart in detail their authoritarian tendencies, the representativeness of the groups studied does not matter. In fact, for such research, representative cross sections are not likely to be studied.

In general, only the neurotic, the mentally disturbed, and specialized groups of students have made themselves available for prolonged psychological testing. Although the research of

[2] That the Berkeley group was aware of this problem is shown by their distinction between genuine conservatism and pseudo-conservatism, in their interpretative sections.

the Berkeley group achieved greater representativeness than usual, even there the samples examined were admittedly limited and self-selected.

Findings from their samples can hardly form the basis for a description of where in the American social structure authoritarian traits tend to predominate. Only by developing an instrument that might be administered through nation-wide surveys could more representative populations be investigated. This implied modifying the original "F" scale to make it suitable for inclusion in a typical attitude survey.

A battery of questions designed to measure authoritarianism had been developed by Fillmore Sanford (1950) for inclusion in an attitude survey in the Philadelphia area. Most of the items for this personality scale were selected from the long battery of the Berkeley "F" scale and modified. Since one of these items was subsequently discarded as manifestly making no contribution to the scale, the personality scale analyzed in this paper is based on six questions in the form developed by Sanford.[3]

[3] The wording of Sanford's statement is as follows: (a) Human nature being what it is, there will always be war and conflict; (b) A few strong leaders could make this country better than all the laws and talk; (c) Women should stay out of politics; (d) Most people who don't get ahead just don't have enough will power; (e) An insult to your honor should not be forgotten; and, with the responses scored inversely, (f) People can be trusted. Respondents were asked to agree or disagree and then permitted to state the intensity of their attitude. Thus a six point, Likert-type scale was obtained for each question.

These items are roughly comparable to the following Berkeley "F" scale items: (a) Human nature being what it is, there will always be war and conflict; (b) What this country needs most, more than laws and political programs, is a few courageous, tireless, devoted leaders in whom the people can put their faith; (c) No weakness or difficulty can hold us back if we have enough will power; (d) An insult to our honor should always be punished.

For the remaining items on Sanford's scale, no close analogue can be found in the Berkeley list, except for the following Berkeley item which parallels a Sanford question omitted by us in making the present scale: Obedience and respect for authority are the most important virtues children should learn. We discarded this measure because over 86% of our population gave at least some agreement with it.

In particular, these questions measure tendencies to respond to ambiguous social reality in terms that reveal attitudes of authoritarian submission and preoccupation with power and toughness. Drawing upon the theories of dynamic psychology, we assume that projective-like questions are likely to reveal underlying psychological reactions of which the individual is not aware. The greater the tendency for an individual to agree with the ambiguous slogans and stereotyped sentiments in the attitude scale, the more authoritarian he is said to be.

Since 1945, the University of Michigan Survey Research Center has conducted a series of nation-wide surveys of public opinion on American foreign policy. In November 1949, the sixth of these studies took place. In May 1950, additional information was gathered by reinterviewing a sub-sample (58 per cent) of the group first interviewed in the previous November.[4] On this sub-sample, responses of 341 persons to Sanford's simplified battery of questions measuring authoritarian tendencies were gathered.[5] In another survey conducted by the Survey Research Center, at about the same time and largely concerned with economic attitudes,[6] the same battery of questions was included. Thus, in establishing the incident of authoritarian tendencies for differ-

---

[4] Cf. "American's Role in World Affairs: Patterns of Citizen Opinion, 1949–50." (Survey Research Center, University of Michigan, 1952, mimeographed.) This survey was directed by Burton R. Fisher, George Belknap and Charles A. Metzner.

[5] The Survey Research Center, in conducting nation-wide surveys, employs a cross-sectional, area probability sample design with carefully controlled selection procedures. In both the November and May surveys such sampling controls were used, with an additional criterion introduced for the May sub-sample: only that portion of the original sample which scored "consistently" on a scale of intervention-isolation attitudes toward Europe was eligible for the May reinterviewing. Although a nation-wide sample was obtained, it was not necessarily a fully representative sample.

[6] Cf. Big Business from the Viewpoint of the Public. (Ann Arbor, Michigan: Survey Research Center, University of Michigan, 1951.) This survey was directed by Stephen Withey and Ivan Steiner. The sample for this study was both nation-wide and representative.

ent social groups, a replicating group of 1227 cases was available. It is of central importance that in every single relevant social relationship the findings based on the second sample population confirmed the conclusions based on the first sample population—the political attitude survey sample.

In both samples, each of the six questions elicited a wide range of responses. Conveniently, enough persons consistently agreed and enough consistently disagreed with the slogans about which they were questioned to permit division of the population into three groups of approximately equal size, without "watering down" the extremist groups.[7] Thus a low authoritarian group was distinguished at one extreme, each member of which disagreed with at least four of the six slogans. A high authoritarian group was distinguished at the other extreme, each member of which agreed with at least four of the six. Finally, the intermediate group that remained was made up of persons none of whom either agreed or disagreed with more than four of the six items in the index.[8]

[7] We used the six questions as a composite battery measuring "authoritarian tendencies" in both primary and secondary relationships. Three of the questions constitute what seems to be a "primary relations" authoritarianism index; none of these three makes *explicit* reference to a social context and all three suggest situations involving a face-to-face evaluation. The other three questions constitute what appears to be a "secondary relations" authoritarianism index; each of these three makes explicit reference to situations involving secondary social institutions.

Using the political attitude survey sample, the distribution of responses from strong agreement to strong disagreement on the two sub-indexes proved to be much alike. An analysis was made to ascertain whether or not the social characteristics (age, education, occupation, income, religion) of persons classed as "authoritarian" on the primary relations sub-index differed from the characteristics of those classed as authoritarian on the secondary relations sub-index. No important differences were found.

[8] Our requirements for classification in one of the extreme categories are more rigorous than this summary statement might suggest. Two criteria were used: cumulative score on all six questions, and ratio of agree to disagree responses. Numerical equivalents from 1 to 6 were assigned to responses ranging from strong agreement to strong disagreement. A low cumulative score for all six responses—a score of less than 19—was necessary in order to be classed as a high authoritarian while a high cumulative score—a score of at least 25—was necessary for classification as low au-

This mode of analysis permits us to characterize an important predisposition in roughly one fourth of the adult population of the nation. Authoritarianism in these relative terms does not, therefore, refer to a marginal extremist group. The quarter of our nationwide samples classified as highly authoritarian is of crucial importance and direct relevance for understanding Amercan political behavior.

TABLE 1
DISTRIBUTION OF AUTHORITARIANISM

	Political Survey		Replication Survey		Total	
	No.	%	No.	%	No.	%
High Authoritarian	107	32	262	23	369	25
Intermediate	117	34	437	39	554	38
Low Authoritarian	117	34	430	38	547	37
	341	100	1129	100	1470	100

SOCIAL PROFILE OF THE AUTHORITARIAN

Before relating personality traits to political behavior, it seems necessary to attempt to locate where in the social structure the authoritarian individuals are concentrated. What is the social setting in which the anti-democratic personality is most likely to be found?

In the Berkeley research, either subjects or the voluntary associations through which they were recruited had to be persuaded to submit to investigation. "Save for a few key groups, the subjects were drawn almost exclusively from the

---

thoritarian. The intermediate group thus included persons whose scores ranged from 19 through 24. To be classed as low authoritarian, it was not enough to have disagreed with at least four of the six items; it was also necessary that the four disagreements be "strong" enough to yield a cumulative score of 25 or more when taken together with the two agreement responses. Similarly, to be classed as high authoritarian, both criteria had to be met: at least four agreement responses, and a cumulative score of less than 19. In the political survey sample, only six cases meeting the ratio of 4:2 failed to qualify for extreme classification because the cumulative score criterion was not met; in the replication survey sample, only the cumulative score criterion was applied.

middle socio-economic class."[9] As such, little could be said by them about the manner in which authoritarian tendencies would vary with age, education, or socio-economic class. Our more representative cross section of the American population makes it possible for these points to be investigated somewhat more adequately.

Age, education, occupation, and income emerge as key sociological indicators locating the authoritarian in American society[10] (see Table 2).

First, there was a statistically significant tendency for younger people to register as "low authoritarians" more frequently than older people.[11] Also a clear and significant relationship between education and authoritarian tendencies emerged. Those with limited education tend more frequently to be high authoritarians while those with fuller education tend to be low authoritarians (see Table 2). These two findings are in line with the implications of the Berkeley group, and are what one would expect.

However, we did not find that middle class persons are the main carriers of authoritarianism.[12] The data from our samples suggest that middle class persons were no more authoritarian than lower class persons. In fact, what differences were found indicated that high authoritarianism occurs more frequently in the lower class. Likewise, the middle class displayed

[9] Adorno (1950:23). The Berkeley group administered questionnaires to a total of 2,099 persons, the great majority of whom lived in San Francisco, with smaller groups sampled in Oregon and in the area around Los Angeles. Their population also included about as many college graduates as persons who had not completed high school. Moreover, the great majority were young people, ranging in age from 20 to 35. For the purpose of validation, approximately 100 subjects were given clinical interviews.

[10] For all analysis, Negroes and Jews were removed from the political survey sample, since they are the objects of much antidemocratic sentiment and constitute a special analytical problem. Negroes were also removed from the replication survey sample, but it was not possible to identify Jews for this population.

[11] Except where otherwise noted, all differences which are reported as statistically significant are at the one per cent level of confidence.

[12] In this respect, our findings closely support conclusions reached in the companion research to *The Authoritarian Personality,* namely, *The Dynamics of Prejudice,* by Bettelheim and Janowitz (1950).

TABLE 2
SOCIAL CORRELATES OF AUTHORITARIANISM

Age	Political Survey Sample Under 45	45 or Older	Replication Survey Sample Under 50	50 or Older	Composite Sample Younger People	Older People
High Authoritarian	31%	36%	21%	26%	24%	28%
Intermediate	30	37	38	41	36	40
Low Authoritarian	39	27	41	33	40	32
	100	100	100	100	100	100
Number of Cases:	(189)	(126)	(679)	(379)	(868)	(505)
Education*	Limited Education	Fuller Education	Limited Education	Fuller Education	Limited Education	Fuller Education
High Authoritarian	42%	23%	25%	18%	28%	20%
Intermediate	33	33	40	36	39	35
Low Authoritarian	25	44	35	46	33	45
	100	100	100	100	100	100
Number of Cases:	(168)	(147)	(803)	(326)	(971)	(473)

* In the political survey, limited education means less than four years of high school; in the replication survey, a slightly different definition was necessary, viz., not more than four years of high school. Correspondingly, in the political survey, fuller education means at least high school graduation while in the replication survey it means more than high school graduation.

Social Economic Class**	Lower Class	Middle Class	Lower Class	Middle Class	Lower Class	Middle Class
High Authoritarian	35%	26%	26%	20%	28%	21%
Intermediate	37	29	37	36	37	35
Low Authoritarian	28	45	37	44	35	44
	100	100	100	100	100	100
Number of Cases:	(133)	(122)	(436)	(413)	(567)	(535)

** In both surveys, by middle class is meant those persons engaged in non-manual occupations and by lower class those engaged in manual occupations. Farmers were excluded from this analysis.

a significantly greater concentration of individuals with low authoritarian scores than did the lower class[13] (see Table 2).

Next we attempted to locate more precisely the authoritarian by considering income differences within class strata. Both the middle and the lower class were subdivided into upper and lower income groups, thereby delineating four socioeconomic strata.[14] From the data, it emerges that within the middle class the lower income group was considerably more vulnerable to authoritarianism than the upper income middle class group. This finding is in line with many contemporary studies of social stratification that point to the lower middle class as being particularly susceptible to authoritarianism because of their thwarted aspirations. Political scientists have often noted that extremist movements tend to attract such lower middle class authoritarians. As far as the lower class is concerned, there too the lower income group displayed more authoritarianism than the more advantageously situated upper lower class group. However, the difference was not as striking as that found between the upper and lower middle class (see Table 3).[15]

TABLE 3
AUTHORITARIANISM BY CLASS AND INCOME LEVEL

Combined Samples:	Lower Class		Middle Class	
	Lower Income	Upper Income	Lower Income	Upper Income
High Authoritarian	32%	24%	34%	18%
Intermediate	36	39	29	37
Low Authoritarian	32	37	37	45
	100	100	100	100
Number of Cases:	(253)	(319)	(130)	(395)

The question now emerges: was the lower middle class the most authoritarian of all the socio-economic groups? The answer is that the lower lower class was almost as authoritarian.

[13] In the replication survey, the difference is significant at the five per cent level.
[14] By lower income is meant less than $3,000 a year and by upper income is meant at least $3,000 a year.
[15] All of the findings reported for the combined samples in Tables No. 3, 4, 5, 6 were also significant for each of the nation-wide samples taken separately.

It might be argued that because the lower middle class presumably includes more people who are politically articulate, the incident of authoritarianism in that group is more serious to the stability of American political life.

Since in actuality these sociological correlates do not work independently, the next step is to ascertain whether combinations of them have a particular tendency to produce authoritarianism. Although many more variables need to be investigated, one important pattern seems to emerge. The social circumstances that condition authoritarianism seem to differ for different social classes. Age and education as correlates of authoritarianism appear to have a different significance for middle class and lower class people.

a. We have seen that age by itself was related to authoritarian tendencies; likewise that social class was related to authoritarianism. Within classes, however, age does not significantly affect authoritarianism. Only between classes is age significant. The older group in the lower class is significantly more authoritarian than the younger middle class group.[16] In fact, reading across the table, a consistent increase in authoritarianism emerges. It seems reasonable to interpret these data as indicating that old age to a lower class person maximizes the social insecurity and frustration which presumably encourage authoritarian tendencies while youth to a middle class person minimizes this predisposition (see Table 4).

TABLE 4

AUTHORITARIANISM BY CLASS AND AGE

Combined Samples:	Middle Class		Lower Class	
	Younger	Older	Younger	Older
High Authoritarian	20%	25%	28%	30%
Intermediate	35	36	33	37
Low Authoritarian	45	39	39	33
	100	100	100	100
Number of Cases:	(343)	(167)	(371)	(171)

b. In a similar way educational status by itself was related to authoritarianism, just as was age. Yet the link between education and authoritarianism is clarified by comparing

[16] Significant at the 5 per cent level.

people of different age groups with comparable educational status. The younger group with fuller education has a significantly lower concentration of high authoritarians than the older group with full education. On the other hand, despite the advantage of their youth, younger people with limited education display authoritarian tendencies significantly more often than younger people with fuller education. To older people, lack of education does not appear to be a significant factor encouraging authoritarian tendencies (see Table 5).

c. Again, the link between authoritarianism and educational status emerges as operating differently for the lower and middle classes. For the middle class, fuller education brings about a significant drop in the level of authoritarianism while for the lower class more education appears to have no significant effect on authoritarian tendencies. There can be little doubt that we are measuring more than formal educational training here. The educational system operates as part of the status system. In achieving the desired values and aspirations of American society, lack of education is obviously a disability in the middle class whereas it seems to make little difference in the lower class (see Table 6).

TABLE 5

AUTHORITARIANISM BY AGE AND EDUCATIONAL STATUS

Combined Samples:	Younger People		Older People	
	Limited Education	Fuller Education	Limited Education	Fuller Education
High Authoritarian	29%	16%	27%	31%
Intermediate	37	35	42	35
Low Authoritarian	34	49	31	34
	100	100	100	100
Number of Cases:	(540)	(342)	(400)	(127)

TABLE 6

AUTHORITARIANISM BY CLASS AND EDUCATIONAL STATUS

Combined Samples:	Lower Class		Middle Class	
	Limited Education	Fuller Education	Limited Education	Fuller Education
High Authoritarian	28%	31%	31%	16%
Intermediate	36	28	35	35
Low Authoritarian	36	41	34	49
	100	100	100	100
Number of cases:	(446)	(96)	(220)	(290)

d. Finally, when educational status is considered in connection with a detailed breakdown of class strata, the social incidence of authoritarianism is thrown into sharper relief.[17] We were able to compare the incidence of authoritarianism in "advantageously situated" social groups and in "disadvantageously situated" groups. Limiting ourselves to those groups with the lowest and the highest concentrations of authoritarianism, we found that the lowest concentration of authoritarianism was in the well-educated upper middle class group. This was true for both samples. For the combined samples, only 13 per cent of such persons were highly authoritarian. On the other hand, and again for both samples, the highest concentration of authoritarianism appeared in two groups: the poorly educated lower lower class, where 33 per cent of the combined samples were highly authoritarian; and the poorly educated lower middle class, where 39 per cent of the combined samples were highly authoritarian (see Table 7).

First, let us compare the lowest authoritarian group—the well-educated upper middle class—with the poorly educated lower-lower class. This is a comparison that cuts across class lines. It juxtaposes that portion of the middle class that is most advantageously situated against the group in the lower class that is most disadvantageously situated.

Authoritarianism in these terms is clearly and significantly linked to those social and economic class cleavages which have long been recognized by political scientists as pervasively affecting American politics.

Second, let us compare the least authoritarian group—the well-educated upper middle class—with the poorly educated lower middle class group. This is a comparison within the middle class; the differences in authoritarian tendencies found were at least as great as the comparison was across class lines. One explanation could be that frustrated social mobility, thwarted status aspirations and inadequate purchasing power appear to produce in the poorly educated lower mid-

---

[17] The detailed breakdown of class strata involved dividing both the lower and the middle class groups by level of income, as previously indicated. Thus we have four strata: upper middle, lower middle, upper lower, and lower lower.

TABLE 7

INCIDENCE OF AUTHORITARIANISM BY SOCIAL GROUPINGS

Combined Samples	Well-Educated Upper Middle Class	Poorly Educated Lower Lower Class	Poorly Educated Lower Middle Class
High Authoritarian	13%	33%	39%
Intermediate	36	36	32
Low Authoritarian	51	31	29
	100	100	100
Number of Cases:	(236)	(224)	(75)
Political Survey Only			
High Authoritarian	17%	42%	67%
Intermediate	30	27	22
Low Authoritarian	53	31	11
	100	100	100
Number of Cases:	(60)	(45)	(18)
Replication Survey Only			
High Authoritarian	12%	31%	30%
Intermediate	39	38	35
Low Authoritarian	49	31	35
	100	100	100
Number of Cases:	(176)	(179)	(57)

dle class the highest incidence of authoritarianism in any social group. Within this group, too, it seems likely that there are upwardly mobile individuals from the lower class whose adult psychological responses are linked to the problems they face of ridding themselves of values acquired previously and incorporating the values of their new middle class position.

We cannot explain why particular sets of social circumstances prove to be conducive to authoritarianism. It is hardly a simple matter of economic insecurity; on the other hand, it is clearly not frustration *per se* in a strictly psychological sense. Modern society apparently needs to be viewed in terms which interrelate functionally its various strata and status segments. There is no need either to single out the personality syndrome of authoritarianism or to point to the frustrating social circumstances in an effort to determine the cause. Our data in any case do not permit making such a refined judgment. The social and psychological elements of which the "authoritarian response pattern" is composed stand in mutual interdependence. A consistent pattern of authoritarian responses is then seen as a mode for the release of tensions created in persons who have accepted the goals of our society but who find it difficult to adapt to the democratic processes by which they are achieved.

The data from our political survey reveal the social profile of the authoritarian. These data, confirmed in every respect by the replication survey, help to identify the different social groups who display the highest concentration of this response pattern. On the basis of this social profile one can analyze the authoritarian's response to politics.

POLITICAL PERSPECTIVE OF THE AUTHORITARIAN

Although a voter's view of a particular candidate may involve considerations that are both particularized and transitory, his attitudes toward "politics" are more likely to reflect his inner self. For example, participation in the political life of a democratic nation—even the minimum participation of voting—is both an expression of self-confidence and a calculation of self-interest. These facets of the individual are as deeply rooted in his personality as any syndrome of authoritarianism. This is what was encountered. Authoritarianism operated to condition a person's basic approach to politics as well as his general political attitudes.

Attitudes toward American foreign policy will illustrate the matter. Are persons who were generally isolationist in attitudes toward American relations with Europe more authoritarian than those persons who had a generally interventionist attitude? A series of questions were asked: Should we give the European countries money? Should we give them arms? And, strongest of all, should we aid them if they are threatened? Answers to these questions scaled well and served to distinguish isolationist proclivities from interventionist ones.

Although a significant link was found between authoritarianism and isolationism, the data confirm the frequently made observation that the isolationist is by no means always the "reactionary." Only that minority of the isolationists characterized by high authoritarianism seem appropriately classifiable as "reactionaries" (see Table 8).[18] Thirty-two individuals or less than one tenth of the total sample fell into the category of high authoritarian and generally isolationist. These individuals correspond to the "reactionaries" in terms of general political usage.[19]

TABLE 8
AUTHORITARIANISM AND ISOLATIONISM

	High Authoritarian	Intermediate	Low Authoritarian
Generally Isolationist	45%	34%	22%
Generally Interventionist	55	66	78
	100	100	100
Number of Cases:	(71)	(82)	(81)

Another type of question investigated was whether a person felt himself powerless in influencing government action, and what he thought could be done by groups he belonged to. Since these questions seek to tap basic political orientations, it is of high importance for political behavior research to note that authoritarianism is significantly and directly related to feelings of political ineffectiveness (see Table 9).

TABLE 9
AUTHORITARIANISM AND ATTITUDES OF POLITICAL EFFECTIVENESS

	High Authoritarian	Intermediate	Low Authoritarian
Believes Influence Is Impossible	63%	59%	41%
Believes Influence Is Possible	37	41	59
	100	100	100
Number of Cases:	(90)	(96)	(99)

[18] Cf. "America's Role in World Affairs: Patterns of Citizen Opinion, 1949–1950" (Fisher et al. 1952:156–159).
[19] Political isolation again was associated with authoritarian tendencies when the question was whether America should admit at least some of Europe's war refugees.

Perhaps the most crucial relation was found between authoritarian tendencies and voting behavior. The findings furnish a meaningful glimpse into certain dynamics of the political process. So far as the 1948 presidential election was concerned the authoritarian syndrome was less relevant in explaining party preference among those who voted than it was in predicting non-voting. Party preference involves not only the voter's basic approach to politics but a number of particular considerations about the issues and candidates as well. On the other hand, non-voting was expected to be closely linked to authoritarianism since authoritarianism was postulated to be an expression both of thwarted self-interest and lack of self-confidence. These are the two underlying facets of individual personality—self-interest and self-confidence—that receive expression partly through participation in the political processes.

In fact, in 1948 individuals with high authoritarian scores did vote significantly less than the rest of the population. Nevertheless, among those who did vote, the incidence of high authoritarianism was in no way significantly linked either to the Truman vote or the Dewey vote[20] (see Table 10).

TABLE 10

AUTHORITARIANISM AND VOTING BEHAVIOR

	Did you vote in 1948?		For whom did you vote?	
	Voters	Non-Voters	Truman	Dewey
High Authoritarian	25%	40%	26%	26%
Intermediate	40	27	33	47
Low Authoritarian	35	33	41	27
	100	100	100	100
Number of Cases:	(199)	(92)	(190)	(81)

[20] The incidence of low authoritarianism, on the other hand, was significantly related to a preference for Truman. By itself this relationship is difficult to explain and assumed significance only through more elaborate analysis. Methodologically, this table illustrates rather well the advantage of treating "high authoritarian" and "low authoritarian" groups separately, with "intermediates" in between. Had we worked with mean levels of authoritarianism, as in the previous research on this subject, differences due to the presence of many high authoritarians could not be distinguished from differences due to the absence of low authoritarians.

Another way of demonstrating the link between authoritarianism and non-voting emerges if the social groups in the population which were characterized either by very high or very low authoritarianism are examined. The well-educated upper middle class had the lowest incidence of authoritarianism, only 17 per cent in the political survey sample; this is the group with only 20 per cent non-voters. On the other hand, the poorly-educated groups in the lower middle class and lower lower class had the highest incidences of authoritarianism, 67 per cent and 42 per cent respectively in the political survey sample; each of these groups had at least 55 per cent non-voters.

For the nation-wide sample as a whole, authoritarianism helped very little to explain candidate preference in the 1948 presidential election. But for the three specific groups having the highest and the lowest incidences of authoritarianism, an important inference emerges. When we compared the two middle class groups with high and low authoritarianism respectively, the same proportions voted for Dewey and for Truman. On the other hand, those who did vote in the other highly authoritarian group—the poorly-educated lower lower class—voted overwhelmingly for Truman[21] (see Table 11).

Support of the "liberal" policies of the Fair Deal was not incompatible with authoritarian tendencies in the lower lower class. On the other hand, neither Dewey nor Truman in 1948 presented a program overwhelmingly appealing to the disadvantageously placed persons in the middle class.[22] Since in 1952 the campaign issues were related as much to the tensions generated by external threats to national security as

[21] This difference is significant at the one per cent level of confidence.

[22] These data suggest the hypothesis that personality reactions to "politics" are manifested not merely in the choice between participation or non-participation, but also depend upon the meaningfulness to the individual of the available political alternatives. In the 1948 election, both highly authoritarian groups—those in relatively disadvantageous circumstances manifested a similar lack of participation. But the available political alternatives, emphasizing as they did socio-economic cleavages, led those in the lower lower class who did vote to an overwhelming preference for Truman.

to socio-economic cleavages, the link between authoritarianism and political behavior seems certain to have changed. These changes are being investigated by the University of Michigan Survey Research Center.

TABLE 11
CANDIDATE PREFERENCE BY SOCIAL GROUPS

	Well-Educated Upper Middle Class	Poorly Educated Lower Middle Class	Poorly Educated Lower Lower Class
Voted for Truman	40%	22%	31%
Voted for Dewey	40	22	9
Non-voters	20	56	60
	100	100	100
Number of Cases:	(60)	(18)	(45)

In summary, the application to nation-wide samples of the techniques used in this study indicates the feasibility of considering personality tendencies as dimensions of American political behavior. At least three conclusions underline the desirability of continued study of these personality tendencies in different political situations: (a) Personality tendencies measured by authoritarian scale served to explain political behavior at least as well as those other factors traditionally included in political and voting behavior studies (age, education, class); (b) It was possible to locate in the national population a number of social groupings characterized by very high and very low authoritarian reactions. The social origins of authoritarianism, however, varied for different classes and status groups; (c) The incidence of authoritarianism not only was significantly related to political isolationism and to feelings of political ineffectiveness, but also to non-voting. Authoritarianism was helpful in explaining candidate preferences.

Dogmatism and Presidential Preferences in the 1964 Elections
Gordon J. DiRenzo

The thesis has been frequently advanced that politicians differ in the public image which they present and that individuals who score relatively high on measures of authoritarianism will be attracted to those candidates who either are authoritarian in personality structure or are so perceived. Studies on the relationship between authoritarianism and preferences for presidential candidates, however, have yielded contradictory results. Williams and Wright (1955) showed that the F syndrome was unrelated to the choice of presidential candidates in the 1948 national elections, and Paul (1956) found no relationship between authoritarianism scores of undergraduates and their choice of presidential candidates immediately prior to the 1952 elections. On the other hand, Milton's study (1952) of college students' preferences of the 1952 convention candidates (MacArthur and Taft) of the Republican party and Wrightsman, *et al.*'s (1961) of undergraduates in the 1960 elections revealed significant relationships between presidential preferences and F scale scores.

How are these contradictory results to be explained? In the light of the considerable number of behavioral studies which have demonstrated an intimate relationship between authoritarianism and political behavior of various forms (see DiRenzo, 1967b), I submit that these inconsistencies may be

Reprinted by permission of the publisher from *Psychological Reports,* Volume 22, 1968, pp. 1197–1202.

explained in part by the fact that in some instances (studies and elections) the particular political issues and candidates involved did not offer sufficiently specific and differentiated stimuli to permit a significant interaction of the analytical variables. Other questions may be raised about the methodological apparatus (specifically, the personality inventory) and its underlying conceptual structures, as well as the specific type of subjects, namely use of undergraduate students who do not represent voting-age citizens.

This study proposes some clarification of these substantive and methodological problems by certain improvements aimed at a greater specification of the political stimuli (issues and candidates) and a refinement of the measuring instruments. The first of these improvements was made possible in part by the "clear choice" which the candidates in the 1964 election offered in terms of ideological polarity.

METHOD

Conceptual Orientation

The focus of the personality element in this study is on the conceptual orientation of dogmatism which has been offered by Rokeach (1954, 1960) as an alternative approach to that of *The Authoritarian Personality* (Adorno, *et al.*, 1950). Rokeach (1960) has made a conceptual distinction which allows for different kinds of authoritarianism by avoiding reference to the specific or substantive content of authoritarian ideologies and by concentrating instead on formal content, that is, what they seem to share in common, and, even more particularly, by concentrating on the *structural* properties common to various authoritarian ideologies. With the concept of dogmatism Rokeach is concerned essentially with the organization of belief systems and more especially with what he calls the openness and closedness of belief systems. Dogmatism is defined as "a relatively closed cognitive organization of beliefs and disbeliefs about reality, organized around a central set of beliefs about absolute authority which, in turn, provides a framework for patterns of intolerance and qualified tolerance toward others" (Rokeach, 1954:195). The intention, therefore, is to delineate that personality structure which is associated with opened and closed belief systems respectively, that is, the extent to which an individual's belief systems are prone to accept or to reject others (Rokeach, 1960:19). Rokeach describes the closed-minded individual as one who has a closed or dogmatic way of thinking about any ideology regardless of its content, is rigid in regard to opinions and beliefs, makes an uncritical acceptance of authority, rejects those who disagree with him, and makes a qualified acceptance of those who agree. Thus it is not so much *what* one believes as *how* one believes that distinguishes the dogmatic personality structure.

Subjects

In October, 1964, a quota sample of 144 voting-age male undergraduates in a small, private Eastern University was administered Form E (complete version) of the Rokeach Dogmatism Scale as part of an interview schedule concerned with interest and activity in the presidential campaign and the forthcoming election. Only 38 (26%) of this sample were not registered voters. Of the 106 subjects who were registered voters, all but 8 either voted (by absentee ballot) or intended to vote in the election. The entire sample, moreover, had an extremely strong interest in the election as revealed by the fact that on a measurement of this variable utilizing a five-point Likert-type scale the mean response was 4.3.

Directions for answering the Dogmatism Scale were basically the same as those used by Rokeach (1960) in his original work; however, the dogmatism scores were computed on a positive or negative basis within a possible score range of -120 to $+120$.

Hypothesis

The general hypothesis was that dogmatism is significantly and differentially associated with political ideology and party preferences, but that—in part because of this association—a more precise interaction of the dogmatism syndrome exists in terms of more specific preferences for particular political candidates. Our specific hypothesis is that there is a significant association between the dogmatic personality structure and preferences for the Republican party, and an even greater significant association between preferences for the Republican presidential candidate; corresponding associations are hypothesized between non-dogmatic personality structures and preferences for the Democratic party and its presidential candidate.

RESULTS

Although the general thesis of the study is upheld, our hypothesis is substantiated only in part. A number of studies (see Rokeach, 1960; DiRenzo, 1967a; McClosky, 1958) have shown that support for conservative doctrines is highly correlated with authoritarian personality patterns. Our findings do not confirm these results insofar as Republicans are more likely to be neither dogmatic nor non-dogmatic in personality structure; but, on the other hand, the data suggest that Democrats are significantly distinguished by non-dogmatic personality scorers as a modal type. As may be seen in Table 1, the chi-square distribution is statistically significant at the .05 level. These findings are consistent with those of a

TABLE 1

PERSONALITY STRUCTURE AND POLITICAL PARTY PREFERENCE

Party Preference	Non-dogmatic Scorers	Dogmatic Scorers	Total
Democrats	66	25	91
Republicans	16	16	32
Total	82	41	123

$$\chi^2 = 5.11,\ df = 1,\ p < .05.$$

similar but unpublished study utilizing a large random sample selection of the same university population (DiRenzo, 1965).

The principal hypothesis was that the interaction of dogmatism and presidential preferences, notwithstanding the correlation with party preferences, is of much greater magnitude. It is assumed that some Democrats would prefer Goldwater and that some Republicans would prefer Johnson. Consistent with our general theoretical orientation, we are hypothesizing that there is a differential and significant cross-over pattern for the two parties on the basis of personality structure. These data are given in Table 2.

TABLE 2
PERSONALITY STRUCTURE AND PARTY CROSS-OVER

Party Cross-over	Non-dogmatic Scorers	Dogmatic Scorers	Total
Democrats Selecting Goldwater	5 (8%)	9 (39%)	14 (16%)
Republicans Selecting Johnson	5 (31%)	2 (13%)	7 (23%)
Total	10 (12%)	11 (29%)	21 (18%)

Our findings show that 21 subjects (18%) out of 119 (there were four non-respondents for the candidate question) crossed party lines in making a presidential preference: 16% of the Democrats and 23% of the Republicans. Now the more important consideration is the role of personality in party cross-overs for presidential preferences. Our data are in the hypothetical directions for both parties. Only 9% of the non-dogmatic Democrats selected Goldwater in contrast to 39% of dogmatic Democrats. For the Republicans who selected Johnson, 13% were dogmatic scorers, while 31% were non-dogmatic respondents. Thus cross-overs in the hypothetical direction of congruent personality structure average about 35% for both Democrats and Republicans which is considerably greater than the average cross-over in either direction of about 20% for each party. For dogmatic scorers there was a 29% cross-over in contrast to a cross-over of only 12% for the non-dogmatic subjects. These data then, to repeat, are in the expected directions and suggest support for our principal hypothesis.

The interaction of dogmatism and presidential preferences is of much greater magnitude than that for dogmatism and party preference. The chi-square distribution (Table 3) is statistically significant ($p=.001$). Our findings show that non-dogmatic scorers overwhelmingly (80%) selected Johnson; while dogmatic scorers, although remaining somewhat evenly divided in their preference for presidential candidates, yielded findings in the expected direction by a slightly greater preference (58%) for Goldwater. As the distribution in Table 2 shows, the cross-over of dogmatic Republicans is counteracted by that of the non-dogmatic Democrats. Hence, the stronger interaction of personality and presidential preference seems primarily a result of greater cross-over activity by dogmatic Democrats.

TABLE 3

PERSONALITY STRUCTURE AND PRESIDENTIAL CANDIDATE PREFERENCE

Candidate	Non-dogmatic Scorers	Dogmatic Scorers	Total
Johnson	65	16	81
Goldwater	16	22	38
Total	81	38	119*

$\chi^2=17.29$, $df=1$, $\rho<.001$.

* Omits 4 non-respondents.

Our data show, then, that while general party preference is significantly related only to non-dogmatic personality structure, the more specific preference for presidential candidates is significantly related to both dogmatic and non-dogmatic personality structures.

No differences in the above findings obtained for registered and non-registered voters or for those subjects who had voted and those who intended to vote.

DISCUSSION

These findings suggest that personality structure is more clearly related to concrete political ideology than to general party preferences or affiliations. The two principal parties in the United States are ideologically more amorphous and less differentiated than those of other countries. Party preference thus frequently tells little about the precise nature of one's political orientation and hence the relationship of this to personality. But significant differences in political ideology—however rare—may be found more readily *within* specific parties, such as in the form of ideological and methodological orientations of their different candidates. Hence, as our results show, the interaction of personality structure and political behavior is more likely to be observed in these respects. This implies a postulate of receptivity that, where the stimulus-field is sufficiently diversified, the voter will select those political alternatives that have the greatest functional value in meeting the requirements of his personality system (Levinson, 1959). Our data suggest that party cross-over appears to be much more of a phenomenon for dogmatic scorers than for the non-dogmatic scorers. Such a finding, of course, is consistent with the dogmatism variable: the closed-minded personality, being rigidly intolerant of opinions and beliefs which are not compatible with his own ideological behavior, is motivated to seek a more cognitively consonant situation when the opportunity is permitted; non-dogmatics, on the contrary, are more open-minded and theoretically more tolerant of cognitive dissonance, such as the opposing views of a presidential candidate from an opposition party. We submit that this kind of phenomenon may explain, at least in part, the political dynamics of "frontlash" and "backlash" which political analysts allege to have taken place in the 1964 elections and which are revealed in the justaposition of the tabular data presented above.

These findings offer some substantiation for the position that voting behavior may be a function of some measure of identification between the political elector and the political candidate. Sanford (1951) suggests that this relationship is determined by the voter's psychological needs and, accordingly, that the political candidate, if he is to win functional acceptance and support, has to meet these "needs." This, of course, would be particularly operative where the voter has a sufficiently diversified stimulus-field from which to make his selection. Thus, the acceptance and the rejection of political candidates are, at least in part, functions of the congruence/incongruence between the personality structures of the political electorate and those of the political candidates. This evidence is consistent with the more general thesis that the structure and the function of the polity are themselves in part dependent upon the personality structures of the political functionaries recruited into it and the congruent interaction of both the psychological and the sociological structures (see DiRenzo, 1967a: Chapter 9).

Personality and Decision-Making:
John F. Kennedy in Four Crisis Decisions
Thomas M. Mongar

INTRODUCTION

What is the role of personality in the political process? The least exclusive answer to this question is that some conditions encourage the expression of individual attributes more than others (Greenstein, 1967b). First, before personal characteristics can shape events, they must be liberated from the normative and praxiological constraints that normally homogenize human differences into patterns of behaviour. In other words, a person must be temporarily emancipated from the ever-present forces of morality and conventional rationality. Second, a person must be in a position to influence political events, which means he must command the resources necessary to intervene strategically and decisively in the political process.[1]

These criteria narrow the number of political situations in which personality may become causally significant. Perhaps the most obvious and interesting would be the crisis decision-making of modern chief executives. I have in mind a situation in which a president (or prime minister, or other leader) be-

Reprinted by permission of the author and publisher from the *Canadian Journal of Political Science*, Volume 2, 1969, pp. 200–225.
[1] The most complete and informed discussion of the principle of strategic intervention is to be found in Kotarbinski (1965).

comes the target of a personally "resonant"[2] policy stimulus, for example one that simultaneously challenged the will of a nation and the self-esteem of its leader. Under these circumstances, the decisional process of the executive system could easily become *fused* with the psycho-dynamic processes of the executive, and the resolution of a policy crisis could ultimately depend on the outcome of a personal emotional crisis. In other words, politics could become a matter of psychotherapy.

In order to demonstrate the heuristic merit of this approach, I have chosen to examine (in purely hypothetical and impressionistic terms) the impact of John F. Kennedy's personality on four crisis decisions: the Cuban missile crisis, the steel price fiasco, the Bay of Pigs crisis, and the Meredith case.[3] Execution of this conceptual experiment requires exposition of an integrated model of personality,[4] description of Kennedy's personality in terms of the categories of the

---

[2] The term "resonance" denotes deep personal significance. A discussion of the term can be found in Greenstein (1967b).

[3] These decisions were selected from a sample of sixteen which were originally examined because they seemed intuitively *representative* of the salient aspirations of Kennedy administration. The sixteen were classified along foreign/domestic and command/consent dimensions, yielding four categories (s=success, f=failure, and d=delay): I. *Foreign consent*: Test ban treat (s), Alliance for Progress (s), Trade expansion (s) and Peace corps (s); II. *Foreign command*: Cuban missile crisis (s), Berlin crisis (s), Postponement of nuclear testing (s), Bay of Pigs (f); III. *Domestic consent*: Medicare (f), Aid to higher education (f), Department of Urban Affairs (f), Civil rights (d); IV. *Domestic command*: Steel crisis (s), Racial ban in federal housing (s), Wage/price guidelines (s), Meredith case (f). The four decisions examined were in the command category, as stipulated by the model; each decisional area is represented by one case. The existence of failures in both the domestic and foreign categories would appear to rule out "decisional arena" as a significant causal variable.

[4] The concept of personality adopted here is basically sociological (or organizational) and can best be described as an integrated model because it attempts to bring some rather disparate strands of modern psychology together into the same framework. Motivation, cognition and perception, ego structure, performance and learning are viewed as internal parts and processes of a cybernetic system. The use of these concepts in this way is consistent with the description of personality put forward by McClelland (1961b).

model,[5] and conjectural exploration of the dynamics of the model to demonstrate how specific elements in Kennedy's personality determined the outcome of each decision. I emphasize the term "conjectural exploration" because no attempt will be made to state and verify hypotheses. My strategy of investigation is designed to demonstrate possibilities, not to settle burning theoretical or empirical questions. Nothing in this essay is meant to add or detract from either the reality or the myth of John Fitzgerald Kennedy.

A CYBERNETIC MODEL OF PERSONALITY

Kleinmuntz defines personality as the "unique organization of factors which characterizes an individual and determines his pattern of interaction with the environment" (Kleinmuntz, 1967:8). This would be a perfectly acceptable definition if it did not evade the fundamental question of structure. Most psychological theorists posit some structure, but no firm consensus has so far emerged concerning its exact shape. We have one indication of rough agreement on the salient dimensions of personality in the high frequency with which certain terms appear in the more recent literature of social psychology: motivation, perception and cognition, ego structure, performance, and manipulation. Although it provides only one answer to the problem, my thesis is that these dimensions stand in a stable and functional relationship to one another, the precise character of which is determined by the cybernetic organization of the central nervous system. Thus, personality denotes *unique content* organized by (and within) a *universal cybernetic structure*.

Conceived in cybernetic terms personality is organized into four major component systems: a motivational (energy) system; a perceptual/cognitional (detection/evaluation) sys-

---

[5] Data used to describe Kennedy's personality and decisional behaviour were drawn from the following sources: (a) Kennedy (1963); (b) Kennedy (1956); (c) Whalen (1964); (d) Burns (1960); (e) Cutler (1962); (f) Fay (1966); (g) Kennedy (1965); (h) Sorensen (1965); (i) Schlesinger (1965); (j) Lincoln (1965); (k) Dinneen (1959); (l) White (1961).

tem; an ego (selector) system; and a skill (effecting) system.[6]
The function of the personality is the disposal of motivational stimuli in ways that enhance the biological, neurologi-
cal, and emotional welfare of the individual. The action of
the personality can thus be reduced to the internal management of motivational stimuli evoked either internally or
externally. In terms of general process, the stimulus first ar-
rives at the detecting system where it is evaluated for meaning and forwarded on to the selecting system where alternative methods of disposal are considered. Disposing of a
stimulus involves deciding what values to pursue, when
and how. This means choosing among available value alternatives and formulating a course of action capable of
acquiring the value chosen at the least cost.[7] When the
proper situation emerges, the action scenario chosen is put
into operation by the effector system. At this point, the motor
system becomes a source of performance and manipulation.
When the desired value is gained at (or near) the predicted
cost, the whole pattern of relationships between personality
items that produced success is reinforced through a "feedback loop"; in this context, feedback is another way of saying "leaning" (Skinner, 1953). Successful repetition of the
sequence gradually creates a stable response pattern, which
means that when the person is similarly motivated under
similar conditions he can be expected to make similar choices
and perform similar actions. Patterns of response evolve
from a mixture of sign conditioning and latent learning.[8] The

[6] Although somewhat mechanical in structure and operation, the
cybernetic model is consistent with the conception of man as a
complex information-processing system found in March and Simon
(1958:9–11). In my model, concepts like motivation, perception
and cognition, ego structure, and skill traits provide a convenient
method of classifying items of information about personality in
terms of functional relationships. The model and the way in which
information about Kennedy is classified are purely speculative. A
readable discussion of cybernetic systems can be found in Kuhn
(1963:42–47).
[7] For a formulation of the principle of least effort in terms of
economic exchange, see Curry and Wade (1968).
[8] The distinction between "sign conditioning" and "latent learning" (thinking) is found in Polanyi (1964).

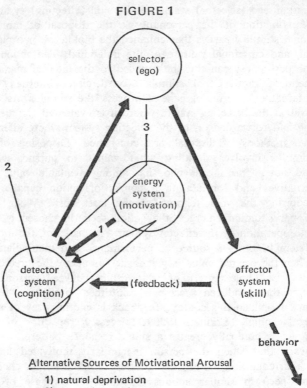

FIGURE 1

Alternative Sources of Motivational Arousal

1) natural deprivation
2) external arousal
3) internal cognitive arousal

basic structure and process envisaged for the model are presented schematically in Figure 1.

KENNEDY'S PERSONALITY: A STATIC DESCRIPTION

Motivation

The primary function of a motivational system is to deploy the motor activities of the organism automatically toward the acquisition of those values necessary for survival and well-being. The basic constituents of motivational systems are needs, which fall into three general classes: biogenic, neurogenic, and emotional.[9] Because needs define what is important, values also fall into three classes: material values, activities, and sentiments.[10] Biogenic and neurogenic needs are presumably innate and universal to all species possessing complex vegetative and associational systems; emotional needs are distinctly human, and are acquired through conditioning.[11] They account for most of the motivational variation in human population. Perhaps the most significant and widespread motivational pathology is a *neurosis,* which involves the internalization of two conflicting emotional needs. By "conflicting" I mean that anything done in service of one need tends to undermine whatever is done in service of another (Horney, 1937).

The available secondary data suggest strongly that John F. Kennedy suffered for most of his life from the effects of a neurosis caused by a deep conflict between two emotional needs: an overpowering fear of failure (*infavoidance*) and a generalized need for assistance (*succorance*).[12] The infavoid-

[9] This classification was borrowed from Fuller (1964:42–53).

[10] For an analysis of sentiments see Homans (1961:164–180).

[11] Biogenic and neurogenic needs are presumably functional for the maintenance and efficient operation of the vegetative and associational systems: see Altman (1966: Chapter 15). Emotional needs are "implanted" by the surplus sentiments that habitually accompany material values and activities during the socialization process. When a child is finally capable of improved discrimination, sentiments become independent sources of motivational arousal. (McClelland, 1961b.)

[12] Definitions of infavoidance and succorance were borrowed from Murray (1938b:182–191). Concealment of disfigurement is taken as evidence of infavoidance: a person hampered by a fear of failure is apt to present himself to others in ways that encourage them to believe he is perfect and whole. Kennedy (*a*) underplayed the seriousness of his Addison's Disease; (*b*) never discussed his back injury with even his most intimate colleagues; (*c*) frequently hid his crutches from constituents; (*d*) always took his pills in private; (*e*) avoided his glasses in public and in the presence of photographers; (*f*) refurbished his tan with a sun-lamp when the beach was unavailable (Sorensen, 1965:38–49; Lincoln, 1965:53 and 234; Burns, 1960:154).

ance need was the result of a continuing failure in boyhood competition with his older brother, Joe, Jr. Competition between the children was deliberately fostered in the Kennedy household by the elder Joseph Kennedy to prepare his sons for protracted conflict with the WASP establishment. The senior Kennedy was convinced that only superior preparation could break the pattern of exclusion that had denied the Kennedy clan social and political recognition commensurate with obvious financial and political accomplishments. His cynical social darwinism apparently led him to the conclusion that the best method of ensuring competitive superiority was to expose his children, especially his sons, to a demanding and competitive family environment. His entrepreneurial instincts led him to identify the American presidency as the "line of least resistance" because of its strategic importance for the entire social structure. Kennedy senior openly nurtured presidential ambitions, but if he could not be president himself, at least he could prepare the way for his first-born son (Joe, Jr.). One can envisage his corporate mind defining the presidency as a family enterprise, in which his other sons would form the necessary reserves to perpetuate the new political dynasty.

Because Joe, Jr. was given the mantle of family aspiration early in life, he gained an obvious competitive advantage over the other children. His status in the family appears to have been more a matter of ascription than of achievement. Kennedy senior introduced him to friends as a future president of the United States. Mother Rose held him up as a

---

Helplessness is taken as an indicator of succorance: a person who wishes to be cared for is apt to feign helplessness and dependence to elicit nurturant responses. Kennedy: (*a*) became notorious for his lack of order and sloppiness at Choate; (*b*) could not remember names, telephone numbers, and appointments in the presence of his Senate secretary, Evelyn Lincoln; (*c*) took his boyhood nanny (Margaret Ambrose) with him to Washington as housekeeper. According to Lincoln, Mrs. Ambrose "babied him like a mother hen with her brood" and she wondered whether Mrs. Ambrose "had as much difficulty picking up after the Senator at home as I had at the office" (Whalen, 1964:166–167; Lincoln, 1965:21–26).

model for the other children, especially Jack, and gave him an unsupervised role in disciplining the other children. Under these circumstances, it was inevitable that Jack would choose his older brother as a target of confrontation to earn an equal (and requisite) share of attention, recognition, and affection; it was equally inevitable that Joe, Jr. would ruthlessly subordinate Jack in order to retain his own superior status. But Joe was older, stronger, faster, more accomplished, and more self-confident (probably because he had the unequivocal emotional support of his parents). No matter how hard he tried, Jack could neither conquer his older brother nor equal his competitive triumphs outside the family arena.

The reason for Kennedy's failure in these confrontations, and to some extent his fear of failure, was the succorance need, which was reinforced as a consequence of chronic childhood illnesses.[18] I say "reinforced" because the need to be cared for is presumably present in every infant, but disappears slowly as the child begins to gain control of the environment. Kennedy undoubtedly discovered that illness released many of the values he could not win competitively, and hit upon the strategy of feigning helplessness as a way of avoiding the costs of competitive failure. Failure evoked the helplessness ruse, which deprived him of the opportunity to develop the poise, wit, and self-assurance necessary to compete effectively. Because the environment conceded the highest rewards for competitive spirit and winning, Kennedy was persistently driven to compete again, only to fail again because he was so ill-prepared for the contest. Each failure increased his fear of failure and encouraged even greater reliance on helplessness as a substitute for preparation and success. The result was a hopeless motivational dilemma: confrontations to suppress the fear of failure ended in failure because of the manner in which his succorance need undermined his capacity to perform.

[18] These included scarlet fever, diphtheria, an appendectomy, a chronic allergy of the stomach, two bouts with jaundice, and a serious back injury. His illnesses typically struck while he was away attending school: Choate, the London School of Economics, Princeton, and Harvard. Schlesinger (1965:80).

Ego Structure

The selector component of the personality is an ego system, which performs executive functions (Bucklew, 1960:34–36). In general this means three things. First, intensive and programatic reality testing which keeps operational beliefs in tune with situational change. Second, discovery and selection of value alternatives and lines of co-ordinated activity best calculated to achieve values at a profit. Third, the co-ordinated management of the components of the personality necessary to see a given course of action through to completion. Moreover, the ego performs each of these functions in ways that are relevant to the disposal of motivational stimuli. The skill with which these functions are performed and the degree to which the internal resources of the individual are focused on a given disposal problem refers to personal competence (see White, 1959). Personal competence rests on self-esteem, which is in turn the product of the historic ratio between success and failure. Success (regardless of source) increases self-esteem, and the inflation of self-esteem improves the probability of successful confrontations with the environment in the future.

Ego structures are of two basic types: "satellizing" and deviant.[14] The kind of structure a child acquires depends upon the quality of his early relationship with his parents. All children presumably experience the same initial ego developments. This involves the inflation of the infant's self-concept through permissive and indulgent nurturing by parents. Infants are obviously incompetent and lack of refined perceptual discrimination leads them to attribute their apparent success in the world to their own efforts. At some point the parents assume socialization roles, and begin to make rewards contingent on conformity to socially acceptable patterns of behaviour. The structure of the child's ego is determined by

[14] Ausubel et al. (1954). The authors have produced suggestive experimental evidence for the dichotomy between the satellizing and what I have chosen to call the deviant ego. My derivations are purely speculative.

the manner in which he conceptualizes his relationship with his parents when this traumatic turnabout in parental behaviour occurs. If the child thinks he is *intrinsically* valued, he will deflate his self-concept, align with his now powerful parents, and begin to develop aspirations consistent with his limited capacity for performance. This is the "satellizing" ego. Alternatively, if the child thinks he has been *extrinsically* valued, he will protect his omnipotent self-image through fantasy, resist identification with parents and other social agents, and will attempt to increase his capacity to perform to meet the burden of vastly inflated aspirations. This is the deviant ego.

In dynamic or causal terms, intrinsic valuation produces an *ascribed status,* which gives the child a feeling of being loved regardless of his failure to perform adequately. This provides the security necessary to risk a truly experimental and tutorial relationship with his parents. Increasing dependence on parental gratifications reduces the child's tolerance of frustration, which means that frustration can be employed by the parent as an incentive for deflating aspirations and inflating performance skills simultaneously. Extrinsic valuation reverses the process because the child knows he is acceptable only when his performance meets parental standards. He is forced to achieve his status, which gives him a larger range of personal and social challenges from which to choose. This freedom may encourage a number of consequences. First, the child is apt to develop eclectic and highly personalized standards of achievement, which emancipates him from social and parental ideology. Second, the child will develop a strong resistance to frustration, which means that the parent cannot easily manipulate incentives to encourage deflation of aspiration. In fact, given the uncertainty injected into the environment by parental rejection, unrealistic aspirations become invaluable motivational benchmarks that substitute for the goals the parents have attempted to impose. Fantasy and ritualistic conformity are apt to be employed to nurture the omnipotent self-image and protect unrealistic aspirations against the persistent threats of reality. Finally, the search for balance between aspirations and skills will be oriented toward the inflation of performance capacities.

Kennedy's "ego profile" is almost a perfect representation of the deviant structure. In other words, his behaviour patterns exhibit the external indicators (omnipotent self-concept, unrealistic aspirations, resistance to frustration, ideological independence of parents) of ego deviance and his early socialization experiences occurred under the conditions posited for the deviant structure (extrinsic valuation, manipulation of fantasy to maintain self-esteem, and constructive inflation of performance traits). The existence of an omnipotent self-concept is revealed in the staggering fact that Kennedy coveted the most demanding and inaccessible role in American politics (the presidency) and finally sought the office in spite of the barriers of chronic illness[15] and political obscurity.[16] The intensity and magnitude of his aspirations are revealed in his disdain for anonymity,[17] his tendency to act brashly in order to attract attention and exploit opportunities,[18] and his willingness to undertake exceptionally difficult

[15] Kennedy sustained his second spinal injury when PT 109 went down in the Solomons. During early convalescence prior to being discharged from the Navy, he contracted malaria and sciatica. After his first unsuccessful operation, he acquired Addison's Disease. He nearly died from hepatitis during a Congressional junket to the Far East in 1951. A staphylococcus infection after the second spinal operation became so serious that he was given the last rites of his church twice. Subsequent novocaine treatments to ease his pain caused anemia. Orthopedic shoes and a back brace brought his spinal difficulty under partial control (his left leg was almost an inch shorter than his right and produced spinal pressure when he walked). Nutritional supplements cured his anemia, and cortisone kept the Addison's Disease in check. (Sorensen, 1965:38–42; Schlesinger, 1965:95–96.)

[16] Not only was he Catholic, but he was only forty-two. Among "realistic" contenders (Stevenson, Humphrey, Johnson) he was the least distinguished.

[17] Kennedy thought of his years in the House as "boring" and was offended by the unpromising committee assignments allocated by the Senate leadership (Sorensen, 1965:27 and 43).

[18] Kennedy permitted publication of a poorly written bachelor's thesis a year after his graduation from Harvard. He ran for the House at twenty-nine, the Senate at thirty-five and the vice presidential nomination at thirty-nine. His impulsive entry into the VP race seems to have been partly motivated by the loss of his seat on

and risky investments to gain higher political office.[19] His capacity to resist failure has become legendary,[20] and there is ample evidence to suggest that he struggled to cast off the trappings of his father's conservative social and political ideology (Whalen, 1964:402–404 and 425–426). Extrinsic valuation was clearly present, especially in light of the emphasis his parents placed on competition and winning, and the special position in the family accorded Joe, Jr. If Kennedy came to resent his brother's advantages in the family, he could easily have defined his own position in extrinsic terms. Although muted by affection and respect, his resentment was obvious (Burns, 1960:28). That he viewed his situation as an extrinsic one is supported by constant references to the fact that he was merely a replacement for his older brother.

Kennedy's situation as a child would also have been ideal for the manipulation of fantasy to protect his image of greatness. These images should have been shattered by competitive failures, but instead they were sustained by the comforts of illness, which included a diet of epic novels, any one of which would have provided sufficient reinforcement for

---

the Harvard Board of Overseers in 1955, a seat highly prized by the clan because his father had failed to acquire it in 1936. Kennedy's drive for the vice presidential nomination was so hastily organized that it collapsed when his supporters discovered that Stevenson preferred a Protestant running mate. When Stevenson unexpectedly turned the decision over to the convention, Kennedy plunged back into the race with less than twenty-four hours to regroup his forces. (Whalen, 1964:222; Sorensen, 1965:78–92.)

[19] Instead of relaxing after the 1956 election, Kennedy launched his own drive for the White House immediately, subsisting on "hamburgers and milkshakes" as he travelled the country for the next three years in a gruelling search for the support of potential delegates. (Sorensen, 1965:99–106.)

[20] His first back injury at Harvard ruled out continued competition in contact sports, so Kennedy turned to swimming. He practised the backstroke secretly while confined to the infirmary with influenza; his friend Torbert McDonald drove him to and from the pool because he was too weak to walk. He managed to graduate *cum laude* from Harvard in spite of two earlier years of marginal work. And when his back injury caused him to fail the Army's physical examination, he exercised until he could pass the Navy's. (Kennedy, 1965:22; Schlesinger, 1965:85–86.)

his self-image.[21] Later reading put the flesh of reality on his images of heroism; his favourite books during adolescence and early adulthood were the biographies of gifted and eccentric political leaders.[22] The strong continuity between childhood and adult reading patterns, and his own book on courage, give partial support to the thesis that he harboured romantic images of greatness.

The deep conflict between infavoidance and succorance called Kennedy's self-image and high aspirations constantly into question. His emotional health would have eventually required an adjustment of the gap between high pretension and poor performance. However, certain alternatives were foreclosed from the outset. Deflation of aspiration was ruled out because of the neurotic pressures for achievement from the family. The pressure to prepare for a career ruled out continued use of fantasy. The only remaining alternative was a massive effort to inflate his performance capacities, which required a strategy of managing the symptoms of his neurosis and turning his weaknesses into competitive assets. Kennedy began his experiment with self-reformation during his last two years at Harvard, and projectively reported the conceptual basis for his strategy in his bachelor's thesis.[23] Three lines of adjustment were followed. First, the effects of succorance (helplessness, sloppiness, lack of order) were rigor-

[21] Kennedy could remember liking *Ivanhoe, King Arthur, Scottish Chiefs,* and *The White Company* (Schlesinger, 1965:80 and 105).
[22] Especially Marlborough, Melbourne, Quincy Adams, Lincoln, Calhoun, Talleyrand. *Ibid.,* 80, 105.
[23] The original title, *Appeasement at Munich,* was changed to *Why England Slept* when the thesis was published. His central theme was that in struggles with totalitarian regimes, democracies are handicapped by institutional weaknesses which can only be compensated for by superior leadership. This could easily have been a restatement in political terms of the conclusions Kennedy had reached about the solution of his own problem, namely that disciplined and learned self-management, based on merciless self-criticism, was the only way to suppress his destructive succorant tendencies and finally rival the accomplishments of an insensitive and "pugnacious" brother. The book's projective title should have been *Why Jack Kennedy Slept.* Kennedy's Inaugural Address is also full of metaphors that appear to have projective meaning. For example, *"Ask not what Kennedy can do for you, but what you can do for Kennedy."*

ously confined to intimate settings, like the family, where they were not only tolerated but encouraged. In this way, helplessness could be removed as a barrier to career proficiency.[24] Second, latent abilities capable of contributing to successful competition were defined, embellished, and developed. These included a disarming shyness, a probing curiosity, and a capacity for personal detachment. Kennedy's shyness and good looks made him attractive company. His exaggerated need to know, which undoubtedly emerged as an intellectual compensation for motor deficiencies, removed much of the drudgery from the routine of preparation required to improve personal competence. He enjoyed discovery, and the sense of impending adventure in some new experience became a constant motivational stimulus. This may account for his restlessness and the fact that in intellectual situations he tended to be precocious. Personal detachment allowed him to find the heart of an issue and still find aesthetic enjoyment in the peripheral aspects of controversy. The third strategy was to openly accept or find especially difficult tasks, and to disarm criticism of pretension by modestly calling attention to minor shortcomings. This witty self-derision, which reflected a merciless introspection, undermined criticism early and at the same time elicited reassurance and support from other people.

Perception and Cognition

The detector component of the personality is a perceptual/cognitional system capable of constructing and testing com-

---

[24] This meant having the family near when he was away from home, or if this was not possible (as during the war) to create a surrogate family. During the war and for most of his life thereafter, the surrogate was the PT Rat Pack. The personal significance of the Rat Pack is demonstrated by the fact that "Shafty" Kennedy appointed "Bitter Bill" Battle Ambassador to Australia, "Red" Fay Under Secretary of the Navy, "Jim Jam Jumping" Jim Reed Assistant Secretary of the Treasury, and Byron "Whizzer" White Associate Justice of the Supreme Court. All were undoubtedly able public servants, but Kennedy's motive in bringing several of them to Washington was primarily personal. See Fay (1966).

plex symbolic representations of the world upon which to base value-oriented action, and of evaluating information. I have intentionally unified perception (sensory experience) and cognition (understanding and thinking) on the philosophical assumption that the manner in which the world is understood ontologically prefigures the organization of most perceptual experience. Ontological maps place boundaries around inherently ambiguous and initially meaningless information, and in doing so construct unified perceptual experiences.

Two types of conceptual (linguistic) implements are involved in cognitive processes: *operational* and *ontological* beliefs.[25] Operational beliefs may be thought of as testable approximations of immediately relevant events; ontological beliefs attempt to interpret the unknown and to supply guidelines for dealing with the moral aspects of social behaviour. Operational beliefs are important because the more a person understands his immediate environment, the higher the probability that his choices and actions will be adapted to the objective requirements of value situations. Ontological beliefs are equally functional because the more a person thinks he understands what cannot be known in an immediate sense, the greater his cognitive security. Cognitive security is undoubtedly related positively to adaptive potential. Ontological beliefs also enable people to recognize profitable options with respect to the moral expectations of the community, in addition to providing those important moral justifications without which decisions could not be made and pursued. Operational beliefs are open to revision, but ontological beliefs are generally resistant to change, except under condi-

[25] My treatment of cognition represents a modification of a line of thought first developed by Rokeach (1960). The distinction between operational and ontological beliefs contradicts the descriptive orientation in cognitive psychology which generally fails to identify beliefs in terms of functions performed. The implication of my analysis is that the cognitive system can be altered in highly selective ways, which means that some beliefs (operational) can change without affecting others (ontological). A person can alter some aspects of his political behaviour without making corresponding adjustments in his basic values. Thus, conflict is possible at the operational level without disturbing the ontological or normative consensus of a group.

tions of stimulus deprivation.[26] Thus, all men are simultaneously open-minded and dogmatic. The relative importance of ontological and operational beliefs in the overall content of a person's detector system will certainly define which factor (open-mindedness or dogmatism) predominates.

At an ontological level, Kennedy was a genuine Aristotelian, with an ethical commitment to the golden mean, especially in the regulation of passion. He disliked passion in politics and feared the undisciplined intellect it was thought to encourage. Like many of his contemporaries, Kennedy extrapolated directly from the moderating aspects of the golden mean to the balance of power as a principle for understanding and responding to social change. He characterized himself as an "idealist without illusions," a proposition that captures the delicate balance in his own cognitive system (Sorensen, 1965:32). Kennedy also shared the Aristotelian obsession for excellence. He typically defined happiness as the full use of one's abilities along lines of excellence (Schlesinger, 1965:94). The hallmark of humanity was voluntarily to shoulder difficult tasks, to do them with daring and precision, and to accept accolades with modesty when successful. In particular, the stylistic aspects of action were as important ethically as the object of action. This was clearly what he had in mind when he defined courage as "grace under pressure." Altruism, excellence, daring, and modesty dominated his choice of idols, and competence became the sole basis for many of his relationships with other political actors. Competent people were invariably drawn to his service, and exploitation of their abilities extended his own effectiveness as a political operator.[27]

Kennedy's concern for excellence appears to have been affected by a sense of human impotence. He was firmly con-

[26] Kubzansky (1961). If beliefs are acquired through conditioning, then they can only be maintained through continual reinforcement. Stimulus deprivation curtails reinforcement and creates the necessary conditions for "brainwashing."
[27] McGeorge Bundy, McNamara, Rusk, Dillon, Taylor, Bell, Heller, Ball and Murrow acquired important assignments in the administration solely on the basis of distinguished reputations for excellence.

vinced that man was the pawn of powerful cosmic forces, but equally convinced that under special conditions, some men could influence the course of human development. He sensed the dramatic possibilities for influencing events through strategic intervention, and he counted his own generation among the fortuitous and fortunate few to whom the opportunity, resources, and position necessary for exerting influence had fallen. Failure was always more probable than success, but human dignity obliged men to make the effort to change the world with the firm intention of achieving success. Even in failure, man could prove his essential nobility by facing impossible tasks confidently with acknowledged limitations.

At an operational level, Kennedy was a cool, sceptical, pessimistic realist.[28] He was chary of ideological discourse, and invariably fastened on the immediate and practical consequences of a problem. His primary test of relevance for a policy was pragmatic: *can* it be done, can *we* do it, and *how much* will it cost in dollars and power? Feasibility and ease of implementation usually became the primary criteria for adopting value alternatives. For every positive answer he received to each of these questions, Kennedy would ask another question, and frequently pursued answers so relentlessly and in such detail that he literally frightened unseasoned advisers. In most encounters, it became apparent that he knew the kinds of answers he wanted. Most of the time, he was better prepared than opponents or advocates of policy alternatives, and in the presidency digested mountains of information daily in order to maintain informational superiority. Because he enjoyed gaming, the peripheral aspects and nuances of issues and programs interested him, which probably explains his capacity to deal with large volumes of information and why he could find genuine merit in almost every point of view. Too much knowledge of the intricacies of political life reinforced his pessimism concerning the limits of human action. As a consequence he persistently underestimated the possibility of domestic political action, and

[28] These conclusions accord well with assessments offered by Sorensen and Schlesinger, Jr.

overestimated the possibility of affecting the forces of global change. Pessimism and excessive scepticism often undermined his capacity to act, or narrowed his leeway for effective action. On the other hand, these same traits produced brilliant and daring programs of action that were well adapted to the situation. Kennedy faced the problem of developing programs with the patience and reserve of a master craftsman. Everything he knew about people and politics told him to remain doubtful, ask questions, and move slowly and dispassionately.

Skills

The effector component of the personality takes the form of a skill system containing integrative verbal and motor patterns designed to attract interaction (performance skills) and to induce other people to part with desired values (manipulative skills). Because images schedule opportunities for interaction by determining how other people respond to invitations, performance skills are generally oriented toward the creation and maintenance of a positive image for the benefit of other people.[29] The more positive (culturally valued) the image, the higher the probability of attracting interaction. Manipulative skills are tailored to the ongoing process of interaction and involve for the actor discovery and application of those verbal and motor sequences best calculated to gain compliance.[30]

Kennedy appears to have employed his performance skills consciously to generate and maintain substantially different images for two different audiences. The first (his internal

---

[29] For an analysis of the psychology of performances, see Goffman (1959). For the relationship between performances and attractiveness, see Blau (1964:34–42).

[30] As his record of failure in domestic/consent politics clearly indicates, Kennedy was not overly successful in manipulating people who were not attached to him emotionally. In a sense he was an overspecialized political actor, capable of demonstrating his attractiveness but incapable of translating attraction into policy payoffs.

image) was designed to encourage a strong bond of loyalty between himself and the members of his inner circle upon whom he relied for tolerant, competent assistance. Without his staff, Kennedy was virtually impotent. The second image was devoted to the problem of gaining recognition within audiences that controlled access to political nominations: Democratic party influentials (who actually determined nominations), young people (who provided inexpensive campaign energy), and selected elements of the American electorate (especially the newly powerful suburbanites, women, and minority groups in urban industrial areas).[31]

The skills necessary for the creation and maintenance of the internal image involved the careful but limited disclosure of authentic personal characteristics. Every person he knew intimately became aware of his presidential aspirations, the severity of his back pain, and his heroism in the Solomons. These became critical bases of respect and emotional attachment, as did his admiration for competence in other people. Each member filled an important gap in his own skill system, which gave each a sense of importance that could not have been gained in a system organized along functional lines. The core members of his staff realized they were making an indispensable contribution to his career, a feeling that seems to have enhanced their job satisfaction enormously. Kennedy also took direct command of his staff, a situation which gave the members considerable confidence in his judgment. Deep loyalty, high satisfaction, and confidence produced extraordinary initiative and co-operation, and resulted in an exceptionally formidable organization of activity.

---

[31] Kennedy's external skills have been excluded because they have very little bearing on the decisions examined, although his ability to keep routine political engagements during the height of the Cuban missile crisis without alerting his audiences or the press to the situation played a major role in the successful execution of the blockade scenario. Research after the assassination indicates that his efforts at image building were successful. Children and adults remembered him as a person of immense drive and self-confidence; altruism, modesty; intelligence, wit, and competence. See Kaiser (1968). These images were precisely the ones Kennedy wanted his external audience to acquire.

Decisional and Personality Dynamics

The central thesis of this paper is that the decisional process of executive systems can be reduced to the personality dynamics of chief executives. The primary reason for this assumption is that one man (the executive) must ultimately determine the course of action of the system he heads. Buried in this assumption is the further implication that the decisional processes of the personality and the executive system are basically the same.

In the most uncomplicated case, decision-making involves making two choices, first among value options (decisional phase) and then among available lines of action (implementation phase). But psychologically the decisional and implementation phases occur together, forming a *response pattern.* We can think of a response pattern as something that connects five different elements psychologically: a stimulus, a value alternative, a moral justification, an action alternative, and a rational justification. By "connect" I mean that all five elements are *bonded* to one another sequentially by sign conditioning. The stimulus is normally sufficient to evoke the entire sequence. I have included justifications in the model on the assumption that people adopt only rationalized alternatives. When faced with several options, they are likely to choose the most justified, even when that particular alternative possesses an inferior utility.

In each phase, a person can do any one of three things with respect to a given stimulus: accept (yes), reject (no), or postpone consideration (maybe). The strength of the connection between elements in a pattern (the bond) determines the flexibility of the response. Each choice (yes, no, maybe) has a different effect on the strength of the bond, and hence on the overall rigidity of the response. Affirmations increase intensity; postponements moderate intensity; and negations reduce intensity. When a person decides to accept a stimulus, he automatically increases its intensity, and in the process tightens the bonds of the pattern. Where the intensity of a stimulus is already latently strong, we observe a *decisional reflex*. Postponement provides greater opportunity for adjusting relationships between elements. In this case, an actor is free to experiment with novel permutations. The basic point of this model is that variations in the intensity of stimuli determine the amount of leeway a person has to adjust to situational change.

This is an important point because the probability of successful value acquisition rests on the relative fit between value and action choices and the objective properties of a situation. A "good" fit between the two presumably requires that choices have benefit of normative relevance, accurate information, adequate preparation, and sensitive timing (Kotarbinsky, 1965). In order to improve these conditions, a decision-maker must be able to alter relationships between stimuli, value and action states, and justifications. This requirement focuses attention directly on the consequences of a particular class of stimuli, namely those that carry personally "resonant" properties. Resonant stimuli are already latently intense because they affect the personality so deeply; affirmation of a resonant stimulus would undoubtedly fuse the bonds between the elements of a response pattern so tightly as to preclude adjustment. In other words, resonant stimuli provoke decisional reflexes, and in so doing threaten to subordinate the decisional process of the executive system to the psychodynamic processes of the personality. This is easily achieved because the two processes are similar if not identical.

In the four decisions examined, two stimulus conditions (*abrogation* and *no hope syndromes*) appear to have produced two radically different responses even though they were operating on the same response pattern. The pattern in question seems to have had three constants. First, Kennedy's primary method of sorting stimuli was the maintenance of his self-regard in the eyes of other people. Any stimulus that threatened to expose his need for assistance or his fear of failure became "resonant." Second, he responded differently to each stimulus category. When confronted by a stimulus (abrogation syndrome) that robbed him of self-esteem, he reacted decisively (yes) to restore the status quo. Alternatively, when a stimulus offered only the opportunity of failure (no hope syndrome), he rejected it (no), unless some competing stimulus aroused his profound sense of personal responsibility, in which case he would accept the stimulus but only in a weakened form (maybe). Third, in fashioning implementation programs, what I have chosen to call *operational regulators* (pessimism, caution, and scepticism) invariably intervened to dampen the stimulus to a manageable level.

The abrogation syndrome refers to the deceptive abrogation of a policy bargain that Kennedy thought he had reached personally with another political actor. It is the personal element in the bargain that made this kind of stimulus so personally salient. We have (in effect) a personal "double-cross" that threatens psychologically to expose personal weaknesses. The abrogation stimulus played directly on Kennedy's neurosis because a person caught in the bind between infavoidance and succorance experiences such difficulty keeping commitments to himself that he begins to place a negative value on the duplicity of others. Lack of personal responsibility is a negative idea that most people would try to avoid confronting. One method of avoidance would be projection, through which the lack of reliability of self is attributed to others. (Projection is a defense mechanism that shows up remarkably often in Kennedy's verbal and written behaviour.) Placing emphasis on the reliability of other people requires a negative evaluation of duplicity. Bargains are especially important in this regard because they provide succorant people with the security of knowing what the world is going to be like from day to day. Bargains compensate for the lack of reliability of self and the duplicity of others by setting out the exact rules of the game. Giving bargains a positive value and duplicity a negative one, we derive some insight into the possible emotional significance of the deceptive abrogation of a bargain.

Kennedy's response to the abrogation stimulus was to adopt the first rationalized policy alternative that entered his mind capable of recovering the self-esteem lost. This meant restoration of the status quo. In other words, Kennedy made policy choices for psychotherapeutic reasons. The initial resonance of the stimulus required a rapid decision with a minimum of consultation. In the cases examined, the rationale employed was one or another version of the balance of power concept, which was one of Kennedy's central ontological beliefs. A positive reaction to an already resonant stimulus magnified the intensity of the stimulus, placing Kennedy under extreme pressure to adopt the first sensible action program conceived. But at this point, his operational regulators came into play, producing countervailing pressure for postponement of action. The result was that the most evaluated and best adapted scenario considered was eventually adopted. This interpretation coincides with the popular view of Kennedy as being both daring and cool under pressure. The "yes/maybe" pattern appears to have produced relatively chancy value choices supported by exceptionally sensible programs of action. The result was usually success.

The no hope syndrome refers to a situation in which the value alternatives available for managing a stimulus are equally undesirable. In other words, you lose no matter what you do. The no hope stimulus struck deeply at Kennedy's fear of failure. His first response was to terminate consideration. However, when confronted with an ambivalent situation in which he was absolutely *forced* to deal with an unwanted stimulus by competing pressures, his strategy was to postpone, which meant a temporary weakening of the stimulus. However, weakening the stimulus automatically reduced the pressure of action, which worked out concretely to an extension of the implementation process and a relentless probing for unforeseen consequences. Since Kennedy's operational regulators worked the same in all situations, there was more time to consider a larger number of action programs or versions of a single program, and greater incentive to discover problems. There was more time to find more objections, which probably concealed Kennedy's reluctance to act in the first place. The result of dampening an already dampened stimulus was a grossly maladapted scenario, and failure. In the "yes/maybe" pattern, the optimal program emerged as the implementation process ended, but in the "maybe/maybe" pattern, Kennedy usually overshot the optimal program, adopting instead the least effective plan as the implementation process ended.

THE PRESUMED ROLE OF KENNEDY'S
PERSONALITY IN FOUR CRISIS DECISIONS

The Abrogation Syndrome[32]

DECISIONAL PHASE

What support exists in the literature on the Kennedy administration for the proposition that when faced with the deceptive abrogation of a policy bargain, John Kennedy experienced an emotional crisis which he resolved by adopting the first rationalized policy alternative he thought would be capable of restoring the status quo? This is really another way of asking how Kennedy's personality affected the two decisions examined. No final answer will ever be possible for this question, but an analysis of the decisions in terms of the model reveals some interesting possibilities. Specifically, there is strong evidence to support the contention that Kennedy thought he had reached bargains, that he experienced the policy stimuli resonantly, that he thought he had been deceived, that his decisions were taken hastily and with virtually no consultation, and that he was able to find adequate sources of rationalization for his value choices in his own ontological belief system. Moreover, it is difficult to

[32] A fifth decision (postponement of nuclear testing) was also examined, but space limitations require its exclusion here. In many ways, this decision fits the abrogation syndrome more closely than the two reported. The bargain was *explicit*, deception was clearly involved, Kennedy was angry and disappointed, and made an instantaneous decision to postpone the American resumption in order to encourage the Soviet Union not to finish the test series. He justified his decision in terms of preventing a testing race that could upset the nuclear balance of power. His choice eventually mushroomed over a long period of time into the strategy of gambling the American testing option at Geneva in order to give the Soviets an incentive to sign a test ban treaty. The high state of technical knowledge in the field of nuclear weaponry and Kennedy's operational regulations (especially his persistent questioning of the experts) were primary factors in the evolution of the Geneva scenario. (Schlesinger, 1965:451–495.)

account for his behaviour in other ways, such as prior policy commitments. Table I summarizes the essential facts about these two decisions.

TABLE I

Decision	Stimulus condition	Bargain	Value choice
Steel* April 10–13, 1962	$6 per ton increase by US Steel	implicit: violation of wage settlement	rescission of price increase
Missile† October 16–28, 1962	discovery of IRBM sites and crated missiles	implicit: no change in distribution of nuclear weapons	remove missiles

    * Sorensen (1965:434–69); Schlesinger (1965:634–40).
    † Sorensen (1965:667–718); Schlesinger (1965:797–819).

The bargains. While the evidence is far from ironclad, there are strong indications that Kennedy either reached (or thought he had reached) an implicit bargain with the steel industry, namely that if the administration could hold the wage demands of the Steelworkers' Union under 3 per cent, the industry would reciprocate by foregoing an increase in steel prices. According to Grant McConnell (who has done the only case study of the decision), "An implicit term of the pact . . . was that no steel price increase would be forthcoming. The labor settlement had been moderate, more so than any in recent history [2½%]; it was 'non-inflationary' in the administration's view and agreeable to the industry . . ." (McConnell, 1963:5–6). Schlesinger, Jr., and Sorensen both conceptualize the event in terms of the violation of a difficulty won bargain.

There exists no straightforward historical evidence to support the view that Kennedy and Khrushchev reached anything resembling a bargain concerning the deployment of nuclear missiles. However, Kennedy's surprise when informed of the missiles and the astonishment in Moscow over the belligerent American response are convincing bits of evidence that indicate a belief in a bargain, but a misunderstanding of its terms. In other words, these behaviours suggest that both Kennedy and Khrushchev thought they had achieved an understanding which could be generalized to cover the subject of arms deployment. How could such misconceptions have been communicated?

During the Vienna Conference, Kennedy argued vigorously that the best way to avoid nuclear war short of disarmament was for the two superpowers to reduce the number of points of conflict capable of escalating to a nuclear showdown. Since both powers had vital interests in Europe, Kennedy suggested general disengagement elsewhere, especially in Southeast Asia where both powers were steadily becoming more deeply involved in the Laotian war. Kennedy reasoned that reduction of points of conflict to areas of vital national interest would evoke the balance of power, and inject a new rationality into Soviet/American relations. Although unstated, Kennedy clearly included Cuba in his disengagement plea.

Three things could have encouraged Kennedy to believe that Khrushchev had tentatively accepted the balance of power thesis. First, the agreement to disengage in Southeast Asia by co-operating with the United States in achieving a Laotian settlement. Second, adoption of Kennedy's proposal for a moratorium on atmospheric nuclear tests. Kennedy could easily have construed this agreement as evidence of a desire on Khrushchev's part to stabilize the deployment of nuclear weapons. Third, Khrushchev's sudden adoption of the balance of power language on the final day of the conference.

Khrushchev, on the other hand, could easily have concluded that the balance of power was an invitation to deploy missiles outside Soviet territory, especially in view of the fact that the West had been altering the deployment of its nuclear deterrent for years. To emphasize his belief that great powers miscalculate, Kennedy told Khrushchev that the Bay of Pigs invasion had been a "mistake." In the context of the disengagement plea, his candor could have been interpreted as a private renunciation of American influence over Cuba, which was almost like saying: "You cannot place missiles in East Germany because we both have vital interests there, but if you really want to compensate for our changes in missile deployment, Cuba is your spot." Kennedy's conception of the balance of power almost required these kinds of adjustments. Seen from this perspective, the thesis that an implicit but imperfectly understood bargain was the basis for the behaviour of both leaders becomes reasonably attractive. The proposition is obviously open to empirical falsification.

Resonance. The best (perhaps the only) surface indicator of "resonance" is an emotive response. Kennedy's immediate reaction to each stimulus in the abrogation syndrome was unbridled anger. What bothered him most deeply was the fact that he had achieved the bargains personally; the fact they were broken without warning added the element of deception. Kennedy had originally become involved in the Steel negotiations with the tacit approval of steel industry executives, and remained involved, either directly or indirectly, through Arthur Goldberg until a settlement had been reached. The industry was playing a double game by silently exploiting Kennedy to achieve wage restraint and avoid a costly strike. Kennedy's explicit assumption was that in return for wage restraint, the industry would give price restraint. If both wages and prices could be kept within the new wage/price guidelines, it would be a victory for this new strategy of government intervention to control inflation at the source. He felt exceptionally deceived when he discovered the financial justification for the increase had been prepared while the bargain was being struck.

If Kennedy believed the Vienna agreements on Laos and nuclear testing extended implicitly to the subject of weapons deployment, the personal element was also present in the Cuban missile crisis. Kennedy was especially offended by what he believed were false assurances from Khrushchev that the Soviet Union would introduce only "defensive" weapons to protect Cuba from an American invasion. The difficulty this time could have been semantic; Kennedy might have confused the technical with the theoretical meanings of "defensive" and "offensive." Kennedy was clearly using the technical meaning, which distinguishes surface-to-air missiles (defensive weapons) from ICBMs and IRBMs (offensive weapons). However, every nuclear power considers its own long-range missiles as a deterrent or "defence" against attack, and Khrushchev could have been using this more theoretical meaning. In any case, the fact that Kennedy failed to ask Khrushchev for semantic clarification before acting reinforces the proposition that the initial stimulus in this decision was personally "resonant."

Haste and consultation. The term "consultation" refers here to a situation in which a decision-maker asks another person what response should be made to a given stimulus. Although consultation varied in both cases, there appears to have been a constant relationship between the speed with which decisions were taken and the amount of consultation sought. The quicker the decision, the lower the amount of consultation. In the missile crisis, Kennedy's decision to force removal of the missiles appears to have been taken in less than half an hour, and by all accounts just minutes after "he was convinced that it (the photographic evidence) was conclusive."[33] Moreover, he took the decision in the presence of only one person, McGeorge Bundy. There is not the slightest indication in either Schlesinger, Jr., or Sorensen that he asked Bundy for an opinion. The record indicates that the rescission option in the steel crisis was chosen less than an hour after Roger Blough delivered the humiliating *fait accompli*. Minimum consultation also characterized the decision, although Kennedy did ask those present: "What can we do about it?" But after just observing his display of an-

---

[33] Schlesinger (1965:801). Schlesinger's view is supported by that of an "insider" (Hugh Sidey), who reports that Kennedy not only reacted hastily in the choice of a value alternative, but also opted immediately for the use of armed force before consulting his military advisers. The implication is that the surgical strike scenario originated with Kennedy rather than some of his "hawkish" and impulsive advisers, as Sorensen and Schlesinger suggest. When McGeorge Bundy "told Kennedy that there was unmistakable evidence of nuclear offensive weapons in Cuba, the Celt in J.F.K. stirred first. After a few choice expletives, he, like Bundy, with vision narrowed by shock and danger, *declared that armed forces would have to strike Cuba* to remove the threat. From that *perilous summit of passion there was a long slope of restraint and deliberation* that led to the remarkable solution," (Italics mine). Sidey (1968).

ger, few members of his staff could have misunderstood his question as a plea for advice concerning alternative value responses rather than assistance in devising a method of forcing the steel industry to back down. Moreover, there is nothing in either Sorensen or Schlesinger, Jr., to indicate that any of his advisers suggested that he do nothing, or respond in any other way.

Rationalizations. In both cases, the explicit rationalizations evoked by Kennedy to justify his decisions reflected an ontological belief in the value of balance, especially the balance of power. In the steel crisis, Kennedy later expressed concern for the consequence of doing nothing on the prestige of the presidency. If he failed to confront the steel industry, the existing balance between organized centres of power within the American political system would have been altered permanently and negatively. In the missile crisis, Kennedy dismissed all other rationalizations for the decision introduced by subordinates to further justify or challenge the wisdom of his value choice. Some of his military advisers, for example, argued initially for a diplomatic response on grounds that the deployment of missiles to Cuba did not change the fact that all Soviet missiles, no matter where they were stationed, were still under Soviet control, and were therefore under the discipline of Soviet deterrent policy. It would make no practical difference to the outcome where incoming missiles originated if the Soviet Union decided to attack the United States. His reaction was the same to each objection: the missiles had to be removed because of their negative effect on the "global political balance." Kennedy treated domestic political rationalizations in precisely the same manner.

Alternative explanations. The only convincing alternative explanation is that Kennedy was merely living up to prior policy commitments. In the steel case, the administration had not committed itself to any course of action publicly. One could argue, however, that Kennedy assaulted "big steel" in order to pacify "big labor." While Kennedy apologized profusely to David McDonald for the betrayal, there is no evidence in McConnell, Sorensen, or Schlesinger, Jr., to support the idea that his response was oriented toward maintaining the allegiance of organized labour to the Democratic party. This aim could have been achieved by a more ritualistic and less risky response. However, there is an argument for the commitment variable in the missile crisis. Sorensen openly attributes Kennedy's response to the fulfillment of prior public warnings to the Soviet Union that "offensive weapons" would not be tolerated on Cuban soil. The administration was aware of the arms build-up on the island and became very worried by the discovery that the Soviets had installed surface-to-air missiles (SAMs). When queried, Khrushchev admitted their presence, and explained they had only "defensive" purposes. Only one member of the administration conversant with the problem (John McCone) even entertained the possibility that their real purpose was the protection of IRBMs. According to both Sorensen and Schlesinger, Jr., the possibility of "offensive" weapons being introduced in Cuba never entered Kennedy's mind. This implies that the warnings must have been routine, which was in fact the case. The sentence containing the prohibition against "offensive" weapons was inserted in the warning of September 4 as an afterthought, and on the advice of Robert Kennedy. Kennedy could still have taken this "afterthought" as a policy commitment, but this would not explain why he chose to confront the Soviet leadership in a way that could only have ended in nuclear war if neither party had backed down.

IMPLEMENTATION STAGE

John Kennedy typically responded dispassionately to the problem of devising action programs. Even though the burden of implementation was borne by his staff, identifiable, motivational and cognitive traits affected their behaviour directly or indirectly. The direct effects were motivational and ontological. Specifically I refer to the single criterion for participation in the decisional process created by Kennedy's succorance need and his obsession for competence: demonstrable expertise. In general, the implementation groups brought together in crisis situations were superior to

any the White House has ever known. The indirect effects
were largely cognitive, involving the manner in which his
operational regulators structured and expectations of his advisers: Kennedy's pessimism about the probability of failure
sharpened their sense of professional craftsmanship and ded-
ication to sound judgment; his sense of caution produced
a reluctance to act prematurely which usually gave them
more time to work; his natural scepticism encouraged them
to thoroughly question every conclusion and item of information encountered.

Missile crisis. Pessimism, caution, and scepticism were writ
large in the evolution of the blockade scenario. Kennedy
recognized immediately the potential for disaster in a mistaken response, and wanted as much time as possible to
formulate a program. He quickly adopted the judgment put
forward during the initial briefing session of ExCom that the
Soviet leadership would be most responsive to pressure before the missiles became operational. By subtracting the time
necessary to execute a program, Kennedy derived a surprisingly long policy formation period: five days. He later
admitted that shorter time period (24 hours) would "probably" have produced an imprudent choice. Kennedy's pessimism concerning the probability of success was repeatedly
injected into meetings of ExCom through warnings that all
available alternatives had serious disadvantages and that any
one of them could escalate to nuclear war.

Scepticism took the form of bruising debate supported by
careful analysis. Kennedy believed so completely in the creativity of this kind of process that he withdrew from the
working sessions of ExCom in order to avoid stifling conflict. In the initial sessions, it became apparent that only two
of the six alternatives advanced originally had any hope of
success: the surgical strike to destroy the bases and the naval
blockade. Initial analysis focused on the surgical strike, but
as debate continued the disadvantages began to accumulate.
The air strike would kill Russians and could provoke a
Soviet response in Berlin. In any case, the Soviets could
rebuild the bases immediately after a strike. Then the sites
would have to be secured through an invasion. But an in-

vasion would bring American and Soviet forces into direct conflict, in Cuba instead of Berlin. Air strategy required a surprise, but this would certainly be viewed as "sneak" attack, an event that would rally world opinion against the United States.

As the surgical strike became less and less attractive, ExCom began to examine the blockade alternative more intensively. If presented as a "quarantine" on the shipment of missiles and nuclear weapons to Cuba, it would appear both legal and responsible. With flexible interception points and options to escalate, it could be introduced as part of a diplomatic initiative which demonstrated both the capacity and the willingness to undertake military action. It would give the Soviet Union time change policy and mobilize support for the change within the Soviet leadership community. If it failed, a surgical strike and an invasion could be initiated. What was most important, it gave everyone options short of war and plenty of time to choose. When presented with both plans on Saturday afternoon (October 20), Kennedy quickly adopted the blockade scenario, and began allocating tasks to bring it into effect. In retrospect, the decision was a masterpiece of political engineering which permitted a neatly packaged performance that created and controlled events in exactly the sequence required to solidify the American position and to induce the Soviets to back down.

Steel crisis. Kennedy had less than forty-eight hours to prevent the spread of the price increase to other companies. This time limit considerably reduced the influence of his sense of caution, but pessimism and scepticism played a prominent role in the development of the divide-and-conquer scenario. The reason for the shortened decisional period was the speed with which collusive pricing had spread in the past. First, a major producer would announce the increase; then, the other major companies would follow the leader; finally, smaller companies, lacking options, would fall in line. The whole industry could act in two days.

With the time limit clearly in mind, Kennedy convened a meeting of relevant staff members within an hour of US

Steel's decision. The first alternative suggested was the threat of anti-trust suit, but sharp questioning revealed a number of flaws. First, it would take longer than two days to formulate the basis for court action. Second, a suit against US Steel would probably not affect the decisions of the other producers. Third, such threats had failed in the past.

The next suggestion was the divide-and-conquer program. Since the large companies acted as a bloc, the only hope lay in encouraging the small companies to defy the increase, something that could conceivably be accomplished by threatening to divert contracts to companies that refused to increase prices. Faced with the possibility of losing the 10 per cent of the market controlled by government purchases, the large companies might be induced to rethink their positions.

The realization that failure would mean humiliation encouraged Kennedy to probe for additional avenues of pressures. Public pressure on the steel industry would be useful; interpersonal pressure would be equally necessary with the smaller companies; the threat of anti-trust action offered an additional source of leverage. In a very short period of time, Kennedy had come up with a plan which required the simultaneous deployment of a number of resources along a number of different avenues. His sense of pessimism undoubtedly contributed to adoption of this "shotgun" approach. If one program failed, then perhaps another would succeed. Or perhaps all would succeed in small ways, and in the end the small gains would accumulate in victory, which is precisely what happened.

The "No Hope" Syndrome

DECISIONAL PHASE

The Bay of Pigs and Meredith cases were peculiar decisions because the responsibility for choice and action were distributed between different centres of power. The Eisenhower administration had already agreed to underwrite an invasion of Cuba, to be carried out with American support by an exile brigade training in Guatemala (Sorensen, 1965:295). A federal circuit court had overruled a district court decision which supported the refusal of officials to register James Meredith at the University of Mississippi (Schlesinger, 1965: 940–941). There is ample evidence to suggest that Kennedy wanted to avoid dealing with either decision because each implied such obvious risks of failure.[34] My conclusion is that Kennedy accepted the decisions reluctantly because of the presence of competing pressures. In the Meredith case, he could not deny the traditional role of the president as an administrative officer of the federal courts. In the Bay of Pigs, he seems to have experienced difficulty separating the administrative and political functions of the presidency, which would have been understandable in view of the fact that the Bay of Pigs was his first important presidential decision. In effect, he felt bound by the Eisenhower commitment, even though he feared the consequences of attempting to carry it through. He accepted both decisions as given because he felt he had no choice, and on the rather egoistic assumption that he was competent enough to process them with limited cost.

IMPLEMENTATION PHASE

In the abrogation syndrome, Kennedy's operational regulators (scepticism, caution, pessimism) dampened exceptionally intense stimuli to manageable proportions during the implementation stage, with the result that the consideration of alternative actions ended at the point the optimal scenario had been achieved. In other words, the operational regulators persistently challenged the assumptions and consequences of each alternative until a more modest, but well-adapted program had been drafted. In the "no hope" set, the same regulators began dampening a set of stimuli that had already been weakened, with the result that the implementation stage ended long after the optimal scenario had been questioned out of existence. The action alternatives finally chosen were too marginal in conception to have succeeded even under the most favorable conditions.

[34] Sorensen (1965:483) for the costs of the Meredith case, and Schlesinger (1965:238–239) for the costs of the Bay of Pigs.

The Bay of Pigs (January 28–April 17, 1961).[35] The original plan advanced by the CIA on January 28 called for an open invasion of Cuba by an exile brigade with American air and logistical support, and if necessary, the commitment of American troops once a beachhead had been achieved. Kennedy was sceptical, and asked the Defense Department to evaluate the plan on the explicit assumption that there would be no overt military participation by the United States. The Joint Chiefs of Staff reported that the plan "stood a 'fair' chance of success" without military intervention, if the invasion force could hang on long enough to stimulate an anti-Castro uprising among the Cuban people. Between January 28 and the next meeting on March 11, Kennedy was confronted with the problem of disposing of the brigade and with the assessment by the CIA that after June 1 Castro would be strong enough to resist an invasion. The only inexpensive way of disposing of the brigade, Kennedy agreed, was to return them to Cuba. The question was "how?"

At the next meeting on March 11 Kennedy authorized the creation of an invasion scenario, with three stipulations: first, no American military assistance; second, a clandestine infiltration rather than an overt invasion; third, flexibility sufficient to terminate the landings twenty-four hours before they were to begin. The CIA came up with the necessary plan, but before approving it in early April, Kennedy asked his "brokers" in the CIA whether or not the brigade would go ahead with a clandestine operation on the understanding that there would be no overt American military assistance. The answer communicated back was "yes," although, for some reason, the brigade leaders believed the landings would fail without some military support and the exile leadership apparently believed that military assistance would be forthcoming if the invasion ran into overwhelming difficulties. Either the exile leadership dismissed Kennedy's limitation for political rhetoric or Kennedy's "brokers" deliberately falsified this information on the assumption that Kennedy would send military assistance if confronted by the possibility of failure at the beaches.

[35] Sorensen (1965:294–309); Schlesinger (1965:233–286).

The record clearly demonstrates that Kennedy was operating on a number of mistaken factual assumptions: first, there was no escape route to carry the brigade to safety if the landing failed; second, the Cuban underground was too disorganized and weak to stimulate an uprising; third, Castro was exceptionally popular and could have dealt effectively with a much larger invasion. I think Kennedy may have accepted these myths at face value because they confirmed the value of the more modest scenario his operational regulators had already produced. In other words, he had found serious flaws in the original program, and assumed that the new program lacked flaws because it made up for the shortcomings of the old program.

Moreover, Kennedy seems to have had real difficulty mobilizing his own interest in the decision, possibly because he had not been responsible for its initiation. Had the invasion been his idea, his staff would have been more devoted to preventing him from making a mistake, which means they would have had a thorough, intimate, and broad knowledge of the feasibility of the invasion and would have felt confident enough to challenge the expert judgment of the military and intelligence communities. Kennedy was himself awed by the apparent skill and expertise of the CIA and the Joint Chiefs, and assumed (mistakenly) that the expertise of one would regulate and test the expertise of the other. In fact, both groups were committed to the program, and made similar errors in judgment.

Perhaps most important, his lack of interest and his instinct for caution led him to reduce the cost of the invasion to every conceivable value that could have been risked. Had the program been evaluated in terms of firm policy preferences, a predominant value would have been recognized, and other values could have been sacrificed as costs, a strategy that would have produced a clearly defined objective supported by a carefully calculated (and essentially positive) program of implementation. The strategy of reducing or eliminating important facets of the scenario in order to minimize the danger to a variety of values predestined the invasion to failure. The problem was that Kennedy had not been in the White House long enough to work through a set of policy objectives to find priorities.

Meredith case (September 28–31, 1962).[36] Caution and scepticism contributed directly to the riot and bloodshed that Kennedy wanted so much to avoid. Caution produced a reluctance to act decisively and to assume full responsibility for registering Meredith. Governor Ross Barnett had already been cited for civil contempt for turning Meredith away, and by Friday, September 28, it became clear that some display of force would be necessary to gain Meredith's admission. The question was "how much?" Kennedy hoped to use the *threat* of military intervention to encourage Barnett to protect Meredith when he arrived on campus. Kennedy and Barnett finally reached an agreement on Saturday in which Barnett would assume direct responsibility for maintaining order on the Oxford campus, and in return Kennedy agreed to register Meredith at the State Capitol in Jackson. This would have allowed Barnett to save face by claiming that he was actually trying to prevent Meredith's registration again, but had been outwitted by Kennedy. Three hours after the agreement had been reached, Barnett inexplicably cancelled the arrangement. Kennedy responded by federalizing the Mississippi National Guard, ordering federal troops to stand by in Memphis, and arranging for broadcast time on national television early Sunday evening (7:30 PM) to explain his decision to enroll Meredith on Monday morning.

On Sunday morning, Barnett phoned Robert Kennedy with a new proposal which involved a staged capitulation by Mississippi forces to federal forces, an idea that RFK immediately rejected as both "foolish" and "dangerous." Alarmed by the Attorney General's disclosure that the president would reveal Barnett's prior duplicity in his television address later that night, Barnett urged that Meredith be registered that afternoon while the campus still was deserted. He would "pretend ignorance and then protest vehemently from his office in Jackson the following morning." In return, Barnett promised to use state police to ensure Meredith's safety, thus eliminating the need for federal troops. The bargain

[36] Sorensen (1965:483–488); Schlesinger (1965:940–949).

seemed to be a perfect solution for both Kennedy and Barnett.

Then Kennedy committed what must be classified as a serious tactical blunder: he postponed his television address until 10:00 PM. His action was presumably a test of Barnett's sincerity, although there is strong evidence that Kennedy wanted more time to rewrite a section of the speech to "make it clear that the government was merely carrying out the orders of the court in a case it had not brought and was not forcing down the throats of Mississippians on its own initiative" (Sorensen, 1965:484). Barnett responded to the delay with an inflammatory statement accusing Kennedy of sneaking Meredith on campus without his knowledge, informed the White House that "no further forces would be required," and then abruptly withdrew the state police. Hearing that the state police had withdrawn, the mob gathered in front of the Administration Building attacked the federal marshals protecting Meredith, and in the ensuing violence two people were killed and hundreds injured.

Barnett encouraged the conditions for the riot in retaliation for the postponement, which he must have interpreted as evidence that Kennedy was going to exploit the presence of the state police to ensure Meredith's safe arrival on campus, and then expose Barnett's duplicity later in order to rationalize his own decisive action in delivering Meredith to the campus earlier than originally scheduled. Not only was Kennedy's postponement a primary factor in triggering the riot, but it compressed events in a way that neutralized his capacity to react to the riot immediately. The riot began shortly before the speech, which meant that Kennedy was unable to respond to it until his speech was over. As a result, the Army arrived too late to prevent the bloodshed, and through a lack of careful briefing in divisional strength instead of numbers appropriate to the situation.

CONCLUSIONS

This study suggests a number of hypotheses about the relationship between crisis decision-making and personality.

First, decisional stimuli are apt to contain personally resonant properties that are capable of arousing personal emotional conflict; this would be especially true of crisis situations. Second, where emotional conflict is evoked the decisional process of an executive system can easily be subordinated to the psychotherapeutic experiences of an executive. Third, a single response pattern of a personality may produce variable (perhaps even contradictory) outcomes as stimulus conditions change. Fourth, small changes in the configuration of decisional stimuli can produce large differences in policy outcomes. Although the psychodynamic model employed to analyse Kennedy's decisions lacks verification, it suggests nevertheless a number of new ways of looking at familiar events. Kennedy's value choice in the Cuban missile crisis, for example, was conceived as an attempt to restore his self-esteem rather than to correct an implausible disequilibrium in the nuclear balance of power. His operational regulators were seen as sources of success in the missile and steel decisions but as sources of failure in the Bay of Pigs and Meredith cases. Viewed in this light, the Kennedy decisions demonstrate how thin the margin between success and failure can be in a crisis situation and how much the final outcome may depend on psychotherapy. They also indicate how innocently irrational forces can be introduced into decisional situations.

PART SIX

PERSONALITY AND POLITICAL SYSTEMS

Introduction

Are the institutions of government related to the kinds of
personality that are recruited into the political system, or to
those types which are potential recruits for the system?

We are concerned in this section with the relationship of
personality to the emergence, development, function, and
change of political systems. Despite the considerable amount
of research activity in the broad area of personality and
politics, there have been few systematic, empirical studies of
these questions, but the void has been compensated by extensive discussion and controversy of the many related
issues. Hence our considerations in this section are speculative
and theoretical.

Fromm (1941) has argued that the personality types in a
given society serve either as a cement holding the system
together or as an explosive tearing it apart, depending on
the degree to which a given personality type fits the demands of the system and finds satisfaction within it. On this
basis, Fromm argues the principle of congruency, which
maintains a functional dependency, or simply a congenial fit
in some cases, between sociopolitical systems and personality
systems, which is mutually beneficial for the effective and
harmonious operation of both systems.

The fundamental proposition of this argument is that it is
only a half-truth that "It takes all kinds of people to make

the world go around." Rather, for any "social world" to function properly and adequately, it takes certain kinds of people, who must be in certain positions and in certain proportions at certain times. Otherwise there will be dysfunctional consequences—for the social system as well as the individual personality systems involved.

Our general thesis for this section is that the structure and the function of the polity are dependent in part on the personality structure of the political functionaries recruited into it and the congruent interaction of both the psychological and the sociological structures (DiRenzo, 1967a: Chapter 9), and that particular kinds of political systems and forms of government (1) are the result of certain personality types, and (2) functionally require certain kinds of personalities.

The first thorough exposition of the connection between the constitution of a body politic and the character of the individual citizens was made by Plato in his *Republic*. For Plato, as with others after him, such as Tocqueville (1840) and Lasswell (1948), the "right kind" of personality was a functional requisite of the sociopolitical system: the stability of the political institutions requires the molding of the appropriate form of social character or personality.

Our question here has been structured more pointedly by Inkeles. He asks: "Are the societies which have a long history of democracy peopled by a majority of individuals who possess a personality conducive to democracy? Alternatively, are societies which have experienced recurrent or prolonged authoritarian, dictatorial, or totalitarian government inhabited by a proportionately large number of individuals with the personality traits we have seen to be associated with extremism? . . . Almost all the modern students of national character are convinced that the answer to this question is in the affirmative. Systematic empirical evidence for this faith is unfortunately lacking" (1961:193–194).

As Berelson (1952:315–316), for example, states in regard to democracy: "There appear to be two requirements in democratic society which refer primarily to characteristics demanded of the electorate as it initially comes to make a political decision. These are the preconditions for electorate decisions. The first is the possession of a suitable *personality structure:* within a range of variations, the electorate is required to possess the types of character which can operate effectively, if not efficiently, in a free society. Certain kinds of personality structures are not congenial to a democratic society, could not operate successfully within it, and would be destructive of democratic values. Others are more compatible with or even disposed toward the effective performance of the various roles which make up the democratic political system. . . . The second requirement . . . is the factor of *interest and participation;* the electorate is required to possess a certain degree of involvement in the process of political decision, to take an appropriate share of responsibility."

What specific modes of personality, then, are required in a people as a necessary condition for the establishment and the maintenance of either a democratic or an authoritarian political order?[1] The "democratic personality" and the "authoritarian personality" usually are presented as clinically polar types, and the dominant view, as Inkeles (1961:193) states, is that a ". . . general syndrome of authoritarianism, dogmatism, and alienation undoubtedly is the psychological root of that political extremism which makes this type actively or potentially disruptive to democratic systems." Authoritarianism as a personality variable has been associated in the minds of Western social scientists with the "bad guys." As we saw in Part Four, McClosky stated that political conservatives with high scores on authoritarian measures are seen as falling on ". . . the more 'undesirable,' poorly adapted side of the personality variables under study." While this may be true in terms of social preferences, such conclusions, of course, have no theoretical meaning, since the functional value of such personality variables may be positive or negative, depending upon the functional needs of the particular political system which is involved. At any rate, au-

[1] This question of personality, or more broadly psychological, requisites parallels the kind of concerns raised by Tocqueville (1840), and more recently by Lipset (1960), for the social or sociological requisites of democracy.

thoritarian personality traits are conceived to be destructive of both healthy personal adjustment and vital democratic processes; and the authoritarian/dogmatic personality syndrome is believed to contain those allegedly pathological elements which are said to inhibit one's contribution to a democratic society.

There is much objection to this view that the authoritarian or the dogmatic personality is unhealthy, and therefore undemocratic and, furthermore, for this reason, undesirable.[2] Allport (1962:183), for example, challenges this position on the grounds that ". . . it may be possible to manifest an extreme degree of authoritarianism without being psychologically maladjusted." On the matter of psychopathology, Christie and Cook (1958:183), in their exhaustive review of the research on authoritarianism, state that "It still appears to be true that most measures of 'neuroticism' do not correlate with scores on the F or E scales." And, in these respects, Rutherford (1966) provides some evidence regarding the kinds of psychological disturbances that do not hinder political participation—and, in fact, in his view, may even increase it in specific circumstances.

The traditional analysis of political dictatorships has been centered on the motivations of dictatorial leaders, driven by the lust for power and sadistic cravings for domination. As Ebenstein (1961:101) states, "The followers and subjects of a dictatorship are viewed exclusively as 'victims' who just happen to fall into the misfortune of oppressive rule." But certain types of political behavior just do not merely happen. Some people and some nations, it is suggested, are more "dictatorship prone" than others.

Fromm (1941), for example, contends that the "authoritarian character" is the "human basis of Fascism"; and explains the rise of Hitler on the basis of the principle of congruency between the German national character and Nazism. And Dicks, as we saw in Part Four, argued that the success of National Socialism, despite its internal irrationality and self-contradictions, was due to the fact that the typical German character was a type highly susceptible to the style of leader-

[2] See, e.g., Eulau (1963:99–100).

ship that the movement offered, and was extremely vulnerable to the kind of propaganda appeals that it utilized.

Others[3] have offered similar explanations for the rise of Fascism in Italy and Perónism in Argentina, namely, that a sufficient number of people in these fascistic countries shared the values, goals, and attitudes of the respective fascist party. In short, they had the necessary psychological disposition and prerequisites for the emergence and maintenance of these authoritarian political systems.

On the basis of these kinds of considerations regarding the functional requisites of political systems, there has been much concern in the political and social sciences about the attraction of the "right type of political man" in terms of the desired forms of government. The discussions, however, have been concerned nearly exclusively with democracy. Lasswell (1948), for example, maintains that only through a reliance upon a "right man," and a concomitant rejection of the "wrong man," can democracy hope to escape the abuses of power. And Manheim (1959) claims, more pointedly, that the good, democratic society can be realized only with a democratic personality and a democratic structure, not the opposite or a mixture.

Our immediate concerns in this section are to explore this question of the "right man" in terms of several of the explicit and implicit issues. Our first selection is by Spitz, who, while offering a cynical argument against the idea of an appeal to the "right man," brings into focus a number of dimensions and considerations which are involved in this question, and defends the position that such a concept is both elusive and impractical. Although Spitz recognizes that the question of the "right man" is fundamentally one of the "right personality," his argument is presented primarily in ethical and moral terms; accordingly, he argues that it is the situation and not the individual (since the environment, he alleges, can modify the personality of the individual) that is crucial.

One objection which Spitz makes is that the "democratic" and the "authoritarian" personality—as presumably the

[3] See, e.g., Levy (1948) and Linton (1951).

"right" and "wrong" kind respectively—have not been adequately identified or distinguished. The other two selections which we offer in this section address this question.

In our second selection, Frenkel-Brunswik, Levinson, and Sanford ask whether or not an authoritarian, or antidemocratic, personality can be empirically identified, and proceed to provide a description of such a personality type, as well as to answer the question of the determinants in the social development of this kind of personality. These authors, utilizing their work from the noted study of *The Authoritarian Personality* (Adorno, 1950), describe the distinctive ideology and underlying personality needs of the antidemocratic, or authoritarian, individual.[4]

Unfortunately, descriptions of the "democratic personality" have been inferred from, and described in terms antithetical to those of the syndrome of authoritarianism. The democratic personality is postulated at the opposite pole from the authoritarian personality syndrome.[5] In our third selection for this section, however, Lane takes a more direct approach and discusses the "democratic personality" in reference to such dynamics as self-acceptance, self-esteem, and ego strength. Additionally, Lane examines the dysfunctional—allegedly pathological—qualities and dynamics of democratic man, which he classifies into the following categories: (1) self-referential pathologies, (2) interpersonal pathologies, and (3) social and cultural pathologies.[6]

It is highly unlikely that any character type will be associated invariably with a single form of political system. For example, both the authoritarian and the democratic types of personality, though with differential frequencies, are found in authoritarian as well as in democratic societies. First of all, it is possible that all decision-making, from a functional perspective, cannot be the sole result of either democratic or authoritarian processes as the case may be. Certain roles

---

[4] For a statement on the authoritarian personality in contemporary perspective, see Sanford (1973).

[5] Martin (1964) speaks of a "tolerant personality" which is described as a syndrome distinct from the authoritarian personality.

[6] For other statements on the formulation of the "democratic personality," see Lasswell (1948:Chapter 7) and Inkeles (1961).

within democratic types of political systems may need more authoritarian personalities, just as others may need more democratic ones. Authoritarian personalities are useful in some roles in democratic systems, and in many other roles where they are not indispensable, they are at least harmless. Moreover, as Shils (1954:48–49) and Lipset (1960:31) contend, a viable democracy, in that it must attract and receive support from all segments of society, must accommodate all kinds of personalities. Data (see DiRenzo, 1967a, 1967b) do show that authoritarian personalities can and do function in both a democratic system and a democratic fashion. Similarly, authoritarian structures may be functionally dependent to some extent upon more democratic personalities.

The concrete significance of these questions regarding the theoretical value of the "authoritarian" and the "democratic" personality can be exemplified with a question that every now and then, perhaps at least once a decade, for a series of various political events, comes to the fore in our own country: How prone is the United States to authoritarian government?[7]

Of course, "boss rule," though not generally in the public eye, has been, and remains, characteristic of many American towns, cities, and counties. We could mention as well the strong-arm politics which frequently come to the surface in other quasi-political organizations, such as those in the labor field. But, on what could be considered a major scale, Huey Long, the Louisiana governor in the 1930s, established perhaps the closest thing to a fascistic dictatorship in the United States. And, during the forties, the United States experienced, however acceptingly, the quasi-militaristic government necessitated by World War II. Since then the country has witnessed the McCarthyism of the 1950s, the John Birch movement of the 1960s, and so far in the 1970s the Wallace movement. None of these episodes, of course, has

[7] Linton (1951) offers an argument against such a possibility. For a treatment of ". . . the relation of national character to the political systems found in modern national states, and more especially, to the establishment of democracy," see Inkeles (1961).

received sufficient following—however extensive and influential, and hence however potentially successful—to make them alarmingly threatening to the fundamental democracy of the nation.[8] Yet, in the midst of each of these "crises" the whispers and shouts of the intimidating question have been heard.

Nonetheless, in terms of functional consequences for political systems, what is important is that the type and the quality of role performance is related directly to the degree of congruence between the social structure of the political roles and the psychological structure of the personality of the individual agents. As Riesman and Glazer (1961:438–439) state, although "different kinds of character could be used for the same kind of work within an institution, . . . [a] price is paid by the character types that [fit] badly, as against the release of energy provided by the congruence of character and task." The practical significance of this issue may be seen in that political systems may recruit personalities that by and large do not, or cannot, function effectively within particular kinds of structures. Now what happens, as Inkeles (1961:197–198) asks, to a social system that is marked by a substantial lack of congruence (which again is always a matter of degree) between its own functional requisites and the requirements of the personality systems therein? The results would seem to be some degree of dysfunction and/or change in either or both of the systems. A substantial change in one system will mean a correspondingly substantial change in the other. The stability and change of political organizations and systems are to an extent, in this view, a function of incongruity which they share with the personality systems therein. The greater the congruity—the more perfect the "fit"—the more stable is the organization and the more minimal is the change in the sociopolitical systems.

We can see here the relevance of personality, in terms of the principle of congruency, for political and social change. Elsewhere (1970) we have shown that political change and social reform require (1) more generally, change-

---

[8] Levinson (1957) has argued that "One symptom of the trend toward authoritarianism is the rapid decrease in ideological choice now available to the general population." On this point, see Bell (1960).

oriented personalities, and (2) more specifically, personalities that are congruent with the particular modes, methods, forms, and techniques of sociopolitical change. Sociopolitical change produces cognitive ambiguity—a social and psychological state—that in an extreme degree cannot be tolerated by the human person and least of all by the more authoritarian and dogmatic personality. The inability, on the part of certain types of personalities, to adapt to social change is crucial, since this kind of psychological accommodation is one of the most important functional requirements of all modern political systems.[9]

The answer to this intimidating question of authoritarian rule is implicit in the selections of this section: the probability of the rise of authoritarian rule is contingent upon the number and the extent of appropriately congruent types of personalities which exist and/or develop within the nation, or any pivotal segment of it. According to Ebenstein (1961: 101), who quotes from the Adorno research, empirical studies in the United States have shown that ten percent of Americans are strongly authoritarian, and about twenty percent are partly authoritarian. Unfortunately, to make these figures meaningful, what is lacking is the knowledge of which proportion of the population would constitute the catastrophic point at which the nation would be pushed off the cliff of democracy.

Fromm (1941) had predicted that only a minimum of the German workers had the "authoritarian attitudes" that would make them convinced Nazis, but likewise only a small percentage had the democratic attitudes to make them devoted anti-Nazis. The majority of the German people, despite their opinions, were overwhelmingly anti-Nazis, but lacked the emotionally based conviction to oppose the Nazis once Hitler held power. And Dicks (1950) similarly argues that the German character was sufficient and indispensable for Nazism, but not limited to Nazism in its potentiality for functional support. Much of the same conclusions are suggested by Erikson (1950) in his analysis of the typical German character and Hitler's appeal to it. Hence, in these views, not only

[9] See Frenkel-Brunswik (1952) for an elaboration on this point.

may a relatively small number be sufficient for the active, functional support of an authoritarian, or even other type of, political system, but such maintenance also can be provided to some extent by passive support; and, in the face of a silent opposition—which itself provides passive support—such a minority can be all the more effective.

The mass production of authoritarian or democratic personalities, nonetheless, is primarily a function of corresponding kinds of political and social structures. These kinds of structures in the United States, for the most part, have been consistent and congruent with democracy, and consequently have mitigated against any extensive or enduring development of authoritarian government or political systems. Yet the relatively long-term psychological effects of rapid and widespread sociopolitical change—however directed toward the greater establishment of democratic structures—is difficult to determine in this regard. Accordingly, as we look to the future, the issue of authoritarian rule in America not only remains problematical, but one the resolution of which rests in the further explanation of the interactions of personality and politics. The principle of congruency, in this respect, constitutes a sociopsychological dynamic of fundamental importance.

Power and Personality: The Appeal to the "Right Man" in Democratic States
David Spitz

At least from the time of Socrates, in whose ideal state philosophers would be kings, the appeal to the right man has played a major role in systematic reflections on the control of power. For if the right man does rule, Socrates argued, neither institutional nor other controls—*e.g.*, law—need to be employed. Because he is the right man, he will do the right things: he will rule wisely; he will establish or, where already established, he will perpetuate, that order in human affairs that best approximates or achieves justice and secures liberty.

The problem, then, for those who hold this view in democratic states, is not whether the right man should rule, but how he is to be discovered and how he can be assured the reins of political power. Or, to formulate the problem in negative terms, how can we identify and exclude from power those who are the "wrong" men, those who are likely to rule badly and unjustly, those who—because they are, for example, "authoritarians" at heart—may if they achieve positions of power violate the very principles of the democratic state and thereby endanger its existence?

A preliminary—and perhaps crucial—difficulty must be noted. The appeal to the right man may not be altogether compatible with the appeal to democracy. If, for example, the

Reprinted by permission of the author and publisher from the *American Political Science Review*, Volume 52, 1958, pp. 84–97.

right man is subject to democratic controls, primarily to the principle of responsibility, he may be removed from or not elected to office, in which case democracy is revealed to be a form of state in which the "wrong" man can rule by popular approval. If, on the other hand, those who appeal to the right man insist that the right man rule, or that the wrong man be excluded from political power, without regard to what the people want, then the state which adopts their view ceases to be (if it formerly was) a democratic state. Most political philosophers who have looked to the leadership of the right man for political salvation, have seized the latter horn of this dilemma. With Plato and Santayana—to take but two from among the more noted of such writers—they have mocked democracy's trust in public opinion. They have derided what they have contemptuously called the rule of the common (by which they mean vulgar) or average (by which they mean inferior) man. They have appealed instead to a form of the aristocratic state—to a political order in which those few who allegedly know what is right will also, precisely because they "know" (*i.e.,* have wisdom), follow the path of "virtue."

This is not the place to discuss the easy assumptions and many fallacies of the aristocratic appeal to the right man,[1] for, whatever its merits or deficiencies, to the extent that it departs from or negates the principle of democracy it offers no solution (and is therefore irrelevant) to our central problem, which is the control of abuses of power *within* the democratic state. When we turn, however, to democratic expositions of the appeal to the right man—to the doctrines of men who, like Harold Lasswell and Karl Mannheim, take the position that only through a reliance on the right man, and a concomitant rejection of the wrong man, can democracy hope to prevent or to escape from abuses of power—we encounter other, and scarcely less serious, difficulties.

For one thing, who is the right man, and who the wrong man? How, and by what criterion or set of criteria, is such a man to be identified or defined? Secondly, will a reliance on

---

[1] For an analysis and criticism of the various forms of this aristocratic appeal, see Spitz (1949:Chapters 4–9); MacIver (1950: Chapter 5 and 130–133).

the right man, or a repudiation of the wrong man, really eradicate oppressive rule? On the one hand, the right man may succumb to and be corrupted by the normal temptations of power, in which event he ceases to be the right man, or may in retrospect be held never to have been the right man. On the other hand, he may, to retain his office, yield to the pressures of public opinion; he may give the people what they want, or what they say they want, and in this event, should the demand be (say) for oppressive rule over a despised minority group, he would no longer fulfill the purpose for which as a right man he was called. If either of these eventualities were to be realized, we would find that we had but traveled a full circle: for we began by looking to the right man to prevent and even to eliminate the ravages of oppressive rule, and we end by looking for some means to rid ourselves of the man who is no longer the right man, and who may in fact have himself become the worst of oppressors.

To make clear that these are real and probable difficulties and not merely hypothetical horrors, it is necessary to consider each of them in turn.

THE DEFINITION OF THE RIGHT (AND WRONG) MAN

Despite the bitter judgment of Ecclesiastes (7:20), who warned that "there is not a just man upon earth, that doeth good, and sinneth not," some of those who would save democracy from its sins have looked yearningly for a just man, one who would do good and commit no evil. Such a man, in traditional political thought, was not merely the competent but the superior man; he excelled all others by virtue of his merit or achievement.

Merit, to be sure, is an ambiguous term, and has been variously defined. In some constructions it has been equated with learning or wisdom; in others, with that technical training or experience that produces what is commonly called expertise; in still others, with certain intrinsic qualities allegedly associated with blood and breeding; and in others, again, with the prescriptive sanction of a higher authority such as God. Each of these qualities is susceptible, in turn, of different definitions. Thus, while learning to the ancient Greeks meant philosophy, to what is perhaps the dominant strand of contemporary American opinion it means knowledge of such applied sciences as medicine and law; and this knowledge is generally associated less with scholars in the law schools (say) than with practicing lawyers, especially those who for one reason or another have attained a place on the Supreme Court. Similarly, the term achievement is not without considerable ambiguity: for one who has acquired great wealth may not enjoy great fame; one who has achieved fame may not also be wise; and one who is wise may remain always in poverty and relative obscurity. Which is the greatest achievement?

It need not follow, of course, from the fact that traditional political philosophy has produced no agreement as to who is the superior or right man, that there is no such man. One among the many divergent views may prove, ultimately, to be well-grounded. One among the many claimants may emerge as "the" right man.

But the dilemma referred to above would still remain to bedevil those who appeal to this right man. For if, on the one hand they place him beyond popular control, they move out of the realm of democratic theory into the never-never land of what they choose to call aristocracy—a world that can appear real only to one who seriously believes that some men at least are, if not perfect, uncontrolled by passion and by the pursuit of self-interest; that some men are, indeed, possessed of so compelling a sense of duty and so abundant a measure of intelligence as to be motivated only by what is advantageous to all and to be unaffected by the corrupting influences of power; that such men are, consequently, to be unhesitatingly entrusted with the lives and destinies of other men. Unfortunately for such a belief, it ignores certain inconvenient historical truths, not least among them the fact that the very existence of democracy is to be accounted for as a reaction against the demonstrated incompetence and tyranny of "aristocrats" and other self-styled superior men. Not all who have affirmed the aristocratic theory have had the honesty and courage of Santayana, who, while he dared to hope, admitted too that good government—from his aristocratic point of view—has never yet existed (and perhaps can never exist) in this world, that all past aristocracies have in fact been artificial and corrupt (Santayana, 1951:413).

If, on the other hand, the appeal to the right man is limited to an exhortation to the people to select a particular man or type of man on the ground that he is the right man, it is an appeal not to the wisdom of the right man but to that of the popular will, in which case it is the judgment of the latter that is at stake.

Another form of the appeal to the right man, however, has emerged in recent years. This appeal eschews the language of morality—of right and wrong, of good and bad, as ethical terms—and seeks instead, in line with what is conceived to be the approved method of modern science, to use such terms only in relation to a stipulated goal. If that goal is the preservation (or the achievement) of democracy, and more immediately the control of oppressive power, the right man is not one who is abstractly the best or most virtuous man but one who is specifically committed—dedicated, if you will— to the attainment of that goal. He shares "democratic" values, he avoids abusing his power, not because it is fashionable for him to do so or because it may happen to serve his convenience or his purposes, but because he *must,* because he really wants to, do so. He is so constituted, in fact, that he cannot (or at least is unlikely to) think or act otherwise. This is because, in the language of the theorists of this school, he is a "democratic" as distinguished from an "authoritarian" personality; he has the "right" type of character structure.

It would be misleading to imply, as do some of the more extreme formulations of this view, that the appeal to democratic personality altogether neglects or moves outside of the institutional framework. On the contrary, it is most commonly an appeal to personality precisely because that personality is held to be in accord with a particular institutional framework. Thus Mannheim, one of the more sophisticated exponents of this "scientific psychology," assumes as an underlying premise of his argument "a correlation between social organization and personality pattern." He draws a contrast between democratic and authoritarian types of personality and between democratic and authoritarian societies, and insists that only where we have *both* a democratic social structure and a democratic man can we hope to realize the good—*i.e.,* the democratic—society (Mannheim, 1950:231 and Chapters 7–9).

A like argument is advanced by Lasswell. Ideally, Lasswell believes, human freedom requires the elimination of power; it means a world "in which coercion is neither threatened, applied nor desired." Since, however, there is no likely probability that power will be eliminated, the immediate task is to curb its destructiveness, to prevent it from interfering with or deviating from the "network of congenial and creative interpersonal relations" that, in Lasswell's conception, constitutes democracy. To guard against such "antidemocratic and destructive" deviations, he would have us rear, choose, and support "leaders with the personality formation appropriate to democracy." He would have us look not to their beliefs but to their adjustment; and this, of course, makes democratic leadership a function not simply of popular desire but of social psychiatry—"the social psychiatry of democracy." "What is needed," Lasswell insists, "is a *National Personnel Assessment Board* set up by citizens of unimpeachable integrity which will select and supervise the work of competent experts in the description of democratic and antidemocratic personality." For unless we support the one and reject the other, "the equilibrium essential to sustain the democratic commonwealth cannot be maintained" (Lasswell, 1948:108–110, 115–118, 146, 187).

Now the contention that in every society some men are visibly—*i.e.,* impressionistically—more prone than others to resort to arbitrary or "authoritarian" methods is, I think, unexceptionable; as is too the conclusion from this fact that a democratic society, if it is intelligent, should not select cruel and vicious men in the hope that upon attaining power they will succumb to the father-instinct and become shepherds rather than wolves, that it should look instead to the leadership of "decent" and reasonably stable persons. None would dispute such a position. But if I understand Lasswell and

Mannheim correctly, their argument goes further than this. They would have such men selected, or at least initially screened, by "scientific" methods—*i.e.*, tests, questionnaires, interviews, and the like—that would, because they are "scientific," admit of little or no error. And this is quite a different thing.

In the first place, the difference between a "democratic" and an "authoritarian" personality is sometimes not in how he behaves but in how he is treated. In this respect Shaw's conversion of Eliza Doolittle from a flower-girl into a duchess attests to a greater insight than that simplistic psychology which mechanistically reduces adult conduct to its alleged infantile origins, or equates it with a particular type of character structure. No one who has seen the products of prison or reform school brutality, or who has witnessed the frustrations and anxieties imposed on administrators by the formalized routines and other pressures of a bureaucratic system, can doubt that personality is as much molded by the situation in which a person finds himself as it is by the imputed compulsiveness or aggressiveness of his neurotic nature. If, then, a so-called "authoritarian" personality is thrust into a "democratic" environment, it does not necessarily follow that his personality will remain unchanged.

In the second place, it is not at all clear just what a "democratic" or an "authoritarian" personality *is*. Despite the urgency (let alone the confidence) with which Mannheim and Lasswell and others of this school plead their cause, they have nowhere adequately spelled out the specific nature of these conflicting character profiles or personality types. It does not carry us very far, for example, to say, as Lasswell and Mannheim do, that the democratic personality is tolerant, cooperative, and secure, while the authoritarian personality is domineering, resentful of criticism, more prone to resort to violence and other forms of pressure, and burdened by social anxiety. These are, for the most part, tautologous terms; they hide rather than reveal meanings. They also overlook the fact that few if any individuals are in all the facets of their being consistently the one or the other personality type, that nearly every man exhibits a complex of both "democratic" and "authoritarian" behavior traits. It is not unusual, then,

for many who are "democratic" in their social relationships
to be "authoritarian" in their family or professional life. It is,
to revert to our first point, the situation and not the so-called
personality type that is often crucial.[2]

It follows, thirdly, that if we do not know with "scientific"
precision what a democratic or authoritarian personality *is*,
and if what any one person *is* depends on the dynamics of a
situation as much as, and perhaps more than, upon some
static character trait or set of attitudes, then any attempt to
test or to measure an assumed and fixed personality "type"
is bound to be ambiguous or meaningless. And if we turn
from the work of a sociologist like Mannheim and a political
scientist like Lasswell to the tests, questionnaires, and interviews of the professional social psychologists and psychoanalysts, we find that this is precisely what occurs: the tests
do not measure what they purport to measure; the evidences
do not *prove* the existence of a definite "democratic" or
"authoritarian" personality type.

This is true whether we take as our point of departure the
simple though politically meaningless definition of the authoritarian personality given by Erich Fromm (1941:163–164,
168, 236)—that the authoritarian personality craves power
over men but at the same time esteems it in others and
longs to submit to it—or the more complex if somewhat
contradictory definition given by the authors of *The Authoritarian Personality* (perhaps the most influential of recent

---

[2] As Else Frenkel-Brunswik, one of the authors of *The Authoritarian Personality* (Adorno, 1950), put it: "Since every individual
possesses features of the authoritarian as well as of the democratic
personality, though in varying proportions, such objective factors
as economic conditions and such psychological factors as feelings
of dissatisfaction, helplessness, and isolation may decide the issue
in a particular overall situation" (Frenkel-Brunswik, 1952:63; see
further, Frenkel-Brunswik, 1954b).

It ought to be observed in passing that what is true of personality
is true also—in this respect at least—of society: for no society
completely fits into one or the other of these rigid categories of
the psychologist; every society contains both "democratic" and
"authoritarian" elements. Mannheim occasionally pauses to recognize this point, both in relation to personality and to society (see,
for example, 1950:208), but his argument generally ignores or
minimizes the importance of this consideration.

studies espousing this point of view)—that the authoritarian personality is rigidly conventional but is also cynical and destructive, is unimaginative and opposed to the subjective but is also disposed "to believe that wild and dangerous things go on in the world," holds to a deterministic view of man's fate but is also preoccupied with sex and power, and so on.[3] Neither definition is very helpful, for both describe or delineate features that can be found in some measure in nearly every man and hence do not enable us to discriminate among them. Since, moreover, both Fromm and the authors of *The Authoritarian Personality* employ an approach to personality that focuses on attitudes or predispositions rather than (as Mannheim [1950:173–180] urges) on behavior, they run into a larger difficulty—namely, the inability to distinguish (and consequently to measure) opinions or ideology from character. If we add to these limitations the failure of both contributions to take adequate account of the varying intensities with which such attitudes or predispositions may be held, and to relate them to the dynamic situations in which they may emerge or in which they may be present but subdued, we see that neither work can take us very far toward a "scientific" understanding of what the "authoritarian" personality is.[4]

Lasswell, indeed, in commenting on *The Authoritarian Personality*, argues that such a concept as the "authoritarian" personality—which he here defines as the "power centered" or "power oriented" man—is more properly applied to *followers* than to *leaders*, or to those who play comparatively minor rather than major roles in the power structure; conversely, he suggests, "all top leaders in democratic or totalitarian regimes . . . tend to be recruited from fundamental personality patterns that are not primarily oriented toward power" (Lasswell, 1954:220–224). If this hypothesis is valid, it would seem to negate his own earlier thesis as well as to cast into disrepute the entire notion of the appeal to the

---

[3] Adorno (1950:228 and passim). See also Frenkel-Brunswik (1954a:171–202; 1954b; 1952); cf. further Maslow (1943); Allport (1954: Chapter 25); and Saenger (1953: Chapter 9).

[4] For some of these and other criticisms as applied to *The Authoritarian Personality*, see Kecskemeti (1951), and Christie and Jahoda (1954). These findings are summarized in Glazer (1954).

"right" personality (and the concomitant rejection of the "wrong" personality) as the indispensable corrective to the abuse of power.

THE RELEVANCE OF THE RIGHT MAN

It may, however, be argued that these strictures are not permanently binding. I have, after all, conceded that the *idea* of an authoritarian personality has a certain plausibility as an impressionistic or intuitive-apprehending if not scientific fact. Consequently, it may be said, refinements in testing techniques may in time enable us to verify such impressions and reduce them to demonstrable facts. They may help to isolate what is intrinsic to character structure from what is part of the total environment. But whether or not they succeed in doing so, it can be argued, the important fact remains that the authoritarian personality—however men may differ as to its definition—can in some measure be detected even now; hence, this awareness properly becomes, or should become, a guide to political action.

Now the possibility that refinements in testing techniques and in other devices will be achieved, is hardly to be contested. Nevertheless, two problems at least will still plague those who hope to demonstrate through such means the validity of a particular personality typology. One problem derives from the curious but not surprising fact that while the concept of the authoritarian personality has received much attention and can be held to rest on some "scientific" evidences, the concept of the so-called democratic personality hangs very much in the air, and is more likely to remain there. For however difficult the task of defining the authoritarian personality may be, the description of those character traits or attitudes that constitute the democratic personality is a most dubious and controversial—because unscientific—undertaking.[5] The other problem stems from the fact that

[5] Thus A. H. Maslow, who finds it impossible to avoid using the term, admits that "the concept 'democratic personality' is simply not a scientific concept; there is no agreement whatsoever on its meaning" (Maslow, 1957:94). Other recent attempts to describe

the line between the individual and the social cannot be effectively drawn. This, of course, was precisely the point on which Mill's otherwise admirable essay *On Liberty* floundered, and it is by no means evident that psychologists and sociologists since his time have succeeded in establishing a legitimate principle by which to differentiate that which is intrinsic to man from that which is inherited or acquired from society. I do not mean to imply by this that personality cannot be distinguished from culture; for the two, while not separable, are not the same. I argue only that the individual, be he conformist or rebel, is so much a product of his society that his attitudes, values, and behavior are always in some measure socially conditioned; they are always a reflection of his cultural environment. When we add to this the very great complexity, the continuing mystery, of personality itself, we see that no psychology can hope through an analysis of individual character alone to establish a particular typology of democratic and authoritarian personality.[6]

Let us, however, set these objections aside. Let us grant, in the face of our ignorance of future events, that a meaningful distinction may be drawn between democratic and authoritarian personalities, and that adequate tests may be devised to tell us into which category our various political leaders or would-be leaders belong. Can we then really expect the eradication of oppressive rule?

The answer, I fear, must still be negative, and for two reasons pre-eminently. On the one hand, abuses of power are not simply a consequence of some psychological quirk or defect in the ruler; they are also the product of conflicting interests, of long-sustained prejudices, and of established traditions. On the other hand, the right man, once in power, is not likely always to remain the right man. Contrary assumptions,

---

these traits—*e.g.*, by Lasswell (1951b:465–525) and by Allport (1954: Chapter 27)—are quite unconvincing when read in the light of such strictures as those by Kecskemeti (1951) and Glazer (1954) and by Shils in Christie and Jahoda (1954:24–49) on the definition of the democratic personality employed in *The Authoritarian Personality*.

[6] Cf. Bendix (1952); Riesman (1950:172, 178 and passim) and Wrong (1956).

while not wholly false, are insufficiently true to warrant the high expectations that some men have placed in them.

Consider first the view that men who abuse power do so primarily (in some formulations of this theory, exclusively) out of evil intent or vanity or madness. The list of tyrants who meet this view is a long but not an exhaustive one; Attila the Hun and Hitler and others like them are known, after all, only because they were, even among tyrants, unusual men. But, more importantly, the abuses of power that disfigure democratic states are customarily of a different order. They derive not merely from the caprice or malevolence of those who come to power, but also from the fact that those who rule, like the factions of the people who support them, tend all too often to pursue their own narrow or selfish interests; that rulers tend all too easily to identify the good of the whole with the material good of their class or of some special portion of the whole, such as their families and themselves. Thus, unless it can be shown that personality stands in some necessary—or even approximate (understanding by this a highly probable)—relation to policy, so that the right man will by virtue of his "rightness" act justly (*i.e.,* in a way that transcends particularity of interest) and the wrong man will by virtue of his "wrongness" act unjustly (*i.e.,* in a way that sacrifices the rights of the many, or even of the few, to greed and ambition), the appeal to personality is no solution to our problem.

This cannot be shown. There is no demonstrable relation between "democratic" or "authoritarian" personalities and policy such that authoritarian men will line up on one side, and democratic men on the other side, of each conceivable issue. The lines of ideological division do not respect those of personality, whether we look at a particular issue such as desegregation or at more general questions of domestic and foreign policy or even at the basic problem of the form of the state itself. Indeed, if the theory of the authoritarian personality is a valid one, it is precisely among authoritarians that the greatest ideological divisions are likely to occur; for here the driving force is said to be not ideology but ambition, the craving for power, and in this context policies will be supported or opposed not in terms of their relation to one's character structure but in terms of their utility as steps along the pathway to power. The shifting positions on policy questions taken by Communist political parties in all democratic states at the command of the rulers in the Kremlin, most strikingly at the time of the Nazi-Soviet pact and again at the demise and subsequent denuding of their "great leader Stalin," is a continuing illustration in point; as are too the autocratic methods sometimes employed by democrats in combatting those whom they deem to be authoritarians. On the other hand, persons of quite different dispositions may well behave in a more or less uniform manner, as is evidenced, for example, by the wide diversity of personality characteristics to be found in any political movement, including a democratic one.[7]

In fact, to argue that there is a causal relationship between democratic personality and social role, is to imply that the specific undemocratic practices in this country—many and varied as they are—could all be eliminated merely by placing men with democratic personalities into positions of power. But this, surely, is a fanciful expectation. History is not made by the impact of personalities alone. A Carlyle may look to the ablest man in loyal reverence, and decry any institutional or other restraints that lesser men seek to put upon him. But politics in a democracy is more than a matter of heroes and hero-worship. Other influences are also at play: the individual must come to grips with the interests and traditions of parties and pressure groups no less than with the established organs of government; he cannot ignore social conditions and the power of non-political organizations; he must look to the will, however erroneous he may believe it to be, of the electorate which put him in power, and which can vote him out. He is bound, in a word, by historical, political, and economic forces that are not of his own making and that are often beyond his effective control. Consequently, even if the ruler should be the right man, the right personality, it does not follow that he can, in a democratic state, do what he conceives to be the right thing.

Nor should he be permitted to do so. If it is the business of a democratic state to give the people what they want, to satisfy their stated desires rather than their objective needs

[7] Cf. Shils (1954:42–49).

(*i.e.*, what some allegedly wise men conceive their needs to be), then it is the function of the government to meet, not to negate, that demand. This is why, in principle, all the people, and not just a few of them, are given political rights. They need those rights, as Mill (1910:291) said, not in order that they may govern, but in order that they may not be misgoverned. And for this purpose it is not the right or the outstanding man, not the so-called democratic personality, that is required, but the representative man—who is sensitive to the changing tides of public opinion and will faithfully seek to translate them into public policy. This is not to imply that a democratic leader ought never to attempt to mold or to change public opinion, that he ought never to be more than an effective recording device for the popular will. But it is to say that however much he may essay a leading role, he ought not, by and large, to act contrary to the judgment of his constituents. So long as he fulfills this role effectively, it is no proper concern of the public what manner of man he is. In this respect it is the part of wisdom to distinguish, so far as one can, the ruler's public life from his private character.

All of this is not to deny that evil or stupid men can cause great harm, and that those states are fortunate that can keep such men out of power. It is only to argue that since tyrannical policies are not necessarily the result of wrong or authoritarian character structures, those policies can neither be removed nor prevented by a remedy that looks to personality alone.

This conclusion is reinforced when we turn to the second of our two major objections to the relevance of the right personality: that the right man is also prone to do great harm. In part, this is because the temptations of power may sooner or later corrupt him, in which case he ceases to be the right man. But in part too, it is precisely because he is the right man that he may do wrong things.

For if the right man is "right" in the moral sense of the word, and is moved by his intelligence and good will to correct the injustices that exist about him, he is sometimes apt to resent those of lesser talents or firmness of character who disagree with him and who would impede his work. Rather than risk failure, rather than have to say later, as the utopian communist Wilhelm Weitling bitterly said: "If all had followed me as the children of Israel followed Moses out of Egypt, I would have succeeded,"[8] he may endeavor to silence or to override dissent and to impose his own right judgment. Unhappily, in a world of conflicting moral codes, the right man is right for himself and perhaps for some others, but not for all men; and for those whose judgment is at variance with his own his coercive rule is as wrong as it may, in a particular situation, be oppressive. This is not, let it be understood, to argue that it is impossible to obtain a "right" man (i.e., right to those who so conceive him) as a leader in a democratic state, or that it would be undesirable to have such a right man rule. Nor is it to contend that such a right man could not, under any conditions, succeed both in remaining a right man and in ruling wisely. It is only to insist that such a right man *may*, in a particular set of circumstances, insist on having his own way (i.e., the "right" way) even if this requires him to act contrary to the popular will or to violate basic democratic rights.[9]

If, on the other hand, the right man is "right" in the democratic sense of the word, he is prone to respond affirmatively to the dictates of public opinion. But public opinion may bid him on occasion do an undemocratic thing, in which case he must choose between conflicting policies. As a right man, he wants to give the people what they want; but as a right man, he is committed too to the preservation of democracy itself. To remain loyal to the latter obligation is to defy public opinion and thereby to risk dismissal from public office. To accede to the public will is to repudiate his greater allegiance and thereby to retain public office only at the cost of ceasing to be the right man. In the first case, he is right but he may also prove ineffective; in the second case, he is neither right nor effective. In both cases, therefore, the appeal to the right

[8] Quoted in Wittke (1950:234).
[9] In this respect Santayana (1951:436) does no more than barely overstate a basic truth when he argues that "all living creatures become wicked under pressure. Absolute singleness of purpose cannot but be ruthless; it is ruthless initially, because it has no eye for any contrary interest; and it becomes ruthless again deliberately in the end, because all contrary interests seem odious and sinful to its fanaticism."

man, to the leadership of (say) the democratic personality, provides no sure solution to the abuse of power.

I do not mean to carry this self-defeating perplexity too far. The fact that too many men would rather have power than be right does not necessarily imply that all right men will seek at all costs to retain power. Not all power corrupts all men. Some power, in fact, is requisite to the making of a man. Without some autonomy of action, without some delegation of power and the responsibility to administer that power wisely, a man may never grow out of the mentality of a child; he may remain always a dependent animal. And if experience is any guide, the histories of the British and the American democracies make it abundantly clear that, within a respected tradition and an institutional framework that renders rule neither permanent nor absolute, power does not necessarily corrupt; by affording opportunities, it enables many to rule moderately, and some to achieve greatness.[10]

But the temptations of power, though resisted by some, overcome many more. The lure of glory, of pride, of material gain, no less than the conviction that given the power to implement his will one can achieve great things, the right things, for the whole of his people—all these combine to make the pursuit, and later the retention, of power a more than necessary thing. Good men may begin the quest reluctantly, but they rarely end that way. The game is too serious, the weapons too biting, the stakes too high, for them to remain in fact what they strive to appear to be—selfless and genteel servants or would-be servants of the body politic. Those who lack power yearn for what appears now to be well within their grasp, and the failure to achieve it but stimulates them to greater endeavors than before; while the actual conquest and enjoyment of power, despite its bitter fruits, is yet so sweet as to seduce those who possess it into thinking that they were destined for the offices they hold, or (what amounts to the same thing) that their achievements will be destroyed if they surrender their protective role. And always there are the *courtiers*—the flatterers and the sycophants, the profit-seeking groups and the glory-seeking adventurers—whose own possibilities of success are linked to

[10] Cf., for example, Radcliffe (1952).

that of the rulers and who are ready, therefore, always to praise their rulers' actions and to encourage their idolatry of themselves.

It is not, therefore, surprising that even good men should begin to think that their power should be commensurate with their goodness, and that this being (in their own eyes at least) unlimited, they should desire their power to be unlimited too. It is true that many have echoed D'Avenant's warning that "no one man ought to think of being omnipotent, unless he could be omniscient and omnipresent."[11] It is true also that in this respect the American political system has heeded only too well Montesquieu's (1748, Book XI, Chapter 4) warning "that every man invested with power is apt to abuse it, and to carry his authority as far as it will go. . . . To prevent this abuse, it is necessary from the very nature of things that power should be a check on power." But those who look to the guardianship of a right man do so precisely because the power which was designed to check the abuses of a lesser power is seen to require a check on its own abuses in turn. And those who, while recognizing the impossible requirement of omniscience and omnipresence, insist nevertheless on omnipotence (or a near-omnipotence) in the hands of a right man, do so precisely because they are confident that the right man, because he is a "democratic" man, will not abuse his power.

Yet surely it is here, at the level of such absolute or near-absolute power, that the greatest danger of tyranny lies. For while power in itself may have no more than a tendency to corrupt, absolute power, as Mill and Acton said, corrupts absolutely. It gives its holders a new importance, a new set

[11] D'Avenant (1699:270). And compare Tocqueville (1969:I, 252): "Unlimited power is in itself a bad and dangerous thing. Human beings are not competent to exercise it with discretion. God alone can be omnipotent, because his wisdom and his justice are always equal to his power. There is no power on earth so worthy of honor in itself or clothed with rights so sacred that I would admit its uncontrolled and all-predominant authority. When I see that the right and the means of absolute command are conferred on any power whatever, be it called a people or a king, an aristocracy or a democracy, a monarchy or a republic, I say there is the germ of tyranny, and I seek to live elsewhere, under other laws."

of habits. Finding themselves worshipped by others, they soon come to worship themselves. Finding that they can do as they like, they indulge in actions that previously seemed so improbable of achievement as to be put beyond the realm of serious contemplation. This is why it is foolish to assume, as the theorists of "democratic" personality are too often inclined to do, that a man out of power will remain the same man when in power. We must never forget, after all, that temptations come more often to him who is in power, and who can by his indulgence advantage the tempter, than to one who is out of power, and who can therefore indulge but give nothing in return.[12] Or that the removal of restraints on the bad as well as the good parts of one's nature makes possible the release of inhibitions that may work to the detriment of the community (Mill, 1910:252–253).

What requires emphasis here, however, is not the corrupting effects of absolute power; for absolute power, even in the hands of the best, the most "democratic" man, is incompatible with democracy. What must be noted is the more relevant fact that even a limited grant of power works somehow in invidious ways to corrupt many of those who exercise it. It is, therefore, a wise political system that looks not only to the beneficent uses that good men will make of power but also to the unhappy consequences that might flow from power in the hands of those who were the wrong men before they achieved power or who became the wrong men after they obtained it.

I have argued, to this point, two things: first, that those who appeal to the right man to control abuses of power have provided no satisfactory definition of that right man; and second, that even if that right man were adequately defined, he would not necessarily remain the right man or do the right things. I have suggested, conversely, that the idea of the wrong man, of (say) the authoritarian personality, is of no

[12] This is one of the reasons why extreme radicals and reactionaries, when out of power and with relatively little chance of getting into power, are so often men of inflexible principle. They are incorruptible because, in part, no one seeks to corrupt them. They are inflexible because, in part, no one seeks to compromise their differences in order to enlist their support.

real value to a democratic society, and this for two reasons in turn: first, that the definition of the wrong man is hardly less ambiguous or more applicable than is that of the right man;[13] and second, that since oppressive policies are the product of other, and more important, factors than that of personality alone, the repudiation of the wrong man would not necessarily secure the democratic state from the excesses of arbitrary rule.

It remains now only to stress one further point—namely, that it is the very meaning of democracy to accommodate the different personality types (if there be such) on equal terms, and not to discriminate among them. Democracy as a method of resolving differences among equals does not guarantee that the best or the right or the so-called democratic man will be put into positions of power, though it should be added that it is preferable for that purpose to other methods of choice. It is no proper concern of a democratic state that one man resents criticism while another welcomes it, that one man lacks independent and critical judgment while another is a creative thinker, that one man seeks power while another shies away from it, that one man is seemingly "well-adjusted" while another is a solitary and difficult or "ill-adjusted" man. Men with such personality traits are to be found in every society, democratic and oligarchic alike, for there is no demonstrable relation between a democratic man and a democratic society, or between an authoritarian man and an oligarchic society. What history teaches is always, of course, a matter of considerable controversy, but this much at least seems clear: that democratic societies have always produced some "authoritarian" men, and that authoritarian societies have been confronted in every age by men who have been "democrats" both in personality and belief.

Whatever the historical teaching, however, it is the logic of

[13] It ought perhaps to be added that if by an authoritarian personality is meant one who is congenial to totalitarianism, a distinction must be drawn between the kind of personality that seeks totalitarianism (e.g., a rebel or non-conformist) and that which remains under it (e.g., a conformist). Cf. Lauterbach (1954:288). Unfortunately, those who most vigorously press the notion of the authoritarian personality rarely pause to note this distinction, much less to consider what it means.

the democratic principle that all men,[14] and not just a particular few, be admitted on equal terms to the rights of citizenship, to the contest for political power. It is also a part of that logic to insist that even the best men, when in power, be held responsible for their actions; for in no other way can a people hope to correct the errors that even the best, because they are still fallible, men commit. And it is a part of the faith, if not the necessary logic, of democracy, that improvement in human affairs is to be anticipated not when a society is made up of like men, for that is the way of stagnation; but when a society cultivates, perhaps to an even greater degree than we thus far have, those conflicts of values, those differences in personality traits, that give challenge and variety and zest to the otherwise drab and penurious existence that is the everyday lot of so many men.

[14] I except, of course, children and the insane.

The Antidemocratic Personality
Else Frenkel-Brunswik, Daniel J. Levinson, and R. Nevitt Sanford

INTRODUCTION

The present research was guided by the conception of an individual whose thoughts about man and society form a pattern which is properly described as antidemocratic and which springs from his deepest emotional tendencies. Can it be shown that such a person really exists? If so, what precisely is he like? What goes to make up antidemocratic thought? What are the organizing forces within the person? If such a person exists, how commonly does he exist in our society? And what have been the determinants and what the cause of his development?

Although the antidemocratic individual may be thought of as a totality, it is nevertheless possible to distinguish and to study separately (*a*) his ideology and (*b*) his underlying personality needs. Ideology refers to an organization of opinions, attitudes, and values. One may speak of an individual's total ideology or of his ideology with respect to different areas of social life: politics, economics, religion, minority groups, and so forth. Ideologies have an existence independent of any single individual, those existing at a particular time being re-

From *Readings in Social Psychology,* third edition, edited by Eleanor E. Maccoby, Theodore M. Newcomb and Eugene L. Hartley. Copyright 1947, 1952, © 1958 by Holt, Rinehart and Winston, Inc. Reprinted by permission of the publisher.

sults both of historical processes and of contemporary social events. These ideologies, or the more particular ideas within them, have for different individuals different degrees of appeal, a matter that depends upon the individual's needs and the degree to which these needs are being satisfied or frustrated. The pattern of ideas that the individual takes over and makes his own will in each case be found to have a function within his over-all adjustment.

Although ideological trends are usually expressed more or less openly in words, it is important to note that, in the case of such affect-laden questions as those concerning minority groups, the degree of openness with which a person speaks will depend upon his situation. At the present time, when antidemocratic sentiments are officially frowned upon in this country, one should expect an individual to express them openly only in a guarded way or to a limited extent. This most superficial level of expression would afford a poor basis for estimating the potential for fascism in America. We should know, in addition, what the individual will say when he feels safe from criticism, what he thinks but will not say at all, what he thinks but will not admit to himself, and what he will be disposed to think when this or that appeal is made to him. In short, it is necessary to know the individual's *readiness* for antidemocratic thought and action, what it is that he will express when conditions change in such a way as to remove his inhibitions. Antidemocratic propaganda, though it makes some appeal to people's real interests, addresses itself in the main to emotional needs and irrational impulses, and its effectiveness will depend upon the susceptibility existing in the great mass of people.

To know that antidemocratic trends reside in the personality structure is to raise the further question of how this structure develops. According to the present theory, the major influences upon personality development arise in the course of child training as carried forward in a setting of family life. The determinants of personality, in other words, are mainly social; such factors as the economic situation of the parents, their social, ethnic, and religious group memberships, and the prevailing ideology concerning child training might be factors of crucial significance. This means that broad changes in social conditions and institutions will have a direct bearing upon the kinds of personalities that develop within a society. It does not mean, however, that such social changes would appreciably alter the personality structures that already exist.

It was necessary to devise techniques for surveying surface expression, for revealing ideological trends that were more or less inhibited, and for bringing to light unconscious personality forces (Frenkel-Brunswik and Sanford, 1945; Levinson and Sanford, 1944). Since the major concern was with *patterns* of dynamically related factors, it seemed that the proper approach was through intensive individual studies. In order to gauge the significance and practical importance of such studies, however, it was necessary to study groups as well as individuals and to find ways and means for integrating the two approaches.

Individuals were studied by means of (*a*) intensive clinical interviews and (*b*) a modified Thematic Apperception Test; groups were studied by means of questionnaires. It was not hoped that the clinical studies would be as complete or profound as some which have already been performed, primarily by psychoanalysts, nor that the questionnaires would be more accurate than any now employed by social psychologists. It was hoped, however—indeed it was necessary to our purpose —that the clinical material could be conceptualized in such a way as to permit its being quantified and carried over into group studies, and that the questionnaires could be brought to bear upon areas of response ordinarily left to clinical study. The attempt was made, in other words, to bring methods of traditional social psychology into the service of theories and concepts from the newer dynamic theory of personality, and in so doing to make "depth psychological" phenomena more amenable to mass-statistical treatment, and to make quantitative surveys of attitudes and opinions more meaningful psychologically.

In order to study antidemocratic individuals, it was necessary first to identify them. Hence a start was made by constructing a questionnaire and having it filled out anonymously by a large group of people. This questionnaire contained, in addition to numerous questions of fact about the subject's past and present life, and a number of open-answer ("projective") questions, several opinion-attitude scales containing a variety of antidemocratic (anti-Semitic, ethnocentric, reactionary, profascist) statements with which the subjects were invited to agree or disagree. A number of individuals (identified by indirect means) who showed the greatest amount of agreement with these statements were then studied by means of clinical techniques, and contrasted with a number of individuals showing strong disagreement. On the basis of these individual studies, the questionnaire was revised, and the whole procedure repeated. The study began with college students as subjects, and then was expanded to include a variety of groups from the community at large. The findings are considered to hold fairly well for non-Jewish, white, native-born, middle-class Americans.

THE STUDY OF IDEOLOGY

Anti-Semitism was the first ideological area studied. Anti-Semitic ideology is regarded as a broad system of ideas including: *negative opinions* regarding Jews (e.g., that they are unscrupulous, dirty, clannish, power-seeking); *hostile attitudes* toward them (e.g., that they should be excluded, restricted, suppressed); and *moral values* which permeate the opinions and justify the attitudes.

In what senses, if any, can anti-Semitic ideology be considered irrational? What are the main attitudes in anti-Semitism—segregation, suppression, exclusion—for the solution of "the Jewish problem"? Do people with negative opinions generally have hostile attitudes as well? Do individuals have a general readiness to accept or oppose a broad pattern of anti-Semitic opinions and attitudes?

These questions led to and guided the construction of an opinion-attitude scale for the measurement of anti-Semitic ideology. This scale provided a basis for the selection of criterion groups of extreme high and low scorers, who could then be subjected to intensive clinical study. The source material for the scale included: the writings of virulent anti-Semites; technical, literary, and reportorial writings on anti-Semitism and fascism; and, most important, everyday American anti-Semitism as revealed in parlor discussion, in the discriminatory practices of many businesses and institutions, and in the literature of various Jewish "defense" groups trying vainly to counter numerous anti-Semitic accusations by means of rational argument. In an attempt to include as much as possible of this type of content in the scale, certain rules were followed in its construction.

Each item should be maximally rich in ideas, with a minimum of duplication in wording or essential content. In order to reflect the forms of anti-Semitism prevalent in America today, the statements should not be violently and openly antidemocratic; rather, they should be pseudodemocratic, in the sense that active hostility toward a group is somewhat tempered and disguised by means of a compromise with democratic ideals. Each statement should have a familiar ring, should sound as it had been heard many times in everyday discussions and intensive interviews.

The 52-item scale contained five subscales—not statistically pure dimensions but convenient and meaningful groupings of items—the correlations among which should provide partial answers to some of the questions raised above. (*a*) Subscale "Offensive" (12 items) deals with imagery (opinions) of Jews as personally unpleasant and disturbing. Stereotypy is most explicit in the item: "There may be a few exceptions, but in general Jews are pretty much alike." To agree with this statement is to have an image of "the Jew" as a stereotyped model of the entire group. (*b*) Subscale "Threatening" (10 items) describes the Jews as a dangerous, dominating group. In various items the Jews are regarded as rich and powerful, poor and dirty, unscrupulous, revolutionary, and so on. (*c*) Subscale "Attitudes" (16 items) refers to programs of action. The specific hostile attitudes vary in degree from simple avoidance to suppression and attack, with intermediate actions of exclusion, segregation, and suppression. The social areas of discrimination covered include employment, residence, professions, marriage, and so on. (*d*) and (*e*) Subscales "Seclusive" and "Intrusive" deal with opposing stands on the issue of assimilation. The "Seclusive" subscale accuses the Jews of being too foreign and clannish; it implies that Jews can themselves eliminate anti-Semitism (a problem of their own making, so to speak) by greater assimilation and conformity to American ways. The "Intrusive" subscale, on the other hand, accuses the Jews of overassimilation, hiding of Jewishness, prying, seeking power and prestige. These items imply that Jews ought to keep more to themselves and to develop a culture, preferably even a nation of their own.

The total scale is intended to measure the individual's readiness to support or oppose anti-Semitic ideology as a whole. This ideology is conceived as involving stereotyped negative opinions describing Jews as threatening, immoral, and categorically different from non-Jews, and of hostile attitudes urging various forms of restriction. Anti-Semitism is conceived, then, not as a specific attitude (jealousy, blind hate, religious disapproval, or whatever) but rather as a general way of thinking and feeling about Jews and Jewish-Gentile relations.

For two groups, the reliabilities were at least .92 for the total A–S scale, and between .84 and .94 for all subscales ("Intrusive," second group only), except for "Seclusive," for which .71 was obtained (second group only). The correlations among the subscales "Offensive," "Threatening," and "Attitudes" are .83 to .85, while each of these correlates .92 to .94 with the total scale.

These correlations seem to reveal that each person has a rather general tendency to accept or reject anti-Semitic ideology as a whole. The correlations of subscale "Seclusive" with "Intrusive" (.74) and with "Attitudes" (also .74) reveal basic contradictions in anti-Semitic ideology. (All the raw coefficients, if corrected for attentuation, would be over .90.) Most anti-Semites are, apparently, willing to criticize both Jewish assimilation and Jewish seclusion. This is further testimony to the irrationality of anti-Semitism. Also irrational is the stereotyped image of "the Jew" (the item about Jews being all alike was very discriminating), an image which is intrinsically self-contradictory, since one person cannot be simultaneously rich and poor, dirty and luxurious, capitalistic and radical.

The question then presents itself: Are the trends found in anti-Semitic ideology—its generality, stereotyped imagery, destructive irrationality, sense of threat, concern with power and immorality, and so on—also expressed in the individual's social thinking about group relations generally? Can it be that what was found in anti-Semitism is not specific to prejudice against Jews but rather is present in prejudice against all groups?

Considerations such as these led to the study of ethnocentrism, that is, ideology regarding in-groups (with which the individual identifies himself), out-groups (which are "different" and somehow antithetical to the in-group), and their interaction. A 34-item Ethnocentrism scale was constructed along lines similar to those employed for the A–S scale. There were three subscales: (a) A 12-item subscale deals with Negroes and Negro-white relations. The items refer to Negroes as lazy, good-natured, and ignorant; also aggressive, primitive, and rebellious, and so on. (b) Minorities. These 12 items deal with various groups (other than Jews and Negroes), including minority political parties and religious sects, foreigners, Oklahomans (in California), zoot-suiters, criminals, and so on. (c) "Patriotism." These 10 items deal with America as an in-group in relation to other nations as out-groups. The items express the attitude that foreign, "inferior" nations should be subordinate; they include a value for obedience and a punitive attitude toward value-violators, and, finally, they express regarding permanent peace a cynicism which is rationalized by moralistic, hereditarian theories of aggressive, threatening out-group nations.

The reliabilities for the subscales ranged from .80 to .91; and for the total E scale .91. These figures, considered together with the correlations of .74 to .83 among the subscales, and the subscale-Total E scale correlations of .90 to .92, indicate a generality in ethnocentric ideology that is almost as great as and even more remarkable than that found in A–S.

The correlations of A–S with E complete the picture. The A–S scale correlates .80 with the E scale, and from .69 to .76 with the subscales. Through successive revisions there finally emerged a single E scale of 10 items (including 4 A–S items) which had reliabilities of .7 to .9 in different groups of subjects. It is clear that an attempt to understand prejudice psychologically must start with the total pattern of ethnocentric thinking, including both general out-group rejection and in-group submission-idealization.

Space does not permit a detailed discussion of the study of politics and religion. Ethnocentrism is related, though not very closely, to political conservatism ($r=.5$) and to support of the more conservative political groupings. In the responses of individuals scoring high on the conservatism scale, two patterns could be distinguished: a traditional, *laissez-faire* conservatism as opposed to "pseudoconservatism" in which a profession of belief in the tenets of traditional conservatism is combined with a readiness for violent change of a kind which would abolish the very institutions with which the individual appears to identify himself. The latter appeared to contribute more to the correlation between E and conservatism than did the former. The non-religious are less ethnocentric on the average than the religious, although such sects as the Quakers and Unitarians made low E scale means (non-ethnocentric).

THE STUDY OF PERSONALITY

The main variables underlying the various ideological areas above represent personality trends expressed in ideological form. A primary hypothesis in this research is that an individual is most receptive to those ideologies which afford the fullest expression to his over-all personality structure. Thus, a person clinically described as strongly authoritarian, projective, and destructive is likely to be receptive to an antidemocratic ideology such as ethnocentrism—ultimately fascism as the total social objectification of these trends—because it expresses his needs so well.

The attempt at a quantitative investigation of personality variables underlying ethnocentric ideology led to the construction of a personality scale. It was called, for convenience, the F scale because it was intended to measure some of the personality trends which seemed to express a predisposition or deep-lying receptivity to fascism. The items are statements of opinion and attitude in non-ideological areas (not dealing with formal groups or social institutions) such as self, family, people in general, sex, personal values, and so on; they are not tied by official statement or surface meaning to items in the other scales. Any consistency in response to the F and E scales, as indicated by the correlation between them, must be due primarily to the fact that both scales express the same underlying trends, since their surface content is quite different. The main difference between the scales is that the F items are less openly ideological.

Ten main variables guided scale construction, each variable being represented by a cluster of several items. The clusters were partially overlapping, since several items were intended to express more than a single variable. In three successive forms the scale contained 38, 34, then 30 items, but the 10 main variables were always represented.

The cluster variables were as follows: conventional values, authoritarian submission, authoritarian aggression, anti-intraception, superstition-stereotypy, pseudotoughness, power, cynicism, projectivity, and sex.

Three of these clusters may be discussed to illustrate the general approach. "Authoritarian submission" refers to an inability seriously to criticize, reject, or actively rebel against one's main in-group (particularly the family) figures and values. There is a highly moralized and idealized conception of authority-representatives and a submissive relation to them. Examples: "No sane, normal, decent person could ever think of hurting a close friend or relative"; "Every person should have complete faith in some supernatural power whose decisions he obeys without question."

"Anti-intraception" involves opposition to a psychological, insightful view of people and oneself. This includes a rejection of emotion and of attempts to look into one's deeper motives and conflicts. Personal inquiries tend to be regarded as prying, and there is often an exaggerated idea of how much prying is going on. Work and keeping busy are emphasized as ways of "not thinking about yourself." Examples: "When a person has a problem or worry, it is best for him not to think about it but to keep busy with more cheerful things"; "Nowadays more and more people are prying into matters that should remain personal and private."

"Projectivity" refers to the disposition to imagine strange, evil, dangerous, destructive forces at work in the outer world; these imaginings have only the smallest basis in reality but can be understood as projections of the individual's deep-lying sexual and aggressive strivings. Examples: "War and social troubles may someday be ended by an earthquake or flood that will destroy the whole world"; "Nowadays when so many different kinds of people move around and mix together so much, a person has to protect himself especially carefully against catching an infection or disease from them"; "The wild sex life of the old Greeks and Romans was tame compared to some of the goings-on in this country, even in places where people might least expect it."

The successive forms of the F scale involved elimination, modification, and addition of items, based on both statistical considerations and on theoretical requirements of richness of ideas and over-all inclusiveness. The reliability of the scale increased from an average of .74 for the first form to .85 on the last. Each high quartile scorer is high on most items and clusters; on each item and cluster the difference between high scorers (total scale) and low scorers is statistically significant.

Correlations of F with A–S and E increased from an average of about .6 to about .75 in later forms, that is, higher than the correlation of .50 with the conservatism scale. This correlation, in conjunction with the clinical findings reported below, gives evidence of the functional role of personality trends in organizing and giving meaning to surface attitudes, values, and opinions.

Does ethnocentrism help the individual avoid conscious ambivalence toward his family by displacing the hostility onto out-groups (the morally "alien") and thus leave in consciousness exaggerated professions of love toward family and authority? Do high scorers on the F scale (who are usually also ethnocentric) have an underlying anticonventionalism, in-group- and family-directed hostility, a tendency to do the very things they rigidly and punitively oppose in others? What impels an individual to feel, for example, that aggression against his family is unthinkable and yet to agree that "homosexuals should be severely punished" and (during the war) that the "Germans and Japs should be wiped out"? Such contradictions suggest that the deeper personality trends of high scorers are antithetical to their conscious values, opinions, and attitudes. The clinical studies reported below investigate further these and other questions.

The so-called "projective questions" are intermediate between the scales and the intensive clinical techniques. As part of the questionnaire they are used in group studies in order to determine how common in larger populations were the relationships discovered in clinical studies. They are open questions to be answered in a few words or lines; each question deals with events or experiences which are likely to have emotional significance for the individual. The original set of about 30 questions was gradually reduced to 8, which were both statistically differentiating and theoretically inclusive. These deal with "what moods are unpleasant," "what desires are hard to control," "what great people are admired," "what would drive a person nuts," "what are the worst crimes," "what moments are embarrassing," "how to spend your last six months," "what is most awe-inspiring."

The responses of the entire high and low quartiles on the A–S (later the total E) scale were contrasted. For each question "high" and "low" scoring categories were made; a "high" category expresses a personality trend which seems most characteristic of ethnocentrists and which can be expected significantly to differentiate the two groups. A scoring manual, giving the specific categories (usually two to six) for each item, was the basis on which two independent raters scored each response (not knowing the actual A–S or E score of the subjects). Each response was scored "high," "low," or "neutral"—the neutral category being used when the response was omitted, ambiguous, or when it contained "high" and "low" trends equally. Less than 10 percent of the responses received neutral scores.

The scoring agreement for the battery of items averaged 80 to 90 percent on a variety of groups (total, 200 to 300). The high quartiles received an average of 75–90 percent "high" scores, as compared with 20–40 percent "high" scores for the low quartiles. Almost never was an individual ethnocentrist given more than 50 percent low scores, and conversely for the anti-ethnocentrists. For each item the difference between the two groups was always significant at better than the 1 percent level.

The differences between the ethnocentric and anti-ethnocentric groups may be illustrated by the scoring of the item "what experiences would be most awe-inspiring for you?" The "low" categories are: (a) Values which refer to personal achievement (intellectual, esthetic, scientific), contribution to mankind, the realization of democratic goals by self and society, and so on. (b) "Power," as exemplified in man's material-technological achievements and in nature. (c) Intense nature experiences in which there are clear signs of esthetic, sensual-emotional involvement.

The "high" categories for this item, in contrast, are: (a) "Power" in the form of deference and submission toward powerful people; emphasis on a generally authoritarian and ritualized atmosphere (military, superficial religious, patriotic, etc.). (b) Personal power in self, with others playing a deferent role. (c) Destruction-harm of people (e.g., "death of a close relative"; no open hostility). (d) Values which refer to conventionalized sex, material security, ownership, vague sense of virtue, and so on. (e) Dilute nature experiences which differ from those of the low-scorers in that they are matter-of-fact, unspecific, surface descriptions with no indication of sensual-emotional involvement.

Some other general differences between these two groups were found. Deep-lying trends such as hostility, dependency, sexuality, curiosity, and the like exist in both groups, but in the unprejudiced group they are more ego-integrated, in the sense of being more focal, more tied to other trends, more complex affectively, and with fewer defenses. This group is also more aware of inner conflicts, ambivalence, and tendencies to violate basic values. Their inner life is richer if more troubled; they tend to accuse themselves of faults, while the prejudiced group externalizes and engages more in idealization of self and family.

CLINICAL ANALYSIS OF INTERVIEW MATERIAL

As mentioned above, those scoring extremely high or extremely low on the overt ethnocentrism scale of the questionnaire were further subjected to clinical interviews and to projective tests.

The interviews covered the following major fields: vocation, income, religion, politics, minority groups, and clinical data. The directives given to the interviewer listed in each field both the kinds of things it was hoped to obtain from the subject and suggestions as to how these things might indirectly be ascertained by questioning. The former were the "underlying questions"; they had reference to the variables by means of which the subject was eventually to be characterized. The "manifest questions," those actually put to the subject, were framed in such a way as to conceal as much as possible the real purpose of the interview and yet elicit answers that were significant in terms of over-all hypotheses. The manifest questions used to obtain material bearing on a given underlying question were allowed to vary greatly from subject to subject, depending in each case on the subject's ideology, surface attitudes, and defenses. Nevertheless a number of manifest questions, based on general theory and experience, were formulated for each underlying question. Not all of them were asked each subject.

Examples of manifest questions, taken from the area of Income are: "What would you do with (expected or desired) income?" and "What would it mean to you?" The corresponding underlying issues are the subject's aspirations and phantasies as to social status, as to power as a means to manipulate others, as to (realistic or neurotic) striving for security, as to lavish and exciting living, the readiness really to take chances, and so forth.

It was the task of the interviewer subtly to direct the course of the interview in such a way that as much as possible would be learned about these underlying attitudes without giving away to the subject the real foci of the inquiry.

In attempting to achieve a crude quantification of the interview material, so that group trends might be ascertained, there was developed an extensive set of scoring categories, comprising approximately a hundred headings. An attempt was made to encompass as much as possible of the richness and intricacy of the material. The complexity of the categories introduced inferential and subjective elements, but, as it turned out, this did not prevent adequate inter-rater reliability and validity. The categories were arrived at on the basis of a preliminary study of the complete interviews and of all the other available material pertaining to the same subjects. These categories represent, in fact, the hypotheses as to which clinical characteristics go with presence or absence of prejudice.

In order to test all the categories, passages of the interview protocols referring directly to political or social issues and all other data that might indicate the subject's identity or ideological position were carefully removed before two clinically trained scorers undertook the evaluation of the protocols.

Interviews of 40 women were thus evaluated. (A later report will present results from a group of men.) Three kinds of judgments were used for each category: (1) whether the interview revealed attitudes tentatively classified as "high" or as "low"; (2) whether no decision could be reached; or, more often, (3) whether no material was available on the issue in question. A number of categories proved non-discriminating either because "high" and "low" statements appeared with equal frequency in the interviews of those found "high" and of those found "low" on the questionnaire, or because of a large proportion of "neutral" responses.

Some of the most discriminating categories included the following. Of the fifteen interviewed women who were extremely low on ethnocentrism, 0 (none) displayed a conventional "idealization" of the parents, the variable previously assumed to be characteristic of ethnocentrism, whereas 12 showed an attitude of objective appraisal of the parents.[1] On

---

[1] In view of the small number of cases (40) and the frequency of the neutral categories (about 30 percent), these differences between

the other hand, of the 25 women interviewees extremely high on ethnocentrism, 11 clearly displayed the "high" and only 6 the "low" variant (the remaining 8 being "neutral"). This distribution of attitudes toward parents is in line with the general glorification of and submission to in-group authority, on the surface at least, by the high scorers on ethnocentrism. In fact, the corresponding figures on the category "submission to parental authority and values (respect based on fear)" *vs.* "principled independence" are 1 to 7 for the "low" subjects as against 9 to 0 for the "high" subjects.

The "high" women emphasize sex as a means for achieving status; they describe their conquests and—as they do in other fields as well—rationalize rather than admit failures and shortcomings, whereas the "lows" do not shrink from open admission of inadequacies in this respect (8 to 3 for "highs"; 1 to 8 for "lows"). In the same vein we find in "highs" underlying disrespect and resentment toward the opposite sex, typically combined with externalized, excessive and counteractive "pseudoadmiration," *vs.* "genuine respect and fondness for opposite sex" in the "lows" (11 to 4 for "highs"; 2 to 7 for "lows"). Similarly, the attitude toward the opposite sex in the "high" women is power-oriented, exploitative, manipulative, with an eye on concrete benefits hiding behind superficial submission as contrasted with a warm, affectionate and love-seeking attitude on the part of the "lows." Thus, the traits desired in men by "high" women are: hard-working, energetic, go-getting, moral, clean-cut, deferent, "thoughtful" toward the woman; the desiderata mentioned by the "low" women, on the other hand, are: companionship, common interests, warmth, sociability, sexual love, understanding, and liberal values. (For the entire pat-

---

the high and low scorers must be regarded as tentative. However, there is additional evidence that these differences would be found in a large sample. (1) Even with this small number of cases the differences are very striking. (2) The data on men appear to reveal similar differences. This not only provides an independent confirmation, but it will provide a sample twice as large as the present one. (3) The variables considered here are similar to those found to be differentiating in the ideological material, the Thematic Apperception Test, and the projective questions.

tern just described the figures are 14 to 4 for the "highs" and 2 to 10 for the "lows.")

As to attitudes toward people in general, the "highs" tend to assume an attitude of "moralistic condemnation" *vs.* the "permissiveness" shown toward individuals by the lows (14 to 3 for the "highs," 2 to 10 for the "lows"). Of special importance for the problem discussed here is the "hierarchical conception of human relations" in the "highs" as compared with an "equalitarianism and mutuality" in the "lows" (13 to 2 in the "highs" and 1 to 10 in the "lows").

All through the material it was frequently observed that the difference between the high and low subjects does not lie so much in the presence or absence of a basic tendency but rather in the way of dealing with such tendencies. As an illustration from the field of interpersonal relationships, we may refer to the category of Dependence. Whereas the dependence of the high subjects tends to be diffuse, ego-alien, and linked to an infantile desire to be taken care of, the dependence of the lows is focal and love-seeking as can be expected in cases where a real object relationship has been established (11 to 1 in the highs; 1 to 7 in the lows). The traits desired in friends are in many ways similar to those desired in the opposite sex (see above); we find emphasis on status, good manners, and so forth in the highs as compared with intrinsic values in the lows (9 to 2 for highs, 0 to 10 for lows).

In the high scorer's attitude toward the Self, we find self-glorification mixed with feelings of inferiority which are not faced as such, conventional moralism, the belief in a close correspondence between what one is and what one wishes to be, and the "denial of genuine causality" (e.g., an explanation of one's traits or symptoms in terms of hereditary or accidental factors), as contrasted to opposite attitudes in the lows, with figures generally as discriminatory or better than those mentioned above for the other fields.

In the case of more general categories pertaining to personality dynamics an unusually large proportion were found to be discriminating. This might be due to the fact that the scoring of these categories was based on the over-all impression of the subject rather than on a specific piece of information. High-scoring women tend to give particular evidence of

"rigid-moralistic anal reaction-formations" as ends in themselves, e.g., totalitarian-moralistic conceptualization of two
kinds of people—"clean and dirty"—and overemphasis on
propriety and kindliness, often with underlying aggression.
The women with low scores show more evidence of "oral
character structure"; and when such values as cleanliness and
kindliness are present they are of a more functional nature.

As far as aggression is concerned, the high-scoring women
tend toward a diffuse, depersonalized, moralistic, and punitive
type of aggression, whereas the aggression of the low-scoring
women is more focal and personalized, and more often it
seems to be elicited by violation of principles or as a response
to rejection by a loved object.

Ambivalence, e.g., toward the parents, is not admitted
into consciousness by the "high" subjects but is rather solved
by thinking in terms of dichotomies and by displacement onto
out-groups. The ambivalence of the "lows" is more often expressed against the original objects (e.g., parents) or representatives, in reality, of the original objects, e.g., real authority.

There is a strong tendency in the high-scoring women to
display "femininity" exclusively, whereas the low-scoring
women are more ready to accept and to sublimate their
masculine traits.

Some of the categories scored under the tentative assumption of their relevance to prejudice did not prove discriminating. Among these are various "childhood events," e.g., death
or divorce of parents, number of siblings, and order of birth.
The conception of one's own childhood, e.g., image of father
and mother, proved only slightly discriminating, mostly because of the great number of neutral scores due often to
lack of information in these categories. The fact that some
of the categories were not discriminating may be taken as
evidence that the raters were at least partially successful in
their attempt to eliminate halo effect.

As was mentioned above, the over-all contrast between the
highly prejudiced and the tolerant women hinges less than
originally expected on the existence or absence of "depth"
factors such as latent homosexuality, but rather, as seen here
again, on the way they are dealt with in the personality: by

acceptance and sublimation in our tolerant extremes, by repression and defense measures in our prejudiced extremes.

It is because of their repressions, it may be supposed, that the high scorers are found to be outstanding on such formal characteristics as rigidity, anti-intraception, pseudoscientific thinking, and so forth.

The differences between high and low scorers revealed by the several independent techniques of the study reported here are consistent one with another and suggest a pattern which, embracing as it does both personality and ideology, may be termed the "antidemocratic personality."

Notes on a Theory of Democratic Personality
Robert E. Lane

Anchoring political ideology and political practice in personality or national character has a long history and a substantial current literature. Perhaps the foregoing discussion of a single phase of this topic, problems of identity, will assume a more realistic perspective for certain interested readers if we offer a glance at some of the ideas currently being argued. Then, even more briefly, I shall suggest a synoptic concept of undemocratic man, the impoverished self.

THE PATHOLOGIES OF DEMOCRATIC MAN

We may conveniently look at those alleged pathologies said to inhibit a man's contribution to democratic society under three heads: those focusing primarily on the self, those primarily relating the self to others, and those relating the self to society.

Reprinted with permission of Macmillan Publishing Company, Inc. from *Political Ideology* by Robert E. Lane. Copyright © 1962 by The Free Press of Glencoe, a Division of The Macmillan Company.

Self-Referential Pathologies

LOSS OF IDENTITY

One broad category of personal problems comes under the heading of the concept of identity and the loss of identity. Erikson is the inventor and expositor of this concept; for him identity "connotes both a persistent sameness within oneself (self-sameness) and a persistent sharing of some kind of essential character with others." The loss of this identity, in both personal and social senses, says Erikson (1950:114), deprives the individual of his political balance, "for when established identities become outworn or unfinished ones threaten to remain incomplete, special crises compel men to wage holy wars, by the cruelest means, against those who seem to question or threaten their unsafe ideological bases." Erikson notes how modern technological and economic developments have tended to weaken the old identities and thus to jeopardize established orders everywhere. Lucien Pye (1962), influenced by this view, shows in persuasive detail how the loss of identity of the Westernizing elites of Burma makes them distrustful of themselves and others, destroys the basis of their certainty, creates frustrations that cast to the surface the high aggressive potentials in a developing, changing, once-traditional society. But the problem is not limited to these areas; it exists in metropolitan centers as well, and loss of identity, of a clear answer to "Who am I?" tends also to inhibit democratic life in the West.

SELF-ALIENATION

A somewhat different approach is suggested by those employing the concept of alienation as their focus of concern. This is a broad term, with many meanings. The one we focus on here is self-alienation, expressed by Fromm (1955:120–121) in the following terms: "The alienated person is out of touch with himself as he is out of touch with any other person. He, like the others, are [sic] experienced as things are experienced; with the senses and with common sense, but at the same time without being related to oneself and to the world outside productively." According to Fromm this alienation leads a man into apathy and withdrawal and makes him an easy mark for manipulation. But the term may be employed in a somewhat different sense, one closer to Freudian usage. Franz Neumann (1957), for example, uses it to mean "the alienation of the ego from the instinctual structure or the renunciation of instinctual gratification," and believes that this has been encouraged by modern industrial society. Its political implications become manifest as this alienation increases beyond a certain point and produces anxiety. Anxiety, in turn, tends to produce a demand for a new Caesar to relieve men of their worries and fears.

ANXIETY

Anxiety has a life of its own. According to Auden, this is the "age of Anxiety," and hence it comes to the focus of attention in several ways. Lasswell says, "The ideal conception of democratic character includes the specification that the self-system shall have at its disposal the energies of the unconscious part of the personality" (Lasswell, 1951b:503). Anxiety not only reduces the energy available to the individual but also destroys his perspective on life, and releases destructive impulses that otherwise would be well under control. Since "hostile impulses of various kinds form the main sources from which neurotic anxiety springs" (Horney, 1937: 62), it is natural that anxiety should be associated with destructiveness and, consequently, with hostile social acts generally unsupportive of democratic methods.

LACK OF SELF-CONTROL

Some have focused on the problem of lack of self-control. H. V. Dicks (1952), Geoffrey Gorer (1949), and Margaret Mead (1951) all speak of the Russians' great indulgences of their impulses, drinking orgies, and emotional abandonment of all kinds, followed by guilty feelings over this indulgence. Knowing this about themselves, they are said to demand strong external authority to keep them in control of themselves (Mead, 1951:26). Almond (1950:69–115), in a somewhat similar but more modest way, argues that the mood swings of the American public, from optimism to pessimism, from involvement to isolation in foreign affairs, has been dysfunctional for the functioning of the nation's foreign policy. I have argued elsewhere (Lane, 1959:147–155) for the relation between ego strength and democratic participation; it seems to be a close one.

IRRATIONALITY

The capacity of man for rational thought and his tropism toward irrationality, misperception, illogicality, have long been a grave concern among those who doubted whether popular government could ever work (see Wallas, 1909). It is reflected in the contemporary discussion as well. In his earlier work, Lasswell (1930) argued that the mind of political man was essentially furnished with rationalizations of his private and highly personal problems. Displacing these feelings of anger, shame, and hate onto political objects, political man wove a plausible story to legitimize these guilty feelings. Broadening the term, Smith, Bruner, and White (1956:43) speak of political opinions as representing "externalizing" maneuvers. By this they mean more than projection and displacement: "Externalization occurs when an individual, often responding unconsciously, senses an analogy between a perceived evironmental event and some unresolved inner problem. He adopts an attitude toward the event in question which is a transformed version of his way of dealing with his inner difficulty." Obviously this is disruptive of a means-ends rationality in the real contemporary world in which the event takes place. Several perceptual, intellectual, and cognitive malfunctionings have been explored in political contexts: men rationalize the defects of their preferred parties and political leaders (Edwards, 1941); they learn and forget partisan material with speeds that favor their own partisan stands (Levine and Murphy, 1943); they misperceive the positions of political leaders when caught in conflicts between preferred positions and preferred candidates (Berelson, 1954:220–230); they employ stereotypes to save time and protect their illusions (Lippmann, 1922); they repress frightening information (Janis and Feshbach, 1953) and information that makes them feel guilty

(Perry, 1953); there are certain kinds of men who are persistently dogmatic or rigid in their mental functioning, making them inhospitable to new information or making them pervert it to serve a preestablished doctrine (Rokeach, 1960); and there are other men who are persistently "intolerant of ambiguity," making unresolved situations and unclear perceptions and postponed decisions hard to bear (Frenkel-Brunswik, 1949a, 1949b). This latter quality is associated with authoritarianism, and is often incompatible with the democratic way of muddling through.

ANTI-INTRACEPTIVENESS

The authoritarian syndrome is a pattern that includes self-referential, as well as other-referential and societal-referential, elements (Adorno, 1950). Toward the self, the authoritarian is "anti-intraceptive," that is, he is unwilling to explore his own motives and personality—for fear of what he might find. This also makes him generally opposed to psychological inquiry, preferring to employ circumstantial explanations for events. Other qualities of authoritarianism, taken in isolation as well as together in the complete syndrome, seem to offer impediments to democratic functioning: the tendency to stereotype, the aggressiveness and toughness, the exaggerated concern with sex, and much more. Although the concept has been eroded by criticism, much of this criticism seems to have been made in the spirit that unless the research is methodologically correct the concept must fail (Hyman and Sheatsley, 1954), and some of the criticism seems to have been on the basis of a very limited set of tests (Campbell, 1960).

Interpersonal Pathologies

Except for analytical purposes, it is almost impossible to separate qualities that refer primarily to the self and those that refer primarily to others, because the self is, as Rousseau remarked, socially created. Referring to the previous discussion, the reader will observe the alienated man as being "out of touch" with other persons; the loss of identity is partly a loss of a sense of whom I am like and whom I go with! the authoritarian's aggression and toughness may be free-floating, but it is often directed at other people. As is well known, a person learns about himself from what others think and say about him and from how they behave toward him.

MISANTHROPY

In spite of this interweaving of the personal with the interpersonal, there are certain qualities that are more distinctly related to others and that are said to be impediments to democratic attitudes. One of these is misanthropy, or a low estimate of human nature. Lasswell makes the point that a "confidence in human potentialities" is characteristic of democratic man; its reverse, of course, would be the lack of such confidence (Lasswell, 1951b:502–503). Pursuing this point with an attitudinal measure, Morris Rosenberg found that people who tended not to believe that "people can be trusted" also tended, logically enough, not to trust democratic officials or to believe that these officials cared much about the interests of the public (Rosenberg, 1956:691). In a forthcoming work, Gabriel Almond and Sidney Verba (1963) will show that this is, indeed, a cross-cultural phenomenon.

CONSTRICTED EMPATHY

In a somewhat similar vein, Gilbert has shown how through "constricted empathy" the German people were able to endure the oppression of others without much guilt; they simply narrowed down the group for whom they had empathic feelings, retaining it for those whom they admitted to friendship (Gilbert, 1950:278–280). Divorcing this concept from its ally, sympathy, it is possible to think of the more general quality of being able to put yourself in the place of another as an important ingredient of democratic man. Lerner (1958:43–52) shows how, in the Middle East, the capacity to think of oneself in another position, performing another role, was essential for the development of democratic institutions. Those who could not think of themselves, for example, as a newspaper editor or as a governor of a district, turned out to be unfinished material for democracy.

CLOSED EGO

Overlapping with these meanings is a term that Lasswell includes among his personal bases for democratic behavior: the "open ego," by which he means that "the attitude toward other human beings is warm rather than frigid, inclusive and expanding rather than exclusive and constricting . . . an underlying personality structure which is capable of 'friendship'" (Lasswell, 1951b:495). The pathology, from the democratic standpoint, then, is the cold, constricted, closed ego. This is close to the "tenderness taboo," a fear of showing the soft, tender, or idealistic facet of personality, which Dicks (1950) found to be characteristic of the Nazis among a large group of German prisoners of war.

"WE" AND "THEY"

Authoritarianism contains a strictly interpersonal component: the tendency to divide the world into "we" and "they," "in-groups" and "out-groups." This is a product of a more basic tendency to conceive of the world in somewhat hostile terms, in which case the most important question to ask of a person is, "Is he for me or is he against me?" Even relationships based on business or sport or strictly contractual matters are heavily loaded with this perspective. Along with this is the hierarchical view of relations with others: Does he submit to me or do I submit to him? (Adorno, 1950:222–279).

CONFORMITY

Finally, there is the question of autonomy and conformity. David Riesman (1950:370) has argued that it is the conformists and the moralizers who appear to determine our political style and most influence our decisions; "the autonomous, insignificant in numbers, play a minor and scarcely discernible role in our politics." Thus conventionality and unrealistic reform often seem to be the main alternatives available in such a political system. Moreover, the conformism of the masses makes of them so many cheerful robots, easily manipulated by a power elite (Mills, 1959:165–176).

SOCIAL ALIENATION

What is interpersonal is social, but there is something more here. In the concept of alienation, there is a strong theme of something broader than simply a distance from the self and from others. In the Marxian version, and that of Fromm as well, there is emphasis upon the individual's alienation from an uncreative work life, a total alienation from society (see Fromm, 1955:120–151). Kornhauser, whose main concern is the loss of community and pluralistic groups serving as strong links between men and the larger society, argues that these losses produce a mass society. "The central problem posed by the theory of mass society," he says, "is that of *social aliena-tion*, or the distance between the individual and his society" (Kornhauser, 1959:237). It is this combination of social alien-ation, atomistic relationships, and easy manipulability that make him fear for the future of democracy.

ANOMIE

Perhaps the term anomie has born the freight of more re-lated ideas dealing with the sickness of modern urban in-dustrial, and democratic, man than any other. From the original use by Durkheim (1951:246–254), where he referred to the lack of rules to live by and loss of values to pursue, through its extended modern usages there has been a common thread—confusion and loss of internalized values; but the source of this confusion has been variously interpreted. Mer-ton, for example, attributes anomie, in part, to the discrepan-cies between the approved goals and the approved means for reaching those goals in the modern American culture. Some of the expression of this anomie produced in this way has political relevance: both apathy (retreatism) and rebel-lion fall in this category (Merton, 1949:125–149). Sebastian DeGrazia conceives of anomie as analogous to the separa-tion-anxiety of the child; it comes with the loss of faith in the rulers and their codes of behavior. When the common belief system of society, including religion, is challenged and de-moralized, when the rulers lose their closeness to the people and become merely decision-makers or employers, the old panic strikes and people once again suffer this sense of abandonment, losing their own faith and their sense of security. They then may help themselves to synthetic ideologies and false political prophets (DeGrazia, 1948).

CYNICISM

The individual who finds neither in society nor in himself a source of values may take another road. It is described in a variety of ways by Nathan Leites (1961) as he portrays the political culture of the French: "the reign of the self," "the quest for privilege," "deceit, imposture, trickery," "I do as I like." There is an over-all theme here; covered by the word cynicism, a corrosive attitude that makes altrusistic and self-denying motives or behavior evaporate into thin air (see also Leites, 1959).

CONSTRICTED UNIVALUE SYSTEM

A variation of this pathology turns, not on devaluation or on denial of values, but on a constricted univalue system. Lasswell (1951b:497–498) says, "Let us speak of the democratic character as multi-valued, rather than single valued, and as disposed to share rather than to hoard or to monopolize." The sharing of values is necessary in all political systems, but because the democratic system gives scope for the value miser in us all, this quality needs more internal restraint. And so, too, since democracy requires, more than other systems, a tolerance of others with different values, those who respect the pursuits of others for wealth or moral stature or fame, or whatever it may be, make a contribution in many discrete ways.

TRADITIONALISM

The traditionalism of the Middle East in Lerner's (1958) analysis, like the tradition-orientation in Riesman's (1950) typology, forms an impediment to democratic functioning. The concept is one of a passive person on whom society acts but who does not believe that he himself has a right or a capacity to influence affairs. Public affairs are like the natural order of things—they just happen. For Lerner, the antidote lies in the development of psychological mobility; for Riesman in the development, perhaps after a period of inner-direction or other direction, of autonomy.

"THE WORLD IS A JUNGLE"

The authoritarian view is that the world is a jungle; hence, it is appropriate to claw and scratch in a struggle for survival. It is a world where power is the main good and where dominance and submission are the main human postures (Adorno, 1950:222–241).

THE IMPOVERISHED SELF

Most of the above concepts either are or may be framed negatively; that is, they suggest that the impediment to democratic support lies in a missing quality: loss of identity, "being out of touch with oneself," lack of self-control, absence of rationality, and so forth. This further suggests that a synoptic concept may best be framed in the same way, as an impoverishment. What is it that is missing? Are there some core deficiencies that summarize or, better still, cause these human failures?

I have attempted to achieve such a synoptic concept under the term *the impoverished self,* meaning, low self-acceptance, low self-esteem, and low ego strength. Let us examine these briefly.

Low Self-Acceptance

This concept was chosen only after some consideration was given to another related term, self-awareness. The reasons are important. One might easily argue that an awareness of one's personal and social identity is an essential ingredient in meeting the demands of a society in conflict, imposing one's demands upon it, resisting the incredibly insistent demands of others. One of the central explanations of politics relies upon the individual's pursuit of his own "interests," something he can grasp only as he understands "who" he is. But the evidence of Eastport spoke against this argument. There, one of the main personal themes was the objectification of the self, the treating of the self as a somewhat impersonal object with needs and qualities to be appraised from an outside perspective. One had to say, on balance, that the best of the citizens were not intimately or sensitively self-aware, while some of the undemocrats and the alienated men were much more concerned with what was happening inside themselves. Moreover, interculturally, it is said that the ethos of the Latin countries, where democracy struggles to survive, leads to a focus on self-mastery, while the North American ethos, generally supportive of democracy, leads to a focus on mastery of the environment (Romanell, 1952).

Furthermore, in Eastport democracy is built upon a certain social-identity diffusion, a vagueness, not about the personal characteristics of the individual, but about his social membership, his reference groups, his political friends and enemies. When these crystallized, we found the individual politically "frozen" as, for example, an Italian-American or as a member of the working class or as a "lifelong Democrat." These social identities, then, became the touchstones by which almost all social policies, all judgments of politicians were transmuted into friendly or hostile objects. A clear social identity served as a substitute for penetrating observation and thought; the diffused social identity served the community somewhat better.

Upon reflection, then, it appeared that the concept that best expressed the quality we had in mind was not the self-awareness of the individual in the sense that he was in constant communication with his unconscious and clear about his social memberships, but the self-acceptance of the individual that implied that he was not in conflict with his unconscious and not rejecting his social memberships.

Thus clarified, it is easy to see how low self-acceptance, not, perhaps, *in toto,* but in part, creates a situation that fosters the pathologies we have discussed earlier. A person who rejects his impulse life and feels constantly guilty about it cannot have the low moral tension we argued was important for a democratic system. His struggle with himself impairs his capacity to see life "as it really is," because some parts of it are too dangerous to be seen this way; the individual in reliving old struggles and trying to master old situations will create an unreality, will have a faltering reality sense. Yet we said that a democracy requires a firm foundation in empirically verifiable and realistic metaphysics, and particularly in the acknowledgment of impersonal causes. For the same reason his epistemology is distorted and his uses of knowledge are defensive, not instrumental.

In the same way, low self-acceptance is associated with anxiety that what he fears to know about himself—chiefly that he has hostile feelings—will become public knowledge. It is a feature in self-alienation; indeed, that is exactly what the failure to accept some feature of the self really is. It is partially embraced by the concept of anti-intraception, and includes that part of loss of identity that we regard as damaging to the democratic polity. Low self-acceptance, the rejection of some part of the self, rather than low self-awareness, is, it seems, an important source of democratic pathology, and one node in the complex called the impoverished self.

Low Self-Esteem

In a penetrating discussion of the psychology of the American Negro, Kardiner and Ovesey place low self-esteem at the center of a network of psychodynamic constellations. Created by the oppressive character of the social environment, low self-esteem encourages hedonism in some, rebellion in others, neurotic symptoms in still others (Kardiner and Ovesey, 1951).[1] In a somewhat analagous way it is relevant here: it produces in the citizen a sense that he is unworthy to hold opinions, to make demands upon the society, to be treated as an important individual. It is a feature of traditional man, who believes that important matters of state are not the proper concern of the "likes of him." To the extent that men use themselves as a template for others, "recreating" others in their own image, and who, at the same time, believe them-

[1] See also Cantril (1941) and Lane (1959).

selves to be weak or sinful or worthless, these men will adopt several of the pathologies noted above. They will be cynical and they will be misanthropic. They will reject the bad part of themselves, hence self-alienated. But, most important, they will have anomic feelings, for there can be little doubt that the core of devaluational feelings lies in the sense of a devalued self. That is one reason why, in the first and classic study of anomie, the resolution was the destruction of this thing without value, suicide. At the same time it is true that *some* doubt about which values to pursue, some value confusion, and hence some aspects of anomie, are compatible with high self-esteem.

Low Ego Strength

There are many societies where men are self-accepting and self-respecting but where they are not capable of self-government because they are not self-governing. Without self-control, plus a sense of mastery over the environment (the ingredients of ego strength), it is possible neither to pursue a consistent long-term course of action nor to effect much social change. Equally important, without the inner experience of control, a man hardly understands how control processes can work; he projects anarchy or conspiracy upon the world. Political man is asked to become an ally of one group, to work with another, and to help defeat a third. Without a gyroscopic mechanism, a strong ego, he becomes putty; he has no "will" of his own. We have said that democracy works best when men view each other not exactly at arm's length but not fused in the warmth of an intense comradeship either. They must see each other as free-standing units; but this is impossible unless each has the ego strength that makes him free-standing.

Some of the pathologies flow directly from this concept— the lack of self-control, the lack of autonomy. Some emerge indirectly: anxiety troubles the mind when men are unsure of their impulse control. What we called irrationality is often a pursuit of immediate gratifications at the cost of long-run "deeper" and more enduring satisfactions. But ego strength implies just this capacity to schedule satisfactions. On balance, like self-acceptance and self-esteem, ego strength seems central to the democratic personality.

PART SEVEN

PERSONALITY AND POLITICS: THEORETICAL AND METHODOLOGICAL DIMENSIONS

Introduction

Scientific ventures that break new theoretical ground often yield, as indeed they should, more questions and more problems than answers and solutions. Such a situation has been no less true for studies in the area of personality and politics, which, as we indicated in our introductory chapter, is in its early years.

We have come a long way since Lasswell's pioneer efforts to integrate psychological/psychoanalytic and political concepts—and a much longer way since the keen observations of Plato and Aristotle. For a confirmation of this assertion the reader need only take a cursory glance at the rather lengthy, yet partial, bibliography of the field of personality and politics which follows this section.[1] Yet, in the context of this qualified success, what confronts us now is the need for more complex explanatory schemes, involving multifocal analyses that promise greater theoretical and predictive potential.

The relationships of personality to politics, as we have seen in each of the preceding sections, are complex. The various interactions, moreover, are seldom absolute, but rather contingent ones that operate only under highly specified circumstances. Accordingly, one of the principal theoret-

[1] For an interesting and comprehensive bibliographical essay on the field of personality and politics, see Michael Lerner's work in Greenstein (1969). A composite bibliography of over two thousand related items can be found in Knutson (1973).

ical problems that needs to be resolved is the specification of the sociocultural circumstances, including in particular the political situations, in which certain relationships between personality and political behavior obtain—and to specify even further those particular sociopolitical circumstances in which the interaction of personality and political dynamics is increased or decreased, vis-à-vis other variables.

More theoretically sophisticated analyses presuppose more intellectually sophisticated questions and hypotheses. For example, to what extent does a particular society modify a political ideology, such as Nazism or Communism, and, correspondingly, the relationship of personality to it[2]; and, furthermore, to what extent does a particular society constrict or expand the number of political ideologies which are available in a political system, and what effect does this situation in turn have on the interaction between personality and the available ideological options? And, on the related level of social structure, does such a thing as a two-party or a multiparty political system appreciably modify the various kinds of interaction between personality and the polity?

These are some of the questions for which we need definitive answers before we are able to provide the precision of explanation on the relationship of personality to politics which we seek. The achievement of this state of theoretical refinement requires the study and the analysis of a host of political issues and situations without any a priori judgments of theoretical viability. Most of the emphasis, for example, in the analysis of politics has been placed on political cleavage at the expense of political consensus. And the corresponding bias in the study of personality in politics has been the greater use of personality variables to explain deviant, or abnormal, political behavior rather than an extension of this approach to "normal" or regular political behavior of every type and kind.

We have tried to stress in our introductions to the several preceding sections that the theoretical specification and de-

[2] For an elaboration on this point, see DiRenzo (1967a).

velopment which we seek requires, fundamentally, refinements in methodological procedures and techniques for analyzing the precise relations between personality and political behavior. Many of the objections[3] which have been raised against some of the existing methodology (e.g., validity of personality inventories, subjectivity of psychological biography) for the analysis of personality and politics need not be permanent injunctions against further, and more expanded, research in this area of scholarship.

One serious methodological obstacle, unique to research in the field of personality and politics, is that of inducing political man, especially at the elitist levels of politics, to submit to the particular techniques (e.g., time-consuming interviews, clinical and/or projective measurements) and the growing social pressures to safeguard the confidentiality of this kind of data. These kinds of problems are not unsurmountable, but their resolution requires the total commitment and effort of the scientific imagination.

The crucial question in these matters of methodological development is not so much how to study personality, and how to study politics, in more sophisticated and theoretically meaningful perspectives—although to be sure these questions are fundamentally imperative concerns in themselves—but rather it is the more specific one of how to study personality *and* politics simultaneously in an interactive, and interdependent, perspective.

Some excellent advances in these areas of theoretical and methodological expansion have been made in very recent years, and their far-reaching promise immeasurably exceeds the intellectual gratification which they provide for the present. Among these works, special mention should be made of the several contributions by Greenstein (1967–1969, 1971) in which he has attempted "to clear away the underbrush" in order to bring some clarification to many of the conceptual, theoretical, and methodological aspects of the study of personality and politics. And, more recently, Knutson (1973)

[3] See Greenstein (1967b) for an enumeration of current objections.

has compiled a highly interesting and useful set of statements and documents of work in this area.[4]

Our selections in this final section are intended to put into perspective some of the major issues and problems of our concern in these matters of the methodology for the study of personality and politics. In the first selection, Levinson, arguing that political behavior cannot be explained adequately without some understanding of the interplay among intrapsychic influences, sociocultural opportunities and demands, and political dynamics themselves, considers some of the ways in which political behavior is influenced by external social pressures, by internal personality requirements, and by the interaction of these two sets of determinants.

In describing the kinds of analytical tools which are necessary for the theoretical problems at hand, Levinson advocates a "personological" approach—one focusing on deep-lying motivational, cognitive, and conative characteristics—in conjunction with more sociological and historical orientations; he believes that this approach can most effectively combine the psychological and sociocultural dimensions. While advocating no particular theory of personality, Levinson prefers psychoanalytic theory, and he makes his presentation in this context.

Smelser, in our second selection, accepts the now commonplace idea that personality is an important determinant of political phenomena, but his particular intention is to explore some of the problems that arise in attempts to conceptualize how this influence operates, and specifically to articulate how personality mediates between social variables and the behavioral outcomes of politics. His methodological essay, like Levinson's, one with a theoretical rather than an empirical character, deals more with canons for establishing conceptual relations among the elements of systematic explanations rather than with the canons for verifying empirical propositions. Many of the theoretical and methodological questions that have emerged in the preceding sections are put into fo-

---

[4] See the *Journal of Social Issues,* Volume 24 (1968), whole issue, for another set of useful statements on the field of personality and politics.

cus, occasionally challenged, but always elucidated by the kind of discussion that Smelser provides.

One of the major questions in the study of personality and politics is its own version of the chicken-or-the-egg dilemma: which set of variables—the psychological or the political— has primacy? Which variables are the dependent ones and which are the independent ones? The answer to this question is neither simple nor absolute. Actually, either the personality or the political factors may be both kinds of variable—although, or course, at different times. The more specific question, again, is under what circumstances does either variable play one role rather than the other. Smelser provides some strategic advice on how to proceed in the interests of resolving this question in given instances of political behavior.

One particular question that could be explored in this context, especially since the dynamics of the principle of congruency move in two-dimensional space, concerns the origin of different types of political personality. In what way, and to what extent, do the variations in sociopolitical systems contribute to the formation, and/or modification, of distinct personality types?

The theoretical problems with which we are dealing in the field of personality and politics are those of a multifocal nature. These kinds of analytical problems, argues Smith, in our third selection, require ventures into mapping operations. In his view, mapping, given the state of scientific maturity in the behavioral and social disciplines, is the most effective approach that we can use toward the goal of interdisciplinary integration at this time.

The function of a map is to help one to find his way— through unknown, or largely unfamiliar, territory—to a given goal. Smith's essay sketches such a map for the analysis of personality and politics, and it is offered as an attempt to place particular variables and relationships in a context which promises a more fruitful perspective.

Smith's map charts for us the way—admittedly, as a "psychologist's map," only one way—of sorting the broad categories of analysis and linking their relationships to each other. Its chief value, nonetheless, lies in plotting a route that is designed to preclude a reductionistic explanation for political behavior by guarding against the selective emphasis of one kind of category at the expense of others. Of particular importance in this regard is that Smith's map provides a reconciliation for "sociological" and "psychological" variables. He recognizes that the study of situational factors must be taken into account if we are to isolate the distinctive contributions of personality; and, while being intentionally and necessarily selective in terms of perspective and focus, the fundamental worth of Smith's contribution lies in its synthetic schematization of the reality of political phenomena rather than in its complex and comprehensive analysis of it. After all, a map, as Smith correctly points out, is not a theory that can be confirmed or falsified by empirical evidence; rather it is a methodological tool, or a heuristic device which provides a declaration of intellectual strategy, that is to be judged as profitable or sterile rather than as true or false.

Our selections in this final section represent fertile advancements for the kind of methodological and theoretical sophistication which now constitutes the crossroads of scientific analysis and explanation in the field of personality and politics.

The Relevance of Personality
for Political Participation
Daniel J. Levinson

Although the general theme of this paper is "Personality and Political Participation," it is clear that political behavior is a matter of much more than personality. Indeed, there are those who argue that political behavior is all but independent of personality. My aim here is to consider briefly, at a general theoretical level, the ways in which political participation is influenced by external social pressures, by internal personality requirements, and by these two sets of determinants operating in interaction.

Social sciences such as sociology and political economy are of central importance to the psychologist engaged in the study of political participation. They provide essential analytic tools in defining and assessing the broad context within which political behavior takes place. Indeed, the most powerful external forces affecting the individual's political functioning are those stemming from the social, economic and political systems of which he is a part. Every social order, whether of a total society or a specific class, community or institutional complex, influences in countless ways the political participation of its members. The continued stable operation of any system requires at least a moderate degree of ideological and

Reprinted by permission of the author and publisher from *The Public Opinion Quarterly,* Volume 22, 1958, pp. 3–10.

behavioral conformity to its norms. While systems differ in the degree of diversity they produce and tolerate, each one has an apparatus of social control that encourages participation along norm-congruent lines and hinders or actively punishes deviance.

THE SOCIO-CULTURAL MATRIX

Every social order has manifold influences on the individual's political views and overt behavior. It makes available only a limited number and variety of political alternatives; that is, it narrows the range of political choice. It legitimizes only those of the existing alternatives that are reasonably congruent with the prevailing social structure. It has an intricate, often unrecognized, system of sanctions through which legitimized modes of participation are rewarded and others punished. The societal elite groups, which are likely to be identified with the prevailing system, can exert great conformity-inducing influence as a result of their prestige, their control over the indoctrination and communication media, and their politico-economic power. Finally, every society makes possible a distinctive but necessarily limited range of experiences that most of its members cannot transcend. Very often, individuals are systematically prevented from having experiences that might lead them to new modes of thought and action. During the cold-war period, for example, persons on either side of the numerous "curtains" have had practically no opportunity to achieve experiences that would contradict the prevailing stereotypes of the "enemy" (Bauer, 1956; Smith, 1956).

Clearly, the sociocultural matrix, with its weighty traditions and its innumerable devices for moulding the human psyche, presents a truly staggering array of influences on individual thought and action. Shall we propose, then, that political participation is determined almost entirely by the contemporary social structure and its apparatus of social control? Many of us would, I believe, argue against an exclusively social-deterministic viewpoint. Yet there are critics of contemporary social science—one of them, Joseph Wood

Krutch (1954), last year formulated his critique in a prize-winning book—who maintain that social scientists conceive of man as merely a social "object," an unthinking creature continually shaped by, but never influencing, his social environment. According to these harsh critics, social scientists focus on man's norm-abiding tendencies to the exclusion of his capacities for rejecting dominant norms and creating new ones.

It is in many respects a "straw man" social scientist, or perhaps a caricature, that Krutch and others have painted in such dark colors. But I believe that the caricature, despite its distorted and at times even hallucinatory quality, has its elements of realism as well. Many social scientists, including psychologists, have been so impressed with the number and pervasiveness of the mechanisms of social control, and have become so committed to believing in the causal potency of a particular set of social, economic, or cultural variables that they have tended to view political and other participation as determined almost entirely by these variables. They have assumed that within each of the various major social groupings in societies there are clearcut social norms and only limited variability or deviance from these norms. When relatively great uniformity is found, they tend to assume that it is brought about directly by social pressures of the kinds mentioned above, and they have given little consideration to the part played by individual or modal personality in this process. One of the most common tendencies is to introduce personality factors in the hypothetical explanation of deviance, but to assume that personality has little to do with the acceptance of prevailing norms. In this view it is, so to speak, merely "normal" to go along with group pressures, but to deviate is "abnormal" and therefore of personality relevance. We have increasing evidence, however, that the simple "J-curve" model of one dominant normative pattern of political participation and a small deviant minority is seldom realized. There is ordinarily much more variability in modes of political participation within a single grouping that this model can accommodate. And it seems likely that personality factors are important determinants of political participation even within the spectrum of normatively accepted modes.

THE PSYCHOLOGICAL PROCESS

The predominantly social-deterministic theories do not make use of an explicit personality theory. That is, they do not regard enduring personal characteristics (such as character traits, conceptions of self and others, preferred modes of dealing with unconscious wishes or external stresses, and the like) as having a significant influence on political participation. These viewpoints do, however, frequently posit one or another psychological process as a mediating device between social pressure and individual behavior. Perhaps the most commonly used of these mediating devices are "imitation," "conditioning," and "self-interest." The imitation and conditioning theories are represented in caricature by Will Rogers' facetious expression, "All I know is what I read in the newspaper." According to these viewpoints, people take on habits of thought and action by repeating in more or less automatic fashion the responses that their environment presents most often and with the greatest pressure. It is only slightly unfair, I think, to call them *sponge* theories, for they conceive of the individual as a passive material that soaks up whatever ideological liquids the environment provides. These theories have been historically useful in emphasizing the importance of the social context in determining political and social behavior. However, they have largely overlooked the complexities of the external "stimulus field" and they have failed to grasp the varied psychological processes involved in the selection, organization and creation of ideas and modes of participation. They have neglected the role of reason and imagination, and, equally, the myriad ways in which man's intellectual operations are influenced by nonrational and irrational processes. In basing their model of human nature on man's capacity for stupidity and blind conformity, they have overlooked his capacity to be intelligently rational—and to be intelligently irrational.

In the more rationalistic, self-interest theories, it is assumed that an individual's political behavior will be determined primarily by a more or less realistic appraisal of his individual or group interests. This approach is represented in the conceptions of "economic man" and "political man," each hedonistically and rationally pursuing his practical goals. The inadequacy of these conceptions, at least in their simpler forms, has become increasingly clear. They cannot account for the many cases in which an individual's or a group's actions are not in accord with its immediate interests and indeed may be antithetical to them. For example: the low political participation of subordinate strata in our society (Lipset, 1954); the common occurrence of pro-business ideology among workers, and the phenomenon of the upper-class radical. Another problem is the difficulty of determining the "true" interest of a given group. Every group has multiple aims and interests, some of which may limit or preclude the realization of others. And, since every individual belongs to, and is identified with, a variety of groups whose interests will not fully coincide, his behavior will necessarily reflect his personal attempts at compromise or synthesis. Given the existence of multiple groupings in society, of multiple group-memberships and group-allegiances in the individual, and of individuality in the synthesis of preferred goals and modes of participation, we should hardly be surprised to find wide individual differences within any large group in the interpretation of its proper interests and policies.

Clearly, imitation, conditioning, and the rational appraisal of self or group-interest should be taken into account in any sociopsychological theory of political participation. However, not any of these in itself, nor the three in combination, provide an adequate psychological basis for such a theory. The first requirement, in my opinion, is a conception of personality within which the individual's preferred modes of political participation can be seen as intrinsic, functional components —that a *personological* approach be taken in conjunction with sociological and historical approaches. Seen in personological perspective, as an aspect of personality, the individual's modes of political participation can be related to deeper-lying motivational, cognitive, and conative characteristics. A personological approach will, more than any other permit the effective meshing of psychology with the various social sciences.

Various theories of personality are available as starting points for a personological approach.[1] My own preference is to start from psychoanalytic theory while utilizing ideas from other theories as well. The development of a general political orientation and of specific political preferences may be regarded as an *external function* of the ego, that is, as one of the means by which the person structures social reality, defines his place within it, and guides his search for meaning and gratification. Other external ego functions include the choice of an occupation, the development of a characteristic "style," of preferred modes of thinking and relating to others, and so on.

Like the external ego functions, political participation is affected by the ways in which the ego carries out its *internal functions*—that is, by the ego's ways of coping with, and attempting to synthesize, the demands of ego, id, and superego. These internal activities, the "psychodynamics" of personality, include among other things: the individual's unconscious fantasies; his unconscious moral conceptions and the wishes against which they are directed; the characteristic ways in which these tendencies are transformed or deflected in his more conscious thought, feeling and behavioral striving; his conception of self and his ways of maintaining or changing that conception in the face of changing pressures from within and from the external world. I am proposing, then, that *the ways in which the ego carries out its internal functions will heavily influence, though not entirely determine, the individual's selection, creation, and synthesis of modes of political participation.*

This general formulation implies a postulate of *receptivity:* the individual will be most receptive to those available political forms that have the greatest functional value in meeting the requirements of the personality as a system. He will prefer those ways of dealing with external political issues that best gear in with his preferred ways of dealing with internal issues of impulse control, maintenance of self-esteem, fulfillment of esthetic urges, and the like. This approach involves,

[1] See Adorno (1950); Frenkel-Brunswik (1952); Levinson (1964b); Murray and Morgan (1945); Smith et al. (1956).

in addition, a postulate of *immanence:* many of the personality characteristics that influence the individual's political participation are directly reflected (immanent) within it. It is possible through psychological analysis of an individual's political thought and action to derive many of the personality features that have helped to establish and maintain it. As Lowell observed, "Truth is said to lie at the bottom of a well for the very reason, perhaps, that whoever looks down in search of her sees his own image at the bottom, and is perusaded not only that he has seen the goddess, but that she is far better-looking than he had imagined."

The thesis of this paper is that enduring personality characteristics influence political participation; hinder the acceptance of "unappealing" (dynamically incongruent) options, and facilitate the acceptance or creation of others that are personally meaningful. However, there are important variations from one individual to another, and from one sphere of activity to another within a given individual, in the degree to which psychodynamics influence the choice and the specific content of political preferences. Clearly, no single set of behaviors ever engages all of the personality. Political choice is affected from within not by the "total personality" but primarily by the particular facets of personality that are engaged at a given period of time. Moreover, inner compulsions and rigidities are seldom so strong that they permit acceptance of, and total involvement in, only one mode of participation. Every individual has multiple political potentials and is capable of some measure of political change. Such change may come about not only through new knowledge and external circumstances but also as a result of inner changes in ideology-relevant aspects of personality. While acknowledging the importance and durability of the personality structure established by the age of five or six, we must still allow for important new developments and partial restructurings throughout life.

In emphasizing the intimate relation between internal dynamics and political participation, we must keep in mind that this is a two-way process. Political preference is not a "mere" epiphenomenon or super-structure with no causal force of its own. Political ideas and actions play their causal, dynamic role in individual personality as in social structure. They may promote change or they may serve to maintain the internal *status quo;* individual personalities, like societal orders, vary in this regard. To the extent that his political participation is personally congenial, it has significant equilibrium-maintaining functions for the individual: it helps to consolidate his ego defenses, to maintain control over fears and conflictful wishes, and to provide forms of activity that are morally appropriate and emotionally gratifying. However, an individual's political role may not be entirely congenial to him; the fit between role and dynamics is seldom perfect. An incongruent role has the effect of perpetuating and perhaps intensifying inner conflicts and anxieties. In addition, *change* in political ideology or affiliation may have consequences for the personality. New political trends in a society, which emerge in part out of its social structure, have a serious impact on that structure. The same is true for political change in the individual. Although the gradual acceptance of a new political orientation depends in part upon the individual's dynamics when the change began, it may very well have major re-equilibrating effects on the dynamics. For example, the availability of a chauvinistic nationalistic ideology during a period of international crisis may lead, in some of those who accept it, to the active use of projective, aggression-releasing defenses that might, in another ideological climate, be more controlled.

The individual's modes of political participation are not simple reflections of his personality structure, any more than they are direct products of environing social pressures. One's political preferences will, in this view, be most stable and most satisfying when they are congruent with both inner and external requirements. Conversely, political preferences will be most susceptible to change when they are not deeply imbedded in the personality, when they reflect one side of a poorly resolved inner conflict, or when the person is unable to find a significant membership or reference group to provide at least minimal external support for his views.

Personality factors may have a major influence on certain political decisions and a minor influence on others. For example, data from a recent comparative study of teachers in seven Western European nations[2] indicate that, in each country, teachers belonging to Labor (left-wing) parties are significantly less authoritarian on the average than those in right-wing parties, while the average for center-party members lies in between. At the same time, the variance of authoritarianism scores within each party is sufficiently great so that personal authoritarianism cannot be regarded as the chief determinant of party choice. Personality would probably play a smaller part in determining party choice within, say, the English working class, where tradition and current pressures operate so strongly in the direction of Labor Party membership. In this class, however, personality would presumably have a greater influence in determining the particular form of Labor ideology and the preference for one rather than another faction within the Labor Party. Again, in the United States, personality is less related to Republican vs. Democratic Party membership (though it does have some bearing here) than it is to preference for liberal vs. conservative factions within each party (Adorno, 1950; Lane, 1955).

As yet we know very little about the conditions under which the influence of personality on political participation is maximized or minimized. The following two conditions probably increase the importance of intrapersonal determinants.

(1) *A wide range of available (socially provided) alternatives.* The greater the number of options for participation, the more can the person choose on the basis of personal congeniality. Or, in more general terms, the greater the richness and complexity of the stimulus field, the more will internal organizing forces determine individual adaptation. This condition obtains in a relatively unstructured social field and, as well, in a pluralistic society that provides numerous structured alternatives. In assessing the degree of effective choice, we must take into account the nature and the meaningfulness of the alternatives. Thus, in many elections, the differences between opposing candidates are so small that the voter is confronted with an essentially trivial, meaningless choice. It is

[2] These data were obtained in a survey carried out by the Organization for Comparative Social Research. The findings noted here stem from an analysis by Stein Rokkan, Arthur Couch, and myself (unpublished study).

also necessary to take into account the strength of the sanctions for and against each option. For example, the option of refusing to sign a loyalty oath is in a sense "available" to any member of an institution that requires such an oath, but the sanctions operating are usually so strong that non-signing is an almost "unavailable" option to many who would otherwise choose it.

(2) *A high degree of personal involvement in political issues.* The more politics "matters," the more likely it is that political behavior will express enduring inner values and dispositions. Conversely, the less salient the issues involved, the more likely is one to respond on the basis of immediate external pressures. When a personally congenial mode of participation is not readily available, and the person cannot create one for himself, he may nominally accept an uncongenial role but without strong commitment or involvement. This has been true of many political liberals in post-war United States. In this case, however, the person is likely to be apathetic and to have a strong potential for change toward a new and psychologically more functional role.

SUMMARY

In emphasizing the importance of social forces, the author has argued against "sponge" theories which regard political behavior as based upon the simple, mechanical absorption of prevailing modes and opposed rationalistic theories in which political ideology and action are conceived of solely as tools serving group interests. In supporting a personological approach, he has cautioned against "mirage" theories according to which political behavior is seen primarily as a psychic by-product, a result of inner defensive maneuvers, with no (conceptualized) relation to social reality and with no effects on the inner man. Ultimately we must understand the interplay among the intrapsychic influences—rational as well as non-rational and irrational—the socio-cultural opportunities and demands, and the political behavior itself. An inclusive theoretical framework would take account of man's docility and of his creativity. It would comprehend man as a "social product," shaped and standardized to varying degrees by cultural, socio-economic, and ecological forces over which he may have little control. It would also comprehend man's individuality, his capacity for reinterpreting himself and his world and for influencing his own destiny. Finally, it would seek to grasp both the conformity- and the individuality-inducing features of societal patterning. An approach of this kind is essential if social science is to achieve an understanding of politically responsible man in a politically evolving society.

Personality and the Explanation of Political Phenomena at the Social-System Level: A Methodological Statement
Neil J. Smelser

It is a commonplace that the personalities of individual actors are important determinants of political phenomena. Consider the following illustrations:

A discrete action of a single individual—for example, a vote—is evidently determined by the interaction of a number of psychological variables: his motives, his attitudes, the information he possesses, his conception of himself as citizen, and so on. In this example, personality factors are directly *causal*, even though they may have themselves been determined by the individual's past and present social involvements.

When many such actions are aggregated into a rate, and when we attempt to explain variations in this rate by factors that transcend the personalities of any single individual, personality factors still are part of the explanation. For example, if we wish to trace the influence of social class on voting patterns, we employ at least the implicit psychological assumption that people's class positions influence their attitudes, and that these attitudes—thus influenced—determine in part the way an individual decides to vote. In this example personality factors mediate between social determinants and behavioral outcomes.

Reprinted by permission of the publisher from the *Journal of Social Issues,* Volume 24, 1968, pp. 111–125.

When we move to a more general level and attempt to account for certain features of a complex political structure (for example, a bureaucracy such as the State Department), personality factors operate in correspondingly more complex ways. Personality factors determine in part who is recruited into the organization; what kind of impact the structure has on these recruits; whether they do or do not conform to the normative expectations that are part of their roles; how they react to authorities in the structure; whether or not they decide to leave the structure; and so on. In this example personality factors *interact* with other types of determinants.

In this essay I do not intend to elaborate the commonplace *that* personality is an important determinant of political phenomena. Rather I intend to explore some of the problems that arise in conceptualizing how this influence operates. Thus it will be a methodological rather than a substantive essay. But it will be methodological in a theoretical rather than an empirical sense. It will not deal so much with the canons for verifying empirical propositions as with the canons of establishing conceptual relations among the ingredients of systematic explanations. I shall begin the essay by creating a simple hypothetical model of political behavior, indicating how personality variables contribute to the outcomes generated by the model. Next I shall review a number of fundamental theoretical problems involved in incorporating personality variables into the explanation of political—or more generally, social—phenomena, illustrating these problems by some references to "national character". Finally, I shall attempt to draw a few lessons from the foregoing.

THE PLACE OF PSYCHOLOGIAL FACTORS IN THE EXPLANATION OF POLITICAL PHENOMENA

The essential ingredients of an explanation of behavioral phenomena—whether these be political or some other kind of phenomena—are the following: (a) The statement of a problem, which involves specification of a range of behavior, variations in which we wish to explain. The statement of this problem identifies the *dependent variables*. (b) The identification of variables to account for variations in the dependent variables. These are commonly referred to as *independent variables*. (c) The organization of the several variables into some kind of conceptual framework. The simplest way to organize variables is to form *hypotheses,* which relate one variable to another in a causal way. More elaborate forms of conceptual organization are found in *models* or *theories,* which combine a number of variables and hypotheses into a system, on the basis of which various outcomes can be generated. The empirical testing of any explanation involves the identification of indices for each variable, and the attempt to assess the empirical validity of the posited relations among variables. But in this essay I emphasize the conceptual relations among variables.

A HYPOTHETICAL EXAMPLE

The ingredients of an explanatory system can be grasped by following a simple hypothetical example. Let us suppose that our field of interest is municipal politics, and we wish to explain variations in three variables—the level of political corruption, the average municipal tax rate, and the rate of turnover of elected municipal officials. Let us suppose further that the problems of establishing valid and measurable empirical indices for these three variables have been overcome more or less satisfactorily. According to the hypothetical model I am now advancing, the following relations hold among the three variables: When elected officials achieve a reasonably secure tenure through repeated re-election (that is, when there is low turnover) these officials will begin to feel free to dip into public funds to reward relatives, friends, cronies and political supporters. As these practices increase, pressures on public funds begin to accumulate, and the officials find it necessary to hike various municipal taxes to meet these pressures. The tax increases, however, infuriate those portions of the local populace that are not receiving the benefits of patronage. As a consequence, voters begin to turn against the local officials in succeeding elections, and the rate of turnover in office increases. As new officials are elected, they proceed to "clean up" corruption by a series of reforms and are thereby enabled to reduce taxes. In this way they gain the continued support of the electorate and are retained in office in succeeding elections. Having been granted this security in office, however, the new crop of officials begins to indulge once again in corrupt practices, and this initiates once again the complex sequence just described.

In this example the dependent variables are three well-known types of political phenomena—corruption, taxes and turnover. But these variables also turn out to be the independent variables, since each dependent variable is represented as a function of the others. The tax rate is at one time a direct function of the level of corruption, at a later time a direct function of the level of turnover of officials. The level of corruption is a direct function of the rate of turnover of officials. And the rate of turnover of officials is a direct function of the tax rate. In this particular model the distinction between independent and dependent variables becomes completely relative, since each variable is a function of the others. Each variable is assessed as independent or dependent, depending on the point entry is made into the model; moreover, each variable may be considered independent or dependent, or simultaneously both.

I have organized the particular variables in this model so that they stand in *equilibrium* relation with one another; a change in any one variable initiates change in the others, and these changes in turn feed back and produce changes in the initiating variable.[1] These particular relations, moreover, produce a series of interrelated cyclical movements among the three variables. These movements can be represented graphically as presented in Figure 1.

The rate of turnover of officials is represented by the solid line; the level of corruption by the dashed line; and the average tax rate by the dotted line. Continued tenure in office (the level solid line) permits a rise in corruption. After a lag,

[1] The choice of an equilibrium type of model does not make my arguments less general in their applicability. The principle of equilibrium is not something different from other types of explanatory model, but is simply one alternative method of generating explanations and predictions about empirical phenomena.

FIGURE 1

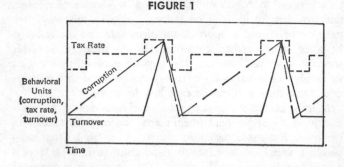

Time

the increase in the tax rate begins, and this in turn precipitates
a turnover of officials at election time. Subsequently all three
variables decrease sharply, but after a time the level of corruption begins to creep upward again, thus initiating the
cyclical pattern for each variable. The contour of each cycle,
however, varies because the units of each variable differ in
their degree of divisibility. It is possible, for example, to represent corruption as rising and falling smoothly, since it can
be increased or decreased by very small increments. By contrast, the tax rate must be represented by a more irregular
contour, since it can be changed only by discrete acts of
legislation. The rate of turnover of officials shows an even
more irregular course, since it can be changed only at election time (say, every two years). Despite these different con-
tours, the cyclical movements are determined primarily by
the functional relations among the three variables.

THE GIVEN DATA—THE PARAMETERS

Up to this point, personality variables have not appeared
in the model. Indeed, the model is represented only as a
series of interrelations among several behavioral indices. How
do personality variables exercise their influence? To answer
this question we must identify yet another ingredient of explanatory systems. Previously we have identified the *variables*
themselves and the *relations* among the variables, from which
were able to generate a number of predictions. But a third

and very important ingredient of any explanatory system is the *given data* or *parameters*. These are phenomena that are known or suspected to influence the relations among the variables—and hence the outputs of the system—but variations in which are assumed to be frozen by analytic controls. In this way their influence on the variables is either held constant or otherwise neutralized. The given data, then, "lie beyond the analytical ambition of the model, in the sense that they are determining rather than determined" (Kuenne, 1963:5). Furthermore, the nature and extent of their determining influence is controlled by conceptual manipulation.

The given data, or parameters, of an explanatory system may be broken down into several subclasses:

(a) Certain assumptions are made concerning the stability of the empirical world lying beyond the limits of the model. For example, the hypothetical model I have developed contains a great many unspoken but important assumptions—that no major economic depression hits the municipalities whose political behavior is being studied; that no major changes are made in criminal law affecting corrupt practices; that no major international war develops; and that the municipalities are free from natural catastrophes and famines. In addition, certain psychological "constants" are tacitly assumed—that the citizenry does not reject the constitutional framework of the municipality as illegitimate, that a majority of the electorate are not ignorant of the political phenomena, and so on.

Any explanatory model rests on an almost interminable list of assumptions about aspects of the "rest of the world" outside the model that do *not* vary. Some of these assumptions are psychological in character. It would be pedantic to attempt to list all such assumptions for every model that is generated; but, notwithstanding, it should be remembered that significant variations in the phenomena ruled out by these assumptions would influence—if not overwhelm—the relations posited in the model.

(b) Certain determinants outside the system are assumed to influence the variables, but in an unvarying way. For example, as indicated, the fact that municipal elections are held only every two years makes for a very irregular rising and falling of the line representing turnover in office, though the cause of the rising and falling movements themselves is found in the interrelations among the primary variables. Or, to take a psychological example, it is assumed that an adequate supply of political motivation exists in the population of the municipality, so that there will be an available pool of motivated individuals to seek municipal offices. Such variables do intrude on the model—and thus differ from the first type of parameter, which is assumed not to influence the model—but this intrusion is of a constant, not a variable character.

(c) Explanatory models also incorporate assumptions that "intervene" between the primary variables. For example, one of the principal connections in the illustrative model is between length of tenure in office and level of corruption. This connection rests on certain psychological assumptions about political officials—namely, that in a secure position they come to feel that they can engage in quasi-legitimate political activities. If this psychological assumption is modified, the relations among the primary variables is modified accordingly. For example, if it is postulated that position in office increases officials' sense of integrity and public obligation, the relation between tenure in office and level of corruption is reversed.

The assumptions that intervene between the primary variables "make sense" of the relations among the variables. If it is asked why tenure of office is positively correlated with increasing corruption, the answer is found in the psychology of the elected officials. In addition, these intervening assumptions provide at least a partial account of the *mechanisms* by which the primary variables influence one another. In the example I assumed that one primary variable (continuity in office) has certain psychological consequences for officials, that the officials will behave in accord with these consequences, and that their behavior will result in a change in another primary variable (corruption). Thus, even though the intervening assumptions do not vary—and thereby fall into the category of "given data"—they provide a service in linking the primary variables to one another.

THE CHOICE OF PARAMETERS

An explanatory model can be legitimately criticized on the basis of its choice of parameters as well as its choice of relations among primary variables. For example, in linking tenure of office directly with corruption, I introduced a psychological view of office holders as primarily opportunistic. On the other hand, in linking the tax rate directly to the rate of turnover of officials, I introduced a psychological view of the electorate as righteously indignant. A critic of my model might well ask whether I have adopted one psychological perspective for political leaders and another for political followers; and, if so, why; and, indeed, whether either perspective is justified. To choose another example: in characterizing the response of the electorate to increasing corruption and tax burdens, I assumed that they would choose to express their dissatisfaction only at the polls, and would not resort to violent assault on political officials or to attempt themselves to seize the reigns of municipal power. A critic might well ask why I chose to view the citizenry as so tame and respectful of law and order; he might suggest further that if I viewed it otherwise, I would be closer to the truth about human nature, and, in addition, would create a very different kind of model.

Having specified these ingredients of an explanatory system —variables, relations and several categories of given data—it is possible to indicate what is involved in the *derivation of hypotheses* from an explanatory model. Derivation consists of systematically and exhaustively specifying the implications of *both* the given data *and* the relations among variables for the variations in the dependent variables. A portion of a variable's variation can be predicted by virtue of the ways in which the parameters—some of which are psychological— constrict or intrude upon the model. Or to put it in other words, "the variables of the model . . . are determined . . . by the constraining interaction of the [given] data and the interrelations that exist among the [given] data and variables by virtue of the natural or behavioral assumptions of the model, or both" (Kuenne, 1963:5).

Finally, it should be noted that the distinction between variables and parameters (given data) is a relative one, and that by relaxing the analytic assumptions that "freeze" the parameters, these may become operative variables, and considered in relation to the other operative variables in the explanatory system. Suppose, for example, I had wished to vary the heretofore constant assumption that the citizenry does not reject the constitutional framework as illegitimate. Having done so, I would have made the level of legitimization into an operative variable rather than a parametric assumption, and could then have traced the influence of its variations on the other variables in the system. Alternatively, operative variables can be converted into parameters by changing the assumptions regarding them. The refinement of an explanatory model consists in part in the selective and systematic relaxation of assumptions—that is, treating new kinds of data as variables and adding to knowledge about the principles governing the working of the system. Furthermore, as is evident from my example, it is perfectly legitimate to convert parameters concerning psychological assumptions into operative variables, thus incorporating psychological factors into the model as primary variables. Of course, there is a limit to the operation of relaxing parametric assumptions; as more and more assumptions are relaxed, the explanatory system becomes conceptually more unwieldy because of the increasing numbers of uncontrolled variables.

PERSONALITY VARIABLES

From what has been said thus far, it would appear that there is no reason to suppose that personality variables cannot be incorporated systematically into the enterprise of explaining social—including political—phenomena. Yet on closer examination a number of difficulties arise. The statements concerning personality in the illustrative model are cast in a very simple form. Mainly they seem to be assumptions that "fit" conveniently between associated aggregated rates and render intelligible their association. In addition, they often seem questionable as empirical generalizations. Surely the assumption that tenure in office breeds personal corruptibility is not true of all office holders; surely a variety of effects of tenure are empirically observable, and this variety depends in part on the personality differences of individuals in office. But if we allow for this diversity of psychological effects, the theoretical rationale for connecting time in office with corruption is weakened accordingly.

A paradox thus emerges from these observations. In explaining aggregated political phenomena it is convenient, even necessary to employ personality variables. Yet at the same time the investigator is apparently forced to rely on oversimple and empirically inadequate formulations of personality. This paradox traces in part to the fact that in constructing explanations the investigator frequently attempts to argue causally across several distinct levels—for example, from personality to aggregated social rate; from personality to social structure; from culture to personality; and so on. I now turn to a brief consideration of the problems involved in moving from one conceptual level to another in constructing systematic explanations.

SOME PROBLEMS IN RELATING PSYCHOLOGICAL VARIABLES TO OTHER VARIABLES

As the various natural and social sciences have developed, there have emerged several distinctive "levels of analysis" of behavioral data—for example, the physiological, the psychological, the economic, the political, the social and the cultural. These several levels represent aspects, or ways of looking at a common body of behavioral data. It should be stressed that the data of the empirical world do not belong inherently to any one of these conceptual systems. An outburst of anger, for example, may have a physiological aspect in that it is associated with various glandular and muscular reactions; it may have a psychological aspect in that it gives rise to recriminations of conscience; and it may have a social aspect in so far as it constitutes a strain on the relations among a group of friends. The conceptual status of an empirical datum, then, is determined by the conceptual system to which it is referred for assessment and explanation (Smelser and Smelser, 1963).

In the behavioral sciences the existing "levels of analysis" are very numerous, and, because these sciences are not adequately codified, they are frequently overlapping and crosscutting. In this essay I intend neither to catalogue the existing conceptual levels in the behavioral sciences, nor to develop yet another version of my own. However, I shall distinguish among several conceptual levels, the relations among which are important for understanding the place of personality variables in explaining political and other social phenomena.

. . . The *personality* level focuses on the individual person as a system of needs, feelings, aptitudes, skills, defenses, or on one or more processes, such as the learning of skills, considered in detail. In all cases the organizing conceptual unit is the individual person.

. . . The *aggregated personality* level also involves characteristics of individuals, but treats these characteristics in terms of their multiple occurrence in many individuals or in a certain percentage of individuals out of a total. Thus, to say that 57 per cent of Americans favor the current conduct of foreign policy is to aggregate a number of individual personality characteristics (in this case attitudes) and to relate this number to a larger population of personalities.

. . . The *structural* level focuses on certain relations that emerge when two or more persons interact with one another. Here the basic units of analysis are not persons as such, but selected aspects of interaction among persons, such as roles (for example, husband, church-member, citizen) and social organization, which refers to patterned clusters of roles (for example, a clique, a political party). This level is similar to what Lazarsfeld and Menzel refer to as "structural properties" of collectives—those properties "which are obtained by performing some operation on data about the relations of each member to some or all of the others" (Lazarsfeld and Menzel, 1961:428). Structure is conceptualized on the basis of relational aspects of members of a population, not on some aggregated version of attributes of the individual members. Much of the literature on roles and social organization in the behavioral sciences is pitched at this structural level.

. . . The *cultural* level, which applies to the values, cosmologies, knowledge, expressive symbols, etc., of social units. The cultural level is an example of what Lazarsfeld and Menzel call "global" properties of collectives (Lazarsfeld and Menzel, 1961:428–429). They are based neither on aggregated characteristics of individual members of a social unit nor on specific relations among the individuals. Being global, they characterize the social unit as a whole, and thus transcend the particular qualities of individual persons and specific structural relations.

Explanations in the social sciences are frequently characterized by the fact that independent variables are conceptualized at a different level of analysis from the dependent variable. The very phrase, "the impact of personality on the political system" suggests just such a transition—from the personality level (whether individual or aggregated) to a certain type of structural level. Or to choose another example, the attempt to explain the content of cultural productions, such as myths and folklore, by reference to personality dispositions laid down in childhood involves a transition from the personality to the cultural level (Kardiner, 1945). Explanatory models that incorporate a number of different variables often involve several such transitions. There is nothing illegitimate in building such transitions into explanatory models—indeed, they are necessary if we are to achieve adequate explanations. But such transitions involve a number of methodological problems, which, if not overcome, can detract from the adequacy of explanations. I shall illustrate some of these methodological problems by reference to some of the conceptions of "national character", as that term has been employed in the past several decades.

IN ILLUSTRATION

Most conceptualizations of national character are of two types:

. . . A global concept characterizing an entire society or civilization (Benedict, 1946b). When national character is conceptualized in this way—as an attribute of an entire social unit—it is difficult to distinguish it analytically from

descriptions of cultural patterns as such. Commenting on the
literature on national character, Nett observed that

> the reader of the materials on both value orientations and
> national character sometimes has difficulty observing the
> differences between the two; he is frequently confronted
> with lists of alleged personality traits ascribed to individ-
> ual persons which coincide with lists of value-orientations
> of nation-societies (Nett, 1957:297).

. . . An aggregated-personality concept, which refers to a
statistical distribution of personality characteristics in a given
social unit. This is the concept most closely associated with
the term "modal personality", which was generated at least
in part as an effort to avoid the confusion between the
personality and the cultural levels, and to provide a distinctively psychological basis for defining and using a concept such as national character (Inkeles and Levinson, 1954:
979–983).

From the definitional standpoint, the second conceptualization is superior to the first, since its definitional units (personality variables) and its level of reference (individual
persons) lie at the same conceptual level. Even if defined as
modal personality, however, a number of difficulties arise
when aggregated personality characteristics are incorporated
into explanatory models. Consider the following illustrations:

. . . A conception of modal personality may be brought to
bear on the explanation of a discrete historical phenomenon;
an example would be the many efforts to attribute the rise of
the Nazi movement to certain authoritarian features of Germans' personalities. Such explanations are necessarily subject
to that kind of indeterminacy that arises when a disposition
is called upon to explain an event. Most of the terms that
enter into personality descriptions are dispositional—attitudes
toward authority, submissiveness, and so on. Most of these
terms have an extended time-reference; indeed, they are the
kinds of dispositions that are transmitted over many generations of child-training. The difficulty that arises can be posed
by the following question: "Even though the logic of the
historical instance (e.g., the Nazi movement) corresponds in

some way with the logic of the personality dispositions (authoritarianism), why did the historical movement occur at one rather than another historical point in time"? The implication of this query is that dispositional concepts should be conceptualized as parameters, which set limits within which other variables interact to determine the precise timing of the event.

. . . A conception of modal personality may be brought to bear on some other type of aggregated personality characteristic. Suppose, for example, the preference for Republican candidates is found to be positively correlated with authoritarianism in a given sample. Such a relationship avoids the dispositional fallacy—since both variables are dispositional —but, if interpreted in terms of a causal psychological connection between authoritarianism and Republican preference, may involve a statistical fallacy, namely reading from associations among aggregated attributes to internal psychological associations. This statistical fallacy is a more general version of what Robinson calls the "ecological fallacy" of arguing directly from ecological distributions of data to individual personality states (Robinson, 1950). The implication of this fallacy is that associations between two sets of aggregated psychological data should be supplemented with research on individuals to establish the validity of the psychological connections that presumably would account for the association.

. . . A conception of modal personality may be brought to bear on the explanation of some sort of political structure or global political value. The typical argument is that certain personality dispositions, generated by childhood, act in some way to sustain a certain structure or set of policies at the national level. Consider two classic examples. Erikson, noting the relatively egalitarian structure of the American family, argues that certain accommodative dispositions regarding conflict and its resolution arise from such a family structure and argues further that political processes in Congress recapitulate the familial mode of problem-solving (Erikson, 1950: Chapter 8). Again, Benedict argues that Japanese attitudes toward hierarchy—themselves a product mainly of familial experiences—sustained the structure of Japanese foreign policy before and during World War II:

> There was anarchy in the world as long as every nation had absolute sovereignty; it was necessary for [Japan] to fight to establish a hierarchy—under Japan, of course, since she alone represented a nation truly hierarchical from top to bottom and hence understood the necessity of taking "one's proper place" (Benedict, 1946a:21).

To put these arguments in the methodological language employed in this essay, they constitute efforts to explain a structural or cultural characteristic (a characteristic of the social unit as a whole) by reference to some aggregation of personality variables (characteristics of the individual members of the social unit).

Such arguments bristle with methodological problems. First, in so far as they rest on loose analogies between, say, family structure and the political structure of the larger society, personality as an operative variable almost disappears, since it appears to be molded uniformly from the family structure and to feed uniformly into sustaining a political structure. In addition, a more subtle problem arises, because the variable to be explained (a political structure, a political value) is an attribute of the entire system—and described at that level— the investigator is tempted to universalize or otherwise oversimplify the impact of the psychological characteristics of the individual members on the structural or cultural characteristic. Even if he qualifies his argument by acknowledging that the personality characteristics are only "modal" and that other personality types exist in the system, the problem is not overcome but rather is translated into a new version of the problem: How large does the "mode" have to be in order to sustain a structure in the social unit? And do the other personality types sustain this structure in different ways, or do they tend to subvert or change it? These problems arise—and cannot be dealt with effectively—because we do not at present have the methodological capacity to argue causally from a mixture of aggregated states of individual members of a system to a global characteristic of the system.

SOME CONCEPTUAL STRATEGIES EMERGING
FROM THE ABOVE CONSIDERATIONS

This essay has raised many more problems than it has resolved, and in the space that remains I cannot hope to do more than indicate a few directions for theoretical formulations and empirical research that might resolve these problems. I would suggest the following strategies:

(a) In any explanatory model it is essential to maintain the distinction between parameters (given data) and operative variables and to acknowledge the different explanatory work done by each. In the hypothetical model discussed above, it became apparent that parameters serve the following functions: to set limits on the explanatory ambition of the model by specifying what variables are *not* operative; to limit the range of outcomes of the model by ruling out many classes of outcomes; and to specify the intervening links among the associated operative variables in the model. Yet the parameters themselves, no matter how carefully formulated, do not determine specific outcomes and specific events. To do this it is necessary to introduce temporal variations of the variables that are conceived as operating within the framework established by the parametric assumptions.

This strategy has implications for incorporating personality variables into explanatory models. Since most personality variables—conceptions of the self, attitudes toward authority, and so on—are dispositional in nature, they cannot be employed effectively to predict the occurrences of specific behavioral outcomes. Accordingly, it would seem appropriate to formulate these variables as parameters in explanatory models, *within* which the interplay of specific events occurs. These personality variables are determinative in that they rule out certain classes of outcome and create a presumption in favor of other classes of outcome, but this determination is general rather than specific. Put another way, dispositional personality concepts set limits and reduce the determinancy of outcomes, but they do not serve as causes in the usual sense of the term. (This reasoning applies to the role of dispositional concepts at the social level as well.)

(b) The preceding paragraphs have two further implications. The first is that whenever patterns of personality dispositions are used to explain social events and situations (for example, the foreign policy of a nation), they should not be treated as simple causes, but should be incorporated into explanatory models that are "open" and make use of conditional predictions. The modal personality pattern of a nation should be conceptualized as encouraging a range of structural or behavioral outcomes, not a specific outcome. If the investigator wishes to make the connection between a personality variable and a specific outcome more determinate, he should do so by attempting to specify *under what additional conditions* this connection is to be expected. This strategy preserves the necessarily indeterminate relation between dispositional personality variables and specific outcomes, but permits the investigator to reduce this indeterminacy by introducing new variables that progressively narrow the range of outcomes.

(c) The second implication is that in relating personality to social-system outcomes it is advisable to dispense with the conventional meaning of "cause"—i.e., one event as caused by another temporally prior event—in favor of some alternative conceptualization. Given the difficulties in establishing simple connections among variables that lie at different levels, it is preferable to rely on conceptions such as probability chains, interactive and feedback systems of variables, and the like.

(d) A final strategy arises in connection with the use of personality variables as intervening concepts that "make sense" of an association between aggregated, structural or cultural concepts. (An illustration is Benedict's notion that hierarchical attitudes toward authority intervene between family structure and foreign policy in Japan.) In assessing the validity of such assertions, the investigator must have available *three* distinct kinds of data—each established independently. The first is evidence establishing that hierarchical attitudes toward authority are in fact a product of experiences within a certain kind of family structure. The second is evidence establishing the intrapsychic connection between these general attitudinal dispositions toward authority and specifically political attitudes about national policy. The third is evidence establishing that such political attitudes are in fact important determinants of national policy. If these types of evidence are assembled, the investigator is able to fill in the imputed causal chain linking family structure and political phenomena. He is also more nearly able to avoid both loose arguments by analogy and statistical fallacies.

A Map for the Analysis of Personality and Politics
M. Brewster Smith

Progress in the social and behavioral sciences has in general not been marked by major theoretical "breakthroughs". As those of us who profess one or another of these disciplines look upon the succession of research and theoretical interests that capture the center of the stage, we may sometimes wonder if there is indeed any progress at all. Particularly if we are fixated on the physical sciences as models of what a good science should be,[1] we can easily become discouraged. As therapy for this depressive mood, however, one has only to scan the textbooks of former generations and some of the earlier landmark contributions to our fields: the fact of progress, of the cumulativeness of understanding that is the hallmark of science, is immediately apparent.

The progress that we see, however, is not on the pattern according to which Einstein included and supplanted Newton, or even on that by which the modern theory of the chemical valence bond makes sense of Mendeleyev's descriptive table of elements. In addition to the development and refinement of research methods and the accretion of facts, our

Reprinted by permission of the publisher from the *Journal of Social Issues*, Volume 24, 1968, pp. 15–28.
[1] Other than meteorology, which in some respects offers such an appropriate model that I am puzzled that social scientists have not picked it up.

kind of progress has involved developing some more or less satisfactory "theories of the middle range" (Merton, 1957), and, especially, a steady increase in the sophistication of the questions that we ask and in our sensitivity to the variables that are likely to be relevant to them.

To codify this kind of progress, and to make our gains readily accessible as we face new problems of research and application, we need something other than grand theory in the old literary style: we are not ready for genuinely theoretical integration, and to pretend that we are is to hamper rather than to aid us in attacking new problems with an open mind. Rather, it often seems most useful for particular purposes to attempt to link the islands of knowledge turned up in the pursuit of middle-range theories and to sort out the kinds of variables that appear likely to be relevant, by means of mapping operations that have only modest theoretical pretensions. When the variables are drawn from the home territory of different academic disciplines, as is bound to be the case in the study of any concrete social problem and is also true of many facets of a context-defined field like political science, ventures in mapping become particularly important. They are the best we can do toward interdisciplinary integration, which in these instances is required of us by the nature of the task.

This essay sketches such a map for the analysis of personality and politics, an outgrowth of my attempts to apply the approach developed in *Opinions and Personality* (Smith, Bruner and White, 1956; Smith, 1958) to the analysis of various social problems involving social attitudes and behavior, particularly McCarthyism, civil liberties and anti-Semitism.[2] While it obviously bears the marks of its origins, I have had to go considerably beyond the range of variables, mainly psychological ones, that Bruner, White and I were dealing with.

[2] In the area of McCarthyism and civil liberties, I prepared an unpublished memorandum for Samuel A. Stouffer in connection with planning for the studies leading to his book on the subject (Stouffer, 1955). The application to anti-Semitism is embodied in a pamphlet (Smith, 1965) on which I draw heavily in the present essay, with gratitude to the Anti-Defamation League of B'nai B'rith for support in the project of which it was a by-product.

A map like this is *not* a theory that can be confirmed or
falsified by testing deductions against evidence; it is rather a
heuristic device, a declaration of intellectual strategy, that is
to be judged as profitable or sterile rather than as true or
false. I have found it personally useful in coming to grips
with topics that were new to me, and in organizing what I
think we know for my students in teaching. Placing particular
variables and relationships as it does in larger context, it may
have the further virtue of counteracting one's natural tendency to stress the exclusive importance of the variables or
theories that one happens to be momentarily interested in.
Many persisting disputes in the social sciences are like the
story of the Blind Men and the Elephant. A good map helps
us to keep the whole Elephant in view.

THE SCHEMATIC MAP

Schematic as it is, the map is too complicated to take in at
a glance. Figure 1 presents the gross outlines—the continents
in their asserted relationships. In Figures 2 and 3, we will look

FIGURE 1

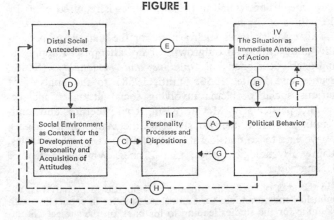

in more detail at particular segments of the terrain. The full
map, given in Figure 4, should then become intelligible. Certain intentional omissions and simplifications must finally be

noted by way of qualification. Illustrations will be provided casually en route, for the most part without documentation from the literature.

The Map in Its Simplest Form

Figure 1 diagrams the major components of a framework for the analysis of personality and politics in terms of five major panels. In keeping with the psychological focus of the map, Panel III (which indicates types of variables relating to the processes and dispositions of personality) occupies the center of the stage. Causal relationships are indicated by arrows. Because we are used to reading from left to right, I have put the payoff in actual behavior (Panel V) at the extreme right. This panel is concerned with personal political decisions as carried into action: voting, information-seeking, policy formation or implementation, influence attempts or—the source of much of our psychological data—question-answering. The data that come from our observations of people, what they say as well as what they do, belong here; only by reconstruction and inference do we arrive at the contents of the central personality panel.

Panel IV represents the person's behavioral situation as an immediate antecedent of action; Panel II includes features of the person's more enduring social environment to which we turn to explain how he has happened to become the sort of political actor that we find him to be; and Panel I represents the more remote or distal facts of politics, economics, history, etc., that contribute to the distinctive features of the environment in which he was socialized and of the immediate situations in which he acts. From the standpoint of the behaving individual, the contents of Panel I are conceptually distal but may be temporally contemporaneous: a political system, for example (Panel I), affects (Arrow D) the political norms about democracy, authority, legitimacy, etc., to which a person is socialized (Panel II); it also affects (Arrow E) the structure of the immediate situations of action that he is likely to encounter (Panel IV)—the alternatives offered on a ballot, the procedural rules in a legislative body, etc. Temporally distal determinants are also assigned to Panel I: thus the history of slavery, the plantation economy, the Civil War and Reconstruction as determinants of the politically relevant environments in which participants in Southern politics have been socialized, and of the immediate situations that comprise the stage on which they perform as political actors.

If we start with behavioral outcomes in Panel V, the arrows (marked A and B) that link them with Panels III and IV represent the methodological premise emphasized by the great psychologist Kurt Lewin: all social behavior is to be analyzed as a joint resultant of characteristics of the *person*, on the one hand, and of his psychological *situation,* on the other. The behavior of a single political actor may differ substantially as he faces differently structured situations; conversely, different persons who face the same situation will respond differently. Both the contribution of the person and that of his situation, in interaction, must be included in any adequate analysis.

For long, there was a disciplinary quarrel between psychologists and sociologists about the relevance and importance of personal dispositions (primarily *attitudes*) versus situations in determining social behavior. To take this feature of our map seriously is to regard the argument as silly and outmoded: both classes of determinants are jointly indispensible. The study of "personality and politics" cannot afford to neglect situational factors, which must in principle be taken into account if we are to isolate the distinctive contributions of personality. In concrete cases in which analysis along these lines is undertaken so as to guide social action, one may ask, of course, whether the personal or the situational component is more *strategic* in terms of accessibility to major influence. It may be more feasible, for example, to influence the normative structure that pertains to interracial relations than to carry through the program of mass psychoanalysis that might be required in order to reverse authoritarian personality trends that predispose people toward prejudice and discriminatory behavior. The practical question of strategic importance and accessibility does not seem to be as charged with disciplinary *amour-propre* as are the theoretical issues that still tend to divide the proponents of personality-oriented and of situational approaches.

The dotted arrows of relationship that leave the behavioral panel require special mention. Political behavior has consequences as well as causes, and for the sake of formal completeness some of these are suggested by the dotted "feedback loops" in the map. As Leon Festinger has argued on the basis of considerable evidence, self-committing behavior may have effects in turn upon a person's attitudes (Arrow G. (Festinger, 1957; Brehm and Cohen, 1962). A political actor who adopts a position for expedient reasons may be convinced by his own rhetoric, or—similar in result though different n the process that is assumed—he may shift his attitudes to accord with his actions in order to reduce feelings of "dissonance". The dotted Arrows F, H and I merely recognize that individual behavior also has effects in the social world. What the person does in a situation may immediately change it (Arrow F); as we integrate across the behavior of many individuals the joint consequences of the behavior of the many eventually alter the social environments that shape and support the attitudes of each (Arrow H). In the longer run (Arrow I), the behaviors of individuals constitute a society and its history.

To be sure, this is a psychologist's map that focuses on the attitudes and behavior of individual persons. A political sociologist would have to give explicit attention to matters that remain implicit in the feedback arrows—to the social structures according to which individual behaviors are integrated to have political effects. His map would necessarily be differently centered and elaborated than the present one.

Panels III and IV

With the broad framework laid out, we can now look at the details of Panels III and IV, still working from the proximal to the distal determinants of behavior (see Figure 2). The contents of Panel IV (The Situation as Immediate Antecedent of Action) remind us that an important component of any behavioral situation is the set of norms or prescriptions

FIGURE 2

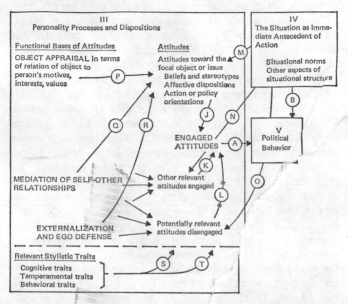

for behavior that are consensually held to apply in it. Students of political behavior at the various levels of governmental organization are concerned with recurring types of situations that confront the citizen as constituent, voter or petitioner: the legislator, the executive, the administrative functionary, the party leader. Much of the variation in personal behavior, not only across types of situations but within the same type in different political structures and different historical periods, will be attributable to differences and changes in the norms that prevail. Apart from the norms, there are of course many other situational features that are also important as codeterminants of action—among them, the competitive or cooperative relations that hold with other actors who participate in the situation, the degree of urgency with which decision or action is required, the contingencies of cost and benefit that obtain (see Thibaut and Kelley, 1959). Lore about the relevant features of political situations is a principal currency of political science.

Turn now to Panel III, Personality Processes and Dispositions. We are concerned here with inferred dispositions of the person that he brings to any situation he encounters, and with their basis in his experience and motivational processes. Social psychologists have come to use the term *attitudes* to refer to such dispositions, when they represent integrations of cognitive, emotional and conative tendencies around a psychological object such as a political figure or issue. Our problem is a dual one: to formulate how a person's attitudes come to bear on his political behavior and how these attitudes arise and are sustained in relation to their part in the ongoing operations of the person's psychological economy.

A first point suggested in Figure 2 is that we cannot take for granted just which of a person's attitudes will become engaged as a codeterminant of his behavior in a political situation. Political scientists are probably less naive than psychologists about this. A citizen's presidential vote for one or another candidate depends, as we know (Campbell, Converse, Miller, and Stokes, 1960), not only on his focal attitude toward that candidate, but also on attitudes toward the alternative candidates, toward party and toward issues. A legislator's vote on a bill will depend not only on situational factors (including whether or not a roll call is involved) and on his attitudes toward the focal issue but also on other relevant attitudes that become engaged—toward tangential issues, toward the party leadership, toward political survival or whatever. The situation plays a dual role here: both as a codeterminant, together with his engaged attitudes, of what he does (B) (the legislator may want to vote for a bill but not dare to), and as differentially activating certain of the actor's attitudes (M and N) while allowing or encouraging other potentially relevant attitudes to remain in abeyance (O). In recent years, issues concerning Negro civil rights have come to be posed in the Congress and elsewhere in such pointed terms that political actors probably find it less feasible than formerly to isolate their attitudes of democratic fair play from engagement—attitudes embodied in the American Creed (Myrdal, 1962) to which most citizens have been socialized to some degree.

Social psychological research may elect to measure and manipulate one attitude at a time for good analytic reasons, but people rarely behave in such a piecemeal fashion. What gets into the mix of a person's engaged attitudes, and with what weighting, makes a big difference. Given the complexity of these relationships, there is no reason to suppose that people's political behavior should uniformly correspond to their attitudes on the focal issue. It is surprising that some psychologists and sociologists have been surprised at the lack of one-to-one correspondence between single attitudes and behavior and have questioned the validity of attitude measurement on these irrelevant grounds.

Moving toward the left of Panel III, we turn from the problem of how attitudes are differentially aroused to that of how they are formed and sustained. The approach taken here is the functional one which posits that a person acquires and maintains attitudes and other learned psychological structures to the extent that they are in some way useful to him in his inner economy of adjustment and his outer economy of adaptation. The scheme for classifying the functional basis of attitudes is one that I have discussed in greater detail elsewhere (Smith, Bruner and White, 1956; Smith, 1968a). It answers the question, "Of what use to a man are his opinions?," under three rubrics: *object appraisal, mediation of self-other relationships* and *externalization and ego defense.*

Object Appraisal

Under object appraisal, we recognize the ways in which a person's attitudes serve him by "sizing up" significant aspects of the world in terms of their relevance to his motives, interests and values. As Walter Lippmann long ago (1922) made clear, all attitudes, not just "prejudice", involve an element of "prejudgment"; they are useful to the person in part because they prepare him for his encounters with reality enabling him to avoid the confusion and inefficiency of appraising each new situation afresh in all its complexity. In the most general way, holding *any* attitude brings a bit of order into the flux of a person's psychological world; the specific content of a person's attitudes reflects to varying degrees his appraisal of how the attitudinal object bears upon his interests and enterprises. This function involves reality testing and is likely to be involved to some minimal degree in even the least rational of attitudes—which on closer examination may turn out to be relatively reasonable within the person's own limited framework of appraisal.

Mediation of Self-Other Relationships

A person's attitudes not only embody a provisional appraisal of what for him is significant reality; they also serve to mediate the kind of relationships with others and the kind of conception of self that he is motivated to maintain. Is it important to the decision maker to think of himself as a liberal Democrat? Then his adopting a liberal stand on any of a variety of issues may contribute to his self regard. Does he rather set much stock in being right in the light of history? Such motivation, by orienting him toward an ideal reference group, may make him relatively independent of immediate social pressures. To the extent that by self-selective recruitment politicians are disproportionately likely to be "other directed" in Riesman's sense (1950), however, they may be predisposed by personality to be especially vulnerable to such pressures.

Eternalization and Ego Defense

Finally comes the class of functions to which psychoanalytic depth psychology has given the closest attention, here labelled externalization and ego defense. This is the functional basis to which Lasswell (1930) gave exclusive emphasis in his classic formula for the political man: private motives displaced onto public objects, rationalized in terms of the public interest. It also underlies the conception of the "authoritatian personality" (Adorno, 1950)—a posture in which

an essentially weak ego puts up a facade of strength that requires bolstering through identification with the strong, the
conventional and the in-group, and rejection of the weak, the
immoral, the out-group. Given the appeal of depth interpretation in the study of personality and politics, there is
little need to expand on these themes; it is more necessary to
insist that externalization and ego defense are only part of
the story.

The arrows P, Q and R raise the functional question about
the motivational sources of any attitude that a person holds.
Arrows S and T, near the bottom of the panel, reflect on their
part a different kind of relationship. A person's attitudes and
the way they engage with particular political situations bear
the mark of his stylistic traits of personality as well as of the
purposes that they serve for him. Intelligence or stupidity,
Kennedy incisiveness or Eisenhower vagueness, zest or
apathy, optimism or pessimism, decisiveness or hesitation—
cognitive, temperamental and behavioral traits like these
may have their own history in the residues of the person's
previous motivational conflicts, but their immediate relevance for his political attitudes and behavior is hardly
motivational. His attitudes and actions in the sphere of politics, as in other realms, inevitably reflect such pervasive
personal qualities, which can have momentous behavioral
consequences. A purely functional account is likely to neglect
them.

Panel II

The foregoing analysis provides us with leverage for
identifying aspects of the person's social environment that
are relevant to the development, maintenance and change
of his political attitudes and his stylistic personality traits,
as we turn to Panel II at the left of our map (Figure 3). To
the extent that a person's attitudes in a particular political
context reflect processes of object appraisal, he should be
responsive to the information that his environment provides
about the attitudinal object or issue (Arrow U). The actual
facts about it will be important in this connection only as they

FIGURE 3

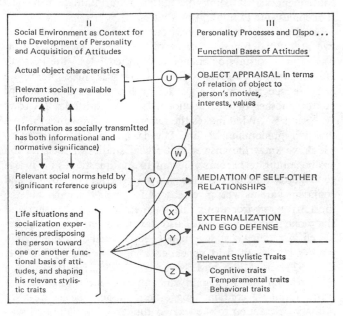

affect the information that is socially available to him, and as we know, the quality and quantity of this information vary widely from issue to issue and across the various niches that people occupy in society.

The information on a topic that reaches a person through the channels of communication has a dual relevance, as the internal arrows in Panel II are intended to suggest: not only does it feed into his processes of object appraisal, but it carries further information—a second-order message, so to speak —about the social norms that prevail. When discussions of birth control begin to percolate through Catholic channels, or debates about the pros and cons of China policy through American ones, not only is new grist provided for object appraisal; the important news is conveyed that these previously taboo topics have become moot and discussable. As Arrow V indicates, the second motivational basis of attitudes—the mediation of self-other relations—then may lead to attitudinal consequences that point to a different resultant in behavior. It becomes safe to think in new ways.

Besides providing the environmental data that the first two attitudinal functions can work with to generate new attitudes or to sustain or change established ones,[3] the person's life situation and socialization experiences may predispose him—in general, or in a particular topical domain—toward one or another of the functional bases of attitudes (Arrows W, X and Y). What makes the rational man, in whom the first function predominates? The Utopia has not yet arrived in which we know the answer, but recent studies of socialization are beginning to become relevant to the question, and it is a good guess that part of the story is rearing by loving and confident parents who give reasons for their discipline. In the shorter run, environments that augment one's self esteem and allay one's anxiety should also favor object appraisal. Research in the wake of Riesman (1950), including the Witkin group's studies of field dependence-independence (Witkin et al. 1962) and Miller and Swanson's (1958, 1960) work on child rearing and personality in entrepreneurial and bureaucratic families, contains suggestions about the sources of primary orientation to the second function, mediation of self-other relationships. As for externalization and ego defense, again the picture is not clear, but conditions that subject the developing person to arbitrary authority, that deflate self esteem, that arouse vague anxiety, that provoke hostility but block its relatively direct expression toward the source of the frustration, seem likely sources.

The final Arrow Z is drawn not to complete the alphabet but to make place for the findings of personality research, as they emerge, concerning the determinants in socialization of personal stylistic traits.

The entire map can now be reassembled in Figure 4. Arrows U to Z, taken together, replace Arrow C in Figure 1.

[3] Environment data play a much more incidental and erratic role in relation to the function of externalization and ego defense.

FIGURE 4

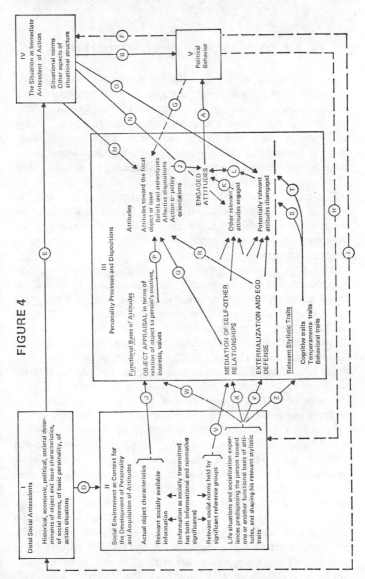

SOME OMISSIONS AND SIMPLIFICATIONS

The usefulness of a map and its inherent limitations are two sides of the same coin: its status as a simplification and schematization of reality. There are many complexities that the present map does not attempt to handle. Some of the major omissions, which I note briefly here, arise from the fact that the role of the basic psychological apparatuses and processes of motivation, perception and learning is assumed implicitly rather than explicitly delineated.

The triadic functional classification attempts to sort out the ways in which a person's attitudes are rooted in his underlying motives and their fusions and transformations, whatever they may be. It assumes but does not spell out a conception of human motivation.

As for perception, it would elaborate the map to an incomprehensible tangle to give due recognition to what we know about perceptual selectivity, the ways in which a person's existing expectations, motives and attitudes affect what he will attend to and how he will register and categorize it. A perceptual screening process intervenes between the environmental facts (Panel II) and what the person makes of them (Panel III); likewise between the immediate behavioral situation as it might appear to an objective observer (Panel IV) and how the person defines it for himself, which in the last analysis is the guise in which it affects his behavior.

In regard to learning, the present formulation makes the broad functionalist assumption that people in general acquire attitudes that are useful, that is, rewarding to them. But it ignores the details of the learning process, and such consequences of learning as the persistence of learned structures beyond their original point of usefulness. Much of the content of political attitudes, moreover, may be acquired by an individual quite incidentally, in his unfocused, only mildly attentive effort to make sense of his world. The culture says, in effect, "This is how things are with (Russia) (China) (Republicans) (Southerners) (Negroes) (socialized medicine)", and in the absence of better information, he takes note.

Such incidentally learned, psychologically marginal "information" may at the time have little real payoff in object appraisal or social adjustment (the person may have no occasion for dealing with the object or issue, and it may not matter enough to his significant reference groups to become part of the currency of his self-other relationships), yet, should the occasion arise, the basis for resonance to certain political positions rather than others has been laid.

Epilogue

In these pages we have attempted to demonstrate that political behavior is, at least in part, and in many different respects, a function of personality.

While personality is a focal element in political behavior, it is not the only instrumental one—nor even necessarily the most important one. Many other kinds of factors—historical, cultural, social, economic, and, of course, political, among others—also contribute to the eventual formation of the concrete dynamics of the political process. Our perspectives, however, have challenged the more strictly sociological approaches that consider personality as simply derivative, secondary, and non-causal. And, by the same token, it has taken issue with the more exclusively psychological orientations that view political behavior as the mere epiphenomena of personality and/or other psychological dynamics.

Our intent has been to explore the particular roles, and the precise analytical value, that personality has in the explanation of politics. We have tried to put personality factors in a realistic perspective in order to show their proper relationship to the many other variables that conjointly account for political phenomena. These considerations move us to reaffirm our basic thesis which we present here, in a somewhat more elaborated form, as a general conclusion to these discussions: the comprehensive analysis and understanding of political behavior—as indeed all other social behavior—remain incomplete, and hence distorted, without the consideration of the structure and dynamics of personality, which constitutes the source of human energy for all political and social phenomena.

BIBLIOGRAPHY

Abel, T. "Is a Psychiatric Interpretation of the German Enigma Necessary?" *American Sociological Review,* 1945, 10, 457–464.

Adler, A. *Practice and Theory of Individual Psychology.* New York: Harcourt, Brace & Company, 1924.

Adorno, T. W., Frenkel-Brunswik, E., Levinson, D. J., and Sanford, R. N. *The Authoritarian Personality.* New York: Harper, 1950.

Alexander, F. *Our Age of Unreason* (revised edition). Philadelphia: Lippincott, 1951.

Allport, G. W. "The Composition of Political Attitudes." *American Journal of Sociology,* 1929–30, 35, 220–238.

———. "What Is a Trait of Personality?" *Journal of Abnormal and Social Psychology,* 1931, 25, 368–372.

———. *Personality and Psychological Interpretation.* New York: Holt, 1937.

———. *The Nature of Prejudice.* Boston: Beacon Press, 1954.

———. "Prejudice: Is It Societal or Personal?" *Journal of Social Issues,* 1962, 18, 120–134.

Almond, G. A. *The American People and Foreign Policy.* New York: Harcourt, Brace & World, 1950.

———. *Appeals of Communism.* Princeton: Princeton University Press, 1954.

Almond, G. A., and Verba, S. *The Civic Culture.* Princeton: Princeton University Press, 1963.

Altman, J. *Organic Foundations of Animal Behavior.* New York: Holt, Rinehart & Winston, 1966.

Atkinson, J. W., Heyns, R. W., and Verkoff, J. "The Effects of Experimental Arousal of the Affiliation Motive on Thematic Apperception," in J. W. Atkinson (ed.), *Motives in Fantasy, Action and Society: A Method of Assessment and Study*. Princeton: Princeton University Press, 1958.

Ausubel, D., Balthazar, E., Rosenthal, I., Blackman, L., Schpoont, S., and Welkowitz, J. "Perceived Parents' Attitudes as Determinants of Children's Ego Structure." *Child Development*, 1954, 25, 173–183.

Baker, R. W. *Woodow Wilson: Life and Letters*. Vol. I. Garden City, N.Y.: Doubleday & Company, 1927.

Barber, J. D. *The Lawmakers*. New Haven: Yale University Press, 1965.

———. "Classifying and Predicting Presidential Styles: Two Weak Presidents." *Journal of Social Issues*, 1968, 24, 51–80.

Barker, E. N. "Authoritarianism of the Political Right, Center, and Left." Unpublished doctoral dissertation, Teachers College, Columbia University, 1958.

———. "Authoritarianism of the Political Right, Center, and Left." *Journal of Social Issues*, 1963, 19, 63–74.

Bauer, R. *The New Man in Soviet Psychology*. Cambridge: Harvard University Press, 1952.

———. "The Psychology of the Soviet Middle Elite: Two Case Histories," in C. Kluckholn and H. A. Murray (eds.), *Personality in Nature, Culture, and Society*. New York: A. Knopf, 1956.

Bauer, R., Inkeles, A., and Kluckholn, C. *How the Soviet System Works*. Cambridge: Harvard University Press, 1956.

Beier, H. "The Responses to the Rorschach Test of the Former Soviet Citizens." Unpublished Report of the Project, Russian Research Center, Harvard University, March 1954.

Beier, H., and Hanfmann, E. "Emotional Attitudes of Former Soviet Citizens as Studied by the Technique of Projective Questions." *Journal of Abnormal and Social Psychology*, 1956, 53, 143–153.

Bell, D. *The End of Ideology*. New York: The Free Press, 1960.

Benda, J. *The Treason of the Intellectuals*. Boston: Beacon Press, 1955.

Bendix, R. "Compliant Behavior and Individual Personality." *American Journal of Sociology,* 1952, 8, 292–303.

Benedict, R. *The Chrysanthemum and the Sword.* Boston: Houghton Mifflin, 1946a.

———. *Patterns of Culture.* New York: Penguin Books, 1946b.

Berelson, B. "Democratic Theory and Public Opinion." *Public Opinion Quarterly,* 1952, 16, 313–330.

Berelson, B. R., Lazarsfeld, P. F., and McPhee, W. N. *Voting.* Chicago: University of Chicago Press, 1954.

Bettelheim, B., and Janowitz, M. *The Dynamics of Prejudice.* New York: Harper, 1950.

Birney, R. C. "The Reliability of the Achievement Motive." *Journal of Abnormal and Social Psychology,* 1959, 58, 266–267.

Bittner, E. "Radicalism and the Organization of Radical Movements." *American Sociological Review,* 1963, 28, 928–940.

Blau, P. *Exchange and Power in Social Life.* New York: Wiley, 1964.

Bonnard, A. "On Political Creed and Character." *Psychoanalysis,* 1954, 2, 55–58.

Borgatta, E. F., and Lambert, W. W. (eds.). *Handbook of Personality Theory and Research.* Chicago: Rand McNally & Company, 1968.

Breckenridge, M. E., and Vincent, F. L. *Child Development.* Philadelphia: W. B. Saunders, 1965.

Brehm, J. W., and Cohen, A. R. *Explorations in Cognitive Dissonance.* New York: Wiley, 1962.

Brickner, R. M. *Is Germany Incurable?* Philadelphia: Lippincott, 1943.

Browning, R. P. "The Interaction of Personality and Political Systems in Decisions to Run for Office: Some Data and a Simulation Technique." *Journal of Social Issues,* 1968, 24, 93–110.

Browning, R. P., and Jacob, H. "Power Motivation and the Political Personality." *Public Opinion Quarterly,* 1964, 28, 75–90.

Bucklew, J. *Paradigms for Psychopathology.* Chicago: Lippincott, 1960.

Budner, S. "Intolerance of Ambiguity as a Personality Variable." *Journal of Personality,* 1962, 30, 29–50.

Burke, E. *Reflections on the Revolution in France*. New York: Harcourt, Brace & World, 1963. Originally published 1791.

Burns, J. M. *John Kennedy: A Political Profile*. New York: Harcourt, Brace & World, 1960.

Campbell, A., Converse, P. E., Miller, W. E., and Stokes, D. E. *The American Voter*. New York: Wiley, 1960.

Campbell, A., Gurin, G., and Miller, W. "Political Issues and the Vote: November, 1952." *American Political Science Review*, 1953, 47, 359–385.

————. *The Voter Decides*. New York: Row, Peterson & Company, 1954.

Cantril, H. *The Psychology of Social Movements*. New York: Wiley, 1941.

Catlin, G. *The Science and Method of Politics*. Hamden: Archon Books, 1964.

Chapman, L. J., and Campbell, D. T. "The Effect of Acquiescence Response-Set upon Relationships Among F-Scale, Ethnocentrism and Intelligence." *Sociometry*, 1959, 23, 69–71.

Christie, R. "Eysenck's Treatment of the Personality of Communists." *Psychological Bulletin*, 1956, 53, 411–430.

Christie, R., and Cook, P. "A Guide to Published Literature Relating to the Authoritarian Personality Through 1956." *Journal of Psychology*, 1958, 45, 171–199.

Christie, R., and Geis, F. L. *Studies in Machiavellianism*. New York: Academic Press, 1970.

Christie, R., Havel, J., and Seidenberg, B. "Is the F-Scale Irreversible?" *Journal of Abnormal and Social Psychology*, 1958, 56, 143–159.

Christie, R., and Jahoda, M. (eds.). *Studies in the Scope and Method of "The Authoritarian Personality."* Glencoe: The Free Press, 1954.

Christie, R., and Nisbett, R. E. "Some Characteristics of College Students for Johnson or Goldwater in the 1964 Election." Paper presented at the Annual Meeting of the American Psychological Association, Chicago, 1965.

Clark, K. B. "The Pathos of Power: A Psychological Perspective." *American Psychologist*, 1971, 26, 1047–1057.

Cole, D. L. "Machiavellianism and Political Behavior." *Journal of Social Psychology*, 1972, 87, 159–160.

Costin, F. "Dogmatism and Conservatism: An Empirical Follow-Up of Rokeach's Findings." *Educational and Psychological Measurement*, 1971, 31, 1007–1010.

Crutchfield, R. S. "Conformity and Character." *American Psychologist*, 1955, 10, 191–198.

Curry, R. L., Jr., and Wade, L. L. *A Theory of Political Exchange: Economic Reasoning in Political Analysis.* Englewood Cliffs: Prentice-Hall, 1968.

Cutler, J. H. *"Honey Fitz": Three Steps to the White House.* New York: Bobbs-Merrill Company, 1962.

Dahl, R. A. *Who Governs?* New Haven: Yale University Press, 1961.

D'Avenant, C. *An Essay Upon the Probable Method of Making a People Gainers in the Balance of Power.* London: James Knapton, 1699.

DeGrazia, S. *The Political Community: A Study of Anomie.* Chicago: University of Chicago Press, 1948.

Dicks, H. V. "Psychological Foundations of the Wehrmacht." British War Office Research Memorandum, 1944a.

———. "German Political Attitudes." British War Office Research Memorandum, 1944b.

———. "National Socialism as a Psychological Problem." British War Office Research Memorandum, 1944c.

———. "The Ten Categories." Internal Memorandum, German Personnel Research Branch, Control Commission for Germany, 1945.

———. "The Psychological Approach to the German Problem." The Royal Institute for International Affairs, Private Memorandum, 1947a.

———. "Why the Germans Became Nazis." (B.B.C. Broadcast) *The Listener*, 1947b.

———. "Personality Traits and National Socialist Ideology." *Human Relations*, 1950, 3, 111–154.

———. "Observations on Contemporary Russian Behavior." *Human Relations*, 1952, 5, 111–175.

Dinneen, J. F. *The Kennedy Family.* Boston: Little, Brown & Co., 1959.

DiPalma, G., and McClosky, H. "Personality and Conformity: The Learning of Political Attitudes." *American Political Science Review*, 1970, 64, 1054–1073.

DiRenzo, G. J. *Student Imagery at Fairfield University.* Monographic publication of the Social Psychology Laboratory, Fairfield University, Connecticut, 1965.

———. *Concepts, Theory and Explanation in the Behavioral Sciences.* New York: Random House, 1966.

———. *Personality, Power and Politics.* Notre Dame: University of Notre Dame Press, 1967a.

―――. "Professional Politicians and Personality Structures." *American Journal of Sociology,* 1967b, 73, 217–225.

―――. "Personality Structures and Political Consensus-Cleavage." *Research Reports in the Social Sciences,* 1967c, 1, 13–27.

―――. "Dogmatism and Presidential Preferences in the 1964 Elections." *Psychological Reports,* 1968, 22, 1197–1202.

―――. "Personality Typologies of Students and Modes of Social Change." Paper presented at the Eighth World Congress of Sociology, International Sociological Association, Varna, Bulgaria, 1970.

―――. "Dogmatism and Presidential Preferences: A 1968 Replication." *Psychological Reports,* 1971, 29, 109–110.

Dorris, R. J., Levinson, D. J., and Hanfmann, E. "Authoritarian Personality Studies by a New Variation of the Sentence Completion Technique." *Journal of Abnormal and Social Psychology,* 1954, 49, 99–108.

Downs, A. *An Economic Theory of Democracy.* New York: Harper, 1957.

Drake, D. "A Psychoanalytic Interpretation of Social Ideology." *American Imago,* 1955, 12, 193–196.

Durkheim, E. *The Rules of Sociological Method.* Chicago: University of Chicago Press, 1938. Originally published 1895.

―――. *Suicide: A Study in Sociology.* Glencoe: The Free Press, 1951. Originally published 1897.

Ebenstein, W. *Today's Isms.* New York: Prentice-Hall, 1961.

Edinger, L. J. *Kurt Schumacher: A Study in Personality and Political Behavior.* Stanford: Stanford University Press, 1965.

Edwards, A. L. "Political Frames of References as a Factor Influencing Recognition." *Journal of Abnormal and Social Psychology,* 1941, 36, 34–50.

Eintorn, H. J., Komorita, S. S., and Rosen, B. "Multidimensional Models for Evaluation of Political Candidates." *Journal of Experimental Social Psychology,* 1972, 8, 58–73.

Erikson, E. H. "Hitler's Imagery and German Youth," in C. Kluckhohn and H. Murray (eds.), *Personality.* New York: A. Knopf, 1948.

―――. *Childhood and Society.* New York: W. W. Norton, 1950.

————. "The Problem of Ego Identity." *Journal of the American Psychoanalytic Association*, 1956, 4, 56–121.

————. *Insight and Responsibility.* New York: W. W. Norton, 1964.

Eulau, H. *The Behavioral Persuasion in Politics.* New York: Random House, 1963.

Eysenck, H. J. *The Psychology of Politics.* London: Routledge & Kegan Paul, Ltd., 1954.

————. *The Psychology of Politics.* New York: Praeger, 1955.

————. "The Psychology of Politics and the Personality Similarities Between Fascists and Communists." *Psychological Bulletin*, 1956, 53, 431–438.

Fainsod, M. *How Russia Is Ruled.* Cambridge: Harvard University Press, 1953.

Farris, C. D. "Authoritarianism as a Political Behavior Variable." *Journal of Politics*, 1956, 18, 61–82.

Fay, P. B., Jr. *The Pleasure of His Company.* New York: Harper & Row, 1966.

Feldmesser, R. "The Persistence of Status Advantages in Soviet Russia." *American Journal of Sociology*, 1953, 59, 19–27.

Fenichel, O. *The Psychoanalytic Theory of Neurosis.* New York: W. W. Norton, 1945.

Festinger, L. *A Theory of Cognitive Dissonance.* Chicago: Row, Peterson & Company, 1957.

Fischer, G. *Soviet Opposition to Stalin.* Cambridge: Harvard University Press, 1952.

Fisher, B. R., Belknap, G., and Metzner, C. A. "America's Role in World Affairs: Patterns of Citizen Opinion, 1949–1950." Survey Research Center, University of Michigan, 1952.

Fox, W. T. R. *The Superpowers.* New York: Harcourt, Brace & World, 1944.

Frenkel-Brunswik, E. "A Study of Prejudice in Children." *Human Relations*, 1949a, 1, 295–306.

————. "Intolerance of Ambiguity as an Emotional and Personality Variable." *Journal of Personality*, 1949b, 18, 108–143.

————. "Interaction of Psychological and Sociological Factors in Political Behavior." *American Political Science Review*, 1952, 46, 44–56.

————. "Environmental Controls and the Impoverishment of Thought," in C. J. Friedrich (ed.). *Totalitarianism.* Cambridge: Harvard University Press, 1954a.

————. "Further Explorations by a Contributor to 'The Authoritarian Personality,'" in R. Christie and M. Jahoda (eds.). *Studies in the Scope and Method of "The Authoritarian Personality."* Glencoe: The Free Press, 1954b.

Frenkel-Brunswik, E., and Sanford, R. N. "Some Personality Correlates of Antisemitism." *Journal of Psychology,* 1945, 20, 271–291.

Frenkel-Brunswik, E., Levinson, D. J., and Sanford, R. N. "The Antidemocratic Personality," in E. E. Maccoby, T. M. Newcomb, and E. L. Hartley (eds.), *Readings in Social Psychology.* New York: Holt, Rinehart & Winston, 1958.

Freud, S. "Character and Anal Eroticism," in his *Collected Works.* Vol. II. London: Hogarth Press, 1950.

Fried, M. "Some Systematic Patterns of Relationship Between Personality and Attitudes Among Soviet Displaced Persons." Unpublished Report of the Project, Russian Research Center, Harvard University, 1954.

Fried, M., and Held, D. "Relationships Between Personality and Attitudes Among Soviet Displaced Persons: A Technical Memorandum on the Derivation of Personality Variables from a Sentence Completion Test." Unpublished Report of the Project, Russian Research Center, Harvard University, 1953.

Friedman, M. "Lange on Price Flexibility and Employment: A Methodological Criticism." *American Economic Review,* 1946, 46, 613–631.

Friedrich, C. J. *Totalitarianism.* Cambridge: Harvard University Press, 1954.

Froman, L. A. "Personality and Political Socialization." *Journal of Politics,* 1961, 23, 341–352.

Fromm, E. "A Social-Psychological Approach to 'Authority and Family,'" in M. Horkheimer (ed.), *Studien über Autorität und Familie.* Paris: Librarie Félix Alcan, 1936.

————. *Escape from Freedom.* New York: Holt, Rinehart & Winston, 1941.

————. *The Fear of Freedom.* New York: Holt, Rinehart & Winston, 1942.

————. *The Sane Society.* New York: Holt, Rinehart & Winston, 1955.

Fuller, J. L. *Motivation: A Biological Perspective*. New York: Random House, 1964.

Gage, N. L., Leavitt, G. S., and Stone, G. C. "The Psychological Meaning of Acquiescence Set for Authoritarianism." *Journal of Abnormal and Social Psychology*, 1957, 55, 98–103.

George, A. L. "Some Uses of Dynamic Psychology in Political Biography." Unpublished paper, 1960.

———. "Power as a Compensatory Value for Political Leaders." *Journal of Social Issues*, 1968, 24, 29–50.

George, A. L., and George, J. L. "Woodrow Wilson: Personality and Political Behavior." Unpublished paper prepared for the Annual Meeting of The American Political Science Association, 1956a.

———. *Woodrow Wilson and Colonel House: A Personality Study*. New York: John Day, 1956b.

Gerth, H. "The Nazi Party: Its Leadership and Composition." *American Journal of Sociology*, 1940, 45, 517–541.

Gerth, H., and Mills, C. W. *Character and Social Structure*. New York: Harcourt, Brace & World, 1953.

Gilbert, G. M. *The Psychology of Dictatorship*. New York: Ronald, 1950.

Glad, B. "Contributions of Psychobiography," in J. N. Knutson (ed.), *Handbook of Political Psychology*. San Francisco: Jossey-Bass, 1973.

Glazer, N. "New Light on 'The Authoritarian Personality.'" *Commentary*, 1954, 17, 289–297.

Goffman, E. *The Presentation of Self in Everyday Life*. Garden City, N.Y.: Doubleday & Company, 1959.

Goldhamer, H., and Shils, E. A. "Types of Power." *American Journal of Sociology*, 1939, 45, 171–182.

Gooch, G. P. *History and the Historians in the Nineteenth Century*. London: Longmans, 1952.

Gorer, G. "Themes in Japanese Culture." *Transactions of the New York Academy of Sciences*, 1943, 5, 106–124.

———. *The American People: A Study in National Character*. New York: W. W. Norton, 1948.

———. *The People of Great Russia*. London: Cresset, 1949.

Gottfried, A. "The Use of Socio-Psychological Categories in a Study of Political Personality." *Western Political Science Quarterly*, 1955, 8, 234–247.

Gough, H. G. "Studies of Social Intolerance: I." *Journal of Social Psychology*, 1951, 33, 237–246.

————. *Manual for the California Psychological Inventory.* Palo Alto: Consulting Psychologists Press, 1957.

Gough, H. G., McClosky, H., and Meehl, P. E. "A Personality Scale for Dominance." *Journal of Abnormal and Social Psychology,* 1951, 46, 360–366.

————. "A Personality Scale for Social Responsibility." *Journal of Abnormal and Social Psychology,* 1952, 47, 73–80.

Gouldner, A. W. *Patterns of Industrial Bureaucracy.* Glencoe: The Free Press, 1954.

Greenstein, F. I. "Personality and Political Socialization: The Theories of Authoritarian and Democratic Character." *Annals of the American Academy of Political and Social Science,* 1965, 361, 81–95.

————. "Personality and Politics: Problems of Evidence, Inference, and Conceptualization." *The American Behavioral Scientist,* 1967a, 11, 38–53.

————. "The Impact of Personality on Politics: An Attempt to Clear Away Underbrush." *American Political Science Review,* 1967b, 61, 629–641.

————. "The Need for Systematic Inquiry into Personality and Politics: Introduction and Overview." *Journal of Social Issues,* 1968, 24, 1–14.

————. *Personality and Politics.* Chicago: Markham Publishing Co., 1969.

Greenstein, F. I., and Lerner, M. (eds.). *A Sourcebook for the Study of Personality and Politics.* Chicago: Markham Publishing Co., 1971.

Groesbeck, B. L. "Toward Description of Personality in Terms of Configuration of Motives," in J. W. Atkinson (ed.), *Motives in Fantasy, Action, and Society: A Method of Assessment and Study.* Princeton: Princeton University Press, 1958.

Guilford, J. P. *Psychometric Methods.* New York: McGraw-Hill, 1954.

Hailsham, Q. M. *The Conservative Case.* Harmondsworth: Penguin, 1959.

Hall, C., and Lindzey, G. *Theories of Personality.* New York: Wiley, 1970.

Hanfmann, E. "Social Perception in Russian Displaced Persons and an American Comparison Group." *Psychiatry,* 1957, 20, 131–149.

Hanfmann, E., and Beier, H. "Psychological Patterns of Soviet Citizens." Unpublished Report of the Project, Russian Research Center, Harvard University, August 1954.

Hanfmann, E., and Getzels, J. G. "Studies of the Sentence Completion Test." *Journal of Projective Technology,* 1953, 17, 280–294.

———. "Interpersonal Attitudes of Former Soviet Citizens as Studied by a Semi-Projective Method." *Psychological Monographs,* 1955, 69, Whole Number 4.

Hargrove, E. C. *Presidential Leadership: Personality and Political Style.* New York: Macmillan, 1966.

Harned, L. "Participation in Political Parties: A Study of Party Committeemen." Unpublished doctoral dissertation, Yale University Press, 1957.

———. "Authoritarian Attitudes and Party Activity." *Public Opinion Quarterly,* 1961, 25, 393–399.

Hartz, L. *The Liberal Tradition in America.* New York: Harcourt, Brace & World, 1955.

Hearnshaw, F. J. C. *Conservatism in England.* London: Macmillan, 1933.

Heberle, R. "Changing Social Stratification of the South." *Social Forces,* 1959, 38, 42–50.

Heinberg, J. G. "State Legislators." *Annals of the American Academy of Political and Social Science,* 1938, 195, 1–252.

———. "The Personnel Structure of French Cabinets." *American Political Science Review,* 1939, 33, 267–278.

Hennessy, B. "Politicals and Apoliticals: Some Measurements of Personality Traits." *Midwest Journal of Political Science,* 1959, 3, 336–355.

Hobbes, T. *Leviathan.* New York: Macmillan, 1947. Originally published 1651.

Hoffer, E. *The True Believer.* New York: Harper, 1951.

Hofstadter, R. M. *The Paranoid Style in American Politics.* New York: A. Knopf, 1965.

Hogg, Q. *The Case for Conservatism.* West Drayton: Penguin Books, 1947.

Homans, G. C. *Social Behavior: Its Elementary Forms.* New York: Harcourt, Brace & World, 1961.

Horkheimer, M. (ed.). *Studien über Autorität und Familie.* Paris: Librarie Félix Alcan, 1936.

Horney, K. *The Neurotic Personality in Our Time.* New York: W. W. Norton, 1937.

Horst, P. "Correcting the Kuder Richardson Reliability for Dispersion of Item Difficulties." *Psychological Bulletin,* 1953, 50, 371–374.

Hughes, E. C. "Personality Types and the Division of Labor." *American Journal of Sociology,* 1928, 33, 754–768.

Huntington, S. P. "Conservatism as an Ideology." *American Political Science Review,* 1957, 51, 454–473.

Hutchinson, T. W. *The Significance and Basic Postulates of Economic Theory.* London: Macmillan, 1938.

Hyman, H. H. *Political Socialization.* Glencoe: The Free Press, 1959.

Hyman, H. H., and Sheatsley, P. B. "The 'Authoritarian Personality,' A Methodological Critique," in R. Christie and M. Jahoda (eds.), *Studies in the Scope and Method of "The Authoritarian Personality."* New York: The Free Press, 1954.

Inkeles, A. "Stratification and Social Mobility in the Soviet Union: 1940–1950." *American Sociological Review,* 1950, 15, 465–479.

———. "Personality and Social Structure," in R. K. Merton, L. Broom, and L. S. Cottrell (eds.), *Sociology Today.* New York: Basic Books, 1959.

———. "National Character and Modern Political Systems," in F. L. K. Hsu (ed.), *Psychological Anthropology.* Homewood, Ill.: The Dorsey Press, 1961.

———. *What Is Sociology?* New York: Prentice-Hall, 1964.

Inkeles, A., and Bauer, R. "Patterns of Life Experiences and Attitudes Under the Soviet System." Russian Research Center, Harvard University, October 1954.

Inkeles, A., Hanfmann, E., and Beier, H. "Modal Personality and Adjustment to the Soviet Socio-Political System." *Human Relations,* 1958, 11, 3–22.

Inkeles, A., and Levinson, D. J. "National Character: The Study of Modal Personality and Sociocultural Systems," in G. Lindzey (ed.), *Handbook of Social Psychology.* Cambridge: Addison-Wesley, 1954.

Jacob, H. "Initial Recruitment of Elected Officials in the United States—A Model." *Journal of Politics,* 1962, 24, 708–709.

Janis, I. L., and Feshbach, S. "Effects of Fear Arousing Communications." *Journal of Abnormal and Social Psychology,* 1953, 48, 78–92.

Kaiser, H. F. "Image of a President: Some Insights into the Political Views of Children." *American Political Science Review,* 1968, 62, 208–215.

Kardiner, A. *The Psychological Frontiers of Society.* New York: Columbia University Press, 1945.

Kardiner, A., and Ovesey, L. *The Mark of Oppression: A Psychosocial Study of the American Negro.* New York: W. W. Norton, 1951.

Kecskemeti, P. "Prejudice in the Catastrophic Perspective." *Commentary,* 1951, 11, 286–292.

Kecskemeti, P., and Leites, N. "Some Psychological Hypotheses on Nazi Germany." Washington, D.C.: The Library of Congress, Document No. 60, 1945.

Kennedy, J. F. *Profiles in Courage.* New York: Harper & Row, 1965.

———. *Why England Slept.* New York: W. Funk, Inc., 1963.

Kennedy, R. *John F. Kennedy: As We Remember Him.* New York: Macmillan, 1967.

Kerlinger, F., and Rokeach, M. "The Factorial Nature of the F and D Scales." *Journal of Personality and Social Psychology,* 1966, 4, 391–399.

Kirk, R. *The Conservative Mind.* Chicago: H. Regnery Co., 1953.

Kleinmuntz, G. *Personality Measurement: An Introduction.* Homewood, Ill.: The Dorsey Press, 1967.

Kluckhohn, C. "Navaho Witchcraft." *Papers of the Peabody Museum of American Anthropology,* 1944, 22, 33–72 and 145–150.

Knight, F. H. *Risk Uncertainty and Profit.* Boston: Houghton Mifflin, 1921.

Knutson, J. N. (ed.). *Handbook of Political Psychology.* San Francisco: Jossey-Bass, 1973.

———. *The Human Basis of the Polity.* Chicago: Aldine-Atherton, 1973.

Kogan, N. *The Government of Italy.* New York: T. Y. Crowell, 1964.

Kornhauser, A., Sheppard, H. L., and Mayer, A. J. *When Labor Votes,* New York: University Books, 1956.

Kornhauser, W. *The Politics of Mass Society.* New York: The Free Press, 1959.

Kotarbinsky, T. *Praxiology: An Introduction to the Science of Efficient Action.* New York: Pergamon, 1965.

Krutch, J. W. *The Measure of Man.* Indianapolis: Bobbs-Merrill, 1954.

Kubzansky, P. "The Effect of Reduced Environmental Stimulation on Human Behavior: A Review," in A. Biderman and H. Zinner (eds.), *The Manipulation of Human Behavior.* New York: Wiley, 1961.

Kuenne, R. E. *The Theory of General Economic Equilibrium.* Princeton: Princeton University Press, 1963.

Kuhn, A. *The Study of Society: A Unified Approach.* Homewood, Ill.: The Dorsey Press, 1963.

La Barre, W. "Some Observation on Character Structure in the Orient: I. The Japanese." *Psychiatry,* 1945, 8, 319–342.

————. "Some Observations on Character Structure in the Orient: II. The Chinese." *Psychiatry,* 1946, 9, 215–237.

Lane, R. E. "Political Personality and Electoral Choice." *American Political Science Review,* 1955, 49, 173–190.

————. *Political Life.* Glencoe: The Free Press, 1959.

————. *Political Ideology.* Glencoe: The Free Press, 1962a.

————. "Notes on a Theory of Democratic Personality," in his *Political Ideology.* Glencoe: The Free Press, 1962b.

————. "Political Personality. Part One," in the *Encyclopedia of the Social Sciences.* New York: Macmillan, 1968.

————. "Patterns of Political Belief," in J. N. Knutson (ed.), *Handbook of Political Psychology.* San Francisco: Jossey-Bass, 1973.

Lange-Eichbaum, W. *Genie, Irrsinn und Ruhm.* Munich: Reinhardt, 1935.

Lasswell, H. D. *Psychopathology and Politics.* Chicago: University of Chicago Press, 1930.

————. "Collective Autism as a Consequence of Culture Contact: Notes on Religious Training and the Peyote Cult at Taos." *Zeitschrift für Sozialforschung,* 1935, 4.

————. *Power and Personality.* New York: W. W. Norton, 1948.

————. *The Political Writings of Harold D. Lasswell.* Glencoe: The Free Press, 1951a.

————. "Democratic Character and Politics: Who Gets What, When and How," in *The Political Writings of Harold D. Lasswell.* Glencoe: The Free Press, 1951b.

————. "The Selective Effect of Personality on Political Participation," in R. Christie and M. Jahoda (eds.), *Studies in the Scope and Method of "The Authoritarian Personality."* Glencoe: The Free Press, 1954.

———. "Political Constitution and Character." *Psychoanalysis and the Psychoanalytic Review,* 1959, 46, 3–18.

Lasswell, H. D., and Kaplan, A. *Power and Society.* New Haven: Yale University Press, 1950.

Lauterbach, A. "Totalitarian Appeal and Economic Reform," in C. J. Friedrich (ed.), *Totalitarianism.* Cambridge: Harvard University Press, 1954.

Lazarsfeld, P. F., and Menzel, H. "On the Relation Between Individual and Collective Properties," in A. Etzioni (ed.), *Complex Organizations: A Sociological Reader.* New York: Holt, Rinehart & Winston, 1961.

Leites, N. *On the Game of Politics in France.* Stanford: Stanford University Press, 1959.

———. *Images of Power in French Politics.* Multilithed, 1961.

Lerner, D. *The Passing of Traditional Society.* New York: The Free Press, 1958.

———. *Sykewar.* Cambridge: M.I.T. Press, 1971. Originally published 1949.

Levine, J. M., and Murphy, G. "The Learning and Forgetting of Controversial Material." *Journal of Abnormal and Social Psychology,* 1943, 38, 507–517.

Levinson, D. J. "Authoritarian Personality and Foreign Policy." *Journal of Conflict Resolution,* 1957, 1, 37–47.

———. "The Relevance of Personality for Political Participation." *Public Opinion Quarterly,* 1958, 22, 3–10.

———. "Role, Personality, and Social Structure in the Organizational Setting." *Journal of Abnormal and Social Psychology,* 1959, 58, 170–180.

———. "Personality, Sociocultural Systems, and the Process of Role-Definition." Paper presented at the Symposium of the Section on Social Psychology, Annual Meeting of the American Sociological Association, Los Angeles, 1963.

———. "Toward a New Social Psychology: The Convergence of Sociology and Psychology." *Merrill-Palmer Quarterly of Behavior and Development,* 1964a, 10, 77–88.

———. "Idea Systems in the Individual and in Society," in G. K. Zollschan and W. Hirsch (eds.), *Explorations in Social Change.* Boston: Houghton Mifflin, 1964b.

————. "Chauvinistic Nationalism: Toward a Sociopsychological Analysis." Paper presented at the Annual Meeting of the American Psychological Association, Los Angeles, 1964c.

————. "Political Personality: II. Conservatism/Radicalism," in the *International Encyclopedia of the Social Sciences*. New York: Macmillan, 1968.

Levinson, D. J., and Sanford, R. N. "A Scale for the Measurement of Antisemitism." *Journal of Psychology*, 1944, 17, 339–370.

Levy, D. M. "The German Anti-Nazi: A Case Study." *American Journal of Orthopsychiatry*, 1946, 16, 506–515.

————. "Anti-Nazis: Criteria of Differentiation." *Psychiatry*, 1948, 11, 125–167.

Lewin, K. *Field Theory in Social Science: Selected Theoretical Papers*. D. Cartwright (ed.). New York: Harper, 1951.

Lincoln, E. *My Twelve Years with JFK*. New York: David McKay, 1965.

Linton, R. "The Concept of National Character," in A. H. Stanton and S. E. Perry (eds.), *Personality and Political Crisis*. Glencoe: The Free Press, 1951.

Lippmann, W. *Preface to Politics*. New York: Mitchell Kennedy, 1913.

————. *Public Opinion*. New York: Macmillan, 1922.

Lipset, S. M. *Political Man*. New York: William Heinemann, Ltd., 1960.

Lipset, S. M., Lazarsfeld, P. F., Barton, A. I., and Liz, J. "The Psychology of Political Voting Behavior," in G. Lindzey (ed.), *Handbook of Social Psychology*. Cambridge: Addison-Wesley, 1954.

Maccoby, M. "Polling Emotional Attitudes in Relation to Political Choices." Unpublished manuscript, 1969.

MacIver, R. M. *The Ramparts We Guard*. New York: Macmillan, 1950.

Manheim, H. L. "Personality Differences of Members of Two Political Parties." *Journal of Social Psychology*, 1959, 50, 261–268.

Mannheim, K. *Freedom, Power and Democratic Planning*. London: Routledge & Kegan Paul, Ltd., 1950.

March, J., and Simon, H. *Organizations*. New York: Wiley, 1958.

Martin, J. G. *The Tolerant Personality*. Detroit: Wayne State University Press, 1964.

Maslow, A. H. "The Authoritarian Character Structure." *Journal of Social Psychology*, 1943, 18, 401–411.

———. "Power Relationships and Patterns of Personal Development," in A. Kornhauser (ed.), *Problems of Power in American Democracy*. Detroit: Wayne State University Press, 1957.

Matthews, D. R. *Social Background of Political Decision-Makers*. Garden City, N.Y.: Doubleday & Company, 1954.

———. *U. S. Senators and Their World*. Chapel Hill: University of North Carolina Press, 1960.

McClelland, D. C. "The Use of Measures of Human Motivation in the Study of Society," in J. Atkinson (ed.), *Motives in Fantasy, Action, and Society: A Method of Assessment and Study*. Princeton: Princeton University Press, 1958.

———. *The Achieving Society*. Princeton: Princeton University Press, 1961a.

———. *Personality*. New York: Holt, Rinehart & Winston, 1961b.

McClelland, D. C., Atkinson, J., Clark, R. A., and Lowell, E. L. *The Achievement Motive*. New York: Wiley, 1953.

McClosky, H. "Conservatism and Personality." *American Political Science Review*, 1958, 52, 27–45.

McClosky, H., and Schaar, J. H. "Psychological Dimensions of Anomy." *American Sociological Review*, 1965, 30, 14–40.

McConaughy, J. B. "Certain Personality Factors of State Legislators in South Carolina." *American Political Science Review*, 1950, 44, 897–903.

McConnell, G. *Steel and the Presidency: 1962*. New York: W. W. Norton, 1963.

McGranahan, D. V. "A Comparison of Social Attitudes Among American and German Youth." *Journal of Abnormal and Social Psychology*, 1946, 41, 245–256.

Mead, G. H. *Mind, Self and Society*. Chicago: University of Chicago Press, 1934.

Mead, M. *Soviet Attitudes Toward Authority*. New York: McGraw-Hill, 1951.

Merton, R. K. "Social Structure and Anomie," in his *Social*

Theory and Social Structure, New York: The Free Press, 1949.

―――. *Social Theory and Social Structure.* Glencoe: The Free Press, 1957.

Meyers, J. S. (ed.). *John Fitzgerald Kennedy As We Remembered Him.* New York: Atheneum, 1965.

Meynaud, J. "General Study of Parliamentarians." *International Social Science Journal,* 1961, 8, 513–543.

Michels, R. *Political Parties.* New York: Collier Books, 1962.

Milbrath, L. W. "The Political Party Activity of Washington Lobbyists." *Journal of Politics,* 1958, 20, 339–352.

―――. "Predispositions Toward Political Contention." *The Western Political Quarterly,* 1960, 13, 5–18.

―――. *Political Participation.* Chicago: Rand McNally, 1965.

Milbrath, L. W., and Klein, W. W. "Personality Correlates of Political Participation." *Acta Sociologica,* 1962, 6, 52–66.

Mill, J. S. *Utilitarianism, Liberty, and Representative Government.* New York: Dutton, 1910, Originally published 1861.

Miller, D. R., and Swanson, G. E. *The Changing American Parent.* New York: Wiley, 1958.

―――. *Inner Conflict and Defense.* New York: Holt, Rinehart & Winston, 1960.

Mills, C. W. *The Sociological Imagination.* New York: Oxford University Press, 1959.

Milton, O. "Presidential Choice and Performance on a Scale of Authoritarianism." *American Psychologist,* 1952, 7, 597–598.

Mishler, E. G. "Personality Characteristics and the Resolution of Role Conflicts." *Public Opinion Quarterly,* 1953, 17, 115–135.

Money-Kyrle, R. E. *Psychoanalysis and Politics.* London: Gerald Duckworth & Co., Ltd., 1951.

Mongar, T. M. "Personality and Decision-Making: John F. Kennedy in Four Crisis Decisions." *Canadian Journal of Political Science,* 1969, 2, 300–325.

Montesquieu, C. *The Spirit of the Laws.* Book XI. New York: Hafner Publishing Co., 1959. Originally published 1748.

Morgenthau, H. J. *Politics Among Nations.* New York: A. Knopf, 1956.

Murphy, G. *Personality: A Biosocial Approach to Origins and Structure*. New York: Harper, 1947.

Murray, H. A. (ed.). *Explorations in Personality*. New York: Oxford University Press, 1938a.

Murray, H. A. "Variables of Personality," in H. A. Murray (ed.), *Explorations in Personality*. New York: Oxford University Press, 1938b.

Murray, H. A., and Morgan, C. D. "A Clinical Study of Sentiments: I and II." *Genetic Psychology Monographs*, 1945, 32, 3–311.

Mussen, P. H., and Wyszynski, A. B. "Personality and Political Participation." *Human Relations*, 1952, 5, 65–82.

Myrdal, G. *An American Dilemma* (revised edition). New York: Harper, 1962.

Nett, E. "An Evaluation of the National Character Concept in Sociological Theory." *Social Forces*, 1957–58, 36, 297–303.

Neumann, F. *The Democratic and the Authoritarian State*. New York: The Free Press, 1957.

Neumann, S. "The Political Lieutenant," in his *Permanent Revolution: The Total State in a World at War*. New York: Harper, 1942.

Niemi, R. G. "Political Socialization," in J. N. Knutson (ed.), *Handbook of Political Psychology*. San Francisco: Jossey-Bass, 1973.

Nomad, M. *Rebels and Renegades*. Freeport, N.Y.: Books for Libraries Press, 1932.

Norbeck, E. (ed.). *The Study of Personality*. New York: Holt, Rinehart & Winston, 1968.

Parker, J. D. "Classification of Candidates' Motivations for First Seeking Office." *Journal of Politics*, 1972, 34, 268–275.

Paul, I. H. "Impressions of Personality, Authority and the Fait Accompli Effect." *Journal of Abnormal and Social Psychology*, 1956, 53, 338–344.

Payne, J. L., and Woshinsky, O. H. "Incentives for Political Participation." *World Politics*, 1972, 24, 518–546.

Perry, H. S. "Selective Inattention as an Explanatory Concept for U.S. Public Attitudes Toward the Atomic Bomb." *Psychiatry*, 1953, 17, 78–92.

Pfister-Ammende, M. "Psychologische Erfahrungen mit Sowjetrussischen Flüchtlingen in der Schweiz," in M. Pfister-Ammende (ed.), *Die Psycholohygiene: Grundlagen und Zeite*. Bern: Hans Huber, 1949.

Polanyi, M. *Personal Knowledge: Towards a Post-Critical Philosophy*. London: Routledge & Kegan Paul, 1958.

―――. *Personal Knowledge: Towards a Post-Critical Philosophy*. New York: Harper, 1964.

Pye, L. *Politics, Personality and Nation Building*. New Haven: Yale University Press, 1962.

Radcliffe, C. J. *The Problem of Power*. London: Seeker and Warburg, 1952.

Rees, J. R. *The Case of Rudolph Hess*. New York: W. W. Norton, 1947.

Reich, W. *The Mass Psychology of Fascism*. New York: Orgone Institute Press, 1946.

Reitman, W. R. "Motivational Induction and Behavior Correlates of the Achievement and Affiliation Motives." *Journal of Abnormal and Social Psychology*, 1960, 60, 8–13.

Rieselbach, L. N., and Balch, I. (eds.). *Psychology and Politics*. New York: Holt, Rinehart & Winston, 1969.

Riesman, D. *The Lonely Crowd*. New Haven: Yale University Press, 1950.

Riesman, D., and Glazer, N. "The Lonely Crowd: A Reconsideration in 1960," in S. M. Lipset and L. Lowenthal (eds.), *Culture and Social Character*. New York: The Free Press, 1961.

Robinson, W. S. "Ecological Correlation and the Behavior of Individuals." *American Sociological Review*, 1950, 15, 351–357.

Rodnick, D. *Post-War Germans*. New Haven: Yale University Press, 1948.

Rogow, A. A. "Psychiatry as a Political Science." *Psychiatric Quarterly*, 1960, 40, 319–332.

―――. *James Forrestal: A Study of Personality, Politics and Policy*. New York: Macmillan, 1963.

―――. "Toward a Psychiatry of Politics," in A. A. Rogow (ed.), *Politics, Personality and Social Science in the Twentieth Century*. Chicago: University of Chicago Press, 1969.

Rokeach, M. "The Nature and Meaning of Dogmatism." *Psychological Review*, 1954, 61, 194–204.

―――. "Political and Religious Dogmatism: An Alternative to the Authoritarian Personality." *Psychological Monographs*, 1956, 70, Whole Issue.

————. *The Open and Closed Mind.* New York: Basic Books, 1960.

Rokeach, M., and Fruchter, B. "A Factorial Study of Dogmatism and Related Concepts." *Journal of Abnormal and Social Psychology,* 1956, 53, 356–360.

Rokeach, M., and Hanley, C. "Eysenck's Tendermindedness Dimension: A Critique." *Psychological Bulletin,* 1956, 53, 169–176.

Romanell, P. *Making of the Mexican Mind: A Study in Recent Mexican Thought.* Lincoln: University of Nebraska Press, 1952.

Roseborough, H. E., and Phillips, H. D. "A Comparative Analysis of the Responses to a Sentence Completion Test of a Matched Sample of Americans and Former Russian Subjects." Unpublished Report of the Project, Russian Research Center, Harvard University, April 1953.

Rosenberg, M. "Misanthropy and Political Ideology." *American Sociological Review,* 1956, 21, 690–692.

Rosenblatt, D., Slaiman, M., and Hanfmann, E. "Responses of Former Soviet Citizens to the Thematic Apperception Test (TAT): An Analysis Based upon Comparison with an American Control Group." Unpublished Report of the Project, Russian Research Center, Harvard University, August 1953.

Rossi, A. "Generational Differences Among Former Soviet Citizens." Unpublished doctoral dissertation, Department of Sociology, Columbia University, 1954.

Rossiter, C. *Conservatism in America.* New York: A. Knopf, 1955.

Rosten, L. C. *The Washington Correspondents.* New York: Harcourt, Brace & Company, 1937.

Rutherford, B. M. "Psychopathology, Decision-Making and Political Involvement." *Journal of Conflict Resolution,* 1966, 10, 387–407.

Saenger, G. *The Social Psychology of Prejudice.* New York: Harper & Row, 1953.

Sanford, F. *Authoritarianism and Leadership.* Philadelphia Institute for Research in Human Relations, 1950.

————. "Public Orientation to Roosevelt." *Public Opinion Quarterly,* 1951, 15, 189–216.

Sanford, N. *Issues in Personality.* San Francisco: Jossey-Bass, 1970.

————. "Authoritarian Personality in Contemporary Perspective," in J. N. Knutson (ed.), *Handbook of Political Psychology*. San Francisco: Jossey-Bass, 1973.

Santayana, G. *Dominations and Power*. New York: Scribner, 1951.

Sartori, G. "Parliamentarians in Italy." *International Social Science Journal*, 1961, 8, 583–599.

Schaffner, B. *Father Land: A Study of Authority in the German Family*. New York: Columbia University Press, 1948.

Schlesinger, A., Jr. *A Thousand Days*. Boston: Houghton Mifflin, 1965.

Schoenberger, R. A. "Conservatism, Personality and Political Extremism." *American Political Science Review*, 1968, 62, 868–877.

Schulze, R. "A Shortened Version of the Rokeach Dogmatism Scale." *Journal of Psychological Studies*, 1962, 13, 93–97.

Schumpeter, J. A. *Capitalism, Socialism and Democracy*. New York: Harper, 1950.

Schwartz, D. C. *Political Alienation and Political Behavior*. Chicago: Aldine Publishing Co., 1973.

Scott, W. A. "Correlates of International Attitudes." *Public Opinion Quarterly*, 1958–59, 22, 464–472.

Selznick, G., and Steinberg, S. "Class and Ideology in the 1964 Election: A National Survey." Unpublished manuscript.

Sherif, M. "The Concept of Reference Groups in Human Relations," in M. Sherif and M. O. Wilson (eds.), *Group Relations at the Crossroads*. New York: Harper, 1953.

Sherif, M., and Cantril, H. *The Psychology of Ego-Involvements*. New York: Wiley, 1941.

Shils, E. A. "Authoritarianism: 'Right' and 'Left,'" in R. Christie and M. Jahoda (eds.), *Studies in the Scope and Method of "The Authoritarian Personality."* Glencoe: The Free Press, 1954.

Shils, E. A., and Janowitz, M. "Cohesion and Disintegration in the Wehrmacht." *Public Opinion Quarterly*, 1948, 12, 280–315.

Shipley, T. E., Jr., and Verkoff, J. "A Projective Measure of Need for Affiliation," in J. W. Atkinson (ed.), *Motives in Fantasy, Action and Society: A Method of Assessment and Study*. Princeton: Princeton University Press, 1958.

Sidey, H. "The Presidency: A Classic Use of the Great Office." *Life*, 1968, 65, 4.

Siegel, S. "Certain Determinants and Correlates of Authoritarianism." *Genetic Psychology Monographs*, 1954, 49, 187–230.

———. *Nonparametric Statistics*. New York: McGraw-Hill, 1956.

Singer, J. David. "Man and World Politics: The Psycho-Cultural Interface." *Journal of Social Issues*, 1968, 24, 93–109.

Skinner, B. F. *Science and Human Behavior*. New York: Macmillan, 1953.

Small, D. O., and Campbell, D. J. "The Effect of Acquiescence Response-Set upon the Relationship of the F-Scale and Conformity." *Sociometry*, 1960, 23, 69–71.

Smelser, N. J. "Personality and the Explanation of Political Phenomena at the Social System Level: A Methodological Statement." *Journal of Social Issues*, 1968, 24, 111–126.

Smelser, N. J., and Smelser, W. T. (eds.). *Personality and Social Systems*. New York: Wiley, 1963.

Smith, B. L. "The Political Communication Specialist of Our Times," in B. L. Smith, H. D. Lasswell, and R. D. Casey (eds.), *Propaganda, Communication and Public Opinion*. Princeton: Princeton University Press, 1946.

Smith, M. B. "Opinions, Personality and Political Behavior." *American Political Science Review*, 1958, 52, 1–17.

———. *Determinants of Anti-Semitism: A Social-Psychological Map*. New York: Anti-defamation League of B'nai B'rith N.D., 1965.

———. "Attitude Change," in the *International Encyclopedia of the Social Sciences*. New York: Macmillan, 1968a.

———. "A Map for the Analysis of Personality and Politics." *Journal of Social Issues*, 1968b, 24, 15–28.

Smith, M. B., Bruner, J. S., and White, R. W. *Opinions and Personality*. New York: Wiley, 1956.

Sorensen, T. *Kennedy*. New York: Harper & Row, 1965.

Sorokin, P. A. *Social Mobility*. New York: Harper, 1927.

Spitz, D. *Patterns of Anti-Democratic Thought*. New York: Macmillan, 1949.

———. "Power and Personality: The Appeal to the 'Right Man' in Democratic States." *American Political Science Review*, 1958, 52, 84–97.

Spranger, E. *Types of Men*. Halle: Max Niemeyer Verlag, 1928.

Srole, L. "Social Integration and Certain Correlates: An Exploratory Study." *American Sociological Review*, 1956, 21, 709–716.

Stalin, J. *Leninism*. Vol. I. New York: Modern Books, 1933.

Stouffer, S. A. *Communism, Conformity and Civil Liberties*. Garden City, N.Y.: Doubleday & Company, 1955.

Talmon, Y. "Pursuit of the Millennium: The Relation Between Religious and Social Change." *Archives Européennes de Sociologie*, 1962, 3, 125–148.

Taylor, I. A. "Similarities in the Structure of Extreme Social Attitudes." *Psychological Monographs*, 1960, 74, Whole Number 2.

Thibaut, J. W., and Kelley, H. H. *The Social Psychology of Groups*. New York: Wiley, 1959.

Titus, H. E., and Hollander, E. P. "The California F-Scale in Psychological Research: 1950–1955." *Psychological Bulletin*, 1957, 54, 47–64.

Tocqueville, A. *Democracy in America*. Garden City, N.Y.: Doubleday, 1969. Originally published 1840.

Vacchiano, R. B., Strauss, P. S., and Hochman, L. "The Open and Closed Mind: A Review of Dogmatism." *Psychological Bulletin*, 1969, 71, 261–273.

Verkoff, J. "Power Motivation Related to Influence Attempts in a Two Person Group." Unpublished paper, 1956.

———. "Development and Validation of a Projective Measure of Power Motivation," in J. W. Atkinson (ed.), *Motives in Fantasy, Action and Society: A Method of Assessment and Study*. Princeton: Princeton University Press, 1958.

Viereck, P. *Conservatism from John Adams to Churchill*. New York: Van Nostrand, 1955.

Wahlke, J. C., Eulau, H., Buchanan, W., and Ferguson, L. C. *The Legislative System*. New York: Wiley, 1962.

Wallas, G. "Impulse and Instinct in Politics," in his *Human Nature in Politics*. Boston: Houghton Mifflin, 1909.

Weber, M. *The Theory of Social and Economic Organizations*. New York: Oxford University Press, 1947.

———. *Essays in Sociology*. H. H. Gerth and C. W. Mills (eds.). New York: Oxford University Press, 1958.

Whalen, R. *The Founding Father: The Story of Joseph P. Kennedy*. New York: New American Library, 1964.

White, R. J. (ed.). *The Conservative Tradition*. London: Kaye, 1950.

White, R. W. "Motivation Reconsidered: The Concept of Competence." *Psychological Review*, 1959, 66, 297–333.

———. "Ego and Reality in Psychoanalytic Theory." Monograph No. II of *Psychological Issues*. New York: International Universities Press, 1963.

White, T. *The Making of the President, 1960*. New York: Atheneum, 1961.

Williams, P. J., and Wright, C. R. "Opinion Organization in Heterogeneous Adult Populations." *Journal of Abnormal and Social Psychology*, 1955, 51, 559–564.

Wilson, F. G. *The Case for Conservatism*. Seattle: University of Washington Press, 1951.

Wilson, Glenn D. (ed.). *The Psychology of Conservatism*. New York: Academic Press, 1972.

Withey, S., and Steiner, I. *Big Business from the Viewpoint of the Public*. Survey Research Center, University of Michigan, 1951.

Witkin, H. A., Dyk, R. B., Faterson, H. F., Goodenough, D. R., and Karp, S. A. *Psychological Differentiation: Studies of Development*. New York: Wiley, 1962.

Wittke, C. *The Utopian Communist: A Biography of Wilhelm Weitling*. Baton Rouge: Louisiana State University Press, 1950.

Wolfenstein, E. V. *The Revolutionary Personality: Lenin, Trotsky, and Gandhi*. Princeton: Princeton University Press, 1967.

Wrightman, L. S., Jr., Radloff, R. W., Horton, D. L., and Mecherikoff, M. "Authoritarian Attitudes and Presidential Voting Preference." *Psychological Reports*, 1961, 8, 43–46.

Wrong, D. "Riesman and the Age of Sociology." *Commentary*, 1956, 21, 331–338.

———. "The Oversocialized Conception of Man in Modern Sociology." *American Sociological Review*, 1961, 26, 183–193.

Yinger, J. M. "Anomie, Alienation, and Political Behavior," in J. N. Knutson (ed.), *Handbook of Political Psychology*. San Francisco: Jossey-Bass, 1973.

Zaleznik, A. "Power and Politics in Organizational Life." *Harvard Business Review*, 1970, 48, 47–60.

Ziller, R. C. "The Political Personality," in his *The Social Self*. New York: Pergamon Press, 1972.

Index

Index